MISTRESS OF RIVERSDALE

Mistress of Riversdale

THE PLANTATION LETTERS OF

Rosalie Stier Calvert

1795–1821

EDITED BY
MARGARET LAW CALLCOTT

The Johns Hopkins University Press   Baltimore and London

The Johns Hopkins University Press
701 West 40th Street, Baltimore, Maryland 21211
The Johns Hopkins Press Ltd., London

The paper used in this book meets the minimum requirements of American
National Standard for Information Sciences—Permanence of Paper
for Printed Library Materials, ANSI A39.48-1984.

Library of Congress Cataloging-in-Publication Data
will be found on the last page of this book.

Frontispiece: Rosalie Stier Calvert and daughter Caroline Maria. Portrait by Gilbert
Stuart, 1804. Private collection; photo courtesy of Maryland Historical Society,
Baltimore.

Contents

List of Illustrations

Preface

I FIRST ENCOUNTERED ROSALIE STIER CALVERT as a legend—a shadowy figure reputed to have been mistress of the decaying old Riversdale mansion in Prince George's County, Maryland, near the District of Columbia. The Riversdale Historical Society was attempting to restore the house, and there I heard tales of the aristocratic European origins of the property's first owners, of an impressive art collection they brought to this country, and of castles and châteaus left behind in Belgium.

The accounts were appealing, but their documentation was sketchy. Then, gradually, Rosalie Calvert's correspondence came to light—more than two hundred thirty letters written in the early years of the nineteenth century to her family in Belgium. Rosalie's letters surpassed all expectations, confirming the romantic background, but far more important, revealing in rich detail the intelligent, high-spirited, rather haughty woman who had lived at Riversdale and the kind of life she led there.

Rosalie Calvert's American letters, always treasured by her European family, have been carefully preserved by their descendants for over one hundred seventy-five years. The letters might still lie hidden away in family archives near Antwerp except for a Belgian archivist who came across them in the 1970s while cataloguing the family's centuries-old manuscript collection. The archivist, Dr. Alfons Bousse, wrote an article in Flemish about Rosalie and her family's emigration to America, a flight from the French Revolution's Reign of Terror, which was spilling over into their native country. Bousse's article came to the attention of the

Riversdale Historical Society, which, with his help, secured copies of her letters and other family papers. Mrs. Calvert's vivid portrayal of a woman's life in the early years of our nation's history convinced the society to share the rich resources in their possession with a wider audience. This book brings together the bulk of Rosalie Calvert's extraordinary correspondence, translated from French and arranged so that the letters form their own chronological narrative.

Rosalie Stier was only sixteen when she, her wealthy parents, five other family members, and two servants arrived in Philadelphia. The Stiers soon moved on to Annapolis, where Rosalie met and married the planter George Calvert, whose ancestors, the English lords Baltimore, had been proprietors of the Maryland colony. Rosalie and George Calvert went to live at his Prince George's County tobacco plantation, while Rosalie's father, Henri J. Stier, began construction of Riversdale, near Bladensburg, just outside the nation's new capital. As the fires of revolution in Europe cooled, the Stiers filtered back to Belgium, and by 1803, all of Rosalie's family had returned. Rosalie and George, with their two small children, remained in America and took charge of the unfinished Riversdale plantation. It was at this point that Rosalie Stier Calvert began the remarkable correspondence that continued until her death in 1821.

Mrs. Calvert wrote remarkably straightforward accounts of her life and what was happening around her. Her letters convey a sense of immediacy that might have been lost by a writer overly concerned with matters of style. She was not writing for posterity, posturing, or looking over her shoulder as she wrote. She was speaking directly to her family about her way of life, her thoughts, and her emotions. Sometimes she worried that she was being too honest in her expressions; at one point she asked her sister to burn all her letters, and she warned several times not to reveal what she had written.

Rosalie and George Calvert were active participants in the social life of the nation's young capital city. They knew many of the political figures of their day and counted the George Washingtons and the Washingtons' Custis grandchildren among their relations; Carrolls, Ogles, Tayloes, Lloyds, and Lowndeses were among their friends. Rosalie had strong conservative opinions born of the upheaval that revolution had wrought in her life, and she was not hesitant in voicing them. The Jefferson regime filled her with foreboding. She viewed the Madisons with both political and social distaste. Not until the Monroes were in the President's House did she feel comfortable with the young nation's leadership.

Mrs. Calvert's greatest contribution to our understanding of these early decades in our nation's history, however, lies in her accounts of day-to-day family and social life. Entirely too rich and too European to qualify as representative, she was far from a typical plantation mistress, yet certain of her experiences were universal to her class and sex. She recorded the details of the work-filled life of a plantation mistress, overwhelming at times, particularly as recurring illness and repeated pregnancies wore her down. She had nine children and at least one miscarriage during her twenty-one years of marriage. She lost four of these children, not as infants but as young children who had imprinted themselves strongly on her heart, and she grieved for each. She was not indulgent, but she was a fond and caring mother.

While the Calverts had many slaves on their various plantations, Mrs. Calvert always felt overworked and underserved. This was a common lament of the plantation wife, and in her case the complaints had a real basis. Life for the plantation mistress was not one of ease and indulgence, as Rosalie's letters show. A large plantation was both a manor and a factory, and its mistress bore clearly defined responsibilities for many aspects of its operation. She and her husband were co-workers in a joint economic venture, and the well-being of their family and slaves depended on how successfully both performed their tasks.

Mrs. Calvert was never entirely comfortable with her slaves, and she hired white servants for her own and her children's personal service. She did not, however, appear to have any reservations about the slave system itself. She never raised questions about its morality, and she bought and sold slaves without hesitation. A hauteur and a failure to regard her servants as individuals is evident in her writings. She rarely called her slaves by name or gave them personality, discussing them almost entirely in terms of whether their service to her was satisfactory. Rosalie added an element of distance between the classes, part of her European heritage, to the harshness of the slave system.

Rosalie Stier Calvert took on responsibilities that most women of her time would not have attempted. She came from a family well-established for many generations in the capitalist and mercantile circles of Antwerp and Amsterdam. While her relatives were in the United States, they invested large sums of money they had brought with them and lived on the income. When the rest of the family returned to Europe, most of the Stiers' American investments remained intact, and Mrs. Calvert was left in charge of managing them. Beginning with simple record-keeping, she progressed to making major investment decisions concerning stocks, bonds, and real estate. She took pride in educating herself about investment opportunities in the United States and became her family's valued adviser.

Rosalie's father always encouraged her to take an active role in managing her own financial destiny. There was no sense that such a course would be unwomanly, although she was advised to be tactful in dealing with her husband on such matters. She had a good head for business and Henri Stier thought that she should use it. Her parents prided themselves on treating their children, male and female, equally. Her father disdained what he called the system of "milord *Anglais*," a system favoring the first-born male. The Stiers practiced the equality they preached, both in the marriage portions they settled on their children and in the final disposition of their estates.

One of the delights of Mrs. Calvert's letters is their revelation of the different roles that she assumed toward her three principal correspondents—her father, her brother, and her sister. Toward her father, she was the dutiful daughter, striving for approval but asserting herself as she matured and gained confidence. Toward her brother, she was the arch and playful little sister, sharing artistic and literary interests, but gradually becoming more like an elder sister as her worldly responsibilities increased while his did not. And toward her sister, Isabelle, ten years her senior, she was most herself, revealing her sorrows and delights, her vanities and frustrations, her loneliness and fears.

All of Rosalie Stier Calvert's letters have been preserved by descendants of her sister, Isabelle Stier van Havre, who have provided copies of the material in their possession for use in this manuscript and to further restoration of the Riversdale house. I have worked from copies in preparing this manuscript, but I have visited and examined the original collections in two of the three family archives. Because Mrs. Calvert usually numbered her letters, we are reasonably sure of having a complete set. Copies of all materials provided by the Belgian sources are in the collection of the Riversdale Historical Society, 4811 Riverdale Road, Riverdale, Maryland.

Mrs. Calvert's some ninety personal and a dozen business letters to her father are in the van Havre Family Papers at the Château du List, Schoten, Belgium. Her few letters to her mother, who died in 1804, are preserved with those to her father. Mrs. Calvert's letters to her sister, Isabelle van Havre, fifty-nine in number, are in the Calvert-Stier Papers in the archives of the van de Werve family at Viersal, Belgium. The

Calvert-Stier Papers at Viersal also contain Mrs. Calvert's occasional letters to her brother-in-law, Jean Michel van Havre, and miscellaneous letters of George Calvert and Caroline Maria, the Calverts' daughter. In addition, there is a fine set of copybooks kept by H. J. Stier from 1803 to 1821, recording, sometimes verbatim, his correspondence with Mrs. Calvert. A small group of letter-drafts made by Isabelle van Havre of her correspondence with Mrs. Calvert is also found in the van de Werve Archives. All of this material, except George and Caroline Calvert's correspondence, is in French.

In addition, the van de Werve Archives contain correspondence from members of the Calvert family to their Belgian relatives after Mrs. Calvert's death. The most important are letters from her son George Henry Calvert from 1824 to 1834, and from her son-in-law, Thomas Willing Morris, from 1833 to 1848, addressed to Charles J. Stier, both groups in English. There are miscellaneous papers too numerous to detail, including such items as death notices, an invitation to dine at Mount Vernon, and catalogues of paintings offered for public sale.

Another major source of material for this work was the Henri J. Stier Papers at the Maryland Historical Society in Baltimore, which contain originals, in French, of letters from Stier to Mrs. Calvert from June 1803 through August 1807. This collection includes a sixty-three-page type-script in English of letters addressed to Charles J. Stier from 1797 to 1828; forty pages contain Rosalie's letters to her brother, some thirty-five in number, from 1797 to 1819. The work of an unknown translator, the copy was made in 1905 for John Ridgely Carter, a Calvert descendant, from original letters in his possession and since lost. This typescript remains the major source of Mrs. Calvert's letters to her brother, ex-cerpts from which, edited by William D. Hoyt, Jr., appeared in "The Calvert-Stier Correspondence," in the *Maryland Historical Magazine* 38 (1943). Thirty-four original letters in French from Mrs. Calvert to Charles Stier are available in the Calvert Family Papers in the Rare Book and Manuscript Library at Columbia University, New York City, along with some twenty items of other family correspondence.

Finally, the papers of Charles J. Stier in the Baron Henry de Witte Archives in Antwerp are especially rich in information about the Stier family's years in America. This interesting collection contains over six hundred pages of correspondence, primarily in French, received by Charles Stier from 1795 through 1805. There is also a daybook, in English, kept by Charles during his first years in America, with entries from October 13, 1794, through December 23, 1795, and from November 3, 1800, through September 19, 1801. The collection also contains miscellaneous business correspondence, accounts with American merchants, and doctors' bills, most of them in English.

In footnotes and chapter endnotes I have used the following references to these primary sources:

Calvert-Stier Papers, van de Werve Archives, Viersal, Belgium (Cal S-V).

Calvert Family Papers, Rare Book and Manuscript Library, Columbia University, New York City (Calvert, CU-NYC).

Typescript translation made for John Ridgely Carter, Henri J. Stier Papers, Maryland Historical Society, Baltimore (Carter Trans-MHS).

Charles J. Stier Papers, Baron Henry de Witte Archives, Antwerp (CJS-A).

Henri J. Stier Papers, Maryland Historical Society, Baltimore (Stier-MHS).

Van Havre Papers, Château du List Archives, Schoten, Belgium (Van Havre-S).

In order to allow Mrs. Calvert's letters to form a narrative, I have arranged them chronologically. I have broken some letters, which were written over a period of time, into separate entries, noting the procedure in each case. Chapter 1, describing the Stier family's arrival and nine-year sojourn in America, is mostly in my words. In chapters 2 through 11, the main body of the book, Mrs. Calvert tells her story in her own words, and I have merely provided an introductory headnote for each. Chapter 12, recounting what happened to the Calvert family after Rosalie's death, is again primarily in my words.

Because Rosalie could never be certain that a particular letter would reach its recipient, especially during the years of wartime interference with shipping, she had no qualms about repeating herself. I have removed a good deal of such repetition, sometimes entire letters. For this reason I have not attempted to reproduce her system of numbering letters to her three main recipients.

I have translated Mrs. Calvert's letters in a fairly literal manner, but I have made some correction in her spelling of names, her capitalization, and her punctuation. For misspelled names and places, I have used her spelling in the first instance followed by a correction in brackets, and thereafter I have used the corrected form. I have modernized place names, using "Bladensburg" for "Bladensburgh," for example, and "Georgetown" for "George Town." Mrs. Calvert's capitalization generally follows modern usage, but she had a tendency to capitalize certain English words, such as "Hogshead" and "Overseer," which I have dropped to lower case. I have adjusted both her punctuation and her paragraphing, since her sentences and paragraphs are overly long by modern standards. I have made minimal changes in reproducing the Carter translation's version of Mrs. Calvert's letters to her brother, Charles. I have noted some apparent errors and have made some silent punctuation and paragraphing changes.

I have received help from many people in preparing these letters for publication, but no one has been more generous with his time and talent than Dr. Alfons Bousse of Ittre, Belgium. Bousse not only rediscovered Rosalie's letters but also persuaded their owners to share them with the Riversdale Historical Society. He has also provided invaluable help over many years, answering questions, tracking down information, and sharing his knowledge of the language, the Stier family, and Belgium.

My thanks to Baron Henry de Witte of Antwerp and to the van de Werve family of Viersal for allowing use of the letters in their possession and for permitting me to examine their archives. Baron J. R. de Terwangne of Brussels assisted us in securing copies of Mrs. Calvert's letters to her father, for which we are most grateful. Mrs. Rosalie Eugenia Calvert Ray of Fayetteville, North Carolina, graciously allowed us to see helpful Calvert family papers in her possession.

I became involved in the publication of these letters through work with the Riversdale Historical Society. I am grateful to the members of this organization for their encouragement, particularly to Ann Ferguson, their president, whose enthusiasm for this project never flagged. Many others have contributed their time and knowledge in supporting this project. My special thanks to Fred DeMarr for sharing his knowledge of Prince George's County history, to Rebecca Meriwether for her early assistance and encouragement, and to Katherine Looney, John Ferrell, Chantal Couronné, and Conrad Berger for their skillful assistance in translation. My largest debt is to my husband, George, who has been my chief critic and main support throughout the course of this project.

For the most part, however, the words of this book were written long ago. They belong to Rosalie Stier Calvert, a woman whose short but fascinating life greatly enriched my own.

MISTRESS OF RIVERSDALE

The Stier Family in America

THE STIER FAMILY FLED BELGIUM in the summer of 1794 as the army of Revolutionary France advanced on their native Antwerp. Rosalie Stier's father, Henri Joseph, had begun plans for the family's departure the previous spring, when he instructed his agents in Amsterdam and London to begin converting his European funds into gold or American currency. The Reign of Terror that had sent thousands to their death in France was advancing into Belgium. Many of the Stiers' aristocratic friends and relatives were also beginning to leave, but few would go as far as the Stiers or stay as long. In June the family made their way to Amsterdam, where they contracted for a ship to take them to America. The ship was the *Adriana,* and Captain Kieran Fitzpatrick agreed to transport them and their belongings for thirty-six hundred florins, with departure set for August. The American consul in Amsterdam, Sylvanus Bourne, and the American minister to England, Thomas Pinckney, provided the Stiers with letters of introduction and safe conduct prior to their departure.[1] The *Adriana* sailed on August 26 and six weeks later arrived in Philadelphia. The family's arrival was noted in Philadelphia's *American Daily Advertiser* on October 13, 1794:

"Yesterday arrived the Ship *Adriana,* Capt. Kieran Fitzpatrick, from Amsterdam. In the *Adriana* came passengers:

Mr. H. J. Stier D'Artsalaer and Lady,

Mr. J. M. Vanhavren [*sic*], Lady and Child,

Mr. C. J. Stier and Lady,

Miss Stier and two Servants."

The arriving family members were Henri Joseph Stier and his wife, Marie Louise Peeters, and their three children—twenty-six-year-old Isabelle, twenty-four-year-old Charles Jean, and sixteen-year-old Rosalie. With Isabelle came her husband, Jean Michel van Havre, and their three-year-old daughter, Louise. Charles brought his new bride, Marie (Mimi) van Havre, who was Jean Michel's younger sister.

For the next nine years the family sought a new home and life in the New World, first in Philadelphia and then in Maryland and Virginia. But it was only the youngest member of the family, Rosalie, who was to find a permanent home in America.

PHILADELPHIA

"America displeases me more and more every day—you meet only scoundrels. It is going to be very difficult to become accustomed to the way of life here."[2] Thus did young Rosalie Stier pronounce judgment on her new home in June of 1795, after eight months in the United States. Rosalie was writing from Philadelphia, the capital of the United States and by far its most cosmopolitan city, but she was not impressed.

The Stiers had given up much in their flight to America. They had left behind a handsome townhouse in Antwerp on the Rue de Venus, a château at Brasschaat, a few miles north of Antwerp, which Stier had built in 1780 and named "the Mick," and a fourteenth-century castle, Cleydael, at Aartselaar to the south of Antwerp, which was part of Marie Louise Peeters's inheritance. There were other properties leased out to various tenants. As important as all these material possessions was the network of family, social, religious, and business ties built up over countless years, which had been left behind.

The Stiers brought enough monetary assets with them to enable them to live like gentry in the new land. They also brought two of their servants, a huge quantity of luggage, and the finest collection of paintings that had ever crossed the Atlantic. The collection was that of Rosalie's maternal grandfather, Jean Egide Peeters, whose widow had entrusted the Stiers with its safekeeping. The sixty-three paintings included works by such masters as Peter Paul Rubens, Anthony Van Dyke, Titian, Rembrandt, David Teniers, and Jan Brueghel.[3] The collection was in appreciative and knowledgeable hands. Henri J. Stier was a direct descendant of Peter Paul Rubens; Stier's great-great-grandmother had been Hélène Françoise Rubens, the painter's granddaughter.[4]

Despite Rosalie Stier's comment about meeting only scoundrels in

America, the family was quickly accepted into the best circles in Philadelphia. Rosalie's brother, Charles, kept a daybook during the first year of the family's stay in America, and from his entries we learn that the Stiers were soon in contact with the social and business leaders of the city—the Binghams, the Willings, the Peters, the Penns, and the Morrises.[5] In November 1794, the entire family settled into a rented house at the corner of Fourth and Walnut streets, and later that month Rosalie accompanied her parents on a trip to New York.[6]

On their return they began a round of social activity that culminated in their "Introduction at Mrs. Washington's Drawing Room by Mrs. Gen'l Knox" on the day after Christmas. Their sponsor was Mrs. Henry Knox, wife of the former secretary of war and a close friend and adviser to the president. Six days later the Stiers attended the president's New Year's Day levee, and a week later they received a personal visit from Mrs. Washington.[7] It was the beginning of a long association with America's first family.

Social and business contacts were interwoven. The Stiers received a visit from William Bingham, founder of the Bank of North America, only days after their arrival in Philadelphia. This was followed immediately by a social call from Mrs. Bingham and then an invitation to dinner at the elegant Bingham home. Anne Willing Bingham was Philadelphia's recognized social leader, a beautiful and cultured lady; she and her husband had spent five years abroad and would have found much to discuss with the Belgians. The Stiers called on Anne's father, Thomas Willing, president of both the Bank of North America and the Bank of the United States, and soon were invited to the Willing home for dinner. H. J. Stier bought stock in the Bank of North America, and Bingham approached the Stiers to explain a land speculation in Maine in which he was involved.[8]

Bingham wasn't the only speculator interested in the new arrivals; Charles Stier records meetings with James Greenleaf, Thomas Law, whom he identified as a "Speculator in Wash: City lots," and Théophile Cazenove, agent for a group of Dutch bankers speculating in United States securities and buying up millions of acres of land in western New York State and Pennsylvania.[9]

The Stiers had numerous contacts with the French émigré community in Philadelphia. They met the exiled Talleyrand in January 1795 at a dancing party and later paid him a visit where they discussed land speculation. The wily Talleyrand, former president of the French National Assembly and future minister of foreign affairs for Napoleon, was at a low point in his career, working with Théophile Cazenove selling American real estate to French investors. The Stiers also met the Vicomte de Noailles, Lafayette's brother-in-law, the Duc de la Rochefoucauld-Liancourt, and Omer Talon, all members of Talleyrand's circle in Philadelphia.[10]

The Stiers took advantage of Philadelphia's cultural life, attending the handsome Chestnut Street theater with its marble colonnade and visiting Charles Wilson Peale's museum in the new quarters provided it by the American Philosophical Society. Charles Stier called on the Italian sculptor Giuseppe Ceracchi, who was working in Philadelphia on a bust of President Washington, and also met miniaturist-painter Archibald Robertson. The entire family enjoyed walks in the landscaped State House Yard, a public green only blocks from their house, with its high-walled enclosure of graveled serpentine walks wandering among a planting of one hundred young elm trees.[11] It was on such a promenade that they first encountered two American bishops, Roman Catholic bishop John Carroll and Protestant Episcopal bishop William White, soon after arriving in Philadelphia.[12]

The Stiers, devout Catholics, attended St. Mary's Church, established in 1763, one of three Catholic churches in the city. St. Mary's was the fashionable church and the one favored by the French-speaking émigrés. Charles Stier records frequent contacts with merchant George Meade and businessman Thomas Fitzsimons, who were trustees of St. Mary's. The church, austere and unassuming on the exterior, was richly ornamented inside and had special pews reserved for the French, Spanish, and Portuguese ministers to the United States. Rosalie Stier found one of the priests to be a hard taskmaster. She warned her sister-in-law, Mimi, to "take care to eat fish on Friday and Saturday and go to mass on holy days because when Madame v[an] H[avre] and I went to conf[ession], for penance we were required to attend mass for eight days in succession—and for nothing other on my part than having eaten meat two or three times and forgotten once to attend mass. Can you imagine our outrage! The horrid fellow—that Irishman—he wants to make us into pious little puppets. Never will he see me again—nor I him, I assure you. It is abominable—dreadful—shocking, etc. These are some of the insults we are voicing."[13]

St. Mary's had had three priests serving its sizable congregation in 1793, but two of them had died in the great yellow fever epidemic of that year. Only Father Keating survived to resume his duties, and he was probably the Irishman who was the object of Rosalie Stier's wrath. Two hundred members of the congregation also perished in the epidemic, and the St. Mary's cemetery was still being covered with extra loads of soil as a sanitary precaution after the numerous burials of that dreadful year.[14]

Illness was a constant concern, and Philadelphia was considered a dangerous city, especially during the summer and early autumn. Everyone who could make arrangements to leave for the countryside during that time did so. Each fever was viewed with suspicion and every patient examined for the telltale yellow cast.

The Stiers chose the famous Benjamin Rush, professor of medical theory and practice at the University of Pennsylvania, as their physician. Dr. Rush was a neighbor, a veteran of the 1793 epidemic, and noted for his bleeding and purging treatments. Modern historians have credited Rush's heroic treatments with considerably increasing the mortality rates during the Philadelphia epidemic. Charles Stier, in a bout with fever in 1795, noted being bled repeatedly, purged, blistered, and dosed with "english bark" by Dr. Rush.[15]

The Stiers ordinarily spoke and corresponded with one another in French, so language was one of the problems that complicated adjustment to their new home. Charles Stier and Jean Michel van Havre could express themselves in English verbally and in writing. H. J. Stier relied heavily on his son's command of English in transacting business and legal matters.

Rosalie Stier was undoubtedly the most proficient of the women of the family, and possibly of the entire family. She had spent over four years, from the time she was nine until she was fourteen, under the tutelage of English nuns at a convent school in Liège. Her sister, Isabelle, had attended the same school, but only for a year and was never comfortable in English. The English canonesses of the Holy Sepulchre recorded that "the Youngest Miss Stier came here upon the 29 November 1787. She was from Antwerp & pay'd 21 Guineas per An[num]. She left us ye 26th of May 1792."[16] Rosalie's ease in the language facilitated the family's social life and probably helped her father in conducting business when Charles was away on trips.

Rosalie got her first taste of revolution at the convent in Liège. The town was racked by unrest from 1789, when an uprising of the poor overthrew the town's established civil authority, to early 1791, when imperial troops restored order. The convent and school were not damaged, but social disorder outside the walls posed a constant threat to the institution. When order was restored, the nuns of Holy Sepulchre and their students, thirteen-year-old Rosalie Stier among them, mounted a joyous celebration with a massive illumination of their church—seventeen pyramids, each constructed of fifty candlelit tin lamps. Joy was short-lived, however, as French revolutionaries invaded Liège the following year; in 1794, the nuns closed their convent and fled to England.[17] Rosalie had left school by the time the French came to Liège, but her convent years left her with a lifelong fear of revolution, an abiding admiration for the English, and a facility with their language.

Charles and Mimi Stier, with an eye to establishing a mercantile business in America, took an extended tour in the spring of 1795 through Pennsylvania, Delaware, Maryland, and Virginia, making contacts and investigating possibilities. Their route led them through Chester, Chichester, and Wilmington, on to Elkton, North East, and Charlestown in Maryland, through Havre de Grace to Baltimore. Charles observed that Baltimore, only "raised within these 30 years, [was] yet increasing in every part," and that "trade, industry & culture [were] equally growing," but he disliked its "unholdsome [*sic*] Climate prevented by fire in Evening."[18] Jean Michel van Havre joined the young Stiers in Alexandria, where Charles admired the buildings and industry, and they journeyed on to Norfolk together.

Rosalie, meanwhile, reported from Philadelphia that "we are much more comfortable with the people here. Last week we went to see Mrs. Peeters [*sic*] at her country place. At first we were all somewhat constrained, but gradually relaxed, and the conversation became quite interesting and the afternoon passed very pleasantly. They don't live so splendidly. They eat and drink a lot. We ate a big dish of strawberries with cream there which was excellent."[19]

Rosalie chided her brother: "How is it that having two sisters who love you equally well, you always write the one and not the other? That will never be forgiven. It is true that our Madame van Havre is an excellent sister . . . and that Rosette [Rosalie] annoys you sometimes, even quite frequently I must confess, and with no regret afterwards, but I have always heard that a brother ordinarily prefers the sister who torments him the most. I am going to mend my ways and will be completely changed when you return. . . . We are talking a lot about going to the country, but are finding great difficulties about our baggage, the servants, horses, coaches, etc. Really, everything here is so disorganized and the people of the country so strange that we don't know what to do."[20]

The Stiers were planning to leave Philadelphia. In July 1795, H. J. Stier wrote his son that he had leased a country place of 170 acres outside of

Annapolis from a Mr. Thompson for one hundred pounds a year. He asked Charles to go by Annapolis on his way back from Virginia and check out both the town and the property. He observed that "when we arrive we will need a carriage, horses, a coachman, gardener, cook, provisions of all kinds, and some furniture such as bedsteads, chairs, etc. Can wine and oil be had there? Please inform yourself. Is there someone there who rents state-carriages? Anyone to cut the hay at the country property? Are there people living in the small houses on the property?"[21]

It was odd to lease such an establishment sight unseen, and not everyone was pleased with the decision. Isabelle van Havre definitely did not want to live in the country, and she said that economy was one of the motivating factors in her father's decision—that by deciding to reside at "an inferior court" like Annapolis, he would not have to augment his fortune and could live on what he had.[22] H. J. Stier had his reasons for feeling financially strained at the time; he had just had distressing news from his agent about the taxes being imposed on émigrés by the French in Belgium. He had already been assessed a tax of forty thousand francs when the French took over Antwerp, and some of his properties had to be sold to satisfy that levy.[23] Now it seemed that there might be more or that they could lose all their properties. If they stayed in Philadelphia, they would need both a town and a country house, and the cost of keeping up with their social set there would be high. A quieter and more economical life in the country probably had much appeal at this time.

ANNAPOLIS

By September 1795, the senior Stiers and Rosalie had settled into their new country home, Strawberry Hill, about two miles by road from Annapolis. The house, built about 1765, was a frame dwelling of two stories with two-storied wings and occupied an enviable location on Dorsey Creek, overlooking the Severn River and the town.[24] The van Havres and the Charles Stiers were still in Philadelphia, but by the end of 1795, both had moved to Alexandria, Virginia, where for a time they shared a house.

The autumn of 1795 was an unsettling time for the family. Several members, both in Annapolis and in Philadelphia, came down with fever, but it was malaria and not the dreaded yellow fever. Charles was ill in Philadelphia; Isabelle and Mimi, visiting at Strawberry Hill, became ill; and Rosalie caught it too. Van Havre, who had come to take his wife back to Philadelphia, had to content himself with escorting Mimi back to Charles, since his own wife was still too sick to travel. In late October

H. J. Stier reported to Charles, "Our *ménage* goes about the same. Betzi [Isabelle] is still sick; the cook often drunk and in bad accord with Joseph. The cuisine, however, goes well, thanks to my 'overseer,' Rosette [Rosalie], who is making great progress in this skill."[25]

There was more bad news from Europe. The Stiers' agent in Amsterdam, Henri Lambert Louvrex, wrote urging their return; he reported that French soldiers had been billeted in their vacant Antwerp townhouse and at their Château du Mick and that damages to their properties were great. With the annexation of the Belgian provinces to France in October 1795, French law became applicable, and the possessions of émigrés were to be sold for the profit of the Republic. Stier took defensive action, drawing up papers contesting this action, arguing somewhat disingenuously that he was not an émigré but had left the country for business reasons and because, he added with special irony, he feared the tyranny of the British.[26]

The thought of returning to Europe pleased Rosalie, who, after more than a year, was no more reconciled to America than before. She wrote Isabelle:

"You say that you are more content and that if we cannot return next year, you will not hang yourself. In that regard you are far more reasonable than I. I cannot stand the idea of staying here forever, not even for two more years. When I think about it, I detest America and it depresses me. You are in quite a different situation from me; it is less dreadful to be deprived of the comforts and pleasures we miss so much when one has enjoyed them for a long time, than to be deprived at the very time when one would have begun to enjoy them, which is my case. Oh, my dear Sister, I cannot answer for myself if ever it is decided that we must remain here.

"What happiness can one expect in a country where everyone is a scoundrel, where no one can be trusted, even in the smallest matter? The women, I find, are generally insincere, unintelligent, without talent or education. This is only natural since they are always with each other without the company of men, and their conversation revolves solely around their households, children, and clothes. No, verily, I would prefer to live in mediocrity in a pretty European town than to live here in great wealth."[27]

Most of her dissatisfaction, however, was simply a young girl's boredom with the family's new country life routine. As Mrs. Stier said, they had been living "like nuns in a convent" since moving to Strawberry Hill; Rosalie's mother vowed that she had not been a mile outside their fences in the five months since they moved. She and Rosette amused themselves reading English romances, a popular diversion in nearby Annapolis, where bookshops were well stocked. Rosalie complained to Charles that Mama had taken her current novel and was reading it day and night, even on Sunday, but Mama said she wasn't reading it "for the pleasure of the very tender English amours, but in order to learn English."[28] Elsewhere Rosalie reported a surfeit of reading about romance, saying she was "up to her eyes in romances—at the moment I have eleven in the house."[29]

Rosalie was also being introduced to housekeeping skills and was not enthusiastic about either the pursuit or her progress:

"As for me, dear Sister, I could become an excellent housekeeper if I wanted to (Mama says I do it very well). However, I find it is a calling much beneath my grandeur . . . and it wastes too much time which could be better employed. Meanwhile our household is coming along—it couldn't be better. Fanny is an excellent cook. She can make all sorts of cakes, pastries, sausages, bread, etc. By the way, Papa bought two pigs which we have salted. It is a pleasure, my dear Sister, to see that done, and then from the lard they make some pies which are better than those made with butter, and from the head they make something whose name I don't know and which you would take for a block of granite, but which is excellent [served] cold for breakfast. . . . What do you think of my knowledge of cooking? Mama says I do it well, but that's not really true. I only occupy myself with it in the morning, up til 10 o'clock, then I get dressed and am a grand lady for the rest of the day."[30]

When Isabelle told her that she must learn to manage a household if she expected to become a good wife, Rosalie replied that in her present situation it did not seem that would ever come to pass, so "it would be a waste of my time, and I don't like learning useless things."[31]

H. J. Stier reported that his house servants in January 1796 consisted of two black men and two black women. Fanny was the cook, and despite her occasional intemperance, Stier agreed with Rosalie that she was invaluable. Fanny's husband, Joseph, was one of the two men and Jacob the other. At least two of the four servants, and probably all, were leased by the Stiers from their owners. Jacob was leased for seven dollars a month and one of the women for three dollars.[32] There was no housekeeper; as Mrs. Stier lamented, it was hard to find a good one.

A glimpse into the relationship between the Belgians and their new black servants is provided by Rosalie's advice to her older sister on their proper handling:

"It seems to me, dear Sister, that you are giving severe reprimands to your blacks. You need to be more indulgent. It is quite uncharitable not to allow your cook to have a lover. Ours fought heartily with another woman in order to have her husband. That is certainly worse and we would have prevented it if possible.

"I must tell you a funny story—the other night Papa goes to the kitchen just before bedtime to see if everything was in order. He finds the staircase door open, even though he had carried the key up to his room. He goes to the door of the kitchen, which he could not open; he calls but no one replies. He opens the door to the small courtyard and sees the old negro, Fanny's husband. Papa asks him about Jacob, to which he replies that [Jacob] apparently is in the kitchen, and he goes to open, with no difficulty, the door which Papa couldn't budge. At the same time [Papa] sees the window wide open, at which point he conducts the negro upstairs (because you must understand that all our Armenians sleep in two lofts) and comes to tell us about this affair. Mama and I come down to examine everything, and Papa goes to check on the little houses at the bottom of the hill. He got no further than the dairy when he heard music—they were giving a party in one of these houses! Papa came back, and we didn't want to upset them further since it was an innocent enough thing and something that masters permit occasionally. But the next day every single one of them was reprimanded and all is well now. I find that it is not necessary to treat these people harshly in order to be well served. You must only be firm."[33]

By January 1796, the family was beginning to make social contacts in Annapolis, but the Stiers were reserved and even suspicious of new friends. Rosalie reported to Isabelle:

"At least everyone is extremely courteous to us. You will say that this is merely self-interested politeness, which is very true. We had a proof of it the other day in a person I didn't suspect of such baseness. You know all the courtesies Mrs. O[gle] has extended to me. I saw no self-interest there even though she said she much liked having a young lady near her in order to attract more company. I never believed any other intent of her, but she just leased us a negress for $3 a month whom she had promised us for $2, which is the ordinary price. Since she has recompensed herself so well, I shall no longer blush to accept her civilities and shall take advantage of them."[34]

The self-interested Mrs. Ogle was seventy-three-year-old Anne Tasker Ogle, widow of Maryland's colonial governor Samuel Ogle. Mrs. Ogle lived in Annapolis and maintained an active social life. Rosalie could not have found a patroness better able to open any door, not just to the social life of the small but affluent town but to that of the entire state and region. Her family was allied with the state's oldest and finest families, and her son Benjamin Ogle would become governor of Maryland two years hence.

Mrs. Ogle seems to have effected a veritable revolution in young Rosalie's attitude toward her new home. Only a month after her description of Mrs. Ogle's "baseness," Rosalie wrote Charles:

"I have always faulted you, my Brother, for wanting to stay in this country for six years. Now I forgive you for it and will grumble no more if this must be our lot. Truly, I don't have the slightest desire to return now. This astonishes you, doesn't it, and you ask what could be the reason for this great change? *Voilà,* I will explain it to you: I have stayed for two days at Mrs. Ogle's, and I have been to three dancing parties which have completely reconciled me to America. Society here really is delightful, and if I could have three or four admirers—which I lack and which are necessary here—I assure you that I could amuse myself better than at Antwerp.

"There is only one disagreeable aspect and that is the tedium of dancing for the whole evening with the same person. You must not forget to bring a nice suit of clothes for the ball. . . . Take care also, my dear Brother, to bring a pair of trusty and elegant pistols because since I have been to several parties and plan on going to more, it could happen that— for the novelty of it—some idiot might pay court to me. And you should know that occasionally it comes to pass here that when a young lady refuses a man, he duels with her brother to console himself. Sometimes even the fathers fight, not with their fists, like you—they are too noble for that in Annapolis, that is for tradesmen like you Alexandrians—but either they break each other's heads politely in the English manner, or they shoot off each other's pigtails with pistols. Isn't that quaint? There is a young man here who has engaged in one or two such escapades and I assure you that he is quite a nice boy, amiable and most intelligent, and has been to Europe. You can see that I am almost 'in love' myself."[35]

While the young men of Annapolis made a favorable impression and made life in America bearable, the young women came in for a different assessment. "The women of Annapolis are very obliging about personal criticism, which is their principal occupation," she wrote Charles. "Sometimes when one sees the women assembled, one would say that they are the best of friends, the way they talk with one another. But they are not apart for one minute before each one begins to speak ill of the others. You remember that scene of the director at his wit's end when the two actresses embrace each other and then turn to say: (one) 'How uncouth she is!' (the other) 'How I hate her!' It is just like that."[36]

In May 1796, Isabelle van Havre gave birth to her second child, a boy whom she named Edward. Mrs. Stier went over to Alexandria to help out, and the Stiers were pleased with their little "American" grandson. Jean Michel van Havre asked his father-in-law's advice about inoculating the baby against smallpox; Stier replied that van Havre must, of course, make his own decision, but that he saw nothing unsuitable in deferring it. "I cannot imagine that the epidemic could touch an infant at the breast since no one would come near him who could communicate this illness to him. I cannot believe the air would be fatal to him."[37] Stier's advice was better than it might appear, for in England that same year Edward Jenner was conducting his first successful experiments with cowpox as an inoculating agent against smallpox; practice prior to Jenner's success was to use matter from smallpox itself in an attempt to induce a light case—a risky and controversial procedure, but one that had spread in the United States.

The good weather of spring and early summer raised everyone's spirits. H. J. Stier reported that the farm was overflowing with abundance, one day a calf, another some pigs, then chicks, and that the garden was an earthly paradise. He was even looking ahead to next year and placed an order for hyacinth and tulip bulbs to be sent from Holland. In April he brought over the seventeen-year-old son of his gardener at the Château du Mick to train him to be his American gardener. He paid the boy no wages but sent a yearly sum home to his father. This arrangement was challenged by the young man in the fall of 1797, and Stier sought Charles's advice, but before he could reply, the matter had been worked out.[38] Stier also bought two beautiful new riding horses that spring, and Rosette obliged them all by giving a sample of her riding skill.[39]

In June there was more distressing news from Belgium. Grandmother Peeters—Mathilde van den Cruyce—had died. The death was not unexpected; Madame Peeters had been infirm for several years, but the passing caused Marie Louise Peeters to reflect that with her mother gone, her last compelling tie to her homeland was broken. Reports from relatives in Belgium indicated that life under the French was difficult; Rosalie's aunt Jeanne Guyot Stier wrote that "we have been enjoying a liberty which is much worse than slavery, and if it lasts much longer it will ruin us altogether. All of the decent people are oppressed; it is only the knaves who go around with their heads held high and fill their purses."[40]

Late summer and autumn of 1796 found several members of the Stier family ill with fever again. Isabelle and her two children, who were visiting at Strawberry Hill, were all ill. Mrs. Stier was not well, and after a long bout with fever himself, H. J. Stier wrote that they could never adjust to the climate and must seek a more suitable place to live. He complained, "It is rare that we are all at the table together—more often half the family is in bed," adding that "I don't anticipate being able to remain here where we are incessantly ill. . . ."[41] Stier said that he would like to move by midsummer of the following year, but was unenthusiastic about Charles's suggestion to live in Alexandria.

Charles was engaged in various wholesale mercantile activities and traveled a good deal in pursuit of business. His father gave him a steady stream of advice on business and financial matters and not infrequent criticism. "You are singularly unfortunate and clumsy in matters of commerce," Stier wrote his son in reference to Charles's importation of a shipment of lace from the Low Countries for resale in the United States. The shipment had arrived in Baltimore a month previously and had sat idle owing to Charles's inactivity. Now, as Stier pointed out, "the balls are beginning, the dresses made, the money spent," and Charles would be hard put to sell his lace.[42] Investments provided the major source of income for both H. J. and Charles Stier. The senior Stier invested in government bonds and bank stocks, especially the Bank of the United States. After his move to Alexandria, Charles became an investor in the Bank of Alexandria, and his father later followed suit. Charles came to know William Herbert, who became president of the bank in 1796.

In his early years in the United States, H. J. Stier showed no interest in investing in real estate. When Charles, dissatisfied with his living arrangements in Alexandria, wanted to purchase a house, his father strongly advised against buying a house, a lot, or any slaves, saying that money in the bank was better.[43] Later, when his son-in-law, van Havre, ignored his advice and bought a house in Alexandria, Stier counseled his son against doing the same thing, warning that a slave uprising could force the family to leave at any time and that money invested in a house would be lost.[44] Stier was aware of the slave uprisings taking place in Haiti at this time and voiced fears about the large number of blacks in Maryland and Virginia. Over a third of the population of these two states was black, and blacks constituted nearly half of nearby Annapolis's twenty-two hundred inhabitants. The Belgians had never lived in a slave society before, and the elder Stier, meeting with little success in managing his few leased servants, was understandably nervous. Stier's son-in-law did not share his worry about the problem, saying that there was little to fear, since "one white was worth three blacks."[45]

After another bout of illness at Strawberry Hill in April 1797, Stier was sure that he wanted to move into Annapolis. "I have been bled, purged, and blistered, and I'm still alive!" exulted Stier. His physician, Dr. John Thomas Shaaff of Annapolis, "had to ply me with rhubarb, senna, castor oil, and jalap to get relief."[46]

Springtime was also restorative, and by May, Mrs. Stier reported that her husband was well and was working with his flowers; he had met three other flower-lovers who were also intelligent people. One of these was Dr. Upton Scott, who became a good friend, and another was William Faris, craftsman and tavern-keeper, who kept meticulous records of his horticultural pursuits. Faris visited Stier's garden in April 1797 and reported that Stier had the best collection of hyacinths he had seen. The two men began an exchange of plants and gardening information, and in 1798 Faris recorded planting four thousand narcissus bulbs that he had gotten from Stier.[47]

For Rosalie, there were other pursuits to enjoy during this last spring at Strawberry Hill. When Charles and Mimi Stier came to visit, Charles spent time sketching the views while Mimi and Rosalie went riding. Rosalie's horse was named Brilliant, and her riding outfit was "a Spencer of nankeen from the Indies [with] a skirt made from the same material."[48] Rosalie's riding style was said to be very bold and a source of constant worry to the young cavalier who accompanied them. It was sometime during this last year at Strawberry Hill that Rosalie Stier met George Calvert, a descendant of the lords Baltimore who had founded Maryland and a member of the state legislature from Prince George's County.

In early August 1797, Stier wrote Charles that he had settled on the rental of the "Jeninks house" in Annapolis at 130 pounds a year.[49] Now known as the Paca House, this fine home had been built in the 1760s by William Paca, a signer of the Declaration of Independence and later governor of Maryland. In 1780, Paca sold the house to attorney Thomas Jennings, who occupied it until his death in 1796. Rosalie described it to her brother:

"Our new house is enormously big, four rooms below, three large and two small ones on the second floor besides the stairhalls, and the finest garden in Annapolis in which there is a spring, a cold bathhouse well-fitted up, and a running stream! What more could I wish for? I do not think we will move before the great heat has abated, and then I trust that

Paca House, the Stiers' Annapolis home from 1797 to 1800. Photographer unknown.

Collection, Paca House

my dear sister Mimi will come to help me furnish and arrange everything, for Mama says she will not undertake any part in it."[50]

It was a grand house, a two-story brick with two single-story wings, and a garden with terraced falls down to a naturalized area on the lowest level. In celebration the family bought a pair of carriage horses and made the rounds in their coach. The rounds would have included some of the loveliest homes in America, a remarkable collection of Georgian town-houses built in the town's colonial golden age and still gathering-places for the small state capital's constant swirl of social activity. The Stiers by this time knew many of the town's prominent residents—the Carrolls, Ogles, Lloyds, Scotts, Murrays, and Keys—and were doubtless welcome additions to the pleasure-loving Annapolitans' social scene.

The move into the Paca-Jennings house was viewed only as a short-term expedient, however, because of news from Belgium. Stier learned in August 1797 that both he and Charles had been taken off the émigrés' list, provided that Stier paid his tax arrears. His agent, Louvrex, complied, and Stier wrote Charles that he was determined to return home the following May or June.[51] Rosalie asked Charles how he felt about the return but did not indicate what her feelings were. She was excited at the prospect of a spring trip from Bath to Niagara Falls prior to their return, however.

The move into town took a good deal of work, and there were the usual delays owing to illness. Stier had to sell off his animals; in October he advertised for sale "four horses, six milch cows, two heifers, and four calves of this year, also two boats, one of which is as good as new."[52] Rosalie's Brilliant was among those sold, but they kept two carriage horses and a pet pony. There was also a round of parties with the November marriage of two socially prominent young people, Edward Lloyd V and Sally Murray, daughter of Dr. James Murray of Annapolis. Stier reported "a great bustle of merriment" occasioned by this marriage, with parties given by the Scotts, the Keys, the Cookes, and the Carrolls.[53] The General Assembly reconvened in the fall, and that always enlivened the social scene. George Calvert was among the returning members of this body, which Stier described as "made up nearly entirely of very frivolous young people of the aristocratic and democratic parties, but both in unison to please the belles who gratefully assist at the legislative assemblies by way of return."[54]

By November 1797, the Stiers were in their new house, and Rosalie urged Charles and Mimi to come and visit, saying that "the household is moving smoothly and we have a very fat cook who makes delicious tarts."[55] Mrs. Stier entertained at a tea party; Calvert was among the guests. She told Charles that their new drawing room was so well arranged, "that entertaining goes quite effortlessly. Besides, I don't worry anymore about the Americans—they think everything Europeans do is fine."[56]

The family's happiness and plans to return to Belgium in 1798 were shattered by a letter from their agent in December 1797. Louvrex reported the collapse of the moderates in France and their succession by a more rigorous regime. The government was voiding return permits, and émigrés who had returned were being ordered back out of the country under pain of court-martial and execution. Further, churches in Antwerp were closed, no services were being held, the French were removing all religious statues from public places, and priests who refused to take the required oath were being deported. "Only God knows," said Louvrex, "how this will end and when you will be able to return to Antwerp."[57]

At this point, H. J. Stier began to think of purchasing property in America and of establishing a permanent home for his family. Despite the fact that he had just moved into one of Annapolis's finest houses and had entrée into the city's highest social circles, Stier rejected permanent settlement there. "If we must remain here, we have concluded that Annapolis is declining too much to establish ourselves here and that the Federal City would be more suitable."[58] Stier was correct; during the 1790s, Annapolis had been displaced by Baltimore, first as an economic and then as a social center. There had even been a move, unsuccessful, to transfer the capital to rapidly growing Baltimore. Annapolis, except for its government-related activities, had become a provincial backwater.[59]

The van Havres also were looking for a more comfortable place to live and in 1798 purchased a newly built house on Cameron Street in Alexandria.[60] Stier urged Charles to become a citizen of the United States in order to facilitate the family's holding of real estate. Worried about the rash of laws proposed against foreigners in 1798, he wrote Charles that "we need to take every precaution to prevent being caught up in this general proscription of foreigners."[61] In June 1798, Charles traveled to Richmond to be naturalized.[62]

ROSALIE'S COURTSHIP AND MARRIAGE

Rosalie Stier was enjoying herself in Annapolis. She was now twenty years old, and George Calvert had become a serious suitor. Calvert, ten years her senior, was the son of Benedict and Elizabeth Calvert of Mount Airy, Maryland, a family with extensive landholdings. Calvert's father, an illegitimate but acknowledged son of Charles Calvert, the fifth Lord Baltimore, had been well provided for both in lands and in revenues by the Lord Proprietor. George Calvert was also connected by marriage to the Washington family, for his older sister Eleanor had married John Parke Custis, who was Martha Washington's son by her first marriage. Eleanor and John Parke Custis had four children, so that George Calvert was "Uncle Calvert" to Martha Washington's four Custis grandchildren, two of whom were living at Mount Vernon.

In early 1798, Calvert, who was going to Mount Vernon on family business and wanted to meet the rest of Rosalie's family, offered to carry mail from the Annapolis Stiers to those in Alexandria. H. J. Stier gave Calvert a letter for Charles in which he wrote that Calvert had asked for Rosalie's hand, but that he had told him plainly of the obstacles to his suit. Stier was still undecided about remaining in America and was loath to make a decision that might separate him from his youngest daughter. But his refusal was not a rejection of Calvert personally, and he cautioned

Charles to receive him warmly: "I do not consider this young man an adventurer, so you will do well to make him as welcome as you can."[63]

Calvert enlisted the aid of his illustrious kinsmen, the Washingtons, in his pursuit of Rosalie. George Washington's diary for Sunday, March 18, 1798, records that "Mr. Steer Senior & Junior Miss Steer & Mrs. Vanhaven dined here and returned to Alexandria afterwards."[64] A family dinner with Washington, whom Stier greatly admired, would scarcely have hurt Calvert's prospects.

Rosalie, meanwhile, was basking in all the attention and was in high spirits. She wrote her sister-in-law, Mimi, about coming to Annapolis for a spring visit: "You need a pretty outfit for making morning calls every day. For receiving visits, a silk would be best and do bring a good supply of elegant bonnets and laces. I have made the most marvelous plans in the world for when you are here. If you want to help me in a little intrigue, we will turn Annapolis completely upside-down, but you must come quickly."[65]

Mimi Stier spent a great deal of time in Annapolis with her in-laws while her husband was traveling, and she reported regularly on her sister-in-law's social and romantic activities: "This afternoon Rosette has been to a party at Madame N[icholas] Carroll's in the country. They had dancing on the green there and she was highly entertained."[66] Tea parties were frequent, and Mimi told Charles of an especially interesting occasion at Miss [Catherine] Carroll's where Rosalie and Mimi stole two beaus away from the tea and attended the theater with them, "which annoyed Miss Carroll so much that she did not ask Rosette to go to the theatre with her the next day."[67] But Mimi also found Rosalie moody and unpredictable—"she is by turns gay, sad, angry, in good humor, then bad, sometimes quite flushed and the next moment pale. I think all she needs is a good husband to her liking."[68]

George Calvert persisted, and by the spring of 1799, his tenacity was producing results. Rosalie's mother wrote Charles: "C[alvert] has come calling again with gifts. He gains ground every day. We try to defer his visits as much as possible, but these lovers always find a thousand pretexts for coming together. It is surprising how tenderly he courts her and with such sustained attentions. If I were a girl I would make him court me for six years! All this only augments our difficulty."[69]

Mimi also thought that George Calvert was a graceful suitor, and she described some of the gifts he showered on Rosalie: "He brought his portrait which is very prettily set in gold with a lock of his hair [surrounding it], and on a chain to wear around her neck. He was very embarrassed about presenting it to her; nonetheless, it was given and accepted, and I had to place it around her neck. The scamp!—he looked as if he enjoyed seeing it placed there. Then in place of the ring he had given her came another with locks of his hair and his monogram. He presented it as prettily and tenderly as could be. It is a pleasure to see him pay court."[70]

A week later Calvert returned, "more amorous than ever," according to Mimi. "He presented [Rosalie] an extremely pretty kerchief pin [bearing] his monogram, surrounded with pearls and with locks of his hair. The pin is of his own design and in very good taste. He is a man who cannot be resisted, and my sister loves him well and rightly so. He woos her so tenderly and with such gallantry that a girl must yield. I didn't think it possible for an American to be so amiable or that Calvert could be so gallant."[71]

The personal nature of these gifts indicated that the couple had overcome parental opposition, but even so, Mimi reported that "Papa was in very low spirits about the whole thing," and she urged Charles to come and cheer him up.[72] There were preparations to be made, and one of the most important, at least to H. J. Stier, was drawing up a marriage contract for his daughter.

Such contracts were common among aristocratic families in Europe when titles and vast estates were involved, and they were also reasonably common among rich Americans, since without them American law generally provided that joint property belonged solely to a husband. Rosalie Stier was an heiress with important financial prospects, and Stier intended to protect her interests in this marriage with the American.

The six-page agreement Stier had drawn up was a four-way contract between himself, Calvert, Rosalie, and attorney William Cooke of Baltimore. It specified that Calvert was to receive a legacy of five thousand dollars belonging to Rosalie—a bequest from her aunt the Baroness de Schilde—on their marriage. In return, Calvert put up all of several tracts of land in his possession—over four thousand acres—for William Cooke to hold in trust until the marriage should take place, and afterwards to hold in trust for the joint use of Calvert and Rosalie during their lives. If Calvert should die first, Rosalie would have dower rights to all the properties, and after her death the lands would revert to Calvert's heirs. Since Rosalie stood to inherit considerable sums of money and other properties from her father, Calvert pledged that anything she inherited would go to her children on his own death, and if there were no children or if the children were of minor age, the inheritance would revert to H. J. Stier or his next of kin. There were provisions for an equal sharing of any increase in property or property value after the marriage. The contract also stipulated that the children of the marriage were to be brought up in the Roman Catholic religion. If the couple separated, Calvert was to receive custody of all male children and Rosalie of all female children, and Rosalie was to receive all of the fortune she brought to the marriage plus one-half of any property or increased property value acquired after the marriage.

On June 8, 1799, the four principals signed the contract before Judge Gabriel Duvall of Prince George's County with Charles J. Stier and Benjamin Ogle II serving as witnesses.[73] Two days later, George and Rosalie obtained a marriage license in Anne Arundel County, and the following day, June 11, the couple was married.[74]

No description of the ceremony is known to exist, but weddings of the time were generally simple affairs, usually occurring at home with only members of the immediate family as witnesses. Nelly Custis, Calvert's niece, had been married in just such a ceremony at Mount Vernon the previous February, with Calvert in attendance. Since there was no Catholic church in Annapolis at that time, it is likely that Paca House was the setting for George and Rosalie's marriage. The Reverend Mr. William Vergnes, a secular French priest serving White Marsh Parish, performed the ceremony.[75]

The newlywed Calverts traveled to Alexandria and on to Mount Vernon on their wedding trip. George Washington recorded in his diary a large dinner there on June 20, 1799, with the George Calverts, the Henri Stiers, the Charles Stiers, and Mr. van Havre as guests, along with Chief Justice of the United States Oliver Ellsworth, the Ludwell Lees, Mrs. Corbin Washington, and others. The Calverts spent two nights with the Washingtons, and they were joined for part of this time by George Calvert's sister, Eleanor Custis Stuart, and her second husband, Dr. David Stuart. The Calverts and the Stuarts left together on the morning of June 22, 1799, presumably to continue the wedding trip at the Stuarts' plantation.[76]

Calvert's principal plantation and the home to which he brought his young bride was his two-thousand-acre tobacco farm on the Patuxent River, north of Marlboro and near the now-dead town of Queen Anne. Rosalie Calvert always called this plantation Mount Albion. Calvert had inherited the property from his father, who had died in 1788, but he did not have full title until after the death of his mother in 1798. He had probably been managing the property, however, for the ten years following his father's death. The home he built for his bride was a two-story,

George Calvert. Portrait by Gilbert Stuart, 1804.
Private collection; photo courtesy of Maryland Historical Society, Baltimore

Federal-style brick house of Flemish bond, situated on a prominent hill.[77] The Calverts had seventy-six slaves on their Mount Albion plantation at the time of their marriage.

BLADENSBURG

With Rosalie settled in a home of her own, H. J. Stier turned his attention to providing himself with a suitable living arrangement. For several years he and Charles had been drawing up house plans and following the auction of lots in the Federal City and in Georgetown. Charles designed a house for himself and submitted the plan to his father. Stier said he thought it was far too expensive for his son and that he should be content with a simple house like van Havre's. Stier then took his son's plan, expanded it with wings and piazzas, and informed Charles that he had improved it so much that he wanted it for his own use.

Stier worried that the lots in the Federal City were too small for the house he wanted to build. Mrs. Stier preferred the neighborhood near the President's House, but after a week-long excursion into the city to look at lots with her husband in the fall of 1798, during which it rained the entire time, she seemed pleased to be back in Annapolis again.[78] And even as he planned his dream house, Stier worried about staffing it: "Even while planning a house, I think about the problem of having proper service. . . . I have given up the hope of being properly served by either freemen or slaves. This is a problem that worsens daily. I find it impossible to cultivate even a small garden of flowers."[79]

Other aspects of American life were becoming more appealing to him, notably the American system of government. He thought that the American system could withstand revolution because of its elective nature, and he admired both federalism and the separation of powers. "All government ought to have two essential parts, legislative and executive," he wrote, and he saw safety in what others called weakness. "The dismemberment of federalism cannot occur. Each part of the whole is too weak to sustain itself. America will not make war because she is impotent. No nation will attack her because it cannot maintain itself here, and anyhow there is nothing to make conquest worthwhile. So I don't see anything to fear."[80] He often debated with Americans who, he observed, regardless of party, seemed consumed with fear of the dissolution of the union, but he remained certain that such a thing would not happen.[81]

Stier thought that the Americans would honor their public debt, and he put a large part of his fortune into United States bonds. On the other hand, he saw Europe struggling in a morass of paper money. While paper money was also a threat in America, he thought it was backed more adequately by real assets here: "The national debt rests on an endless fertile land and a growing population, [and] the banks are buttressed by houses and industry."[82]

In January 1800, Stier learned from a local newspaper that the Paca-Jennings house he was renting in Annapolis was to be sold. "No doubt they want to force me to buy it, but they don't know much about my ability to resist compulsion," he fumed.[83] The incident had its bright side, however, for his son-in-law Calvert came by shortly afterwards, bearing news of a substantial property near Bladensburg for sale at a sheriff's auction. Bladensburg, a prosperous port in the eighteenth century until silting of the Anacostia River had deprived it of this role, still boasted some of the amenities of a small, established town. Situated on the main road between a thriving Baltimore and a promising Federal City, it was a reasonable choice for someone seeking a country place convenient to the new capital. Calvert himself had recently bought land in this vicinity, and he reported that the soil was rich, the woodlands good, and the Northeastern Branch of the Anacostia River, along which this property was located, a superb stream. There was even a sawmill on the property, which the present owners could not continue to operate.[84]

Stier went with Calvert to inspect the land and found it to his liking, but the sale, which had been set for January 24 at Dougherty's Tavern in Bladensburg, did not take place as expected. There were legal challenges, and the sale was postponed indefinitely. Discouraged, Stier talked of renting a house in the Federal City.[85] Back in Annapolis, the Paca-Jennings house was put up for auction in February 1800, but when no serious buyers materialized, the owners had to buy it back. Stier said that he remained "aloof and silent" at the sale and refused to rent for more than one month at a time.[86]

George Calvert encouraged Stier not to give up hope of acquiring the Bladensburg property and put him in touch with attorney William Steuart, who was now handling the sale.[87] Stier's desire to acquire the property was growing. He was tired of living in rented houses with inadequate service and not knowing from one day to the next whether he would be out on the street. "I feel the need to have an actual base of operations and that property offers an excellent site for development," he wrote Charles.[88]

News from Europe seemed to hold out little hope of a return home for the Stiers. Bonaparte's overthrow of the Directory and establishment as consul so upset Stier that he told his son he scarcely knew what he was writing.[89] "If he intends to usurp power for himself, he will be another Robespierre, detested by all. I think the fate of this revolution is probably being decided as I write—it will either be a monarchy or a reign of terror and massacres. . . . We should abandon Europe to its fate and devote our attention to the country in which we are living."[90]

There was yet another reason for the Stiers' heightened desire to settle down in the United States. The number of their American grandchildren was increasing. Isabelle van Havre had given them their first American grandchild, Edward, in 1796, and in the spring of 1799, young Charles Jean van Havre followed. Now, in 1800, Rosalie was expecting a child, and in July she returned to her parents' house in Annapolis to have her baby. Her midwife was a Mrs. Somers, and the Calverts' first child, Caroline Maria Calvert, was born on July 15, 1800. Mimi Stier wrote Isabelle van Havre an account of her birth:

"Tuesday night Rosalie began to have a little pain and summoned us. At first we feared this would be a long process, but at five [A.M.] the pains increased and at eight a small demoiselle made her joyous entry into the world—without making her Mama, who showed much courage, suffer too much.

"The baby is small and thin, [has] a tiny round face with brown eyes, and will be fair so we can expect her to be pretty, provided she doesn't have crossed-eyes or birthmarks. Rosalie does not have much milk since her delivery, and the little monkey doesn't want to suck so we need you here to teach her how to nurse. [Rosalie's] nipples are not at all prominent, and since her baby is not as vigorous as yours, it lacks the strength to take the breast. My sister feels as well as could be under the circumstances, not especially weakened, and she is a very pretty *accouchée*. [Calvert] was not here. He came on Wednesday—hours too late."[91]

It must have caused Mimi some pangs of envy to witness her young sister-in-law's successful delivery since, at age thirty, she was now the only childless Stier female. Mimi had repeated pregnancies but always miscarried, and the process was proving extremely deleterious to her general health. Dr. Shaaff found her suffering from a persistent cough and oppression of the chest and informed Charles that she needed a change of air. He prescribed a trip to the seacoast, and Mimi's brother pressed Charles to go: "All this cupping, powders, drugs, etc. are chips in the porridge. Only the sea air and amusement occasioned by the journey will do her lasting good. There is a physician in Dumfries who has made use of an herb called fox glove with exceptional success. You may suggest it to Dr. Shaaff."[92]

In the late summer of 1800, H. J. Stier learned that the public sale of the Bladensburg property he was interested in would take place on September 18. Determined to buy it this time, he made plans to go to the sale and asked Charles to meet him and to arrange for cash on hand for the purchase.[93] He also set about renting a house in Bladensburg to occupy while he was building his plantation residence. The house he settled on was the town's most imposing, Bostwick, built by prominent merchant Christopher Lowndes in the 1750s and now owned by Secretary of the Navy Benjamin Stoddert and his wife, Rebecca Lowndes.[94]

The sale took place as scheduled, and Stier was the successful bidder. The purchase comprised 729 1/4 acres of land, plus six lots in the town of Bladensburg, and the purchase price was seventy-two hundred Maryland pounds, or approximately twenty thousand dollars.[95] Stier noted that his new property and Calvert's land were separated only by a small farm of approximately one hundred acres belonging to a widow named Peggy Adams.[96] The Stier property was put in the name of Charles Jean Stier of Fairfax County, Virginia, presumably for the safeguards conferred by Charles's status as a United States citizen, although later the same year the senior Stier himself was naturalized by a special act of the Maryland General Assembly.[97]

The move from Annapolis to Bladensburg was accomplished in a surprisingly short time. On October 4, 1800, Stier wrote his son that he had just arrived in Bladensburg and was awaiting his baggage, which was coming with Jacob, the gardener, by boat. Part of the baggage consisted of Stier's collection of bulbs, which he hoped to have Jacob plant at the new property before December. Mrs. Stier went to visit Rosalie at Mount Albion during the move and remained there until everything was unpacked. Stier asked Charles to come by stagecoach to join him and to bring a fine saddle and two bridles, one ornamented in silver, for the two riding horses that Stier was buying. Stier was already purchasing cattle and sheep.[98]

Stier had begun purchasing slaves by this time, too. He wrote Charles about buying an old black woman, but evidently there were many more whom he did not mention. The 1800 United States census listed him as a head of household residing in Prince George's County with one white female over forty-five years of age [Mrs. Stier] and fifteen slaves.[99] In late

Bostwick, Bladensburg, the Stiers' residence from 1800 to 1802, while Riversdale was under construction
Library of Congress

November, after the move to Bladensburg, Mrs. Stier wrote that she and Mimi were working frantically "to outfit our people against the cold weather."[100]

Various members of the family came to visit after the Stiers were established in their Bladensburg home. Charles and Mimi were the first visitors, arriving in early November; they had an accident with their horse and chaise en route, which left Charles nursing a sprained knee for a month. The van Havres came for an extended visit from mid-November to mid-December, bringing along all their family and Mimi, too. The day before Christmas the Calverts came to join Rosalie's parents and Charles and Mimi for the holidays.[101] Stier was exceedingly busy and complained to Charles: "I haven't got all my bulbs planted, my mill never stops giving me problems with repairs, and everything is behind here. . . . I am always the first up and the last to bed."[102]

The family visiting back and forth exactly suited Mrs. Stier, who reveled in an idyllic vision of country life: "Since Holy Writ commands us to seek the Kingdom of Heaven first of all, I shall begin by building a chapel. [Father] Varens will come to celebrate the Mass every Sunday, and you [Charles] will come, too, along with the van Havres and all their children. You will spend the whole day with us, unless you have other things planned. Papa will provide the first seeds for your garden. When a sheep or a calf is butchered, he will send a quarter to each of you, and you, in turn, will do the same, so we will have fresh meat often. We'll share poultry as we need to and dine at each other's homes on moonlit nights on roast turnips, cream cheese, and ice-creams, since we will all have fine dairies. We will have the best fruits in the county, wonderful cider, and beer which we will brew jointly. We'll plant tobacco in order to [buy] wine, tea, sugar, and coffee. We will always have a horse ready to mount, a sulky for two to make visiting easy, a fine carriage or coach to take us to the city and to do our errands. All we have to do is get started."[103]

Stier was also extremely impatient to begin building his new house. He had decided on the basic design. Deeming a square building unattractive and unsuitable for a country house, he was determined to have a house with wings. He asked Charles, who had given him several designs to study, to proceed with the winged plan and to have it drawn up by Benjamin Henry Latrobe, the country's foremost professional architect.[104] Stier specified general dimensions for the central salon of the house and for the two rooms on either side of the salon.[105] Charles Stier, who had some drafting ability, drew up a rough draft of Stier's house plan and sent it to Latrobe, probably in December 1800.

The house was to be constructed of brick made on the place. Stier was anxious to hire a brickmaker immediately, even before finished plans were on hand. He discussed terms with a Georgetown brickmaker, but finding him somewhat expensive, he asked Charles to make inquiries in Alexandria about prices for a good brickmaker there. "It is time to dig the clay so he should come as soon as possible in order to select the clay for 3[00] to 400 thousand bricks," he wrote.[106] He asked Charles to get all the information he could about the best woods for various parts of the construction, stressing that he had a sawmill and quantities of white oak on hand.[107] He would need large amounts of lime, oyster shells, and nails, too. He asked Charles to come and help him with placement of the house, the cattle yard, the overseer's house, one slave house, and a blacksmith's shop.[108]

In the midst of all this activity, the Stiers took time to have their portraits done. On January 8, 1801, the English painter Robert Field, who was making a successful career for himself doing portraits in America, particularly miniatures, arrived at the Stiers' Bladensburg residence.

Charles, who was visiting his parents at the time, recorded that Field began miniatures of both Mr. and Mrs. Stier the day after his arrival and completed them a fortnight later.[109]

The home that Stier was building was not the first he had undertaken. He had built the Château du Mick in Belgium in the 1780s. Certain features of Riversdale, the name he would give to his American château, were inspired by the Mick, although Riversdale was much smaller. The reduced size was probably in part a result of the Stiers' continual difficulties with American servants; all of the family complained about the impossibility of getting the kind of service they were accustomed to in Belgium.

Although Henri Stier had definite ideas about what he wanted in a house, he knew that he needed the help of an experienced builder. He lacked knowledge of local materials and where to get them. He lacked the skill to work with a labor force that was part slave and part free. "The work frightens me. I encounter so many obstacles on all sides. In spite of all my exertions I still don't have a single tree cut for the building, and I need 3 to 4 hundred," he confided to Charles in early February 1801.[110]

Benjamin Latrobe still had not sent a plan for the house, and Stier fretted that if it didn't come soon, they would lose all chance of finishing the house that year.[111] By late February, Stier had lost patience and was in touch with another architect and builder, William Lovering of Georgetown, who was just completing Octagon House in Washington. Stier informed Charles:

"Lovering has been here expressly to show me three different plans, rather ingenuous but complicated, and with unattractive facades. . . . He has proposed to direct my construction on such a plan as I will give him, to attend to the progress and the designs in detail, to come twice each week, and that if I want to hire enough workmen to finish it in 12 months, he will do it for $600. . . . I am strongly inclined to accept his proposal. . . .

"I see already that Latrobe is an architect who will not suit us in the future. I imagine he is one of those men who do not finish their work. The best thing is to work on our own and with the help of Lovering. We must write him again that we cannot wait any longer to prepare the wood and to contract with the workers. I want to have my plans returned."[112]

Just one week later, Latrobe did send Stier some plans for Riversdale, but Stier was not impressed. Charles came over to Bladensburg to confer with his father and make some revisions in Stier's original plans. Then, at his father's direction, he wrote to terminate their association with

Latrobe: "Your designs not apearing [*sic*] to answer Mr. Stier's object, the lateness of the Season left no other Choice than to adopt imediately [*sic*] the plan which he had before aproved [*sic*] of." Unfortunately, the Stier plans themselves have been lost.[113]

William Lovering was eager to make himself agreeable to the wealthy Belgian, and all during March he met regularly with the Stiers and gave them tours of his completed houses around Washington. Stier evidently was pleased with what he saw, because on March 24, 1801, he, Charles, and Lovering met in Alexandria to sign a contract.[114]

Stier also hired Robert G. Lanphier, an architect and joiner from Alexandria, to take charge of the carpentry, including the selection of all woods.[115] Throughout the spring of 1801, there was much difficulty assembling all the materials. At one point, Stier considered firing Lovering and retaining Lanphier as his "architect and chief purveyor of all necessary materials," since Lanphier was proving more adept at securing materials for him.[116] Stier was also having disputes with Lovering about various aspects of the plans; Mrs. Stier wrote Charles that they were fighting over the design of the windows, the fireplaces, and the pantry, and that Lovering was "a blockhead."[117]

These difficulties, however, were smoothed out; Lovering remained, and by the end of June they were ready to lay the first brick.[118] The work progressed at a much slower pace than the impatient Stier had reckoned, and he soon saw that there was no prospect of completion within the year. Stier then conceived the plan of finishing one wing for occupancy by winter together with the basic structure of the main building, but even this goal proved unattainable. In late October Stier reported, "The construction has given me so much work that my head is spinning. I am fed up with mistakes and with hurrying the work along, but finally the building is up to roof level and only awaits the carpenter to be covered. Then I can rest easy."[119] It was late December, however, before the end of the roofing process was in sight, and the family remained in Bladensburg and did not move into the nearly finished east wing of Riversdale until the following year.[120]

Meanwhile, events in Europe were again affecting the Stier family. Napoleon was courting the old aristocracy, and in the fall of 1800, the French prefect of the Two Netherlands at Antwerp, the Marquis d'Herbouville, asked the minister of police to remove the Stiers from the list of proscribed émigrés.[121] It is unclear when word of this recommendation reached America, but by mid-March 1801, Charles Stier was thinking of a return to Europe.[122] His wife, Mimi, was homesick for her family;

Mimi's mother was ill, and there were letters from relatives imploring their return. Intending to leave in June 1801, Charles sold his furniture, moved out of his Washington Street house in Alexandria, and dissolved his partnership with van Havre. He delayed his departure until September, when he and Mimi visited Bladensburg for a farewell to their parents and to Isabelle and Rosalie. A few days later they traveled to Baltimore to embark on the ship *Hampton*.[123] Neither Charles nor Mimi ever returned to America. For Rosalie, this was her last glimpse of her much-loved brother.

In early November, following news of the death of his mother, Jean Michel van Havre also left for Europe, leaving his wife, Isabelle, and their three children with the Stiers in Bladensburg.[124] Isabelle could not return with her husband, for she was pregnant with her fourth child, and autumn was not regarded as a good time to cross the sea.

The Charles Stiers arrived safely in Holland in late October 1801, and Mrs. Stier, Isabelle, and Rosalie all wrote to catch them up on the news. Mrs. Stier relayed the political news, noting with displeasure that the Jeffersonians were in the ascendancy not only in Washington but in Annapolis, too: "[Polly Lloyd] can't stand Annapolis anymore. It's true that she is a big Federalist, and Annapolis is completely changed in that regard. They say that [John F.] Mercer, who married Miss Sprigg, will be Governor, and [Charles] Carroll and all the Federals are out of the Senate."[125]

Mrs. Stier's reports of the new national administration reflected both her native conservatism and the views of her Federalist circle: "Jefferson puts himself above the Constitution and Congress talks of nothing except changing [the Constitution]. All the elections are Democratic and all the offices are in their hands. [Jefferson] has removed all the Federalists from office—contrary to the Constitution. . . . [Treasury Secretary] Gallatin takes care of everything and works to suppress the various departments so he can put them under his direction, becoming master of all."[126]

Isabelle's news was more prosaic, explaining to Charles that their mother was frequently ill with a chronic cough, that they had hired a housekeeper who didn't work out, and that most of the housekeeping now fell on her. She said that Papa was "oppressed with work" on the construction and that she herself was in "low spirits." Rosalie came to visit every three or four weeks, bringing Caroline who was beginning to prattle and be quite noisy.[127]

Rosalie, however, wrote in high spirits: "Today I came back from the

Federal City, where we spent several days with Mrs. Law, who is certainly the most charming woman I have met in this country. I was surrounded there by Ambassadors and Ministers. Society will be very brilliant this winter. . . . We come frequently to Bladensburg, which seems to give Papa and Mama pleasure. The house is progressing well, and . . . I think they would be very happy now if you were here. Therefore, dear Brother, fix your return as soon as possible."[128]

The Calverts spent Christmas of 1801 in Bladensburg with the Stiers, and Rosalie reminisced to Charles about the festivities of the previous year: "Following this country's custom we are now with Papa. Do you remember how gay we were at this same season when you were here? It is not so now. I cannot help thinking of how far you are from us. Everything recalls the time we were together—our horseback rides, our stay in your pretty home in Alexandria—memory makes precious every moment spent with you and makes me regret how short they were. When you left, we both promised to keep a daily journal of every interesting happening, but the simple retired life I lead in the country gave me no material, so I have not yet begun. . . .

"Papa is well, but suffers a great deal with headaches and colds. Mama is not so well. She is often ill with the slightest cold she takes. This house they are living in causes the greater part of their indispositions, for neither the doors nor the windows close properly and when it is cold we freeze!

"I must tell you the great event of Annapolis society. Polly Lloyd is to be married next month to Frank Key who has nothing and who has only practiced for two years as an [attorney]. They are going to live near Fredericktown. . . .

"My little Caroline grows charming. She has begun to prattle and is extremely merry and vivacious. Her father idolizes her, but don't be afraid—we don't spoil her at all. My husband just returned from the Federal City and bids me send his love to you and Mimi and to say that there is nothing new in politics which is at all interesting. He witnessed the arrival of the celebrated mammoth coach presented to Jefferson by the Democrats. It was drawn by five beautiful horses."[129]

The Stiers were strongly Federalist in their views and in their connections, and they feared the new ascendancy of the Jeffersonians as the beginning of the kind of extremism which had engulfed their homeland. In January 1802, Mrs. Stier wrote Charles, "Our politics are going quite badly. Jacobinism and democracy increase every day. They removed all the Federalists from office, even the justices of the peace in the villages, in order to put Democrats in. . . . The newspapers are beginning to write strongly against [the Democrats] and to notice all the follies and blunders the present government is making. They especially ridicule Jefferson, who really is only a fool, full of vanity and of desire to pass himself off as a philosopher and a great man."[130] She noted the effects of partisanship on social life, observing that "the City is not brilliant this year—the two parties do not associate with each other"—and the reverse side of this coin, that some Democratic leaders were beginning to have second thoughts because "they are ashamed to be found associating with such an ignorant set of people," and they were being ostracized by polite society.[131]

Mrs. Stier thought that democracy was corrupting the public spirit and making it impossible to get an honest day's work out of the common man. "You know, my dear," she wrote her son, "Papa does everything here himself. I see it more every day—democracy does not make the people more manageable. Jefferson promises them a life of abundance without toil; that lifts everyone's spirits into the air; they don't want to do anything for one another; they think it is contrary to democratic dignity. It is much easier to take without paying. You would not believe how corrupted the public spirit is and what preponderance the Democrats have. Everything they propose passes Congress by all sorts of means."[132]

The New Year brought another addition to the family. Albert van Havre was born at his grandparents' home in Bladensburg in February 1802. Rosalie and Mrs. Somers, the midwife, both came to help Isabelle with the birth. Mrs. Stier said that everyone was disappointed that the new baby was not a girl because Rosalie's Caroline, "the most delightful child I have ever seen—gay, lively, affectionate, full of intelligence and charm, obedient and not the least spoiled—made us all wish for a girl."[133]

With Charles back in Antwerp, the Stiers took the opportunity to have many articles sent from home. Mrs. Stier wanted first of all some religious objects—vessels and linens used for celebrating Mass, which had been hidden from the revolutionary mobs in a walled-up garret at Cleydael. She also wanted barrels of anchovies and stockfish sent in time for Lent, together with a long list of garden seeds for spring planting—red celery, asparagus, early peas, early carrots, beans, red cabbage, and brussels sprouts. Stier wanted Charles to have some marble mantels made for the house, and he sent the measurements for them. The house was now covered, but interior carpentry was going so slowly that Mrs. Stier despaired of moving in before midsummer. She was particularly eager to leave the Bladensburg house, which was plagued by rats, and where she was constantly catching cold.[134]

In Antwerp Charles found that the condition of the Stier properties, which had not been sequestered in their absence and had been used by the government, was not as bad as feared. Cleydael Castle was in basically good condition; soldiers billeted there had ruined some furniture, rifled the cellar, and cut down several trees. The Château du Mick also had suffered only superficial damage, but the Venus Street townhouse had suffered extensive vandalism and destruction with floors, walls, and mantels all damaged. Charles and Mimi lived with Mimi's father, and Charles devoted all of his energies to looking after the family's interests. He wrote of inspecting the family's forests, collecting back rents from tenants, and checking up on the family's gardeners and foresters. The family's legal status was still up in the air; the men of the family were still on the proscribed list, but the women were struck from the list upon swearing allegiance to the Republic, which Mimi had done.[135]

Charles went to Paris, at his mother's urging, "to make a little noise," to see what he could do about getting all their names removed from the list. While he was there, Napoleon proclaimed a general amnesty for all émigrés to reenter freely, if they did so by September 22, 1802. Charles urged his family to return immediately to take advantage of this amnesty, saying it was Bonaparte's invitation to them to return. Charles sent twenty copies of his letter by different routes to be sure the family would receive it as soon as possible. Charles stayed on in Paris and was personally presented to Napoleon by Madame d'Herbouville, wife of the prefect of the Two Netherlands.[136] Charles was favorably impressed with the First Consul, with the Bonaparte family, whom he met at the theatre in Paris, and with the new order of things. He assured his family that Bonaparte was firmly in control and that the Revolution was ended, but he warned that they risked losing all their properties if they did not return.[137]

This news reached Bladensburg in June 1802, but the deadline was too near. Mrs. Stier wrote her son: "How could you think that in the three months time before September 21st, we could find a ship, send everything to Baltimore, arrange our affairs, make provisions for the passage, pay the debts, finish up with the workers . . . or how a man of over 60, worn out from over-work, along with a sick old woman and another woman with four small children, all of whom are on the verge of catching the measles which is already in the house—tell me how, my dear, you could even think of the possibility of our getting there by the 21st of

September?" She said that it would be impossible for Papa to come without them, since that would leave Isabelle, the children, and herself "alone at the mercy of the negroes."[138] H. J. Stier took what measures he could to comply with the amnesty. In July he, Mrs. Stier, Isabelle, and Rosalie all swore an oath of allegiance to the French Republic at the French legation in Georgetown, and he sent medical statements certifying Mrs. Stier's inability to travel to the proper authorities.[139]

Isabelle supplied further insights into the various family members' attitude toward returning to Europe. She said that Rosalie and Calvert were determined to stay and because of that, Stier didn't even want to talk about leaving. Mrs. Stier was undecided, but she herself couldn't wait to leave. Isabelle also reported that Rosalie had been ill for several months with "a type of fever which comes on with the least fatigue or mental or physical agitation. . . . Just between us, I think the air of Flanders would restore her as much as it would me. The life of a woman here is hard and unpleasant. She is, however, very close to her husband. I think she is now about three months pregnant."[140]

Rosalie also wrote Charles about the Calverts' decision. Apologizing for being remiss in writing, she cited her illness as excuse, confiding:

"The doctors thought I was going into consumption, but the outcome is that you will have another nephew or niece in several months.

"We were very surprised to receive your pressing invitations to return. I did not expect Mama and Papa would be so opposed to it. It seems to give them much pain to think of going back to the same country they left with so much regret!

"As for us, my dear Brother, I cannot imagine how you could have thought it feasible for my husband to leave in one month all his property, consisting as it does entirely of real estate. . . . You understand how hard it is to find a good tenant for good estates, and how still more difficult it is to find an industrious honest overseer. And no matter how well they were managed we would not derive nearly as much profit from them as if we remained on the spot."[141]

Rosalie joked with her brother about his seeming disapproval of the new, classically inspired fashions in women's apparel: "I am surprised that an art-lover like yourself should not approve of the clinging dress which gives the painter and sculptor opportunity to contemplate and study beauties formerly left to their imagination. In this more virtuous land only the contours are perceived through filmy batiste—a subtler fashion. Several of your Annapolis acquaintances are married, among others Polly Lloyd . . . and Betsy Cook[e], who married one of the most prominent Baltimore merchants, but it is believed that she will die from a cold she caught at a ball where she wore a Greek dress."[142]

The senior Stiers had noticed the new fashions, too. Mrs. Stier told Charles: "The airiness of French attire has penetrated here, but not to the same degree. The voiles are a little higher and not as transparent. Papa recently came back [from the city] and couldn't stop talking about two ladies who he said reminded him of eels stripped of their skin—without skirt, sleeves, or anything to furnish them some grace. . . . All the men joke mercilessly about them."[143]

Other news concerned the death of Martha Washington in May of 1802. Rosalie said that "young Custis offered to buy Mount Vernon, but Bushrod Washington did not want to sell it (or rather his wife did not agree). I am expecting her [Mrs. Bushrod Washington] here [Mount Albion] in several days to spend the ortolan and blue wing season with us. I remember rather sadly that at the same season two years ago I went to watch the shooting in a wee boat with the best friend I have, now so many thousand miles distant from me!"[144]

Isabelle reported that the Calverts had had their daughter Caroline inoculated against smallpox, using the cowpox matter, and that the procedure was "thoroughly successful." "Calvert has inoculated himself and all of his negroes," she continued, "and it is such a simple matter that everyone should do it. As soon as I can secure the fresh material, I am going to inoculate my little darling."[145]

RIVERSDALE

In August 1802, the Stiers finally moved into their new home, even though it was far from completed. The east wing was ready for occupancy, but the central block was only partially finished. Mrs. Stier's enthusiasm about the house was unqualified, however. "I wish we could transport our new house there [Belgium]," she told Charles, "because we could never find a more comfortable one. Were I to build another tomorrow, I would change nothing. I am completely delighted."[146]

Still, their real home was in Belgium, and sometime in the autumn of 1802 the Stiers determined to return. It was a reluctant and unenthusiastic H. J. Stier who wrote his son of this decision: "We have resigned ourselves to the inevitable decision to return. Since no hope remains of seeing all my family reunited, I must join the greater number. I don't see any possibility that Rosalie can come and establish herself with us."[147] Van Havre, who had returned from Europe, noted Stier's unhappiness with the decision: "Papa don't [*sic*] like the idea of going home. . . . When I speak of anything relative to the voyage, it casts directly a gloom over his countenance. . . ."[148] Nor was Mrs. Stier eager for the return. She complained about the irony of going to so much trouble building the house and then not being able to settle in and enjoy it. She was realistic about Rosalie not being able to accompany them in the spring with a newborn baby, but neither she nor Rosalie seem to have thought that this would be anything other than a temporary separation.[149]

With the 1803 New Year, Rosalie's baby, George Henry Calvert, made an unexpectedly early appearance. Isabelle gave Charles the particulars: "Rosalie intended to be confined here [Riversdale] on the fifteenth of January, but on the second of January an express messenger came to tell us that this Dauphin had made his entry into this world at her home. Mama and I went there through a deep snow. I came back the next day. Mama stayed over for a fortnight, then I went to relieve her, and after three or four weeks Rosalie came with me to Bladensburg where she has been ever since. She is much better since her confinement and does not suffer from the fever she had so badly."[150]

Jean Michel van Havre gave his version of the event: "[Rosalie] was delivered in two hours of a fine healthy boy. She was to come here to do that business, but the note was due before the money was ready and so she deceived us all and herself the most."[151] George Calvert, secure now with the son he had expected the first time, affected a certain indifference: "Rosalie has presented me with a sweet little boy who made his appearance in this world on the second of January last. His mother thinks him very handsome. I do not yet admire him so much as my dear little daughter. She is the sweetest little girl in the world and a blessing to her father."[152]

Rosalie's health was improved by her delivery, but her baby was sickly, and she, Caroline, and the baby stayed on for several months at Riversdale. There she had the counsel and companionship of her mother and sister; the wife of the Stiers' coachman, Will Scott, was engaged to supplement Rosalie's inadequate milk supply for her struggling infant. It was a good time for a daughter to have a family to rely on, and something Rosalie would miss sorely in future years. Meanwhile, spending as much time with her family as possible, even participating in the preparations for their return, helped ease the sadness and sense of impending loss. Her husband seems to have understood and appreciated what she was going through. He wrote Charles: "You will readily suppose that Rosalie and myself had indulged the fond hope of Papa and Mama's remaining on this side of the Atlantic, after having done so much towards fixing a residence by the improvements made upon the farm, but if it cannot be so, we must yield to the necessity and like good republicans submit to the majority who are entitled to decide, and content ourselves with praying for their return accompanied by you and Mrs. Stier. My dear Rosalie seems prepared to meet the event with that fortitude and good sense for which I think she is pre-eminent, and it has not failed (if that were possible) to increase the high regard I have for her, when I consider she parts with all her friends for her husband."[153]

George Calvert went on to explain his reasons for not accompanying the family: "You are well acquainted with the nature and situation of my property, the proceeds of which much depends upon management. This was little attended to before my marriage, since which I have made considerable improvements in the agricultural line which will enable me to make an abundance for our support here, but were I to leave my land at this time I fear the profits would not enable me to live so comfortably in Europe. . . .

"Papa has made considerable improvements upon [his] plantation. There still remains a great deal to do which would serve him for amusement did he remain here. I fear he finds the management of negroes more troublesome than he expected; it certainly requires a large stock of patience. You will see from our public prints that we are still Democratic. It has produced no very bad effects as yet, but there is no telling where it will end."[154]

The Stiers and van Havres planned to leave in May or June, and there were many questions to be resolved before they left. They were especially concerned with getting precise information about bringing their furnishings and valuables, particularly the painting collection, back into the country. What sort of customs duties were they going to encounter? Stier was inclined to take a minimum of household effects home: two or three feather beds, a commode, a lacquered bureau, clocks, candelabra, the Sèvres china, glassware and crystal, table linen, the dining table, silverware, books, rolls of new damask linen, and some harnesses. Most of these things had come with them from Antwerp and presumably would not be subject to duty on reentry. But the paintings were the most important concern, and besides the matter of possible duties to be paid, there were other considerations. Stier thought the collection should be insured for the voyage but was unsure of the amount or who should underwrite it.[155]

Stier had to decide, too, what to do about his American investments and about Riversdale. He determined to keep his investments here intact and to retain his Philadelphia agent, Thomas McEwen, to look after them. Riversdale was put in the care of his daughter Rosalie and his American son-in-law, with the proviso that they could live there if they wished. The slaves he had acquired were put at the disposal of the Calverts with the exception of his gardener and wife with four children, whom he offered for sale.[156] One young slave girl was also coming with them on the voyage to help Isabelle with the children, but she would be sent back to the Calverts.

The remaining valuable to be disposed of was Stier's bulb collection, and to his family's distress, he offered them for public sale, taking out advertisements in the newspapers. He advertised two thousand of "the best hyacinths" and "2 to 3,000 tulips of the first quality"; the sale was first set for April 12, 1803, but had to be postponed until April 18, "on account of the backward season."[157] Isabelle described the sale: "All the hyacinths are nearly in full bloom, which diverts [Papa] and although they cause great loss of time they put him in good spirits. He has advertised them for public sale without reflecting how we should be overrun with people. Now we have to escape them by the door or windows like very Harlequins. There is a Mrs. Carroll of Baltimore who has written asking to see them before the sale. I am afraid we shall have to entertain her here. Doctor Scott is coming, too, and Heaven knows who else besides! The other day a whole [coach] load of ladies and gentlemen came from Georgetown, but [since] we did not know them we were dispensed from very active politeness. Mother is all in a flurry about it, but it prevents her from fretting about something else."[158]

The Stiers' departure from America was saddened by news from Antwerp that Charles's wife, Mimi, after another miscarriage, had died in late February 1803. This unhappy news reached them in May just as they were readying their baggage—twenty-five packing crates—for shipment to Baltimore. More bad news came at the same time. War between France and England had been declared. As Mrs. Stier recounted, "The day before we were to load our baggage we got word that war had been declared. This caused us great anxiety, and we deliberated all day without coming to a satisfactory conclusion."[159] War greatly increased the hazards of the crossing, and they had to rethink all their plans. They had intended to go via England, since that was a shorter and safer route, but that now seemed unwise. There was special concern and indecision about the paintings. If they were shipped, they risked being captured; if they were left, they were exposed to the dangers of being stored in an empty house, since the Calverts had not made a decision about living at Riversdale.[160] The final decision, evidently made at the last minute, was to leave the paintings at Riversdale.

In early June they boarded the *Anthony Mangin* in Baltimore, destined for Amsterdam under Captain Thomas W. Norman. The major part of their baggage went via the ship *Java,* which sailed shortly after their departure.[161]

Rosalie Calvert wrote almost daily letters to her parents while they were waiting in Baltimore for their ship to sail, and they responded in kind. The last chance for communication came when the ship sailed from the Capes before starting the ocean crossing, and the Stiers made sure that their daughter had a message from them.

The return trip was plagued by calms, contrary winds, and challenges from warring British and French ships, and it was not until August 2 that the *Anthony Mangin* reached Holland. The *Java,* with all the Stiers' baggage aboard, was detained by the British at Portsmouth and arrived much later. Charles Stier met his parents and the van Havres in Amsterdam, and Stier's business agent, Lambert Louvrex, welcomed them into his home to stay until they could travel to Antwerp.

The sojourn of the Stier family in America had ended, but the story of the daughter they left in America had really just begun. She left her own record of this story in the numerous letters she wrote over the next eighteen years to her beloved parents, brother, and sister, whom she never saw again.

NOTES

1. For details of the emigration, see Alfons Bousse, "Nazaten van Rubens in Amerika de Gevolgen van een Overhaaste Emigratie," *Noordgouw* 17 (1977), 1–26; and Baron Hervé de Gruben, "Une Famille d'Emigrés Belges aux Etats-Unis pendant la Révolution Française," *Belgium* 1 (June 1944), 7–14.

2. Rosalie Stier to Charles J. Stier (hereafter RS to CJS), [Philadelphia, June 1795], Charles J. Stier Papers, Henry de Witte Archives, Antwerp, Belgium (hereafter CJS-A). These papers constitute the primary source for this chapter.

3. See Appendix for Henri J. Stier's listing of the paintings he brought to America in 1794.

4. Soeur Gladys Guyot, "Un Milieu Rubenien a Anvers Ascendants et Descendants des Peeters D'Aertselaer," *Le Parchemin* 187 (1977), 11–46.

5. Charles J. Stier's daybook covers the period from October 13, 1794, to December 23, 1795, and a second period from November 3, 1800, to September 19, 1801, CJS-A.

6. Daybook, October 21, 1794; November 9, 1794, CJS-A. The house, which no longer exists, was rented from merchant Thomas Ketland and stood on the southeast

corner of Fourth and Walnut. *Stephen's Philadelphia Directory for 1796* lists Ketland's house as 53 South Fourth Street.

7. Daybook, December 26, 1794; January 1 and 8, 1795, CJS-A.

8. Daybook, October 14, 17, 23, and 27, 1794; November 12, 1794; January 8, 1795, CJS-A.

9. Daybook, October 30, 1794; November 25, 1794; January 21, 1795, CJS-A. James Greenleaf (1765–1843) and Thomas Law (1756–1834) were business partners. Théophile Cazenove (1740–1811) lived in Philadelphia from 1790 to 1799 and was the chief agent for what became the Holland Land Company.

10. Daybook, January 27, 1795; March 12, 1795; April 19, 1795, CJS-A. Charles Maurice de Talleyrand-Périgord (1754–1838) spent two and a half years in the United States, 1794–1796. François-Alexandre-Frederic, duc de la Rochefoucauld-Liancourt (1747–1827), Louis-Marie, vicomte de Noailles (1756–1804), and Omer Talon (1760–1811), former deputy from Chartres, all frequented Philadelphia during the same period.

11. Daybook, December 24 and 29, 1794; January 21, 1795; March 21, 1795, CJS-A.

12. Daybook, October 14, 1794, CJS-A. John Carroll (1735–1815) had been ordained in Belgium and spent many years there; he became the first Roman Catholic bishop in the United States in 1790. William White (1748–1836) became bishop of Pennsylvania in 1787.

13. RS to CJS and wife, [Philadelphia, June 1795], CJS-A.

14. Dennis C. Kurjack, "St. Joseph's and St. Mary's Churches," *Historic Philadelphia from the Founding until the Early Nineteenth Century,* American Philosophical Society, vol. 43 (Philadelphia, 1953), 203–5.

15. Daybook, October 22–November 6, 1795, CJS-A. Benjamin Rush (1745–1813) lived on Walnut Street, only a block from the Stiers.

16. Richard Trappes-Lomax, ed., "Records of the English Canonesses of the Holy Sepulchre at Liège, now at New Hall, Essex, 1652–1793," *Publications of the Catholic Records Society* 17 (London, 1915), 166.

17. Ibid., p. 106.

18. Daybook, undated trip account [May–June 1795], CJS-A.

19. RS to CJS, [Philadelphia, June 1795], CJS-A. Rosalie refers to Sarah Peters, wife of Judge Richard Peters (1744–1828), whose Belmont home was noted for its constant hospitality.

20. Ibid.

21. H. J. Stier (hereafter HJS) to CJS, 5 July 1795, CJS-A. The reference is to Hugh Thompson (1760–1826), Baltimore merchant and son-in-law of Richard Sprigg (1739–1796), owner of Strawberry Hill. Thompson inherited the property at Sprigg's death.

22. Isabelle van Havre (hereafter IvH) to CJS, [n.d.] June 1795, CJS-A.

23. HJS to CJS, Philadelphia, [19?] June 1795, CJS-A. See also Gruben, "Une Famille d'Emigrés Belges," p. 12.

24. Built for the Richard Sprigg family, who lived there from 1765 to 1787, the house was situated on the north side of Dorsey (now College) Creek. The house was demolished about 1864, and its site, now a cemetery, is owned by the United States Naval Academy.

25. HJS to CJS, Annapolis, 26 October 1795, CJS-A. Charles is described as having "intermittent fever" (a term for malaria) in a letter from HJS to IvH, Annapolis, 6 September 1795.

26. Gruben, "Une Famille d'Emigrés Belges," p. 13.

27. RS to IvH, Annapolis, 28 January 1796, Calvert-Stier Papers, Van de Werve Family Archives, Viersal, Belgium (hereafter Cal S-V).

28. HJS and Marie Louise Peeters Stier (hereafter MLPS) to CJS with postscript from RS, Annapolis, 8 January 1796, CJS-A.

29. RS to IvH, Annapolis, 8 January 1796, CJS-A.

30. Ibid.

31. RS to IvH, Annapolis, 28 January 1796, Cal S-V.

32. HJS to CJS, Annapolis, 8 January 1796, CJS-A.

33. Ibid.

34. RS to IvH, Annapolis, 8 January 1796, CJS-A.

35. RS to CJS, Annapolis, 19 February 1796, CJS-A.

36. Ibid.

37. HJS to Jean Michel van Havre (hereafter JMvH), Annapolis, 23 May 1796, CJS-A.

38. HJS to CJS, Annapolis, [n.d.] September 1797 and 26 September 1797, Typescript, in English, in the Henri J. Stier Papers, Maryland Historical Society, Baltimore, of letters written by various members of the Stier family, primarily Rosalie Stier Calvert, to Charles Jean Stier. The typescript is a translation made in 1905 for John Ridgely Carter, a great-grandson of Rosalie Calvert; the French originals of these letters have been lost. Hereafter referred to as Carter Trans-MHS.

39. HJS to CJS, Annapolis, 29 May 1796, CJS-A.

40. Quoted in a letter from RS to IvH, Annapolis, [n.d.] June 1796, CJS-A.

41. HJS to CJS, Annapolis, 15 October 1796, CJS-A.

42. HJS to CJS, Annapolis, 20 October 1796, CJS-A.

43. HJS to CJS, Annapolis, 7 August 1797, CJS-A.

44. HJS to CJS, [Annapolis, July (?) 1798], CJS-A.

45. JMvH to CJS, Alexandria, 17 February 1797, CJS-A.

46. HJS to CJS, Annapolis, 11 April 1797, CJS-A. John Thomas Shaaff (1752–1819), one of the state's leading physicians, was a founder of the Medical and Chirurgical Faculty of Maryland.

47. Upton Scott (1724–1814) was the first president of the Medical and Chirurgical Faculty of Maryland. On William Faris (?–1804), see Barbara Sarudy, "The Gardens and Grounds of an Eighteenth Century Craftsman" (Master's thesis, University of Maryland, 1988).

48. MLPS and Marie Stier (hereafter MS) to IvH, [Annapolis, Spring 1797], CJS-A.

49. HJS to CJS, Annapolis, 7 August 1797, CJS-A.

50. RS to CJS, [Annapolis, August (?) 1797], Carter Trans-MHS.

51. HJS to CJS, Annapolis, 12 August 1797, CJS-A.

52. *Maryland Gazette,* October 12, 1797.

53. HJS to CJS, Annapolis, [n.d.] September 1797, Carter Trans-MHS. The party-givers were the Upton Scotts, the Philip Barton Keys, the William Cookes, and the Nicholas Maccubbin Carrolls.

54. Ibid.

55. RS to CJS, Annapolis, 3 December 1797, Carter Trans-MHS.

56. HJS and MLPS to CJS, Annapolis, 31 November 1797, Calvert Family Papers, Rare Books and Manuscript Library, Columbia University, New York City (hereafter Calvert, CU-NYC).

57. Extract of a letter from Henri Lambert Louvrex to HJS, Amsterdam, 23 September 1797, quoted in HJS to CJS, [Annapolis], 8 December 1797, CJS-A.

58. HJS to JMvH, Annapolis, [n.d.] January 1798, CJS-A.

59. See Edward C. Papenfuse, *In Pursuit of Profit: The Annapolis Merchants in the Era of the American Revolution, 1763–1805* (Baltimore, 1975), pp. 156–58, 225–36.

60. Jean Michel van Havre bought the house from Joseph Thornton for $4,000. The house, located at 608 Cameron Street, still stands (1988). JMvH to CJS, Alexandria, 27 June 1798, CJS-A.

61. HJS to CJS, [Annapolis, about Easter, 1798], CJS-A. A highly restrictive naturalization act and the Alien and Sedition Acts were passed in June and July 1798.

62. CJS to MS, Richmond, 9 June 1798, CJS-A.

63. HJS to CJS, Annapolis, 3 February 1798, CJS-A.

64. William Spohn Baker, *Washington after the Revolution, 1786–1799* (Philadelphia, 1898), p. 356.

65. RS to MS, postscript on letter from HJS to CJS, Annapolis, 3 March 1798, CJS-A.

66. MS to CJS, [Annapolis], 4 May 1798, CJS-A. Ann Jennings Carroll (?–1839) was the wife of Nicholas Maccubbin Carroll (1751–1812), heir to Charles Carroll, Barrister.

67. MS to CJS, [Annapolis], 18 May 1798, CJS-A. Catherine Carroll (ca. 1778–1861) was the younger daughter of Charles Carroll of Carrollton.

68. MS to CJS, [Annapolis], 4 June 1798, CJS-A.

69. HJS and MLPS to CJS, [Annapolis], received 2 April 1799, CJS-A.

70. MS to CJS, Annapolis, 30 April [1799], CJS-A.

71. MS to CJS, Annapolis, 4 May 1799, CJS-A.

72. Ibid.

73. Land Records of the General Court of the Western Shore, 1798–1800, Liber J. G. 5, fols. 489–95. Gabriel Duvall (1752–1844) had served as a Maryland congressman prior to becoming a judge of the General Court; he would later serve on the United States Supreme Court from 1811 to 1835. Benjamin Ogle II (1775–1845) was the son of Maryland governor Benjamin Ogle.

74. Anne Arundel County Marriage Records, 1777–1813, p. 73; R. Winder Johnson, *The Ancestry of Rosalie Morris Johnson* (Philadelphia, privately printed, 1905–8), vol. 1, p. 170.

75. Marriage license of George Calvert and Rosalie Stier, Annapolis, 10 June 1799. The original license, in the possession of Mrs. Rosalie Eugenia Calvert Ray of Fayetteville, North Carolina, lists "The Reverend Mr. Vernes" as minister. William Vergnes was a non-Jesuit priest who waged a long but unsuccessful campaign to be admitted to the Select Body of the Roman Catholic Clergy of Maryland (see Thomas Hughes, *History of the Society of Jesus in North America, Colonial and Federal* [London, 1908], vols. 1 and 2).

76. Donald Jackson and Dorothy Twohig, eds., *The Diaries of George Washington* (Charlottesville, Va., 1979), vol. 6, pp. 352–53.

77. The house, uninhabited and in poor condition, still exists (1988); it is located off Claggett's Landing Road in Prince George's County, Maryland.

78. HJS to CJS, Annapolis, 17 and 24 September 1798, [and Fall 1798], CJS-A.

79. HJS to CJS, [Annapolis], 28 September 1798, CJS-A.

80. HJS to CJS, Annapolis, 12 December 1798, CJS-A.

81. HJS to JMvH, Annapolis, [n.d.] January 1798, CJS-A.

82. HJS to CJS, [Annapolis], 20 January [1800], CJS-A.

83. Ibid. See also *Maryland Gazette,* January 16, 1800.

84. Ibid. The notice of sale appeared in the *Georgetown Centinel,* January 14, 21, and 24, 1800. David Ross, Horatio Ross, and Archibald Ross were the owners who were forced to sell because of insolvency.

85. HJS to CJS, [n.p.], 27 January 1800, CJS-A.

86. HJS to CJS, [Annapolis], 17 February 1800, CJS-A.

87. HJS to CJS, Annapolis, 24 February 1800, CJS-A. William Steuart (1754–1838) was the son of Dr. George Steuart of Annapolis and Ann Digges of Prince George's County. The Steuarts and Calverts had longstanding associations dating back to Benedict Calvert's arrival in this country in the 1730s.

88. HJS to CJS, [Annapolis], 31 March 1800, CJS-A.

89. HJS to CJS, [n.p.], 17 January 1800, CJS-A.

90. HJS to CJS, [Annapolis], 4 February [1800], CJS-A.

91. MS to IvH, Annapolis, 16 July 1800, Cal S-V.

92. Dr. John Thomas Shaaff to CJS, [n.p.], [After the winter] 1800, CJS-A, and JMvH to CJS, Alexandria, 13 July 1800, Carter Trans-MHS.

93. HJS to CJS, Annapolis, 26 August and 8 September 1800, CJS-A.

94. Christopher Lowndes (ca. 1713–1785), an Englishman who came to America in the 1830s, made his fortune as a tobacco merchant. His daughter Rebecca (1757–1802), who married Benjamin Stoddert (1751–1813) in 1781, inherited Bostwick at Lowndes's death. Stoddert was appointed the first secretary of the navy by President John Adams in 1798 and served until 1801. HJS to CJS, [Annapolis], 22 September 1800, CJS-A.

95. Prince George's County Land Records, Liber J. R. M. 8, fols. 584–87. The land was located in five contiguous tracts: Charles and Rebecca, 370 acres; Brothers fifth, 296 acres; Taylorsburg, 36 acres; Tide Meadows, 22 acres; and Brothers third, 5 1/4 acres. The six lots in Bladensburg were numbers 24 through 29 inclusive. This land record contains an exception for Tom Dick's store on Lot 24, but the store was later purchased by Stier for three hundred dollars (Prince George's County Land Records, Liber J. R. M. 9, fols. 89–92).

96. HJS to CJS, [Annapolis], 22 September 1800, CJS-A.

97. *Laws of Maryland,* Acts of 1800, chap. 45. Stier's naturalization was in conflict with the federal Naturalization Act of 1798, which required fourteen years' residency before admission to full citizenship, but in 1802 Congress repealed the act and reinstated the five-year residency requirement.

98. HJS to CJS, [Bladensburg], 4 October 1800, CJS-A; HJS to CJS, [Annapolis, late September 1800], Calvert, CU-NYC.

99. Population Schedules of the Second Census of the United States, 1800, Prince George's County, p. 470.

100. HJS and MLPS to CJS, [Bladensburg], 25 November 1800, CJS-A.

101. Daybook, November and December 1800, CJS-A.

102. HJS to CJS, [Bladensburg], 6 December [1800], CJS-A.

103. MLPS to CJS, [Annapolis (?), Fall 1800], CJS-A.

104. HJS and MLPS to CJS, [Bladensburg], 25 November 1800, CJS-A. Benjamin Henry Latrobe (1764–1820) was living and working in Philadelphia in 1800, and business matters between him and the Stiers seem to have been conducted by mail. Latrobe had numerous projects under way in Philadelphia at this time, including the Bank of Pennsylvania, the Philadelphia Waterworks, and several private homes.

105. Stier wanted the central salon to be twenty to twenty-two feet wide and each side room twenty-four or twenty-five feet.

106. HJS to CJS, [Bladensburg, late October 1800], CJS-A.

107. HJS to CJS, [Annapolis], 22 September 1800, CJS-A.

108. HJS and MLPS to CJS, [Bladensburg], 30 January, 8 February 1801, CJS-A.

109. Daybook, January 8, 9, and 22, 1801, CJS-A. Robert Field (ca. 1769–1819) came to the United States in 1794 and painted in Baltimore, Philadelphia, Washington, and Boston. During several years' residence in the capital, he painted many of its foremost citizens and gained social recognition. He left the United States in 1808. The Field miniatures of Henri Joseph Stier and Marie Louise Peeters Stier are in a private collection in Belgium (1988).

110. HJS and MLPS to CJS, [Bladensburg], 12 February 1801, CJS-A.

111. Ibid. There had been correspondence with Latrobe. Charles Stier's daybook records a letter from Latrobe on January 10, 1801, and an answer three days later. H. J. Stier speaks of another letter from Latrobe in his 12 February letter to Charles.

112. HJS to CJS, [Bladensburg], 26 February [1801], Calvert, CU-NYC. William Lovering, a native of Great Britain who became a United States citizen in 1798, worked in and around Washington, D.C., from 1796 through 1802. Lovering built Octagon House for John Tayloe III in the period 1799–1801 under architect William Thornton. He had built several other prominent homes in Washington and Georgetown by this time and was beginning to get contracts for public buildings.

113. Draft of a letter from CJS to Benjamin H. Latrobe, 6 April [1801], CJS-A; Daybook, March 5, 1801, CJS-A. A single sheet of drawings from Latrobe exists in the Calvert-Stier Papers at Viersal. This sheet shows a drawing of a north elevation of a building with a central block and two wings, a south elevation, and a floor plan of the chamber (second) floor; there is no plan for the first floor.

114. Daybook, March 14, 17, and 24, 1801, CJS-A.

115. HJS to CJS, [Bladensburg], 1 June and 19 June 1801, CJS-A. Robert G. Lanphier (1765–1856) had apprenticed with his father, Goin Lanphier, a builder who worked on the enlargement of Mount Vernon in the 1770s. Robert Lanphier submitted an entry in the 1792 design competition for the United States Capitol (see Jeanne F. Butler, "Competition 1792: Designing a Nation's Capitol," *Capitol Studies,* Special Issue (1976), 43–45).

116. HJS to CJS, [Bladensburg, late Spring, 1801], CJS-A.

117. MLPS to CJS, [Bladensburg], 28 June 1801, CJS-A.

118. HJS to CJS, [Bladensburg], 19 June 1801, CJS-A.

119. HJS to CJS, [Bladensburg], 29 October 1801, CJS-A.

120. MLPS to CJS, [Bladensburg], 28 December 1801, CJS-A.

121. Bousse, "Nazaten van Rubens in Amerika," p. 8.

122. Daybook, March 13, 1801, CJS-A.

123. Ibid., June 13, 16, 17, 1801; September 7–19, 1801.

124. MLPS to CJS, [Bladensburg], 16 October 1801, CJS-A. Van Havre sailed on the *Montezuma* from Baltimore to Rotterdam.

125. MLPS to CJS, [Bladensburg], 16 October 1801, CJS-A. Mary Tayloe (Polly) Lloyd was a daughter of Edward Lloyd IV. Democrat John Francis Mercer (1788–1848) served as governor of Maryland from 1801 to 1803; his wife was Sophia Sprigg, daughter of Richard Sprigg, owner of Strawberry Hill. Charles Carroll of Carrollton (1737–1832) served as a Maryland state senator from 1777 to 1800, when he was ousted by the Democrats.

126. MLPS to CJS, [Bladensburg], 28 December 1801, CJS-A. Albert Gallatin (1761–1849) was secretary of the treasury under presidents Jefferson and Madison from 1801 to 1814.

127. IvH to CJS, [Bladensburg], 28 December 1801, CJS-A.

128. Rosalie Calvert (hereafter RC) to CJS, Bladensburg, [late October, misdated December in typescript] 1801, Carter Trans-MHS. Eliza Custis Law (1776–1832) was the oldest of the Calverts' nieces; she was married at this time to Thomas Law, a wealthy Englishman.

129. RC to CJS, Bladensburg, 30 December 1801, Carter Trans-MHS. Francis Scott Key married Mary Tayloe Lloyd on 19 January 1802 in the Chase-Lloyd House, Annapolis.

130. MLPS to CJS, [Bladensburg, January 1802], CJS-A.

131. MLPS to CJS, [Bladensburg, early March 1802], CJS-A.

132. MLPS to CJS, [Bladensburg], 23 March 1802, CJS-A.

133. MLPS to CJS, [Bladensburg, early March 1802], CJS-A.

134. MLPS to CJS, [Bladensburg], 28 December 1801; [Bladensburg, January 1802]; [Bladensburg, early March 1802], CJS-A.

135. CJS to HJS [draft], Antwerp, 11 March 1802, CJS-A.

136. Charles-Joseph Fortuné, Marquis d'Herbouville (1756–1829), was named prefect in 1800.

137. MLPS to CJS, [Bladensburg], 8 March 1802; CJS to HJS [draft], Paris, 16 April 1802; CJS to Uncle [Joseph Stier], Paris, 21 April 1802; CJS to MS, Paris, 19 April 1802; and CJS to HJS [draft], Paris, 21 April 1802, CJS-A.

138. MLPS to CJS, [Bladensburg], 25 June 1802, CJS-A.

139. Stier took his oath on July 1 and the Stier women on July 19, 1802 (see Gruben, "Une Famille d'Emigrés," p. 13). Gruben states that H. J. Stier also took the oath at Versailles on May 31, 1802, but this is an error. H. J. Stier did not leave the United States in 1802.

140. IvH to CJS, [Bladensburg], 1 July 1802, CJS-A.

141. RC to CJS, Mont Alban [Albion], 3 July 1802, Carter Trans-MHS. Mrs. Calvert misspelled "Albion" throughout the first half of her correspondence.

142. Ibid. Elizabeth Susan Cooke, daughter of William Cooke, married Robert Gilmor II in 1802; she died of consumption in 1803.

143. MLPS to CJS, Bladensburg, [May-June, 1802], CJS-A.

144. RC to CJS, Mount Albion, 3 July 1802, Carter Trans-MHS. George Washington Parke Custis (1781–1857) was the youngest of Martha Washington's grandchildren and the Calverts' nephew. Bushrod Washington (1762–1829), associate justice of the Supreme Court and George Washington's nephew, inherited Mount Vernon after Martha Washington's death. Mrs. Bushrod Washington was the former Julia Ann Blackburn.

145. IvH to CJS, [Bladensburg], 8–26 May 1802, CJS-A.

146. MLPS to CJS, [Bladensburg], 26 July 1802, CJS-A.

147. HJS to CJS, [Riversdale, November 1802], CJS-A.

148. JMvH to CJS (in English), Bladensburg, 15 November 1802, CJS-A. Jean Michel van Havre returned to the United States in September 1802. The van Havres remained at Riversdale with the Stiers instead of returning to their Alexandria home.

149. MLPS to CJS, [Riversdale], 17 December 1802, CJS-A.

150. IvH to CJS, [Riversdale], 1 March 1803, Carter Trans-MHS.

151. JMvH to CJS (in English), Bladensburg, 13 January 1803, CJS-A.

152. George Calvert (hereafter GC) to CJS, [n.p.], 20 April 1803, Carter Trans-MHS.

153. Ibid.

154. Ibid.

155. HJS to CJS [Riversdale, November 1802], CJS-A.

156. *Maryland Gazette,* March 31, 1803. The ad offered "a negro man, 35 years of age, with his wife and four children, he has been a waiter, is a very good gardener and shoemaker; the woman is about 30 years of age, a good cook, washer and sews tolerably well."

157. *Maryland Gazette,* March 31 and April 14, 1803.

158. IvH to CJS, [Riversdale], 10 April 1803, Carter Trans-MHS. The two expected visitors were probably Harriet (Chew) Carroll (1775–1861), wife of Charles Carroll of Homewood, and Dr. Upton Scott (1724?–1814) of Annapolis.

159. MLPS to CJS, [Riversdale, May 1803], CJS-A. War between the two countries was officially declared on May 16, 1803.

160. HJS to CJS, Bladensburg, [May 1803], CJS-A.

161. HJS to CJS, Baltimore, 8 June 1803, CJS-A.

On Her Own

W HEN THE REST OF HER FAMILY returned to Belgium, Rosalie Calvert was left alone in America with her husband and two small children. Rosalie had been very close to both of her parents and to her siblings, and their absence left her lonely and depressed; she suffered repeated bouts of depression, which she referred to as her "blue devils." More importantly, she was now left without the support and protection conferred on a young married woman by the close presence of her parental family. No longer could she rely on mother or sister to come and assist her in childbirth, illness, or with household management, or on father and brother to keep a watchful eye on her husband. She had to depend on her own resources and on the kindness of in-laws.

George and Rosalie accepted her father's offer to take over Riversdale. She had a strong attachment to the partially finished home—her father's creation—and she was full of plans for completing and embellishing it. As her father had foreseen, Riversdale's proximity to the Federal City was a source of great pleasure to her. Rosalie Calvert's first three years of marriage had been spent in the relative isolation of her husband's Mount Albion plantation on the Patuxent, and the activities and social life of the new capital excited her. Her husband's well-connected relatives— the Thomas Peters, the Thomas Laws, George Washington Custis— welcomed her into their circle and helped dispel her loneliness and homesickness for her family. Rosalie became especially friendly with her niece Eliza Custis Law, who saw that she met the interesting people of the nation's young capital city.

The move to Riversdale proved beneficial in another way. This new plantation was still in the developmental stage, with few slaves to supervise and to supply, in contrast to Mount Albion, which was an established tobacco plantation with over seventy slaves. Since the work and responsibilities of a plantation mistress mounted as the size of her household increased, Rosalie probably found living at sparsely populated Riversdale less demanding—at least temporarily—than life at Mount Albion. As mistress she had the major responsibility for establishing the garden, which would provide an important source of food for the plantation, and she undertook this work with especial interest and pride. She does not, however, appear weighed down by work or responsibility during her first year at Riversdale. Indeed, with nurses to care for her children, a fine coach and four at her disposal, pleasure-seeking companions, and a fond and indulgent husband, she seems the embodiment of the Southern belle on endless rounds of parties and visits.

Mrs. Calvert's Washington, actually a city in name only, was characterized by great empty stretches of wilderness bound together by rutted, potholed pathways pretending to be roads. Georgetown, the commercial hub of the fledgling capital, was scarcely better; only two years before, First Lady Abigail Adams had pronounced it "the dirtiest Hole" she had ever seen. Still, both Washington and Georgetown were booming. There was much new construction, including some very fine private homes, and interesting people from all parts of the country and the world were flocking to the area.

Mrs. Calvert eagerly relayed news and gossip about events in Washington to her family in Antwerp: the Bonaparte-Patterson romance, the uproar over Jeffersonian protocol raised by the English ambassador's wife, the progress of the Capitol building, and the construction of Arlington House. The activities of President Thomas Jefferson's administration were scrutinized, and generally disapproved of, by Mrs. Calvert and her Federalist circle.

Back home, much work would be needed to make Riversdale livable and profitable. The house had to be finished, the grounds landscaped, more slaves acquired, and crops made. Rosalie Calvert reported regularly to her family on all these matters, and from her letters emerges a vivid picture of the daily routine and social milieu of a Maryland plantation mistress at the beginning of the nineteenth century.

To M. & Mme H. J. Stier

Dear Parents,

This is the first time I have written to you since your departure. . . .
You cannot imagine, dear Parents, what the reality of your departure has
made me suffer. Up to this moment I had always entertained some hope,
and even now I find myself in a kind of dream as if I am daily expecting
your return.

I have been nine days at Mount Albion. Mrs. Peeter [Peter] was with
me during that time, which was a diversion, and making exertions to
amuse her lifted my spirits, but the moment I was alone, I became
depressed.[1] Nothing interests me and everything I do seems to make me
more unhappy. Yesterday, coming here and seeing the house from afar, I
recalled how, when you were here, you were always at the door to welcome me and seemed to have so much pleasure seeing us arrive. What a
change now! A closed-up house where, upon entering, everything reminds me of all those moments I spent here with you. What I wouldn't
give to have them back again that they might be better spent.

Yes, dear Parents, every day I regret not having done more to contribute to your happiness and having often caused you pain. That feeling is
the cruelest I have to bear. Writing to you comforts me a great deal. I will
do it often. I don't hesitate to burden you with my complaints because as
you say in your letter, dear Mama, where can I better deposit them than
in the bosom of my family? I will always write you exactly what I am
thinking and everything I do, and I hope you will do the same. Write me
as soon as you arrive. Tell me how you find [Belgium] and how the
climate affects your health. I assume that Charles came to Holland [to
meet you], perhaps with Uncle and Aunt Joseph.[2] What a great pleasure
to see friends such as they again!

I had to leave my letter, dear Parents, to go into the City where I had
some errands to do and to dine with Mrs. Peter. Everyone asks about
you. Mr. Law is expected back next month.[3] We have a lot of work here
[at Riversdale] which requires my husband's continual presence. He
dined in [Bladensburg] today in order to direct the work on the bridge
they are building on the mill race. Now it will be done properly and will
last for a long time; it will cost between $20 and $25. . . .

In a few days we are going to start [building] the tobacco house;
nobody wants to do it for less than $200, even with Moses to help. I am
very busy cleaning up the garden and taking up the bulbs. They seem to
be in good condition. There are three lots of hyacinths which no one has

Mount Albion, Prince George's County, Maryland, first home of Rosalie and George Calvert. Ruins of an 1830s addition are to the left of the Calverts' original home.
Library of Congress

come to claim—I guess the buyer didn't have the money.[4] All the bulbs are large and have lots of offshoots, so next spring I'll have a beautiful collection.

1. Martha (Custis) Peter (1777–1854) was the wife of Thomas Peter of Georgetown and the Calverts' niece. She was one of the four children of Eleanor (Calvert) Custis, George Calvert's older sister, and John Parke Custis (1753–1781), the only son of Martha (Dandridge) Custis Washington by her first marriage.

2. Uncle and Aunt Joseph were Henri J. Stier's younger brother Joseph (1748–1803) and his wife, Jeanne (Guyot) Stier (1751–1822). The Stiers learned of Joseph's death when they arrived in Europe.

3. Thomas Law had returned to his native England in 1802 to raise capital for his speculations in Washington real estate.

4. The reference is to a public sale of bulbs held at Riversdale in the spring of 1803 prior to the Stiers' return to Antwerp.

To M. & Mme H. J. Stier

[Riversdale], 28 June [1803][1]

I just received your letters, dear Parents. My husband had gone to inspect the work on the bridge in town. I was the first to see him returning, holding your letters in his hand, which he showed me from afar. Imagine how fast I ran downstairs and with what haste I opened them, what happiness for me to learn that you are well and that the sea air is restoring your health. So you were nine days in the Bay. It is with much pleasure, dear Mama, that I saw from the various dates of your letter that you have written me every day. This is a new proof to me of your love and that, even though far away, I am no less dear to you. For my part I will write you very often and will send this one by the *Java*, if it hasn't left.

As you say in your letter, there is no better place for conversation and reflection than on the deck of a ship, and all the places you passed by were interesting: Annapolis, where we lived so long; the Patuxent, which I am sure you did not pass with indifference; then the Potomac, which comes here—after all, each place giving rise to memories of times past. . . .

As you request, I will give you details of all our activities. Taking up the flower bulbs is occupying most of my time. They are not all up yet, but I think I will finish tomorrow. . . . Just now it is too hot to take a walk during the day, but I go out in the evening when it cools off. Day before yesterday I took the same walk along the river that we took together a few days before you left. It is a pretty walk. Caroline came with me. I will follow your advice and keep her with me as much as possible. When I got your letter, she asked me who it was from and when I told her, she replied that it could not be, since you had gone. I told her that was true, but you had written me from the ship. She looked at me very carefully and seemed to think about it for a few minutes. Suddenly she turned, saying, "Then Papa has been to Roup (meaning Europe) this morning!" I talk to her frequently about Grandpapa and Grandmama to help her remember things you did. Her memories of you are too strong for her to forget you. George is fine and quite fat. I give him as much [Blom?] pap as he wants, and as much to drink as he wants, too. He is the happiest and best-humored baby I have ever seen. He laughs and dances all day and is always happy to have someone play with him.

The bushes in front of the house are full of flowers. I am going to pick them and make superb bouquets. I am glad I bought the cook—he is doing very well, and I think he will easily learn what he doesn't know since he is willing. He stews extremely well. . . .

We are going to Bath in a fortnight.[2] Custis said he would go with us, but he still may change his mind as there is no way he can make the other trip if he goes with us.[3] I will try to persuade him to go to Europe and I will send him to you. And since you tell me that nothing would give you more pleasure than to find out that I am enjoying myself, I will write you from Bath where I hope that the <u>waters</u>, the <u>exercise</u>, and especially the <u>company</u> will cure me of my <u>spleen</u>, or "<u>blue devils</u>," which always assails me when I am alone and think of the distance which separates us.

Thank you for the pretty little bonnet, dear Mama—it suits me quite well, and I wear it with more pleasure than any other because it comes from you. Each time I put it on, I remember all the nice things you have done for me. We plan to return to Mount Albion day after tomorrow. I made all the purchases I needed for our trip in Georgetown and am going to organize my wardrobe and the childrens'. *Adieu,* dear Mama, I close this letter by embracing you most tenderly. My husband joins me in wishing you and Papa all happiness and in the hope of seeing you soon again, believe me,

Your affectionate daughter,

R. E. Calvert

P.S. . . . Please number your letters and write me as often as you can.

1. Mrs. Calvert often wrote long letters over a period of several weeks or even months. As noted in the Preface, where she has provided a separate date or salutation for these entries, I have treated them as separate letters.

2. Bath was a popular spa of the day, located at present-day Berkeley Springs, West Virginia.

3. George Washington Parke Custis was the Calverts' twenty-two-year-old nephew.

To H. J. Stier

[Riversdale, 28 June 1803]

Dear Father,

This morning I received your letter of the 17th written from the Capes and I assume sent by the pilot. It took eleven days to reach me. . . .

Yesterday we had a storm and heavy rain. My husband immediately had everyone come up from [Mount Albion], where it hasn't rained enough, to plant tobacco here. . . . The corn looks beautiful and today [the hands] are busy cutting the rye. After that, they will cut the hay. . . . I see you haven't received the letter I sent to Baltimore in which I indicated to you that since you allowed us the liberty of accepting the propositions you made a while back—to take the profits of the plantation and use them toward improvements this year—we think this would be advantageous on all sides. My husband has seen in a few days time that in order to manage [Riversdale], he must be here frequently and to do it well, he ought to live here. Also, he will be able to combine the work of the two plantations profitably.[1]

For myself, dear Father, I feel attached to this place you have created at the cost of so much trouble and where I have spent so much happy time with you. It would be dreadful to me to see it go downhill, which I fear will be the case if we do not persevere until all is put in good order. So we will accept your offers, dear Father, and if Europe does not please you, we will have the pleasure of having worked for you. Do not fear that this could become an obstacle, delaying our trip to come and see you. My husband will have to have a good manager in any event, and for four plantations it will be worthwhile to hire an able, intelligent, and honest man to whom it is worth the trouble of giving directions. We have one in mind who I believe will do well.

I promise myself great satisfaction in completing all the projects of embellishment you planned to carry out here. . . . When I walk in the garden, each tree and rose planted by your own hand is of interest to me, and I take pleasure in watching them grow and caring for them. I am writing this letter on the same table where I have seen Mama write so often—I feel close to her. After all, every object here is dear to me because you used it.

We plan to finish the dining room first. Latrobe, who has come to live in the City, will be able to help us a little with the plans for the cornices and moldings, which I don't know enough about to proceed without an architect's help.[2] If my brother has time, he should send me some ideas. William Birch said he saw you in Baltimore and that you had commissioned him to make some plans.[3]

Adieu, dear Father. . . . Write me as often as possible. Receiving your letters and following the advice you give me will always be the greatest joy I have until I have the happiness of seeing you again. . . .

Your most affectionate daughter,

R. E. Calvert

P.S. If a ship is coming to Baltimore or Alexandria, you would do me a great favor if you would send me a marble mantelpiece for the dining room and a cask of good claret. I will take good care of the five cases [of paintings] until you decide what to do with them. . . .[4]

1. Calvert's Buck Lodge plantation of 1,179 acres adjoined Riversdale. In addition to Buck Lodge and Mount Albion, Calvert also owned 874 acres in Montgomery County.

2. Benjamin Henry Latrobe came to Washington in 1803 at President Thomas

Jefferson's request to serve as surveyor of the public buildings and to oversee construction of the Capitol. No record of Latrobe's help on the interior finish of Riversdale has been found.

3. English artist William Russell Birch (1755–1834) came to America in 1794 and settled in Philadelphia. Birch had visited Riversdale in November 1802 and made a favorable impression on the Stiers (MLPS to CJS, 13 November 1802, CJS-A). Stier had not engaged Birch, but was delighted with the idea (HJS to RC, [n.p.], 26 August 1803, Henri J. Stier Papers, Maryland Historical Society, hereafter Stier-MHS). Birch was employed by the Calverts in 1805 and drew a landscape plan for Riversdale which has been lost.

4. The cases held the painting collection of Jean Egide Peeters, Stier's late father-in-law, which the family had brought to America in 1794 and left behind at Riversdale on their return. See Appendix for Stier's list of the sixty-three paintings.

To M. & Mme H. J. Stier

Riversdale, 12 August 1803

Dear Parents,

. . . In my last letter I wrote you that we were going to Bath in a few days and Mrs. Law was supposed to accompany us. However, on returning to Mount Albion to make further arrangements, I had a kind of a miscarriage (I don't know enough about this to be sure that it was one). It weakened me so that I didn't think I could stand the fatigue of the trip, which is long and tiring. So I decided to come here [to Riversdale] instead. I am taking plenty of exercise and a cold shower bath every day, which has completely restored me. I am feeling better now than I have in three years.

The proximity of the Federal City is a great pleasure for me. I am quite *intime* with Mrs. Law, truly a woman who has no equal. Her husband still has not returned. She dined with us here last Sunday, along with Dick Lowndes and Cramphin—all of whom ask about you and greatly desire your return.[1] On Tuesday I dined at D[ick] L[owndes]'s house on the hill with Mrs. C[harles] Lowndes, her husband, and Dr. Murray of Annapolis.[2] I don't see any member of the Ben Lowndes family. . . .[3]

General Washington's nephew, who married Taloe's [Tayloe] sister, has bought Scott's country property near Georgetown for $16,000, and has just moved there.[4] He is a man who owns a lot of property.

They are busy finishing the Capitol building, which is progressing rapidly, and they have made the road in the woods between here and the City by the method you admired so much—all gravel, which cuts the journey in half.

The waters of Spa Spring have suddenly gained such a reputation that Dougherty's house is not large enough to handle the crowds of the fashionable who come to drink the waters every day.[5] It is also becoming stylish again for married ladies to ride horseback. Mrs. Law and I had riding habits made for our trip to Bath which I will describe to you. Hers is Hussar-style; mine is bottle-green [with] a quite short skirt, with two rows of small gold buttons on the pockets and five rows on the jacket all the way up to the shoulders and gold cord [in a criss-cross design] between the buttons. It is most becoming. The hats are velvet, the same color as the habits, turned up on one side a la Henry IV, with a lovely plume and a cord and pendant of gold.

I was in the City the past two days to talk to the ceiling plasterers who will come to work next Tuesday to finish the dining room. I am annoyed that I don't know what your plans were for the salon.[6] I think the best thing will be to let Latrobe do it.

We have made a lot of repairs to the [saw] mill which was in total disorder. The crank was broken and the wheels wouldn't turn well. They made some alterations and now it works better than ever before. The mill race, which is full of gravel, is also being cleaned. We are being urged to build a grist mill. . . . Mrs. Diggs' [Digges] mill has three times more business than it can do.[7] We sold the sorrel horse to Cramphin for $140, and the white mare for $50. Everyone knew how old [the mare] was and nobody wanted her, even though we tried at Queen Anne and at Marlboro. The old witch Sara and her granddaughter have been sold for $100. We tried to sell her in Baltimore but couldn't; [she was] afraid of being sold to some Georgian and took it in her head to make herself look bad. Finally, she made so many fine promises that she persuaded Ben Lowndes to buy her.

The tobacco that you took such pleasure in seeing planted, dear Papa, has succeeded very well, especially around the dairy house. It is superb—my husband says he has never seen any larger. [The tobacco] growing in the orchard also looks good, as does the corn. . . . the oats and hay have not been as successful—in part, I think, because the pigs were in the fields so much during the spring. My husband had a large number of them slaughtered and [that has helped].

We have five carpenters here now building houses for the negroes, lattice for enclosing the garden, etc.[8] The garden has been a bit neglected, but I will bring my gardener over from Mount Albion in a fortnight and it will soon be put right. I have arranged all the orange trees and geraniums in pots along the north wall of the house, where they make a very pretty effect, and the geraniums, being shaded, bear many more blossoms and are growing well. You probably recall that we planted several orange cuttings together—not a single one was lost and now they are small trees. The hydrangea from my Uncle Joseph hasn't bloomed yet, but I think I am going to have three small ones. . . .

[no signature]

1. Richard Tasker Lowndes (1763–1840) was the third son of Christopher Lowndes, Bladensburg merchant, and his wife, Elizabeth (Tasker). Richard Pottinger Cramphin (1760–1806) was the son of Thomas Cramphin, Sr., of Prince George's County and his second wife, Elizabeth (Pottinger) Bowie.

2. The guests were Charles Lowndes (1765–1846), Georgetown merchant and youngest son of Christopher Lowndes; Charles's wife, Eleanor (1776–1805), daughter of Edward Lloyd IV of Wye; and Dr. James Murray (1739–1819), prominent Annapolis surgeon. Richard Tasker Lowndes was married to another of Lloyd's daughters, Anne (1769–1841); they lived at Blenheim, on the heights just east of the Bladensburg town limits.

3. Benjamin Lowndes (1749–1808) was the oldest of the Lowndes brothers. He and his wife, Dorothy (Buchanan), lived across the street from the old Lowndes family home, Bostwick, which the Stiers had rented while Riversdale was being built, and there had been friction between the two families.

4. William Augustine Washington (1757–1810), son of George Washington's older half-brother Augustine, married Sarah Tayloe in 1790. The property referred to was Gustavus Scott's (1753–1800) Rock Hill estate.

5. Spa Spring was just north of Bladensburg, between Riversdale and the town. Patrick Dougherty was a local tavern and innkeeper.

6. The salon was the large central downstairs room opening onto the south portico. Along with the dining room to the east and the drawing room to the west, these three rooms constituted the formal entertaining area of the house.

7. Catherine Brent Digges (ca. 1772–1835), widow of George Digges, owned a mill which still stands, now called Adelphi Mill, in Prince George's County.

8. When speaking of her slaves, Mrs. Calvert usually used the word *négre;* she also frequently referred to them as "servants," but almost never as "slaves."

To Charles J. Stier[1]

Riversdale, 12 September 1803

Dear Brother,

It has been a very long time since I have written to you, but still longer since I have received a letter from you. It seems, dear Brother, as if you have entirely forgotten your poor little sister! . . .

A little while before Papa's departure, we received the sad news of your wife's death. Be assured that no one felt a more lively sympathy with you than I did in a loss so painful. . . . I feel and share your grief all the more deeply now that I am virtually abandoned by all my relatives and can appreciate better than most how the loss of a living helpmate must touch you. . . . My husband feels the same and would write to you now, but he has so much to do that he must put it off till the next time I write. As he has four plantations now, there is much more work than he can do. Papa's alone requires his continual presence to be kept in good order, so we live there. I feel nearer to my parents in this house. . . .

I am very well now and take much exercise—chiefly on horseback. Mrs. Law comes here three or four times a week.[2] We ride together and several 'Cavaliers' accompany us. . . . Besides our beaux, we both have a servant in livery *à l'Anglaise* who follows us. I have a very fine equipage now with four beautiful brown horses. I go into the Federal City nearly every other day. The road has been made entirely of gravel. Bladensburg has become very brilliant indeed. People come from all directions to drink the waters on Sunday—all Georgetown in particular comes. . . . I must finish now, dear Brother, sending you my tenderest love. . . . Remember that it is the greatest pleasure I could have to learn that you are all well. *Adieu.*

Your affectionate sister and sincere friend,

R. E. C.

1. Carter Trans-MHS.
2. The Carter translation incorrectly renders Mrs. Law's name as "Lewis."

To M. & Mme H. J. Stier

Riversdale, 16 September 1803

Dear Parents,

I had planned to wait to send the tulips until there was a ship going directly to Antwerp, but the season is so far along that I am afraid that would risk sending them too late. So I am going to take advantage of a ship advertised in the Baltimore paper as leaving in a few days for Amsterdam. I hope they arrive without mishap. I have packed them in a double case lined with lead to keep the humidity from affecting them. Those which Mama had marked for herself are in the blue papers at the top of the box. I have sent only about one-half the bulbs, thinking it would be best to send them by two different shipments—surely then one or the other will reach you. I fear that the war will cause many of our letters to be lost; according to the local papers all the ports of Holland and the Scheldt are blockaded.[1]

Here it is almost three months since you left the Capes and I still have not received any news of [your] ship. I am beginning to be a little impatient. . . .

We are very busy here. The dining room is almost finished—the cornice is quite rich and pretty. The salon will take a lot more time—it is not yet begun. Wouldn't it be good to order a parquet for the drawing room? I don't think it would cost much more here than a plank floor.

Recently I have made several friends in the Federal City who often come to dinner here, and I go there more, too. In place of our bad-tempered gray horses, we now have four browns who never refuse to pull. The two lead horses are remarkably handsome and lively. Tomorrow I am going to send the carriage to have some alterations made; they are going to enclose the front with two [pieces of] glass, [put] some cushions up against the Venetian shutters, and [make] a *passé* in the English style. I will have it painted purple. Since I often travel to the City at night, an open carriage is too cold, but changed like this, it will be delightful.

In three months there will be horse races which are going to be quite splendid and will last for five days. The first prize will be $1,600. You will be astonished that I am becoming so completely dissipated, but staying at home all the time I was always looking on the dark side and being melancholy. Getting out in the world lifts my spirits and seeing that other people have more to complain about than I do makes me more content and better able to bear our separation.

Don't think that I think of you any less often for all that, dear Parents—on the contrary, my greatest pleasure is to imagine the time when I will have the joy of seeing you again, and only the hope that this will be soon helps me bear your absence. I realize more and more each day that one cannot have true friends outside one's family.

I must finish this letter. . . . [My husband] has said twenty times that he intends to write you the next time I do, but then my letter is written and he never has time to do it. He really has too much work. He is at Mount Albion now for two days. *Adieu,* dear Parents, believe me,

Your affectionate daughter,

R. E. C.

1. With the resumption of hostilities between France and England in 1803, the ports of the Low Countries, including Antwerp on the Scheldt River, were subjected to blockades and embargoes.

To H. J. Stier

Riversdale, [19] November 1803

Dear Father,

I hasten to respond to your letter No. 5 dated 26 August 1803, which I received yesterday afternoon. I am so happy to learn that you were pleased with [Belgium] and with the way you were received. I sincerely hope that you continue to be happy about your return and that the war does not make your situation difficult. This is the first letter I have had from you since your departure. . . . On hearing that Captain Norman had returned in early October, I made inquiries as to whether he had any of your letters, but all I could find out was that you had arrived safely in Amsterdam. I assumed you hadn't given him any letters and that since he had sold his ship and booked passage, you had made other arrangements for Lucie.[1] I was quite surprised to learn that you had given him charge of this girl and of a second letter, which I have never received. I am afraid that Norman is a rascal who planned to keep the girl, and who for this reason hasn't gotten the letters to me. . . . However, we must not jump to conclusions—he may not be at fault, although appearances are against him. . . .

I am very sorry to have to tell you bad news about your baggage. . . . [William Cooke] sent us a message two weeks ago that [the *Java*] had been seized by the English and taken to an English port—Portsmouth, I believe. I will find out more particulars. . . .

I have received your check on the Bank of Alexandria, and I thank you, dear Father, for the increase you want to make in my allowance.[2] Our affairs here are going pretty well now. My husband sold his last tobacco crop a few days ago for $10 for the best quality and $8 for second quality. He had 51 hogsheads which will bring him more than $4,500, since most of it is the best quality. . . .[3]

We will now have enough income to live splendidly here, to improve our properties . . . and to buy some bank shares from time to time. I want very much to come and see you next spring, dear Father, [and] if I insist on it, I know my husband will not refuse me. Nevertheless, he does not want to go before he has put all his plantations in good order and in as productive condition as possible, and that is not done overnight. He says that when I get there, I will no longer want to return so everything must be arranged accordingly. There is some truth in that. I don't know how to resolve [this problem] and beg you to advise me. . . .

My husband is not at all attached to this country. He has told me a hundred times (and you know he never says what he doesn't mean) that he would prefer to live in Europe if his economic interests didn't hold him here. He often complains about Americans' lack of honesty and good faith, but at the same time he thinks there is no other country where property is as secure. So it would not be possible to persuade him to sell his lands. Please tell me how much you think we would have to spend (liberally figured) to live in Antwerp, and also whether you think my husband could become accustomed to a society and way of life so different from here. He tells me that if he has nothing to do, "he will get into mischief."

. . . Right after the New Year, I will be sure to send you a certificate of life attested by the Swedish consul, Mr. Soderstrom, who lives in the Federal City and who dined here just two days ago.[4] I am enclosing an account of [the $866.80] we have received for you. . . . Following your instructions, my husband will invest it in shares of the Bank of Columbia, although he doesn't think they are the most advantageous shares to buy at present. . . .

I am happy that our decision to come and live [at Riversdale] full time pleases you, dear Father, and do not worry that it will be the slightest obstacle to our coming to see you. The feelings which make me want that so much can never be weakened by any other attachment. My primary and strongest desire will always be to see you again, and if that does not take place next summer, it will be for pressing reasons.

It is hard to calculate what this plantation could produce [on its own], independent of my husband's hard work, but noting down all the costs and income of this year will probably be the best way to figure it out. . . . My husband thinks that $160 [$1,600] a year would not be overestimating [its net income]. . . .[5] He wants very much to begin building a grist mill. A very capable Baltimore mill-builder was here some time ago to look over the land, see what type mill would be best, and now he is busy drawing up plans. It will cost between $3,000 and $4,000, and will yield 20 percent, possibly 25, by leasing it out. Subtracting 3 percent for the cost of repairs would leave 17 percent [return], quite apart from the plaster of paris, which we would supply to be processed—it is more and more in use and its toll would return a great deal.[6] Another big benefit would be not having to produce any Indian corn at all—just contracting with the miller to deliver so much meal for the negroes. A second benefit is that half the cost of the mill has already been expended in the dam and race, which have to be maintained without yielding the return they should. I don't know whether I told you that for $300 we bought a man who is a good carpenter and knows how to keep a mill in good repair.

But, dear Father, I am beginning to think I'll never finish this letter, which I fear must long since have bored you, and still I haven't written half of what I had to tell you. But I will save it for another occasion and close by embracing you tenderly,

Your affectionate daughter,

R. E. Calvert

1. Lucie was the female slave who accompanied the Stiers on their voyage to Europe. Stier wrote Mrs. Calvert that he had sent Lucie back with Captain Norman, paid her passage and even her stage fare to Bladensburg, and entrusted her with a letter and journal of the trip (HJS to RC, 26 August 1803, Stier-MHS).

2. Finding his financial affairs in Belgium in better condition than he had anticipated, Stier wrote his daughter that he could raise her yearly allowance to $2,000 from the $1,200 previously paid her (HJS to RC, 26 August 1803, Stier-MHS).

3. A hogshead of tobacco was approximately one thousand pounds at this time; the prices of $10 and $8 were for one hundred pounds. The crop sold was the 1802 harvest from Calvert's plantations, not from Riversdale.

4. Since there were European investments in her name, Rosalie Calvert had to submit a certificate each year testifying to her continued existence.

5. Mrs. Calvert omits a zero here. She is replying to her father's query as to whether the plantation can clear $1,400 to $1,600 a year (HJS to RC, 26 August 1803, Stier-MHS).

6. Plaster of paris was in demand as a fertilizer for its lime content.

To Mme H. J. Stier

Riversdale, [n.d.] November 1803

Dear Mama,

Yesterday I received your letter written eight days after your arrival in Antwerp. . . . I am very touched by the proof of affection and remembrance you give me by writing such a short time after your arrival and while surrounded with friends hastening to show their pleasure in your return. I have read with emotion all the details you give me about your reception, and all who contributed by their endearments to make the country more pleasant for you are dear to me. The death of my dear Uncle Joseph grieved me very much. [Uncle and Aunt Joseph] were the two I felt closest to. When I read at the beginning of your letter that you were at <u>Madame</u> Stier's house, I suddenly suspected this sad event, and I could not continue reading for a while. It affected me greatly. At my age, especially having had so few adversities in my life, the loss of someone I loved so much is very afflicting. Every day I see people who don't feel anything deeply and I envy their indifference. Surely an over-sensitive heart is an unlucky gift from nature, producing more pain than joy. Please tell my Aunt that I genuinely share her sorrow. . . .

I was pleased that the de Vinck family has been so friendly to you. It must help comfort Papa in the loss of his dear brother to rediscover a sister who has been like a stranger for such a long time.[1] Leverghem, I see, is a person who doesn't like to be bothered—he might be very pleasant in society, but I would not choose him for my friend.[2] So the Baron and Baroness de S. still continue their formal manner; it frequently happens that we don't like people we have wronged. Since neither one is in the least interesting, they are not worth worrying about.[3]

I am delighted, dear Mama, that you gave me so many details. It makes me feel close to you and I accompany you everywhere, which makes me so absentminded that everyone laughs at my responses and *propos rompus*. I am pleased that my Aunt Guyot has been so friendly and that her granddaughter reminds you of Caroline.[4] I kissed [Caroline] several times, telling her it was from you and Papa. . . . She is still extremely lively and easily upset, but she never has a moment of rancor and is remarkable for her good humor.

George is fat and in good health. He can almost walk by himself. His nurse takes good care of him and is quite attached to him. . . .

Since I still haven't gotten the letter you wrote from Amsterdam, I didn't know until this letter about the death of the Baroness Stier.[5] I cannot comprehend why she gave her daughter such a peculiar education—it is very dangerous. Your comparison to the Virgin of St. Peter makes me picture her exactly. I think it will be difficult to prevent her from becoming the dupe of some adventurer, because it won't be easy in their circle to find a rich man sufficiently <u>Romantic</u> to prefer such a woman, whatever her merit.[6]

<u>Jerome</u> [Bonaparte], the great man's brother, has been here for some time and commands no respect. People insult him at every opportunity. He was courting Miss Patterson of Baltimore, but her parents refused to consent to the marriage. The young lady threatened to run away with him, [so] they gave in. The date was set and preparations made, but the evening before the wedding she was driven off to one of her relatives in Virginia under a chaperone's custody. I don't know how this story will end.[7] She is a most extraordinary girl, given to reading Godwin on the rights of women, etc., in short, a modern *philosophe*.[8]

Last week I went to Mrs. Law's to enjoy the horse-races, which lasted for five days and were splendid, with a great number of carriages. I went to a ball where there were 120 women and as many men. Every day we either received company at home, or we went out from morning till evening. I had the satisfaction of seeing my husband's family superior to all others in every respect. Mrs. Stuart was there with her daughters; the oldest is the most delightful person I've met, extremely sweet, pleasant, and well-bred.[9] Mrs. Peter, on her way back to the City, was detained at her sister Mrs. Lewis' house; while she was there, [Mrs. Lewis] gave birth to a boy. A few days later [Mrs. Peter] had a girl. Their <u>mother</u> went back there yesterday for the <u>same</u> reason! As you can see, these women are making certain that the country not become depopulated.[10]

. . . We often give small dinners. The roads are so good now that coming here is no problem. I don't know whether I wrote you that we changed your old carriage; it is enclosed in front now with two pieces of glass and cushions against the Venetian shutters. Since the body of the carriage was too short to put a *passé,* we manage with two postilions in yellow jackets, leather pantaloons, and black velvet caps with gold lace trim. It makes a very fine equipage. The horses near the wheel are sure and <u>steady</u>—the lead horses are extremely lively and handsome. . . .

I get up every morning at daybreak and when the weather is nice, I go out to the garden. We are very busy putting it in order. I have some superb salad in the beds. My gardener John works as hard as four people—he is a good man.

Adieu, dear Mama, I embrace you so many times in my imagination and want nothing more than to do so in reality. My husband sends his regards; he is at Mount Albion, where I haven't been for a long time. Believe me,

Your affectionate daughter,

R. E. Calvert

1. H. J. Stier's younger sister, Hélène Françoise (1746–1807), was married to Jean F. J. de Vinck Westwezel.

2. Joseph Charles H.J.M. della Faille de Leverghem (1754–1822) was the husband of Jean Michel van Havre's half-sister, Catherine.

3. Probably the Baron and Baroness de Schilde, Philippe van de Werve (1748–1834) and his third wife, Marie della Faille. The Baron's second wife, Thérèse Peeters (1749–1789), was Rosalie Calvert's aunt and had left her a bequest at her death.

4. Françoise Jacqueline Guyot (1751–1808[?]) was Mrs. Stier's sister and the widow of Jean Baptiste Guyot.

5. Marie J. (le Candele) Stier (1761–1803) was the widow of the Baron Jean François de Stier (1739–1792), H. J. Stier's oldest brother.

6. Joséphine Isabelle Stier (1785–1850) was the only child of the late Baron and Baroness de Stier.

7. Jerome Bonaparte (1784–1860), Napoleon's youngest brother, was a nineteen-

year-old lieutenant in the French navy in 1803. Sailing to the West Indies at the outbreak of war between France and England, he was forced to seek refuge for his ship in New York Harbor to escape the British. While in the United States he met and married Elizabeth "Betsy" Patterson (1785–1879), daughter of a wealthy Baltimore family. The marriage did not have Napoleon's blessing, and he had it annulled in 1807. By that time Elizabeth and Jerome had a son, born in England in 1805. Napoleon made his brother King of Westphalia in 1807 and required him to marry Catherine, Princess of Wurtemberg. The alliance of Betsy Patterson and Jerome Bonaparte was the talk of the country when it occurred and became the subject of many novels and biographies.

8. Mary (Wollstonecraft) Godwin (1759–1797) was the English author of *A Vindication of the Rights of Women* (1792), which espoused education for women equal to that of men and companionate marriage.

9. Eleanor (Calvert) Custis Stuart (1754–1811), George Calvert's older sister, married her second husband, Dr. David Stuart (1753–1814), in 1783. The Stuarts' oldest daughter was Ann Calvert Stuart (b. 1784).

10. Martha Peter was detained at Woodlawn, the home of her sister, Eleanor "Nelly" (Custis) Lewis (1779–1852). Martha Peter had a daughter, America Pinckney, and Nelly Lewis had a son, Lorenzo, in the autumn of 1803. Their mother, Mrs. Stuart, was remarkable for her fertility; in addition to her four Custis offspring, she had sixteen children by Dr. Stuart.

To H. J. Stier

Riversdale, 25 December 1803

Dear Father,

I am going to take the opportunity of a ship going from Alexandria to Antwerp to send you a box with some seeds of the tulip poplar and red cedar trees. . . . [After your last letter] my husband immediately wrote to Mr. Cooke about your luggage. He replied that the [*Java*] had indeed been brought into Portsmouth on the suspicion that there was French property aboard, but it had been released and arrived at Amsterdam with all the luggage. I was delighted to hear it, fearing you had lost it all. Some time after that, your slave Lucie arrived. Captain Norman took her on board the *Venus* at Amsterdam. . . . So we accused Norman too quickly. . . .

Lucie gave me your letter of 4 August [1803], in which you give a journal of your passage.[1] It was not as pleasant as I had hoped, but considering wartime and the number of ships that stopped you, I think you have been fortunate to be treated so well. There were many false rumors here, among others that you had been put in prison in France. Fortunately, they didn't let me hear of them until after I had received your letter from Antwerp. . . .

Lucie is now in my service. I am going to try to sell her soon for the best possible price. I could not make her say that she had not left the ship, as she tells me about having been on land several times, but I don't think it is important. She really is a very good chambermaid and conducts herself well since she has been separated from her mother. . . . We are busy now getting the tobacco in order, and my husband thinks there will be no more than 8 hogsheads. The weather has been extremely bad, even worse around Mount Albion than here. Planters who usually make 15 to 20 hogsheads are not even making 8. No one can recall such a drought, lasting the entire summer.

Profits will be smaller, too, because of our living here. . . . The workers' time goes to making improvements rather than being devoted entirely to growing tobacco. . . . We bought a negro at auction the other day for $404. There are not anything like enough hands to farm [this plantation] profitably. A little darky arrived here day before yesterday—Betty's production. We also bought a carpenter who is very skilled at sawing for $300.

The brick bridge on the mill race in town is finished. . . . They have made a wooden [bridge] on the Eastern Branch, where you said to put it, but it is not yet completely finished.

The dairy has been moved behind the clumps on the way to Peggy Adams' place, and [the addition of] a brick chimney converted it into a good house for negroes.[2] We are going to build a small dairy near the pump in front of the kitchen.

They are busy making the palings to enclose the garden, which we are greatly enlarging by extending the side near the spring. . . . I am also going to have a small greenhouse built where you planned it—at the wash-house. The cellar makes a very good orangerie.[3] You offered to send me some fruit trees. . . . I hope Louvrex will not forget to send me a cask of red wine. Ordering so many things and making plans for so many improvements here will, I fear, make you think that we are not planning to come and see you. That is certainly not the case. . . . Even if this country were the earthly paradise, I would leave it today with complete content if it were possible. I have little hope that we can come before spring after next. . . .

Your affectionate daughter,

R. E. C.

1. This letter with journal has not been found.

2. Peggy Adams was a widow who had a one hundred-acre farm between Riversdale and the Buck Lodge plantation.

3. The cellar at Riversdale had large windows facing south which could furnish enough light to carry plants over the winter.

George Calvert to H. J. Stier[1]

Riversdale, December 25, 1803

Dear Sir,

It is with great satisfaction I have heard of your agreeable reception in your native country, and it is with sincere pleasure I look forward to the time when it would be in our power to pay you a visit, but this cannot be until we have made one or two Crops more. I am preparing for making one hundred Hogs. next year. If the season is favorable I ought to make that quantity; the last was one of the worst ever known and I shall make fifty.[2] My last year's Crop of fifty Hogsheads I sold at 10 & 8 dollars, which brought me $4,600. Rosalie and myself thank you for the additional mark of your kindness. The money due you here shall be invested in the manner you have directed; Columbia stock is now 55—what a speculation it was when so long not above 30.

With respect to the value of the farm, I cannot speak with any degree of presition [precision;] it would be perhaps more productive under a good manager than with me living upon it, as I cannot help frequently taking off the hands to make improvements which would not be attended to by an Overseer. I think you do not over rate it at 1,600 Dollars with the hands and stock you left upon it; perhaps it may not produce that much net for the last twelve months, but [I] have no doubt it will average that take a few years [from?] then. There was not preparation made for a larger Crop of Tobacco, and the season was remarkably bad. I think we shall make here about 8 Hogsheads. The meadow near the saw Mill did not produce more than 4 tons of hay; I shall put all that in Tobacco and Plaster the old fields in hopes of getting some grass from that.

I send you some seeds and in the Box with them a late publication upon the use of Plaster of Paris. By this you will see how easy it is to get good Crops from our land, and how much better it must be than your European mode of manuring with stable dung. For fear you should not believe the Books, I have sent you some certificates as you may think it necessary to have some proof of clover growing ten feet high.

I shall have some money next summer to spare and I wish to build a Mill to rent near the saw Mill, as I find it will produce me a better interest than in any other investment I can make, and I will be improving the property besides. I wish to know whether you approve of my erecting a Mill there. We shall have a Tobacco house to build for the next Crop; I made use of one at Sheckles' for the Tobacco we made this year.[3] We are preparing to pale in the garden, and if we remain here must finish more of the house. The dining room we have nearly got compleated, and it is much admired. We have a very handsome cornish [cornice] put up, which with its chimatium [cymatium], makes it look very handsome indeed. My dear Rosalie and her sweet little children are very well, having enjoyed very good health since you left us, and should all of us be as happy as mortals are permitted to be in this life, could we but now and then see those who are so deservedly dear to us. You will present my sincere Affection to Mama, my brother Charles, Mr. and Mrs. van Havre and there [*sic*] Children and believe me,

With the greatest Respect & Regard,

Yours, Geo. Calvert

1. Van Havre Papers, Château du List Archives, Schoten, Belgium (hereafter Van Havre-S).
2. This is the crop that Calvert expected to make on his lands, not Riversdale.
3. Samuel Sheckles was Calvert's overseer at his Buck Lodge plantation (Prince George's County Land Records, Liber J. R. M. 9, fol. 46).

⋅◖ SOME OF H. J. STIER'S LETTERS to his daughter in the early years of their separation have survived. Stier did not hesitate to offer his daughter and son-in-law advice on a wide range of topics, and he encouraged Rosalie to develop her natural abilities and look after her interests. Following is one of his letters.

To Rosalie Calvert from Henri J. Stier[1]

[Antwerp, 25 December 1803]

My dear Rosalie,

. . . I am sorry to see that you have been deterred from your plan of a trip to Bath, but glad that you are now feeling better than you have in three years. I urge you expressly to give me an exact description of your condition whenever you don't feel perfectly well. You are subject to nervous illness; a miscarriage is evidence of such a condition and aggravates it. . . .

Marie Louise Peeters Stier and Henri Joseph Stier. Miniatures by Robert Field, 1801.
Copyright Bureau d'Iconographie de Belgique (ANRB), Brussels

I was truly pleased to see that you like being in the vicinity of Washington and that they have improved the road. I predict that in a few years your location will be as agreeable as one could wish for. However, the vogue for Spa Spring will not be so pleasant since you will be subject to inconsiderate and tiresome visits. Beware of opening roads on that side, and above all, of opening the spring in your woods which people say is even better than the other. . . . Do persuade your husband to make the formation of meadows a goal and take care to clear the woods. . . . Observe for yourself how bad the condition of your woods is. In the large number of trees I had cut down there were very few that were not greatly damaged because they were too old. A tree has a time of growth, a time of maturity, and then a time of decay. . . . So it is necessary to clear your woods of all the old and inferior trees in order to give light and [room for] growth to the good ones. . . .

I advise you to begin training a young negro for the garden so that later when you are free of your greatest cares, you can send for a gardener from here. He will cost you perhaps $100 a year, but you will only have to keep him for two or three years, and he can teach your negro.

But these are plans which keep you where you are while we both should be making one to bring us back together. But, alas, my dear, I see little hope of that when I weigh your own personal interest, which frequently concerns Mama and me. We know the difficulty of advising you about the most suitable and advantageous course of action. I think your husband would have trouble adapting to our country where the customs, language, and occupations are so different. I don't know if you yourself, having left at so young an age and having become used to other ways, would find life here more pleasant than there. You could both come here to make the experiment. The future establishment of your children is yet another important consideration. . . .

Mama is writing you to come here this summer. I think it is the best arrangement and I greatly desire it, too. Let's plan on it. Your house will still not be finished—much will remain to be done there. The grounds also won't be finished. You will need plans for all that. You should have them made as best you can by your architects, for the house as well as the grounds. Bring the plans here with you and you can find some models in Paris and London by which to judge them, change them, furnish them. You should take some good managers into your service to take care of your agricultural interests in your year's absence. . . .

I must give you still one more piece of advice: inform yourself about your business affairs. You have sufficient ability to acquire this knowledge if you resolve to do it and seize the opportunities to learn. No capable woman should neglect it. The country in which you live, more than our own, requires that women have that kind of knowledge, and I can't urge you too strongly to acquire it. Your special situation makes it really indispensable because of the inheritances coming to you and their terms set out in a language foreign to your husband. . . .

Wishing you a happy New Year and all possible good fortune to you and your husband. I am

[no signature]

1. From the Henri J. Stier Papers at the Maryland Historical Society, Baltimore. This collection contains correspondence, in French, from Stier to Rosalie Calvert from 1803 to 1807.

To Mme H. J. Stier

Riversdale, 29 December 1803

Dear Mama,

. . . There are so many ships going to Antwerp and Amsterdam now that we can write each other often. I will do my best to be informed about each ship sailing to your port, which is going to become famous again.[1]

We are having a very warm winter after a summer so dry no one can remember being so long without rain. I go out almost every day for a walk to the garden which they are busy leveling out, a process which requires a lot of work. I haven't been to Mount Albion for a long time, although my husband frequently goes for a day or two. All of my excursions nowadays are to Washington which seems only a step away since the roads have been so improved.

Mr. Merry, the new English Ambassador, arrived here a short while ago.[2] He has three different carriages, all of the latest fashion, an enormous amount of furniture, servants, etc., and he has rented two houses. . . . [The Merrys] have made one house out of these two, which is very grand. They plan on living in the most splendid style, which will not be at all agreeable to Mr. Jefferson and his Democratic party who want to introduce a system of equality and economy, thinking by that means to please the populace—in whom they are beginning to find themselves disappointed. [The Jeffersonians] don't like Mr. Merry, and this caused a most ridiculous scene the other day at a dinner given by Secretary of State Madison. [Madison], instead of conducting Mrs. Merry into dinner first, gave his hand to Gallatin's wife, leaving the Ambassador to conduct his own wife. It made a huge uproar—as much as if a treaty had been broken![3]

The Democrats are beginning to lose ground among the people in our county. My brother-in-law, Edward Calvert, has been elected a member of the [Maryland General] Assembly.[4]

Custis has finished a wing of his building, which will be very handsome and will be seen from all points of Washington.[5] I haven't been there yet, but I plan to go soon. My sister-in-law Mrs. Stuart is in the market to purchase Richard Scott's property near Alexandria. Her object in wanting to come and live in that neighborhood is to educate her children and give her daughters more opportunity to go out in society and get married. I'm afraid they won't find husbands easily since they are very difficult to please, and there isn't a good choice nowadays. The eldest [daughter] is a delightful person, extremely sweet and amiable, and as soon as her mother is recovered from her confinement, [Ann] is coming with her sister to spend a few days with me.[6]

Caroline and George are in perfect health—they haven't had the least indisposition since you left. Caroline is still vivacity itself and is beginning to learn her letters and to count a little. Her brother is as big as she, but not as tall. He walks by himself, like a drunk man, and is always in a good humor. He rarely cries. . . .

Tell me how you found the [Château du] Mick and if you still amuse yourself with plants. Tell my brother I do not forgive him. He has forgotten me entirely. He has not written me for two years—his last letter was December 1801. I have written him twice since then. . . .

Your affectionate daughter,

R. E. C.

1. Antwerp was experiencing an economic revival under French domination. The city had been one of the most important trading centers of the world, but after the Treaty of Westphalia (1648) and the closing of the Scheldt, it had steadily lost ground to Amsterdam.

2. Anthony Merry was English minister to the United States from 1803 to 1806.

3. James Madison (1750/51–1836) was Jefferson's secretary of state from 1801 to 1809; his dinner partner was Hannah (Nicholson) Gallatin (?–1849), the wife of Treasury Secretary Albert Gallatin (1761–1849). This incident, and others like it, did stir up a great deal of social and political uproar. Mrs. Merry and Federalist critics of the Jefferson administration were outraged at what they considered a major breach of protocol. President Thomas Jefferson, after noting that Mrs. Merry had "disturbed our harmony extremely," explained his part in the matter: "I had been in the habit when I invited female company (having no lady in my family) to ask one of the ladies of the four Secretaries to come and take care of my company; and as she was to do the honors of the table I handed her to dinner myself. That Mrs. Merry might not construe this as giving them a precedence over Mrs. Merry, I have discontinued it" (Jefferson to James Monroe, January 1804, in John P. Foley, ed., *The Jefferson Cyclopedia* [New York, 1967], vol. 2, p. 549).

4. George Calvert's older brother, Edward Henry Calvert (1766–1846), a Federalist, was elected to represent Prince George's County in the Maryland House of Delegates in 1795, 1803, 1809, and 1815.

5. George Washington Parke Custis was building his home, Arlington House (the Custis-Lee Mansion). The north wing was completed first.

6. The David Stuart family moved from their Hope Park plantation in Fairfax County, Virginia, to Ossian Hall, near Alexandria, in 1804. Ann Calvert Stuart, age 19 in 1803, and her sister Sally were Mrs. Calvert's prospective guests.

To Isabelle van Havre

Riversdale, 30 December 1803

Dear Sister,

. . . Thank you a thousand times for the abundant details you gave me about your landing. I read it with much pleasure and in my imagination participated in all the endearments and loving welcomes our large family gave you. . . .

I see with sorrow that our brother is so grave. He hasn't written me for two years. You must not, dear Friend, let him feed his grief. When one has children, it is unpardonable to remarry, but it is quite the contrary when one does not, and is young and has a large fortune. I fear that my brother is a bit too romantic, and I sincerely want him to find and take a wife who will comfort him for the loss he has suffered. He likes children too much to be deprived of the happiness of having them. . . .

I am often surprised at how we can endure the sadness which comes our way every day. I never reflected as much on human vicissitudes as [I have] since I am left alone here—and nonetheless, one is gay. I am part of a large family on a ladder which we all climb, and from time to time one of us makes a misstep and falls. The others are discouraged for a while, but soon continue climbing until they, too, fall. You know that I have always been subject to the "blue devils" and since your departure, even more. To distract myself, I see as many people as I can and go into Washington often. I am very close to Mrs. Law, who comes here frequently, and I can stay with her with complete informality. Her husband is back from England—the same as ever—he cannot stay still for two minutes.

I now have a very nice team of four beautiful brown horses driven by postilion, and with lanterns on the carriage I am no longer afraid to come home in the evenings. I receive invitations to dances almost every day. According to your description, our fashions are about the same. I wear my sleeves half-way up the arm; those who follow the exaggerated fashion wear them even shorter and very transparent, with gloves of a kind of lace called "patinet," which lets the skin show through. It certainly is flattering. I had the honor of winning the prize of the costume and of the dance the other night at a dance given by Mrs. Law. . . .

I don't visit the ladies of Bladensburg (except Mrs. Dick Lowndes), but the men often dine here.[1] Mrs. Ben Lowndes came to see me the other day and apologized for not coming sooner. I received her imperiously. I will never forgive them for having vexed Papa and Mama so, and I don't want to have any relations with them. They are so jealous of our equipage, our mode of living which surpasses theirs, etc. etc.

Mr. Merry, the English Ambassador who arrived recently, is the news of the day in Washington. Tommy Jeff and his party don't care for him. What do you think of my sister-in-law Mrs. Stuart who, having eleven children alive and being grandmother to seven, is expecting a new addition to her family? Mrs. Dulany of Alexandria separated from her husband who is crazy, but they are reconciled once again.[2] Luxury is increasing greatly here.

You didn't write me anything about your children, in whom I am quite interested. . . . Caroline and George are well. . . . He is fat like his sister, like a little ball, and never cries. I won't wean him before next summer. His wet-nurse takes extremely good care of him and is very attached to him. I sometimes leave him at home [with her] for two or three days without the least problem.

I must finish this letter, dear Sister. . . . Give my kind regards to all who remember me. Tell me what is said about my not coming back with you. Embrace your children for me.

R. E. C.

[P.S.] My husband, who just came in this moment, brought the news that Jerome Bonaparte has been married to Miss Patterson of Baltimore. . . .[3]

1. Mrs. Calvert considered Anne Lowndes, a daughter of Edward Lloyd IV and Elizabeth (Tayloe), her social equal and the two became good friends.

2. Probably Elizabeth (French) Dulaney, wife of Benjamin Tasker Dulaney (1752–1816).

3. The Bonaparte-Patterson marriage took place on December 24, 1803.

A Daughter's Grief

T HE SOCIAL SEASON, ALWAYS AT its peak in the winter months, was enlivened in 1804 by extremely cold weather, which made it easy to travel by sleigh. There were dancing parties and outings, and the revealing new French fashions for women making their appearance in Washington provoked outrage from some, bawdy jokes from others.

Rosalie Calvert enjoyed the season but professed disillusion with the American women of her acquaintance, calling them duplicitous and cold. Her niece Eliza Law, with whom she had been friendly, was pursuing what Mrs. Calvert regarded as an unsuitable course of action by separating from her husband, and they grew apart. The lack of a compatible female friend made Rosalie's loneliness for her absent family more acute, and when she learned that she was pregnant again, she was overwhelmed with longings for them.

Rosalie was also beginning to experience difficulties in running her household. She felt besieged by houseguests, by sewing chores for outfitting her family and the house, and she complained bitterly about the lack of good servants in America. Such complaints were common among plantation mistresses, but Mrs. Calvert seems to have felt at a particular disadvantage in dealing with her black servants, contrasting her experience with that of her husband, who had grown up with the slave system. Rosalie regularly hired white servants to supplement the Calverts' slave labor force and perhaps also to provide a sort of buffer between herself and the blacks she was neither comfortable with nor able to manage.

Mrs. Calvert appears, however, to have accepted the slave system of her adopted country without any introspection or doubts about its morality. She speaks casually in these early letters of buying and selling men and women without hesitation or regret.

The number of slaves held at Riversdale in these early years ranged somewhere between the fifteen that Mrs. Calvert's father had owned in 1800 and the thirty-two reported in an 1806 tax assessment. This labor force was supplemented by moving slaves from the Mount Albion plantation as need arose, to work not only at Riversdale but also at George Calvert's adjoining Buck Lodge holding. The number of slaves at Mount Albion fell from seventy-six in 1800 to fifty-seven by 1806.

With labor-intensive tobacco constituting the Calverts' main crop, there was urgent need for more hands to work the fields and make the improvements a new plantation required. However, when one of the worst floods of the century hit the area, destroying crops, fields, fences, and watercourses, the Calverts experienced a severe financial setback, and economy became the watchword of the day. Some relief came from Rosalie's father, who raised her allowance, but he expected the major portion of this allowance to be earned from the property, and she feared to tell him that in 1804 Riversdale would earn nothing.

The tribulations of plantation life paled before the news from Antwerp in late summer that Rosalie's beloved mother, Marie Louise Peeters Stier, had died. Rosalie Calvert had a strong maternal heritage. Madame Stier, a woman of culture and ability, had come from a privileged background, as had her mother before her. Both Cleydael Castle and the painting collection had come into the Stier family through the maternal line. Rosalie's few letters to her mother reveal an easy camaraderie, a delight in sharing thoughts and emotions, and none of the rivalries or tensions that mar some mother-daughter relationships. Their shared years as exiles in America had undoubtedly brought them closer. Mrs. Calvert's grief at losing "the best of all mothers" was intensified by the guilt she felt over her inability to travel to Europe during her mother's last illness. She envied her sister "the sad happiness" of having been able to assist their dying mother.

The birth of the Calverts' third child in late fall forced Rosalie to put aside these thoughts and turn her attention to her own growing family. Naming this second daughter Marie Louise helped ease her loss. Rosalie had flirted briefly with the idea of using one of the newly fashionable male doctors to assist her with this birth, but her sister objected so

Jean-Egide and Mathilde van den Cruyce Peeters with grandchildren. Rosalie (holding violin bow) with her maternal grandparents at Cleydael. Charles and Isabelle are to the far left and far right; Marie Louise Peeters Stier stands behind her parents. Artist unknown.

Copyright Bureau d'Iconographie de Belgique (ANRB), Brussels strenuously, insisting she engage only a female midwife, that she relented. She hired an old black woman who had belonged to Mrs. Washington and was delighted with her choice.

Rosalie's immediate family was a source of great joy to her, and she had no complaints about her husband, who, she said, always treated her with respect and consideration and consulted her on all matters of importance. Nevertheless, she began to take an interest in her family's monetary affairs and demonstrated a keen awareness of the limitations on a married woman's property rights in America.

To Mme H. J. Stier

Riversdale, 2 March 1804

Dear Mama,

I haven't heard from you in two months. During this time there have been a huge number of ships coming into Baltimore from Amsterdam, and with each one I thought I would finally receive your letters. You can imagine my impatience at being disappointed each time. . . .

We have had a very hard winter. We could cross over the Potomac on horseback! The snow was deep and stayed on the ground a long time, and we had the pleasure of going to Washington by sleigh several times. One night as we were returning home, we met another sleigh carrying Betsy Lloyd—the road was narrow, our horses very lively, and in passing the other too fast, we overturned in several feet of snow.[1] Before the gentlemen in the other sleigh could come to our aid, we were already on foot and ready to go on our way. This makes for a diversion of sorts and is pleasant.

There were several large dancing parties this winter. Mr. Tayloe gave a very nice one a few days ago.[2] He had two bands of good musicians, one for the dancers, the other made up of military instruments, clarinets, kettledrums, etc., etc. They played in the round salon where it made a delightful effect. I like dancing more than ever. There is a ball every Tuesday, alternately at Georgetown and on Capitol Hill. The clothes they wear are extremely becoming, [although] some display a little too much—among others, Madame Bonaparte who wears dresses so transparent and tight that you can see her skin through them, no chemise at all. Mrs. Merry, the new English Ambassadress, is very fat and covers only with fine lace two objects which could fill a fourth of a bushel!

I am enclosing some verses that Mr. Law, who stayed here, gave me the other day. You may not understand all of the humor—you must get my brother to read them to you. The occasion which gave rise to them is this: Mrs. Bonaparte came to a dance given by Mr. Smith, wearing a dress so transparent that you could see the color and shape of her thighs, and even more![3] Several ladies made a point of leaving the room, and one informed the belle that if she did not change her manner of dressing, she would never be asked anywhere again. Our nephew Law, who is a great poet, composed the first verses. Colonel Burr wickedly told the lady that someone had written some very pretty verses about her beauty, and she so insisted on seeing them that the poor poet, in order to keep his eyes, had to write the second verses. . . .[4]

At the moment I am busy making curtains, slipcovers, etc. for the dining room. The curtains [are] of that blue striped English cloth you gave me, [trimmed] with a white fringe intermixed with small blue tassels; there is just enough material for the windows and the sofa. The cornices are white and gilt, [and] I plan to paint the room yellow. The middle bedroom has curtains and bed [hangings] of white dimity with white fringe intermingled with green and red embellishment, which is quite elegant. The carpenter is going to start finishing the other bedroom now. . . .

I want to make the garden my principal amusement this summer. I hope that Charles will send me plans for the lake and for some <u>bridges</u> and <u>gates</u>.

. . . My children and my husband are in good health. Please give my compliments to Papa. . . .

Your affectionate daughter,

R. E. Calvert

[Thomas Law's verses about Betsy Patterson Bonaparte]

I.
I was at Mrs. Smith's last night
And highly gratified my self
Well! what of Madame Bonaparte
Why she's a little whore at heart
Her lustful looks her wanton air
Her limbs revealed her bosom bare

. . . .
. . . .[5]

Show her ill suitted for the life
Of a Columbians modest wife
Wisely she's chosen her proper line
She's formed for Jerom's concubine.

2.

Napoleon full of trouble
Conquers for an empty bubble
Jerom's conquest full of pleasure
Gains him a substantial treasure
The former triumphs to destroy
The latter triumphs to enjoy
The former's prise were little worth
If e'en he vanquished all the earth
The latter Heaven itself has won
For the ador'd Miss Paterson.

1. Elizabeth (Betsy) Lloyd (1774–?) was a younger sister of Anne Lowndes of Bladensburg.

2. John Tayloe III (1771–1828) was the owner of Octagon House in Washington, where this dance was held.

3. Robert Smith (1757–1842), Jefferson's secretary of the navy, hosted this affair. Margaret Bayard Smith gave her account of the same incident: "I think it no harm to speak the truth. She [Madame Bonaparte] has made a great noise here, and mobs of boys have crowded round her splendid equipage to see what I hope will not often be seen in this country, an almost naked woman. An elegant and select party was given to her by Mrs. Robt. Smith; her appearance was such that it threw all the company into confusion, and no one dared look at her but by stealth" (Gaillard Hunt, ed., *The First Hundred Years of Washington Society* [New York, 1906], p. 46).

4. Aaron Burr (1756–1836) was vice-president of the United States, 1801–1805.

5. The lines left blank were probably censored by Thomas Law when he gave the verse to Mrs. Calvert.

To Mme H. J. Stier

Riversdale, [n.d.] March 1804

Dear Mama,

After four months without hearing from you, I finally received your letter of October 3 today. You can imagine, dear Mama, with what impatience I opened it and what pleasure it gave me, but I don't understand why it takes so long—five months—to get here. I am afraid Louvrex forgets to send the letters and leaves them on his desk. . . .

I am very busy with gardening at the moment. Half the garden is leveled off now, and they are working on the palings. Today I planted four groups of cherry trees between the house and the barn, with some rose bushes around. Next I am going to plant several clusters of willows, Italian poplars, and acacias on the north side. There is so much work to do that we don't know where to start. We have extended the garden near the spring so that it is twice as large, but more than half will be planted with fruit trees, currants, raspberries, etc. I have planted a large number of all the varieties of young fruit trees I could find, and I am going to fill the orchard with young apple trees everywhere there is room.

Caroline also has a garden where she works all day long, but she often digs up the seeds she planted the day before. She is beginning to be good company for me and always accompanies me when I go for a walk. She is still extremely lively, but very affectionate and quite reflective. Her questions and answers frequently amuse me.

George is very serious, but I think that comes from the disposition of his nurse whom he is constantly with. When the weather gets nice enough to go outside more, I believe he will play with his sister and Kitty and will become more lively. . . .[1] I had hoped we would be content with these two [children], but it seems not, and I am afraid that next November will not be the most pleasant month of the year.

We continue working on the house. The dining room is finished except for the mantelpiece and the painting. . . . The upstairs bedroom is almost done, but I fear starting the salon.

The painter Stuart—whose paintings Charles admired so much—is in Washington, and I think he has improved.[2] That is to say, he has changed his manner, which was very rude, and has settled down somewhat. He finishes [his paintings] quickly and has a lot of work. . . .

We are quite well-informed about what is going on in Europe. I think Americans have a natural relish for knowing everything that is happening in the four corners of the world. This incursion into England—if it is made—will not be at all advantageous for the Low Countries.[3] Does Papa worry much about political news? Since you take our newspapers, I imagine you are informed about events here.

I gave you an account of our winter entertainments and the clothes [we wear] in my last letters. . . . I am including here a small drawing showing how we do our hair, which is exactly like this, sometimes with a garland of flowers, or the hair is turned up with combs garnished with pearls, or for those who have them, diamonds. . . .

I thank you, dear Mama, for your offer to let me to use the furniture which is in the house. . . . I wrote you how I had furnished the bedrooms; in the back [bedroom] I am going to put the two beds I had at Mount Albion. That is the fashion, and it is sometimes very convenient to have two beds in a bedroom. . . .

Each day I realize more and more that happiness is only to be found in one's family. Although I go out in society more and play a more distinguished role than I have ever done before, nevertheless I am continually disgusted by the maliciousness and the lack of sincerity I meet here. I think that in America there is less attachment between kinsmen than in Europe, and I attribute this to the fact that generally they live so far apart from one another. I can find pleasant acquaintances here, but I have not yet found anyone who could be my friend, either man or woman.

Fortunately, my family is all that I could wish for, as my children enjoy unusually good health and my husband's affection for me increases instead of diminishing. He has all possible consideration for me, lets me do as I please, and he doesn't do anything important without my opinion. . . .

1. Kitty was Mrs. Calvert's white chambermaid (see RC to IvH, 28 September 1804, 5 November 1806, and 6 May 1807, Cal S-V).
2. Gilbert Stuart (1755–1828) came to Washington from Philadelphia in 1803 and opened a studio at F and Seventh streets.
3. A reference to Napoleon's preparations for an invasion of England.

To Mme H. J. Stier

[Riversdale], 5 April [1804]

I didn't have time to finish my letter. . . . Thank you for the trouble you took to choose the mantelpieces. I have written to Baltimore to have them sent to me as soon as possible, and I will get the stonecutter to come from Washington to place them.

You say you ordered [a mantel] for the drawing room, but that it is not finished. Please do not send it when you get it, because I don't think we are going to finish the drawing room so soon. The salon and the two piazzas are more important, and our funds won't permit us to do everything. Besides, we have to make a Spaarpot in order to cross the ocean and to live over there afterwards. . . .[1]

I would be much obliged if you would [send me] . . . I don't know how to say what is called "diaper" here—enough to make four dozen napkins for children and a dozen ells of small lace for everyday bonnets. . . . My regards to Papa. . . . My husband has been in Marlboro for a week on the jury, which he had the honor of serving as president. . . .

Your affectionate daughter,

R. E. C.

1. To make a *spaarpot* (Flemish) means to lay by some money. Mrs. Calvert spoke Flemish in addition to French and English, and occasional Flemish words and phrases appear in her letters.

To Mme H. J. Stier

Riversdale, 12 May 1804

Dear Mama,

I have thought of writing you every day since the beginning of April, but something has always prevented it. For some time my house has been full of houseguests and before that, I was so sick every morning that I couldn't do anything. . . .

It must have been disagreeable to wait so long for your baggage, but nothing surprised me more than what you tell me about my sister who has more work there than she had here! How is that possible? Are the servants not as good as they were in the past? I have a lot of work now, but it is because I don't have a single good servant. Were it not for that, I wouldn't have anything to do, but to keep everything in good order one has to watch them continually, and it is a great torment which I hope you have rid yourself of.

I have Mrs. Lewis and her children, the two Misses Stuart, and young Charles Stuart with me now—which fills the house.[1] They are very nice girls. Their brother Custis is going to marry Chatham Fitzhugh's young-est daughter next fall.[2] It is a good choice which all the family is happy about.

I did not expect to hear that the once cautious Antwerpers were spending so much and going into such huge bankruptcies. They should be sent over here where economy is all the fashion, especially in Wash-ington. In Alexandria, however, it is just the opposite.

There is not the least danger that [our] government would declare war on England. [Our leaders] are quite persuaded it is in their interest to maintain good relations with that power, which is the only one that could be an obstacle to this country. And Jerome B. [Bonaparte] is so generally scorned that he receives all sorts of slights, which he deserves. He has to borrow from various ambassadors in order to live, and he came to Washington with a beautiful carriage and six horses, but later it was discovered that it belonged to his friend, Commodore Barney, who is also disliked. . . .[3]

We are well-informed about what is going on in Europe—sometimes I think we know more than those who are there. I don't like the look of things over there, and I often fear that our unfortunate [Belgium] will suffer another revolution. Although I am convinced that you are better off and happier than you were here, nevertheless I sometimes worry that you will regret having returned. In my opinion, there is only one objection to this country, but that one is dreadful and without remedy—the difficulty we have with servants. Except for that inconvenience, which destroys all other pleasures, America would certainly be the more pleasant country in which to live.

Your little Caroline . . . is the admiration of all who see her. Her reputation is quite widespread. I took her the other day to the home of the painter Stuart, who has a fine collection of portraits. He could not tire of looking at her and said she was exactly like a Mrs. Sheridan of England, a woman famous for her beauty and her lovely voice.[4]

I am amusing myself now with the garden. We have had a frightful spring with continual rain from the beginning of March until now. No one can remember having so much rain and such violent storms. The hail between here and Baltimore even destroyed trees. The day after it had fallen, they brought pieces to my house that were bigger than a hen's egg, and in some places the ground was covered with a layer a foot deep. . . .

You know, I suppose, if you have received my last letter that since I didn't think our family was large enough, I plan to increase it at the beginning of next November. I would have preferred to postpone it a bit longer. Our two nieces, the Misses Stuart, are busy here making pretty little bonnets and baby frocks.

But I must finish, dear Mama. . . . I embrace you a thousand times and think of nothing but the pleasure of seeing and being with you again. Believe me always,

Your affectionate daughter,

R. E. Calvert

1 June [1804]

P.S. I just received your letter No. 6. . . . I see with great anxiety that you have had a recurrence of your old illness, and I hope you will continue to see the same doctor since he gave you relief. If I were not kept here by two <u>imperious</u> reasons, I would leave this minute to be with you. Imagine, dear Mama, how I feel at not being able to even hope of coming before next spring. . . . This thought is so dreadful that I can hardly bear it. You know our situation, and you know I would not delay for a minute setting out if it were possible. . . . Regards from my husband. He learns French very poorly and never expresses himself in it.

1. Mrs. Calvert's houseguests were Eleanor (Custis) Lewis; her children, Frances Parke (b. 1799) and Lorenzo (b. 1803); and Ann Calvert, Sally, and Charles Calvert Stuart (b. 1794).

2. George Washington Parke Custis was engaged to Mary Lee Fitzhugh (1788–1853), daughter of William Fitzhugh of Chatham and Anne (Randolph).

3. Joshua Barney (1759–1818) was an American privateer and naval officer who served under the French flag during the early Napoleonic period.

4. Caroline Henrietta Sheridan (1779–1851), English novelist and daughter-in-law of Richard Brinsley Sheridan, was acclaimed as the most beautiful woman in England.

To H. J. Stier

Riversdale, 14 May 1804

Dear Father,

. . . I am sorry you have become so quickly discouraged with your treatise on agriculture, which would have been very useful for us, and my husband says you are wrong in saying that you don't have any influence on him. On the contrary, he has a very good opinion of your horticultural talents, but [he says] a tobacco planter doesn't have time to attend to the details of a farm because his workers are always and without respite busy [with that crop]. He is applying himself as much as he can to developing meadowland, but to develop the forest according to your plan—which he thinks is a very good one—would necessitate another complete enterprise requiring a great many workers to cut [and] plant, horses for hauling, etc. The result would probably be a big profit, but it would require a large expense to start. We are convinced that your ideas about the degradation of the woods are quite correct, but at the same time it is impossible to remedy because we don't even have time to cut the few trees that are needed for fences. My husband bought [wood] . . . all chestnut, which is the best since it lasts twice as long. The work necessary to grow tobacco employs the negroes every day of the year.

We have planted many fruit trees this year, including all kinds of cherries, but it is impossible to buy any good pear trees from the nurseries. They sell bad pears under good names.[1] Tell me the best tree for grafting pears and plums—is it the <u>quince</u> or the pear itself? We don't have any young negro who seems intelligent enough to become a good gardener, but I will try to buy one.

I have thought often, dear Father, of the comparison you made between our two countries. . . . Considering first our children, there is no doubt that America offers the most advantages. As you observed once, in our venerable city families uphold themselves by always making <u>equal</u> alliances, by <u>strict economy</u>, and by investing in secure stocks. However, the last two of these three foundations seem very precarious, and thus the other becomes so also.

Education in the public colleges of the <u>north</u> here is excellent and offers several outstanding courses of study. Education for girls is usually very poor, but a mother attentive to her family's interest can easily remedy that, especially in the countryside. Education in Europe must be quite neglected at present.

As for our children's future, I don't know which country offers the best prospect. If everything returns to the old footing and the Scheldt stays open, perhaps you have the advantage, but that is so uncertain. . . . The climate here is certainly quite good, and the liberty of everyone to live as he pleases is a great advantage. But the torment with the servants poisons all these pleasures. Perhaps by hiring housekeepers and spending twice as much, we would have less trouble, but I am not in a position to do that. My husband doesn't feel this inconvenience as I do, since he is used to it. . . .

We still have not managed to put our plantations into good enough order to ensure good crops during our absence. We need two or three tobacco houses, a barn and a stable at Sheckles, a stable for the cattle here, plus a corn house and more houses for the negroes, overseer, etc. All this could be done in a short time by using some hired carpenters, but we can't deduct <u>all</u> these <u>expenses</u> from our income, which <u>up to now</u> has always been needed as soon as it is received.

I am following your advice to instruct myself as much as I can in our business, convinced, like you, that it is a big advantage and very necessary in my situation. My husband does nothing important without informing me of it. . . .

Yesterday we sold your girl Lucie to Dougherty for $225. . . .

We had a storm and terrible rain this week that caused a lot of damage. It broke the mill dam and the race in two places, carried off fence logs from here to beyond Bladensburg, which consequently are all lost. It inundated and destroyed all the tobacco beds, except a small one at Sheckles, and part of the oats which had been sown. My garden almost washed away—a dozen tulips were washed out of the ground and carried outside the garden fence. No one has seen such a flood in ten years. . . .

Not knowing if our letters are respected, I never write you about politics, but the news we receive daily from France and Holland causes me much worry. I don't understand why your letters take so long to arrive. I always get them three months or more after their date. . . . I would receive them just as well by ships going to Boston, New York, or Charleston, since the postal service takes them from the ships and distributes them afterwards, so it is not at all necessary to send them to Baltimore. . . .

Your affectionate daughter,

Rosalie E. Calvert

P.S. . . . What you tell me about Mama's health worries me very much. I hope that the summer and the air at the Mick will make her better. . . .

1. Stier advised buying pear trees at Alexandria, planting them in the garden which had "the real soil for pears," and watering them in winter with buckets of cow urine (HJS to RC, [25 December 1803,] Stier-MHS).

To Charles J. Stier[1]

Riversdale, 13 June 1804

Dear Brother,

I received your letter of February 20th by the *Diana,* and I cannot tell you how much pleasure it gave me. I had almost despaired of hearing from you and begun to fear that you no longer cared for your little sister. . . . Your letter, dear Brother, is bittersweet. What you say of Mama's health opens before me a future so hopeless I can hardly bear it, and yet I cannot yield to my desire to fly to her arms. . . . Nevertheless, I am infinitely indebted to you for your frank account of her condition. It is a proof of your attachment and confidence. I trust that the country air and the diet prescribed by the physician from Ghent will restore her and that I shall have the joy of seeing her next spring. . . . I had hoped for a time to be able to come this summer, but after more mature reflection we found it impossible. It will be with great difficulty that we can put everything in order even for the spring, but we are resolved to leave then unless unforeseen events intervene. The French are now treating the

American ships they meet outrageously, ill-using all on board and pillaging like pirates. The state of Europe—if we can form a just estimate from the gazettes—is very alarming. . . .

You paint me such a glowing picture of your Eugénie I am impatient to make her acquaintance.[2] My Aunt Stier . . . described her as the most admired and accomplished beauty of Antwerp. I can therefore only congratulate you, dear Brother, on having made so happy a choice. . . . Although it would be a great joy for me to be present on the day that gives you so charming a comrade, still I hope that it is not so far off and that you will taste this joy a long time before I shall have that of seeing you again. So prepare your Eugénie to love me as I am sure I shall love her. . . .

Your affectionate sister,

R. E. Calvert

1. Carter Trans-MHS.
2. Eugénie van Ertborn (1785–1834), daughter of François van Ertborn and Jeanne (van de Werve) of Antwerp, became the second wife of Charles Stier on July 16, 1804.

To Mme H. J. Stier

Riversdale, 14 June 1804

Dear Mama,

. . . [The news] about your health troubles me very much. . . . Be assured that it is only absolute necessity which keeps me here. . . .

Even if we had been able to arrange our affairs this summer, the condition in which I find myself would not allow me to come in autumn since it is at the beginning of November that I expect to increase our family. As I imagine that you may be worried about this time because I have always been so poorly the other times, I will give you some details about the arrangements. Since I won't have the advantage of your help or that of my sister, I will take a doctor from Washington who is very good at delivery and employed by everybody.[1] The Misses Stuart and Mrs. Law have all offered to come and stay here during that time, and I will choose whomever seems best. If I can get her, I will hire Betty, your old cook from Annapolis, for two months to take care of me. So you see that I am going to take all the precautions necessary for everything to go well, and you don't have to worry about my health which is very good right now. . . .

I know that you are at the Mick and I often imagine myself there with you. I am sorry to hear you say that [the Belgian countryside] is monotonous and sad compared to America. Since you must live there, I would like it to be an earthly paradise. Your spring is much nicer—the delightful nightingales and such a large variety of pretty birds—instead of bull frogs, locusts, and the thousand other detestable insects that we have. I only noticed the unpleasantness of this country since you left it, and I probably imagine Europe more pleasant since you are there. . . .

Adieu, dear Mama. My husband sends his compliments. He has written to Papa three or four times, but I fear you have not received our letters. . . .

Your affectionate daughter,

R. E. Calvert

1. Mrs. Calvert's sister, Isabelle, took immediate exception to this plan: "I see by your letters that you plan to use an *accoucheur* [male midwife] from Washington. I think you were badly advised. . . . I have had some experience and would never use anyone but a woman" (IvH to RC, undated letter draft [probably August 1804], Cal S-V).

To H. J. Stier

Riversdale, 7 July 1804

Dear Father,

. . . I am sorry not to be able to give you agreeable news from Riversdale, but we have had continual rains—no one can remember such a spring. It is impossible to give you an account of all the damage done by five storms, all terrible, but one in particular. We thought it was the second deluge! The water was four feet high in Ben Lowndes' store. . . . Capt. Jones came in a boat through the port right up to his own house. All the gardens in Bladensburg were destroyed and in some places covered with several feet of gravel. Not a single fence log remains between Sheckels [Buck Lodge] and Addison's plantation; some were stopped only at the new bridge over the Eastern Branch at Washington, where thousands have collected. There are only remains of the mill dams, and holes in the race ten feet deep in places; in other places, it is completely full of gravel. My husband had gone to a lot of trouble to collect a large quantity of manure, which he bought from Dougherty, Jones, Clarcke, etc., and almost all of it was carried away. Not only was a big plot of tobacco just planted near the large gate destroyed, but all the soil there was also swept away to the depth it had been plowed. [My husband] was planning to put a section of land north of the house into tobacco; five times it was plowed and prepared, and each time destroyed by the rain. Now he is going to try potatoes there, in order to produce something at least.

I am afraid we will not make even one hogshead here, although we were counting on twenty. The meadows won't produce anything either, nor the oats, and the wheat very little. Edward Lloyd, who grows almost nothing except [tobacco], won't have any at all, nor will others, so we have company in our misery.[1] Never have the fields promised such a good crop before they were destroyed. . . .

In the City two or three men were carried away on Pennsylvania Avenue and would have gone in the river if they had not grabbed onto some tree branches near Yong's house, where they were rescued by horsemen. When all is said and done, it is impossible to conceive the extent of the destruction without being on the spot. We had begun to buy some bank stock and planned to continue, but now we have to sell it in order to repair all the damage as soon as possible. . . .

My husband went to Alexandria yesterday to be present at the marriage of young Custis with Mr. Fitzhugh's younger daughter. . . .[2] I wasn't able to go because the roads are not passable for a carriage. . . .

[continued 8 July 1804]

1. Edward Lloyd V (1779–1834) became governor of Maryland, 1809–1811, and United States senator, 1819–1826.
2. George Washington Parke Custis married Mary Lee Fitzhugh on July 7, 1804.

To Rosalie E. Calvert from Henri J. Stier[1]

[Antwerp], 24 February 1804

My dear,

. . . I have always said, and most emphatically, that since I am equally fond of all my children, I would always treat them with complete impartiality and with generosity. . . . Although I sustained heavy losses here [in Europe], . . . I am happy to find that, without constraining myself, I can increase your dowry to the same level as that [originally] provided your brother and sister—that is, to $2000 a year. . . .

Before leaving America, I offered to leave the plantation with its dependencies to you in exchange for the annual income I was paying you. Further, I would pay for the cost of completing the entrance hall, the middle salon, and the dining room. . . . I had no intention of limiting my contribution to the revenues and profits of the plantation, but rather to take this income into consideration. . . .

You realize that however much I may wish to help, I must govern my calculations by a plan which maintains an equitable level with my other children. For that reason I must take account of what I paid for the plantation, the slaves, the buildings, furnishings, animals and accessories for the farm. . . . You can see by the attached record that the plantation cost $40,000, which, at 4 per cent interest, amounts to $1600 a year. . . .[2] So the plantation will represent a $40,000 capital asset which I imagine will provide you an income of $1600 a year, to which I shall add $400 to bring the annual dowry to $2000. . . .

And now I must reassure you that our plantation . . . will be irrevocably your property, barring only upheavals or unforeseen circumstances necessitating its use by your mother or me. So in order to assure you indisputable ownership, we shall make the necessary depositions very shortly. . . .

Your affectionate Father

1. Stier-MHS.

2. The record that Stier attached gave the following breakdown of Riversdale's cost:

Purchase	$20,105.00
Buildings and other improvements	15,638.32
Slaves left*	3,394.00
Miscellaneous (furniture, cattle)	962.68
	$40,000.00

*No listing or number of slaves left was given. Stier had owned fifteen slaves in 1800 according to the federal census.

To H. J. Stier

[Riversdale], 8 July [1804]

It seems, dear Father, that I need only begin writing you in order to hear from you. This is the third time I have gotten one of your letters just as I was going to send you mine. Since this method works, I am going to employ it more often. . . . [The letter just arrived] is your No. 10 of 24 February [1804] in which you send me a $500 check on the Bank of Alexandria, along with the accounts and arrangement about my allowance. You say, dear Father, that if I think you have been mistaken, or if I have any objections, to tell you. However, I assure you that I am perfectly satisfied, and please believe that I am convinced that you, just as

Mama, act at all times with the greatest generosity and fondness. I know, dear Father—and I never think of it without the keenest regret—that once I caused you to think that I believed myself treated unjustly, but you gave me so many unequivocal proofs to the contrary, and of your affection, that I would be ashamed if I did not remain eternally grateful. . . .

Finally, I have found a way to make my husband keep an [account] book—I began it myself! At the beginning he laughed at me for my awkwardness in doing it. Then he became impatient because I asked him every day how much he had spent. But at last he is going to do it himself, because he says I do it so badly that he will never be able to get away. Now every evening after supper we enter how much has been received or expended during the day. . . .

I thank you for your offer on the matter of a priest, but all things considered, I think it is better to go to a public chapel, especially in my situation [with] a husband of another persuasion.[1] The chapel you attended has been repaired and put in very good condition, and I contribute to its upkeep annually.[2] I plan to go there regularly, and for the same amount I would give for a priest to come here, I can entreat him to go there which will have a double advantage: [it will] provide a far better service than is usually held in a house, and [it will] increase the number of the congregation by furnishing more frequent days of mass and instruction.

Adieu, dear Father. I embrace you most tenderly in my imagination and ask you to believe me,

Your affectionate daughter,

R. E. Calvert

1. Stier had offered to pay part of the cost for a priest to come and offer mass regularly at Riversdale and also to furnish everything necessary for setting up a chapel there (HJS to RC, 24 February 1804, Stier-MHS).
2. This Catholic chapel may have been located at Green Hill, the home built by Catherine Brent Digges in the 1790s. Charles Stier, on a visit to his parents in Bladensburg in 1801, recorded in his daybook for April 10: "Vis: to Mrs. Digges—Plunckett's church." Robert Plunkett was Henri J. Stier's *curé* (Daybook, CJS-A).

To Mme H. J. Stier

Riversdale, [30] July 1804

Dear Mama,

. . . I hope that the air of the Mick will have done you some good and that I will hear from you soon. . . . Take good care of your health which is so precious to me, and as soon as the season permits I will come and offer you another little American. It is in November that I am expecting, but I wouldn't be at all surprised if he played the same trick as last time. I will have everything ready this time, and I plan to use Dr. May of Washington, whose method I know and who is considered very expert in this branch of his art and is widely used. . . .

You ask me how I amuse myself. . . . During the winter I frequently went to parties in Washington. I also took up dancing again. For the last two months I had the two Misses Stuart here, and Mrs. Peter and Mrs. Lewis for a few days.

I find a major flaw in [American] women is that they are extremely cold and incapable of deep feeling, and that they dissemble, which does not suit me at all. I wrote you about Custis marrying Fitzhugh's daughter. John Herbert is to marry Major Snowden's daughter—Major Snowden is dead.[1] But something that will really surprise you is the marriage of Mary Ogle to Beavens [Bevans] whom you knew well in Annapolis.[2] Mrs. Ogle must have lost her mind to have engaged her daughter—completely against [her husband's] will—to marry such a man. Because it is totally [Mrs. Ogle's] fault; she quarrelled with her son and with Mrs. Tayloe because they wanted to prevent it. Mrs. Lloyd was in on it, too—in short, it is an inconceivable affair. Yesterday my husband was with young Ben Ogle, who told him that his father was so grieved he feared he might die, being already in a very feeble state. He is going to take [his father] to Bath for some time.[3]

Mrs. Law and her husband separated amicably.[4] I believe this is the most peculiar affair of this sort that has ever taken place. They don't accuse each other of anything except of not being able to get along together. You know he has always been a little crazy, and I think she is too. My husband has the unpleasant task of having to arrange their affairs for this separation. She will go to live in the country and he, I believe, to England.

America has just had a great loss in the person of Alexander Hamilton who was killed in a duel with Colonel Burr, the vice-president.[5] Even General Washington's death did not produce such a sensation. The City of New York is in an uproar, and if Burr had not fled, they would have made him pay dearly for his vengeance.

You promised in one of your first letters, dear Mama, to send me your and Papa's portraits in miniature. I fear you have forgotten it since. It is something which would give me infinite pleasure, if you are able to have it done. . . .

Your loving daughter,

R.E. Calvert

1. John Carlyle Herbert (1775–1846), son of William Herbert and Sarah Carlyle of Alexandria, married Mary Snowden (1785–1857), daughter of Thomas S. Snowden of Montpelier, Prince George's County.

2. Mary Ogle (1785–1842), daughter of Benjamin Ogle (1748/49–1809), governor of Maryland from 1798 to 1801, and Henrietta Margaret (Hill) (1751–1815), married an Englishman, George Bevans, on July 22, 1804.

3. Besides her father, those opposing Mary Ogle's marriage were her older sister, Ann (Ogle) Tayloe (1772–1855), her brother, Benjamin Ogle II (1775–1845), and even an aunt by marriage, Elizabeth (Tayloe) Lloyd (ca. 1750–1825).

4. Eliza and Thomas Law signed a separation agreement in August 1804. He was granted custody of their daughter, Eliza, and agreed to her full maintenance. He also agreed to pay Mrs. Law fifteen hundred dollars a year (see Allen C. Clarke, *Greenleaf and Law in the Federal City* [Washington, D.C., 1901], pp. 285–86).

5. The Burr-Hamilton duel took place at Weehawken, New Jersey, on July 11, 1804. Alexander Hamilton (1755/57–1804) had played a key role in Aaron Burr's defeat in the race for governor of New York earlier in the year, and Burr, seeking revenge and claiming he had been slandered by Hamilton, challenged him to a duel. Severely wounded, Hamilton died the following day, and Burr fled southward to escape indictment.

··⊰[ON AUGUST 17, 1804, NEWS CAME TO Riversdale of the death of Mrs. Calvert's mother, Marie Louise Peeters Stier, the previous April. With great sensitivity toward the manner of his daughter's learning of this loss, H. J. Stier sent the news first to their friend and neighbor, Richard Tasker Lowndes, enclosing separate letters to George Calvert and Rosalie Calvert. He entrusted George Calvert with breaking the news to his wife.

To George Calvert from Henri J. Stier[1]

Antwerp, 24 April 1804

Dear Sir,

I have the hard task of apprising you and Rosalie of the sad news of the death of her dear mother. I feel to [*sic*] much the effects this loss will have upon you both not to take the necessary precautions in announcing it to you. I entrust you with the care of breaking the matter to Rosalie before you give her my letters. I think it would be best to invite some of your friends who may help you in mitigating her sorrow. . . . You know to [*sic*] well the maternal tenderness of my late wife for her daughter and you to doubt that you hade [*sic*] been both to the last days the object of her tenderest Cares. She has often spoken of you in the last days of her illness, always expressing a firm reliance on your Steady love to her daughter & on your desire and constant endeavors to forward her happiness in this world, but I cannot dissemble you her uneasiness on account of religion, in Consequence of her daughter living in a Country Where it is so difficult to observe the precepts, although persuaded you would by no means trow [*sic*] obstacles in her way in that regard.

She has addressed to heaven the most fervent prayers for you. . . . I join mine most sincerly [*sic*]. . . .

Your affectionate,

H: J: Stier D'artselaer

1. This letter is in English (Stier-MHS).

To Rosalie E. Calvert from Henri J. Stier[1]

Antwerp, 26 April 1804

I must now, my dear, inform you of that fatal event which I hope has already been communicated to you with suitable care. Certainly I am little able to offer you consolation. I know too well that the only comfort at present can be found in our religion. . . . Let us pity our misfortune, but let us not pity your mother. If there were any mortal who could trust in the mercy of their Creator, it is she. Her Christian and exemplary life, her perfect resignation during a long illness which she endured with patience and which ended without anguish on the 22nd of April . . . after the Holy Sacraments of the Church had been administered . . . leave me with the most complete confidence as to her eternal happiness. . . .

I was with her constantly up to the last day and lavished all the care and attention on her I could, with the assistance of two nuns and an excellent and faithful servant who took turns watching over the invalid during the course of her illness. Never have we been more attached to each other as since our return from America, doubtless because of a presentiment of the end. Thus she suffered little during her illness, which she always bore with hope, good spirits and complete resignation. . . .

It is not necessary, my dear, to tell you that you were often the object of her concern as well as of our conversations. Intellectually, we did not regret your establishment in America, even though emotion led us to want to see you near us. We always concluded that your situation was fortunate. Religion is a matter we discussed often . . . and something about which your mother and I have felt some responsibility and which we recommend (at a time when the heart is full) to your special attention and remembrance. I will discuss with you at another time the means of making up for the deficiencies presented by your location. In the meantime, I strongly advise that if you ever become ill, as soon as the sickness is recognized as serious, do not put off calling for a minister of your faith. Convince your husband of the importance of never deceiving you as to your condition. . . .

Your brother's marriage with Mlle van Ertborn had been set for the first of May, but under the circumstances has been delayed six weeks for the customary period of mourning, and consequently will not take place until the 6th of June. . . .[2] It is sad to see the knot tied in such unhappy circumstances. . . .

Your affectionate Father,

H: J: Stier D'artselaer

1. Stier-MHS.
2. Charles Stier's marriage was further postponed until July 16, 1804, because of another death in the family.

To H. J. Stier

Riversdale, 28 August 1804

Dear Father,

. . . The details you give me are a consolation. . . . I always hoped I might have the joy of seeing her again, and I prayed every day for that eventuality. Now that hope so dear has vanished, and I shall never again see the best of all mothers. I console myself by believing that she knew it was absolute necessity which kept me from coming to her—without that I could never forgive myself for not being present during her final hours. . . .

Thank you again for giving me a full account of the circumstances preceding and during her illness. I find a sweet satisfaction in rereading them and consolation in seeing that she suffered little. I am comforted also to learn that you do not regret my staying here. This is a matter, dear Father, that I can never think about without experiencing feelings so contradictory that I can scarcely describe them. If you had stayed in this country, I would never have had a moment of regret, but now separated from all my family, I feel so alone here. Moreover, I have gone from being naturally happy and light-hearted to being quite the opposite. . . .

I have been fortunate in my choice—there could never be another man in the universe more suited to me than my husband. He is as attentive as can be and fully appreciates the sacrifices I have made. He treats me with tenderness and respect on all occasions, and although [he is] impetuous, quick-tempered, and not one to brook contradiction, I don't believe there has ever been a wife with more power over her husband than I. . . . All the members of [his] family are well-off and respectable. They have high regard for me and are attentive, but these are superficial bonds without any heartfelt or real interest. I was too young when we left Antwerp to be a good judge, but it seems to me that there is a stronger attachment between relatives there than here. . . .

I hope you will write me often—the greatest joy I have is hearing from you. . . .

Your affectionate daughter,

R. E. Calvert

To Isabelle van Havre

Riversdale, 29 August 1804

Dear Sister,

. . . The awful certainty that I will never again see the best mother ever is almost more than I can bear. I blame myself for leaving her, although it was impossible for us to accompany you then. But now all I can remember is that I was a daughter before I was a wife and mother. I envy you the sad happiness of being near her in her last moments. . . .

The situation of our dear father preoccupies me greatly. I am sure you are with him often—give me the smallest details of all that concerns him. . . .

Forgive, dear Sister, that my letter is so short. . . . Be assured that I feel the value of your friendship more than ever at this time, but I can write on only one subject and it is a comfort to talk with you about it. . . .

Your affectionate sister,

R. E. Calvert

To H. J. Stier

Riversdale, 15 September 1804

. . . We and the children are well, but all the negroes have been sick, some quite seriously. Our coachman, Will Scott, is dying of consumption. Caroline was ill for several days, but is now fully recovered. I have an excellent white nurse for the children now. George is so attached to her that he never leaves her side, and she loves him as if he were her own. He is quite big for his age.

You perhaps remember our overseer Watson. We discharged him at the end of the year for being good-for-nothing and hired another man who quickly proved to be worse and the biggest rascal. We dismissed him at mid-year and rehired Barett, who is a good, honest man. My husband is quite happy with him. . . .

I wrote you that Mrs. Law is separated from her husband. She is with me at present and is considering buying the Stoddert house.[1] If we were not planning to go to Europe, she wouldn't hesitate to take it right away. It is a sad thing to see two people with a child separate without good reason. You know what an odd man [Thomas Law] has always been. She has a disposition completely opposite to his, and she wasn't sensible enough to put up with his peculiarities. The result is that they are both at fault, which is usually the case. . . .

I live solely in the hope of seeing you. Ever since your departure, America seems a desert to me and everything is disagreeable. What I want most is to arrange things here so that if my husband is able to adapt to living in our country, we will be able to stay there. There is one worrisome drawback: the financial interests of my children surely are tied to their establishment here, especially if our family becomes more numerous. But must I completely sacrifice my own happiness? Another consideration is religion. My husband will not change on this point, and an exact observation of our precepts is most difficult here. . . . Therefore the only way is to try [living in Europe] before making decisions we could regret.

. . . Dear Father, think often of your poor Rosalie who will never be consoled for not having accompanied her Mother, and believe me with the most tender attachment,

Your affectionate daughter,

Rosalie E. Calvert

1. Eliza (Custis) Law did not purchase Bostwick, Benjamin Stoddert's house in Bladensburg.

To H. J. Stier

Riversdale, 28 September 1804

Dear Father,

. . . I see with sorrow that everything seems to perpetuate and remind you of our unhappy loss. I appreciate your bitter grief more than anyone—it is the same as mine. . . . I am unable to concentrate on anything here. My mind wanders to you all the time.

You asked me to send you a deed for the transfer of the plantation since you didn't think you had the proper model for it. . . . For Charles' discharge, it is only a matter of burning the deed of trust he gave you . . . since as soon as the deed no longer exists he cannot be responsible.[1] Another matter I don't understand at all, and that you say should be mentioned in this deed, is that we are receiving this property in place of and on account of my legitimate portion of my mother's estate, and [this is to be] signed by my husband. I am completely unable, dear Father, to comprehend this article, since you are giving me [the plantation] as dowry and not by inheritance.[2] Thus it cannot be necessary to have the act drawn up in any particular way except to mention that it is given to me, Ros. E. Calvert, daughter of Henri J. Stier, because everything I receive in my name can only go to <u>my</u> heirs.[3]

In the same way, I plan on putting the stock we buy out of my principal in my name, which is often done here. Then my husband cannot take offense. I do not desire to be independent of my husband and will always act with the greatest delicacy in these matters, but the laws here give little power to women and it is better to err on the side of too much caution. I must do him justice that he treats me on all occasions different from the custom here, since he does not make any important transaction without consulting me and getting my consent.

I will do what you ask about obtaining an act, when the legislature assembles, to authorize you to hold lands in Maryland. It is good to have the authority, but I don't think it would be advantageous for you to own land here. Land should be under a master's supervision to produce an adequate return. At present it has almost no value here—there is much for sale and no buyers because there is no money. Addison's three plantations and those of Tom Dick, Stoddert, Belt, Tayloe, plus several others whom you don't know [are all for sale]. . . .[4]

I wrote you in my preceding letters how much we have suffered, and to crown it all, a hard frost came to destroy the little tobacco which, in hopes of a late autumn, had been planted after the floods. So we will make literally nothing here, despite many expenses for [repairing] the mill, dams, race, fences, etc. . . .

In addition, everyone in the neighborhood has been ill—a number have died. Dr. Mitchel had so much to do that he contracted a bilious fever which carried him off. Today there is an assembly of all the neighbors to select and invite another doctor who would be good. . . . All the negroes have been ill. Betty lost two of her children. . . .

I am afraid that the things I asked you to send me will cause you trouble. I forgot to tell you that it makes no difference whether you send them to Baltimore or Philadelphia since there are packets coming constantly from both places to Washington. If the packages don't weigh more than 100 pounds, they can come by the stage at a very low rate. . . .

I will also attend to the matter of observing the duties of our religion with more exactitude. As you say, it is very difficult here. The priests make themselves so little respected that religion suffers, and their number is insufficient, too. They tell me that Plunket is dead—I don't know if it is true. . . .[5]

Your affectionate daughter,

Rosalie E. Calvert

1. Riversdale's purchase was complicated. The land was put in Charles Stier's name, since he was the only family member who was a naturalized citizen at the time of purchase. English common law prevailing in Maryland prohibited aliens from holding land. In December 1800, H. J. Stier was naturalized by a special act of the Maryland General Assembly, but it is doubtful whether this act was legal, since it conflicted with provisions of the United States Naturalization Act of 1798. In any event, the family proceeded as if Stier's naturalization were valid, and before his return to Antwerp in 1801, Charles conveyed title to Riversdale to his father (Prince George's County Land Records, J. M. R. 8, fols. 584–87, and J. M. R. 9, fols. 92–93; *Laws of Maryland,* Acts of 1800, chap. 45).

2. Stier explained that the typical marriage contract in his country stipulated that parents give their child a certain sum as dowry at marriage and that this sum must take the place for them of the legal portion of the inheritance of the first of the parents to die. He was merely trying to reconcile this usage and the laws of his country with those of hers, but he acknowledged that it was difficult (HJS to RC, 15 December 1804, Stier-MHS).

3. Mrs. Calvert is relying on her marriage contract in making this statement, and even so, the enforceability of marriage contracts was strictly up to the courts. Under English common law a married woman's property rights were vested in her husband. While a single or widowed woman could buy, hold, and convey property on a par with men, a married woman could not execute contracts, make a valid will, purchase or free a slave. Her husband owned her personal property, her real estate, her wages, and her services. Only by some sort of written conveyance, such as a marriage

contract or deed of trust, could property be held in a separate estate for a married woman (see Suzanne Lebsock, *The Free Women of Petersburg* [New York, 1985], pp. 22–24).

4. Landowners mentioned are John Addison (1770–1835), Thomas Dick (?–1802), Benjamin Stoddert, Benjamin Belt, and John Tayloe III.

5. Robert Plunket [or Plunkett] (?–1815), a Jesuit who headed Georgetown College from 1791 to 1793, had been Stier's parish priest at Bladensburg.

To Isabelle van Havre

Riversdale, 28 September 1804

Dear Sister,

. . . I am sending you a little baby dress of the latest style which I made myself. I made it with pleasure, hoping it would remind you of me every time your little darling wears it. Now it is just about the time you thought you would be having your baby. I fear that I, too, will be caught in October even though I had reckoned it in November. I don't have anything ready, and I don't know why I have so much work because I now have two excellent seamstresses and a white children's nurse who also sews very well. I pay her high wages—five dollars a month—but she is worth it. Never have I seen such patience and good humor about everything. I don't have the least trouble with the children now—she even makes their clothes with very little help from me. I also took on a thirteen-year-old black girl who cleans, makes the beds, etc. Kitty, whom you know, is my chambermaid and an excellent one. She is quite skillful and even puts my hair in curl-papers every night. You see that I am giving you an account of my entire household—and in spite of everything, I am overwhelmed by work. Of course, I have had houseguests constantly since the first of May. In addition, I have undertaken a weighty task, which is to take care of our business affairs, learn bookkeeping, etc. . . .

I don't think you are finding things [in Belgium] as wonderful as we had imagined. I ask you in earnest, dear Sister, to write me openly on this matter, and above all, don't be afraid that anything would keep me from coming, because it is not the country which appeals to me but the people who live in it. Rest assured that if it were paradise here and purgatory over there, I wouldn't hesitate one minute to come as soon as I could. I feel like I'm in prison here since your departure, and even more so since the unhappy occurrence that I can't stop crying about. I don't enjoy anything. My friends, my husband, all try to distract me and in company I try to be cheerful, but it's forced. [Mentally] I am constantly in Europe, and I cannot forgive myself for having left you. No, not so long as I shall live. . . .

I am pleased that my dear [niece] Louise is getting so much out of her lessons. She must be greatly changed. Embrace her for me and tell her that I recommend dancing if she wants to return here—it is the surest way to be noticed. The education of young girls here is quite mistaken at present. They bring them up as if they are going to marry dukes and marquises, and then [the girls] don't ensnare anybody because the men are afraid of their airs and expenses. . . .

I am astonished and cannot imagine you having the "blue devils." Don't you have everything you could want, in the midst of all your family and friends, no household cares, all kinds of amusements without the least trouble? Consider the difference of my situation and you can never complain. . . .

Your affectionate sister,

R. E. Calvert

To H. J. Stier

Riversdale, 4 December 1804

At last, dear Father, I have the pleasure of announcing the birth of another little daughter, who came into the world on the 20th of November at nine in the morning. She is in excellent health, fat, and as pretty as a little angel—and unlike my first two children, she has not yet cried once. I am also in good health and would have written you sooner, but they wouldn't let me. I am expecting M. Vergnes tomorrow to christen her and I hope you will be her godfather.[1] I plan to name her Marie Louise. My husband is a bit disappointed that it is not a boy, but he says he forgives me because she is so pretty. . . .

We have not been able to make any improvements here this summer. The rains have almost ruined us. All the workers were constantly busy repairing the damages. Now they are beginning to repair the three mill dams, of which no trace remains, nor of the race in several places. If the weather remains moderate, they will be able to finish this winter, but if it freezes or snows, they won't be able to continue. . . . We are obliged to buy maize for the negroes at $5 a barrel, which is outrageous. If the winter is hard, we fear distress will be very great. . . .

I will take care of having your petition to hold land presented to the

Maryland Assembly. You asked me to give you my thoughts on this matter. Unless the public bonds become unsafe, I don't see any advantage in buying land. We find that we have too much [land] to give it the attention it requires to be productive. If you rent it out, you have the drawback of not being on the spot, [and] tenants destroy the forest, impoverish the land, and then you can't be sure of being paid. If we could sell some of ours for a good price, we would do it right away and buy some stocks. However, never has there been such distress about money in America, especially in the Federal City, Georgetown, and surrounding areas. All the lands in this district are for sale for half their value—evaluating them at a 4 percent return—and still there are no buyers. My sister-in-law Mrs. Stuart recently bought a plantation in Virginia, ten miles from Washington, with a good house and all sorts of improvements for a mere trifle. . . .

We had a great number of ortolans, water rails, and blue wings this year and a little boy from Bladensburg went to shoot them for us. Now my husband frequently brings me excellent snipe for supper. Mr. Ogle of Annapolis dined here a few days ago and asked about you. I wrote you that his daughter had married Bevans, that uncouth Englishman whom you saw through so plainly. Your old friend Dr. [Upton] Scott is also interested in you and not at all fond of the French government. He hopes you will return to America. M. Thuriot [Thurreau,] the new French minister, just arrived in Washington.[2]

. . . The democratic spirit seems to be weakening in this country, especially among the people of the countryside. My husband has converted almost all the Democrats of Bladensburg, where he is extremely well-liked (notwithstanding that he kills all your old enemies, the pigs). He has even drawn up a petition to have a law permitting killing any [pigs] found wandering loose in town.[3] [His petition] was signed by all the inhabitants, even though several of them are interested to the contrary. . . .

Your affectionate daughter,

R. E. Calvert

1. The Reverend William Vergnes was the Catholic priest who had married the Calverts in 1799.

2. Louis Marie Thurreau (1756–1816) was French minister to the United States from 1804 to 1811.

3. The town of Bladensburg had had a law since 1791 prohibiting swine from running at large, but obviously it was ineffective.

To Isabelle van Havre

Riversdale, 4 December 1804

I am writing, dear Sister, to announce the birth of my daughter. . . . She came into this world November 20, one hour after I got up, so you can see she was in a hurry to show her pretty face. She isn't large but very fat, and according to everyone, "the handsomest baby that ever was seen." I haven't gone downstairs yet, but I feel extremely well. I had planned on using a doctor from Washington, but after I hired as a nurse an old negress who used to belong to Mrs. Washington and who is highly regarded, I liked her so much that I wanted only her. In any case, I can only applaud myself. I had a kind of foreboding that I wouldn't have time to send for the doctor, and sure enough mademoiselle hardly gave us time to prepare anything. This little old woman is worth her weight in gold. I don't have the least bother—she dresses the child, if the baby wakes at night, she takes her until she falls asleep, and she takes marvelous care of me so that I won't catch cold.

I suppose you are presently in the same situation, and I hope that you have been as fortunate as I. I await your news with impatience. How sad that we can't be together. I feel more each day, dear Sister, the need to be with people I love and with whom I can speak freely. I thought I had found a friend in Mrs. Law, but like all American women she has no sensitivity and her tastes and propensities are completely different from mine. . . .

My compliments to Louise and please ask her for me to be godmother to her little cousin. . . . Are [your sons] already in school? If there aren't any good schools there, send them here. There is an excellent one in Baltimore just for boys under the direction of Bishop Carroll and Abbot Dubourg.[1] Caroline is learning to read. George is greatly changed—he has a face like a full moon with a lot of color, his eyes are yours exactly, and [he has] curly blond hair. If his nose were a little longer, he would be a very handsome boy. . . .

Your affectionate sister,

R. E. C.

1. John Carroll (1735–1815) was Roman Catholic bishop of Baltimore from 1790 to 1808, when he was appointed archbishop. Louis William Dubourg (1766–1833), a French émigré priest, opened a school for boys in Baltimore in 1799 in conjunction with St. Mary's Seminary. In 1805, the school received a charter from the State of Maryland as St. Mary's College and had an enrollment of over 125 students. St. Mary's was a prestigious Catholic preparatory school until its closing in 1852 (see Christopher J. Kauffman, *Tradition and Transformation in Catholic Culture* [New York, 1988], pp. 46–52, 69).

Straitened Circumstances

THE RIVERSDALE PLANTATION, WITH so many improvements
needed and the losses caused by the previous year's floods, proved a
drain on the Calverts' resources. The situation worsened in 1805, when
the Calverts experienced difficulties selling their tobacco. Large planters
like George Calvert dealt directly with European merchants in mar-
keting their tobacco, but they needed and usually got cash advances on
their consignments. It was not forthcoming this year, however, with trade
sluggish, money in short supply, and bankruptcies mounting. Rosalie's
dream of returning home to Belgium had to be postponed again.

Rosalie cut back expenses as best she could, forgoing the social life of
the city and withdrawing to a quiet existence in the country. She noted
the increasing conveniences and luxuries of the city, but seemed content
to live simply. She painted a picture of happy domesticity, with husband
and wife spending evenings seated before the fireplace playing with their
children. She and her husband also took more practical economic measures. They put the carriage horses to plowing, sold excess butter at
market, and began to manufacture some cloth at Riversdale to clothe the
slaves.

Mrs. Calvert described her daily routine beginning a little before
sunrise when both she and her husband rose, and he went out to check
on the workers. Breakfast was between six and seven, after which she
attended to her children and household duties until ten or eleven. She
then dressed for the day, worked or strolled in the garden, or read. Before
sunset she and her husband took a walk together and retired by nine in

the evening. The life she depicted was not arduous, but she had plenty to do. Her husband, faced with starting up two plantations while maintaining a third, had a heavier work load at this time than she.

Rosalie was still experiencing difficulty managing her servants. She dismissed her gardener, John, for "insolence" and refused to take him back even though he begged her repeatedly. John had been brought up from Mount Albion, and he was probably sent back to work in the tobacco fields, a harsher life than tending the kitchen garden for the mistress. Another of her male slaves, Sam the cook, was difficult to deal with, although she had nothing but praise for her coachman. She expressed a preference for young slaves because they were more docile. George Henry's wet nurse must have displeased her mightily, for she vowed she would never have another black one since they were "not capable of genuine attachment to a child." Rosalie was successfully nursing her own baby for the first time and found it a distinct pleasure, especially since little Marie Louise was such a good baby.

The Calverts were making important decisions about production at their various plantations. George Calvert decided to follow his father-in-law's advice to stop growing tobacco at Riversdale, realizing that Riversdale's soil and its tendency to flooding made production of good tobacco crops there unlikely. Riversdale was to be devoted to animal husbandry with meadowland and woodlands predominating and oats, clover, hay, and corn the principal crops. Calvert was not giving up tobacco, however; he continued to produce the staple at Mount Albion and attempted to grow it at Buck Lodge. Wheat, the Calverts' other major cash crop, was leased out, grown by certain of their tenants, but it is not clear where.

George Calvert was an excellent farmer who recognized the importance of conserving and replenishing his soil. He bought up quantities of manure, lime, and wood ash to apply to depleted soil. He diversified his crops, releasing himself from dependence on the vicissitudes of a single crop economy, and he laid the basis at Riversdale for what eventually would become an agricultural showplace. Still, he remained at heart a Maryland tobacco planter, his prestige wrapped up in this crop, so long grown and once so immensely profitable in the state, and now in fast decline except in southern Maryland, where Calvert and his neighbors pursued it still. The Calverts had overseers at all three of their plantations, two of whom George Calvert fired in 1805 for incompetence. Overseers generally had a short tenure, caught as they were between the demands of the master and the resistance of an enslaved labor force.

Even with overseers, however, Calvert had to spend much time traveling from one plantation to another, checking on the demanding culture of tobacco. With tobacco's year-round schedule of unremitting labor and the crucial timing decisions it required, the staple exacted a heavy toll on slave, overseer, and master.

As events in Europe led inevitably toward general war, Rosalie Calvert saw that her plans to return to Belgium would have to be postponed indefinitely. She blamed Napoleon and his overweening ambition for this disappointment, worried about the safety of her European family, and tried to persuade them to return to an America she described as much improved. Her distaste for the French and their new emperor was marked, and she chided her brother for dancing attendance at his coronation. She gave a full account of the scandalous behavior of the French minister in Washington.

Mrs. Calvert's European family was slow to understand her financial situation. Her father reminded her of her responsibility for preserving her family's fortune, warned against the spendthrift ways of Americans, and called for strict economy. She replied testily, pointing out that while her European relatives were attending plays, balls, and concerts, she was diverting herself making butter to sell and cloth to clothe her servants.

To H. J. Stier

Riversdale, 5 January 1805

. . . I am upset that we were not able to have your petition [to hold land] passed at the Assembly. My husband worked hard to persuade the members who have the most influence. He went to Annapolis expressly for that purpose and did succeed in converting several, but in the end they didn't want to grant it. They said that such a law has never been passed for anyone. . . . If you had obtained it, I would not have advised you to buy land, even though you could purchase much which would produce more than 4 percent. . . . We think that we have too much land, and I would like to be able to convert a portion into stocks, but there is no way of selling anything here. Nobody has any money. Its lack is so great and so widespread that no one feels obliged to pay their debts this year.[1]

After a most unfavorable summer for agriculture, we are having an extremely hard winter. Distress is great among the people. Wood in Washington is at $10 and $12, because the rivers are frozen and the draft animals generally in bad condition. Corn meal is $2 a bushel, hay is $2.12 the hundred [pound], and they say may go to $3. Everything else is proportionately high.

[continued 25 January 1805]

1. Mrs. Calvert was speaking literally when she said that no one had any money. A severe shortage of metallic currency caused great problems during this period. The bimetallic rate of 15 to 1, established in 1792, overvalued silver, and by 1800 gold coins had practically disappeared from circulation. It was also difficult to keep silver in circulation as silver dollars drained to Latin America. Resort to foreign coins and barter was widespread and retail trade was especially hampered.

To Isabelle van Havre

Riversdale, 5 January 1805

. . . You wouldn't believe, dear Sister, what pleasure I feel each time you write me, so please do it often. . . . Let's tell each other all our feelings and ideas freely, and be assured that everything you tell me will always remain secret and that I do not show your letters to anyone. I hope you do the same with mine. . . .

I had been certain of coming this spring. I had even already made some preparations, but I am afraid it is going to be postponed once again. With three small children, and one so very young, the month of May—or June at the latest—is the only season I would dare to risk it. Only one obstacle holds us back—it is finances. We can't sell, without sacrificing it, our last year's tobacco crop, which amounts to 52 hogsheads. They only want to buy it on a six month's credit which wouldn't be payable until June. This year we made more than 50, so in the spring there will be over 100 [hogsheads] and no way to convert them into cash in time to leave before the season [for sailing] is too far advanced. We had a lot of expenses this year repairing the damage of the rains and terrible storms at Riversdale. [Riversdale] will not bring us any profit this year (but this must remain between us—it could cause Papa pain). So I am afraid that again this year I will be deprived of the happiness of seeing you. . . .

I have lived a very withdrawn life recently and take pleasure in economizing in order to be reunited with everyone dear to me. My greatest amusement now is to sit by the fireplace with my husband, Caroline and George playing together, and my little Louise on my lap. She's the prettiest little baby I ever saw and very fat. I was extremely lucky this time— she scarcely gave us time to get ready to receive her. I went downstairs a fortnight after [her birth] and have felt quite well since. . . . I find the best way to recover quickly is not to let anyone come in the room the first week except the nurse. Nothing is worse than talking or listening to a lot of conversation. . . .

I am glad to hear that Papa is doing well and that you are with him so often. You say in your letter you have almost given up all your friends, but it must be a most pleasant feeling to be able to soothe our father's sorrows. One can always have friends. . . . Perhaps in Europe the word friend means more than here and its attributes are more respected. I see people every day who call themselves close friends and who find fault with and talk about each other with the most perfect indifference. I cannot tolerate this kind of friendship. . . .

Thank you, dear Sister, for the trouble you took to execute my commissions. . . . I hope to receive them soon because I'm in desperate need of linens. . . .

My best wishes for your happiness during the coming year and for that of your husband and children. . . .

R. E. Calvert

P.S. I am sending a box of [tulip poplar] seeds to Papa. In the box are two little jars of strawberries, as we agreed, and a glass of fox grape marmalade, along with the baby frocks and bonnets. I hope you like them—you may find them expensive, but everything is this year.

To H. J. Stier

[Riversdale], 25 January 1805

My letter remained here, dear Father, because there was no opportunity to send it. All the rivers are frozen, as is the Chesapeake Bay. I have had the tulip poplar seeds ready for a long time but I don't know when they can be sent. . . . Have you tried the plaster of paris yet? My husband is more attached to it than ever—four years experience reinforces his good opinion of it. . . . Speaking of the plaster, my husband discovered that for maize, putting on a small quantity (as you remember they did with a spoon) does more harm than good. The reason is that while the roots were young and short, they got nourishment from the plaster and the plant grew vigorously at first. However, this nourishment was used up before the grain was formed and thus [the plant] produced a lot of leaves but much less grain. Now we use it mainly on the clover.

My husband's eagerness to procure manure reminds me of how much trouble you had getting it at the Mick. He collects almost all of Bladensburg's [manure]. He is going to put a large portion of the land north of the house into meadowland and is putting the manure there, since it is better for timothy [grass] than anything else. Although we lost the hay in the meadows this year, [the meadows] in Bladensburg improved a lot. In some places there was five inches of black mud on the land, so I hope we will have a good harvest next summer. . . .

Like you, my sister complains of having too much to do. For myself, I can scarcely find time to write you—it seems to be a general malady. I thought, however, it was only in America that we complained all the time of having too much to do, since in your country you don't have so much trouble with your households. That is what takes all my time here, because the servants are so bad. Luxury increases [here] daily—in the cities one can now live as well as in Europe. We have some excellent restaurant-keepers, confectioners, pastry shops, but all that is a disadvantage for those who live in the country and it unavoidably increases the expenses one has to make. . . .

Your affectionate daughter,

R. E. Calvert

To Charles J. Stier[1]

Riversdale, 25 January 1805

I have taken up my pen three different times to write and by some strange trick of fate did not once succeed in finishing my letter. . . . Finally today, I have armed myself with a very good pen, a little round table just large enough to hold my paper, and I have filled my inkstand, determined to break the spell which has so long prevented me from chatting with my little brother. . . .

I received your letter of 12 August . . . and it is with sincere pleasure that I learn the amiable Eugénie van Ertborn has become your wife. The description you have given me leaves no doubt in my mind that with her you will enjoy that perfect happiness which few people experience for any length of time. May it continue without interruption is the sincere wish I make for you. But lest my little brother imagine that it is on his word alone that I am going to believe that his Eugénie is pretty, kind, sensitive, etc.—no, no, I know too well that the little god is blind. I get my information from more reliable sources. It is from the testimony of more disinterested people who are not under her influence that I know she is all of this. So I congratulate you most sincerely in this event which gave you a companion and at the same time gave me such an interesting sister.

I regret very much that I cannot look forward with certainty to the time when we will be together, but I am beginning to fear it will not be this spring as I had expected. You ask what it is that prevents us from coming. It is the Elements, my dear friend, which all conspire against me, especially water—not of the sea, but of the heavens which we had in such abundance last summer that Riversdale and Buck Lodge were almost carried away. So instead of being surrounded by improvements, as you seem to think in your letter, we are surrounded by <u>ravines</u> and desolation!

I see that you spent the summer diverting yourself, going from fête to fête, and finally to Paris. I cannot refrain from smiling at this moment— <u>going to see</u> the coronation of the Emperor <u>Bounaparte</u>! I fear finding you completely Frenchified. The empty heads of France are easily turned by <u>Puppet Shows</u>—but my philosopher-brother!—that, I must admit, frightens me a little. Here we are entirely English, especially in our family. The contemptible conduct of his imperial majesty's brother in this country contributes in no small degree to increase the contempt which the English have for that nation. You know that in my youth I always had a penchant for the English; their manners, ideas, sentiments have always been to my taste, even before I knew them well enough to experience their superiority. In short, a Frenchman would not know how to please me. . . .

We are having a very hard winter, but it is delightful for sleighing. I made an excursion into Washington yesterday. The diversions are not very sparkling this year. I am expecting my sister-in-law with her daughters tomorrow to spend several days here. . . .

Your affectionate sister,

R. E. Calvert

1. Calvert, CU-NYC.

To Isabelle van Havre

Riversdale, 18 February 1805

. . . I have your complaint, dear Sister—low spirits—and everything contributes to augment them. I feel better when I can chat with you by letter. I had planned so much pleasure this summer breast-feeding my little Louise, who is the most delightful child possible. My first two cried from morning till evening and gave me only trouble, but this one smiles the moment I take her. [Yet] I fear I will be obliged to wean her or take a wet nurse, since I think I am pregnant again. Isn't that depressing. I am afraid to continue nursing her for long [for fear] of hurting the other one, and it is hard to get a wet nurse whom you really know. I never want to have a black one again—they are not capable of attachment to a child. In short, I simply cannot make up my mind. . . .

Mrs. Law has been with me since August, but a month ago she went to her sister Mrs. Peter's home. I have never told you the story of this peculiar person, and you may be surprised that she lives here. Since childhood, Mrs. L demonstrated a violent and romantic disposition. Her father recognized that her singular personality would bring her unhappiness and he tried to correct it, but he died while she was still very young. Her mother remarried and from a number of lovers made a very prudent choice for the welfare of her children. Mr. Stuart took care of them both as if they had been his own and also watched over their estate which was considerable.[1] When Mrs. L entered society, she was very pretty, rich, and quite intelligent. Her relatives and connections were the most respectable. Consequently, she was greatly admired and flattered. She never cared about the compliments she was given on her beauty, but she was always very vain about her mind and knowledge. After rejecting some brilliant offers, she married Mr. L, whom you know well, against the wishes of all her relatives.[2] Never were two people less suited to live together, but during the life of her grandmother Mrs. Washington, to whom she was most attached, they restrained themselves in order to spare her pain. After [Mrs. Washington's] death, Mr. L went to England, and soon after his return they decided to separate. Never was anything stranger because they only reproach each other about their manners and dispositions. Mrs. L's biggest fault is that she has such a high opinion of herself that she is contemptuous of everyone else. Of all her relatives only my husband has her trust and the power to tell her the truth about herself. She wants to buy a small property in the country and dabble in agriculture. In her tastes and pastimes she is more man than woman and regrets that she can't wear pants.

You asked me to tell you the local news. Betsy Lloyd just married a little man from Annapolis named Harry Harwood who wasn't received in society when we were there. . . .[3] None of our [Stuart] nieces are married yet nor ever will be, I fear. Their mother paid scant heed to their education and brought them up as if they were to marry English lords, and I don't believe they accept the offers made to them. At present everybody is flocking to Washington on account of a proceeding against the Justice Chace [Chase] by the Democratic party.[4] All the most important attorneys in the United States are there and many foreigners have come to hear them. Benj. Dulaney has become completely crazy—he tried to kill one of his children. His wife has left him. . . .

We are quite close to the Dick Lowndes family—his wife is very nice and a respectable woman. Dr. Mitchel died and a better doctor with more experience came in his place. . . . My regards to all who remember me.

Your affectionate sister,

R. E. C.

1. Eleanor (Calvert) Custis married her second husband, Dr. David Stuart (1753–1814), in 1783. The Stuarts brought up the two older Custis daughters, Eliza and Martha; the two younger Custis children, "Nelly" and George Washington Parke, were brought up at Mount Vernon by George and Martha Washington.

2. Eliza Custis and Thomas Law were married in 1796. Objections to the marriage probably focused on the fact that Law, an Englishman who had come to America only two years before, was unknown. He was also twenty years older than Eliza and a widower with three nearly grown sons. Money and family background were not at issue, since Law, who had made a considerable fortune in India, was the son of the bishop of Carlisle and quite well-connected. One of his brothers became bishop of Clonfert, another bishop of Chester, a third was a member of Parliament, and a fourth, Lord Ellenborough, became lord chief justice of England.

3. Elizabeth Lloyd (1774–?) married Henry Hall Harwood (1774–1839) in 1805.

4. Samuel Chase (1741–1839), a Maryland signer of the Declaration of Independence, had been a member of the Supreme Court since 1796. Chase, a Federalist, had incurred the enmity of the Jeffersonians by his partisan behavior on the bench, and they tried to remove him by impeachment. Despite pressure from Jefferson, he was acquitted on March 1, 1805.

To H. J. Stier

Riversdale, 20 February 1805

. . . The season is now approaching when I had thought to undertake our journey, the expectation of which was all that enabled me to bear our separation patiently. Alas, dear Father, I think it is going to be postponed for another year. Besides the grief this causes me, I worry that you will think there is an unwillingness to undertake it. . . . You cannot conceive that with three plantations and the allowance you give us that a lack of funds keeps us from crossing the sea. Nonetheless, we live with the greatest economy and take each penny into account. The price of tobacco has been very low this year, and we have not sold last year's crop which was 50 hogsheads. This makes us quite pinched. I hope the price will increase this spring, when we will have two years' product to sell. . . .

We had a very hard winter here, but nice weather is beginning and I am going to occupy myself gardening. I had to dismiss my gardener John because he had become so insolent. He has been back three times since, begging me to take him back, [but] I am now without [a gardener]. . . .

I close by embracing you most tenderly in my imagination and with the near certainty of actually doing so within a year, because then at last I think nothing could keep me from coming. . . .

Your affectionate,

Rosalie

To H. J. Stier

Riversdale, 10 April 1805

Dear Father,

. . . I finally received your letter of 1 November [1804]—more than four months in transit, which is inconceivable. . . . I am very impatient to learn news of my sister, and I hope that her confinement was as fortunate as mine. . . .[1]

We have some beautiful [hyacinths] this year, but I am afraid I have lost many of the best tulips from last year's flooding. The water made ravines several feet deep from one end of the garden to the other. You will scarcely believe me when I tell you that I've handed over the care of the tulips to my husband, who has become a great connoisseur and is in the garden four or five times a day to check and mark them, etc. He has grafted a number of fruit trees this year. We extended the orchard beside the woods. . . .

. . . I am living very quietly and haven't been to a party for more than a year. I amuse myself with sewing and with my garden, [and] when I have time I read. My carriage horses are plowing. I have completely recovered my health and feel better than ever. My children are beginning to give me a lot of work, but at the same time much pleasure. The education of girls in the schools here is so objectionable that I do not plan to send Caroline at all, which will cause me a good deal of work and trouble, but I will be rewarded in the long run. . . .

I live solely in the hope of being reunited with my family. . . .

Your affectionate daughter,

R. E. Calvert

1. Eugene van Havre was born in November 1804.

⋅⋅◁ A LONG LETTER OF ADVICE from her father, excerpted below, reached Mrs. Calvert at this time. Stier counseled his daughter on how to manage her marriage, her family, and her fortune.

To Rosalie E. Calvert from Henri J. Stier[1]

[Antwerp] 10 November 1804

My dear,

. . . Your mother and I often discussed your marriage which separated you from us, and we always ended by recognizing the merit of a decision which cost our mutual affection so dear. You know, and your husband also, how much it affected us, how many tears I shed before giving my consent. Foreseeing the possibility of an eventual separation, although improbable at the time, I was under no illusion about your husband's promise to follow us. It would be cruel to require it of him if his happiness were to be thwarted by carrying out such a promise. . . . We considered that you were in the prime of your life, that our return to Europe was not very probable . . . and that you could not gain anything by waiting to establish yourself. . . . Your inclination determined our consent, we have never regretted it, and we would give it again. . . . Whether you come to settle here or whether you stay where you are, establish your happiness on solid foundations, on a perfect union and accord with your husband and your children because it is only within that circle that one can find real and continual happiness. . . .

The power of a wife over her husband is boundless when she knows how to govern with moderation and method. If he slips away now and then, it is easy to bring him back and the only secret consists in making the interests of his family dearer and more interesting to him than all other diversions, in short, in making him find true happiness in his home. . . .

Prepare [your children] now for their fortune by your good management, your good example. . . . The general rule in America is to spend; thrift is considered a vice there. People think only of themselves; they worry little about their families. . . . Try to put your children in as fortunate a position as you yourself have been put. Live nobly but with moderation. Follow the fine examples of a Washington, of a Carroll—yes, of a Carroll whom they so unjustly accuse of avarice, a reproach of which he has been fully cleansed by his generous dowries to his children. . . .[2]

You and your husband have received your wealth by inheritance, and you will find pleasure in likewise transmitting it to your descendants. . . . It is important that you should know your means. . . . You may expect by right of your mother's estate and mine—if no revolution occurs—capital of almost $180,000, of which you have already received $40,000 by the value of the Bladensburg property. . . . This sum . . . is partially the product of our good management, and you should consider it a most substantial inheritance, which has few precedents in any region or country. . . .

Our policy was always to treat our children with complete equality. This is what we have done up to now and what I will continue to do. . . .

I am sending attached the various accounts of what you have received since the time of your marriage. Do not think, my good friend, that in sending these to you and remarking on these matters that it is for the purpose of reproaching you. I only want to point out some things to you and accustom you to accounting. . . . You will see by the list that you have spent $16,171 in the course of five and a half years. . . .

Be sure you understand thoroughly the difficulty of managing and conserving a fortune. . . . [Our fortune] goes back many generations. . . . Only Antwerp offers such an example of families maintaining their inheritances for several generations. Elsewhere it's the wheel of fortune, one goes up and another goes down. . . .

The revolution has brought such great changes in the whole order of things. . . . In some ways we here are suffering the least. Look at England, in what a precarious state she finds herself, more burdened down with charges and duties than we are. Holland is drained to such an extent that all the people of property are obliged to emigrate. Actually, I know of no place other than our city where people maintain themselves in a state of ease and tranquility, one could even say, splendor. . . .

Now compare this to your life in America. On the one hand you have some great advantages—an immense territory which offers future generations resources which will not run out for several centuries. However, these resources are of value only to that class born into moderate circumstances. Those who are affluent can maintain themselves only as they do here—by alliances with those of equal wealth, and because the spirit of thrift is lacking there, those [alliances] are not easily found. Moreover, the oldest sons are favored at the expense of the younger sons and the daughters. . . . Another disadvantage is the present system of government which is a system of individuals [designed] to abase those who are above them.

So these comparisons [between countries] decide nothing. . . . the major difficulty will be to decide what to do with your properties. . . . Your husband is deceiving himself in thinking that he can bring [his plantations] up to such a state of perfection that they are secure from deterioration. . . . if you come here you must be gone for at least a year.

So do come, my dear, and here is how we will arrange things. You will choose a good ship and embark in May. At my house you will find spacious and comfortable quarters for all your family. We will make all possible efforts to make your husband's stay agreeable. . . . We will spend part of the summer in the country. We will travel extensively so he can become familiar with the area. We will make the trip to Paris together, enjoy the pleasures of society here in the winter, and we will await the outcome of all this. . . .

I will always remain,
Your affectionate,

H. J. Stier

1. Stier-MHS.
2. Charles Carroll of Carrollton (1737–1832) was sometimes called the richest man in America.

To H. J. Stier

Riversdale, 19 May 1805

. . . The observations you have offered me made the greatest impression, and I reread them frequently. Be assured, dear Father, that I faithfully follow all your advice. Every day I realize more and more that if I sometimes see things differently from you, in the end I have invariably found that you were right. . . .

It will doubtless please you to learn that the advice you gave about farming Riversdale agrees quite well with my husband's plans. He plans to produce very little tobacco [here], perhaps four or five hogsheads, and to give it up entirely after this year. . . . He is going to apply himself to making meadows. . . .

For the moment we have given up the project of a [grist] mill—it just doesn't fit in with our preparations for the trip. For the same reason we have not made any embellishments around the house. Everything is still as it was when you left. The garden produces a quantity of excellent vegetables and a great variety of flowers, but it still has only a log fence because the [saw] mill hasn't been functioning. It costs so much to cut [fencing] by hand that it is better to wait. We are getting much better at the art of gardening, especially with fruit trees which we planted a large collection of this year. You would scarcely recognize the orchard. The manure which was applied there in 1803 improved it greatly, and young trees have been planted where needed and [the whole thing] extended a lot on the side of the woods. We are also going to surround it with a hedge. It is incredible how they grow here—within seven years they are impenetrable. . . .[1]

I am amazed that my brother is staying so long in Paris. At age 30, one is supposed to behave reasonably, and a love so excessive and exclusive seems to me different from Charles' normal behavior. . . .

Please, when you write, tell me the price of tobacco in Antwerp. We regret not having a reliable agent in Amsterdam to ship to, because there is no way to sell it here. The merchants don't have any money and the banks don't want to discount it. Those who can [afford to] make a safe and extremely profitable speculation by buying it now from small farmers in the country. . . .

My husband is very much looking forward to seeing you again and living near you. He has changed a lot since you left and you two would get along extremely well. He has become as much of a flower-lover as I, and now as I write, he is amusing himself painting five new gates.

You ask me to tell you what we do and how we amuse ourselves. We get up a little before sunrise—a good habit I began some time ago which does me good—and [my husband] goes out first thing to check on the workers. We have breakfast between six and seven o'clock. It's incredible how much time one gains by rising early (but we go to bed regularly at nine). As soon as I'm up, I go downstairs and occupy myself with my household and children until ten or eleven. Then I dress for the day and work, or take a stroll in the garden, or read, etc. A little before sunset, I walk with my husband until the dew forces us to go inside. I go out very rarely. This is the way I pass my time. Once or twice a week Mr. Calvert goes into Washington in the morning, but returns for dinner. . . .

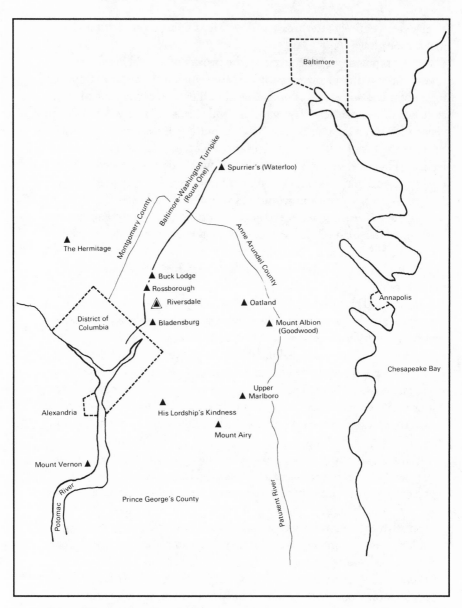

Map of Riversdale and environs

You ask me to write you the smallest details about our health. My husband enjoys a strong constitution and is bothered only occasionally by headaches which you have often witnessed. As for me, I have enjoyed perfect health since Louise's birth and am much fatter. We had our portraits painted by Stuart this past summer, but my good health has so improved my looks that though when painted my portrait was as exact a resemblance as possible, everyone now tells me it doesn't do me justice. . . .[2]

We have a doctor now who is a lot more capable than Dr. Mitchel. He is mature enough to be a good doctor, and he doesn't go to Georgetown every day like Mitchel did. He was chosen by all the neighbors assembled, who would have chosen a real ignoramus without the influence of Mr. Calvert, Richard Lowndes, and [Richard] Cramphin, but with we three saying we would not employ him, he had to quit the field.

Riversdale has great advantages apart from the beauty of its location so close to the capital of the United States: it is on the principal and most traveled road in the country, it is only one mile from the post office, [it is] on the waterway so everything can come and go by boat from Alexandria and Washington, and [it is] close to Baltimore with two or three stages daily from there to Bladensburg. My husband often tells me that there is no other place in America he would rather be.

Dr. [Upton] Scott of Annapolis spent two days here and greatly admired our tulips. I marked one for him and he said then that he would have the prettiest one in Annapolis. Such a pleasure to see your old friend again—it recalled so many memories. He departed quite pleased with us and completely enchanted with the house, especially the bed where he slept, which he couldn't admire enough. . . .

I gather that the situation in Europe, especially in the Low Countries, is most precarious. . . . It oppresses me to think that all your security depends on the life of a single man!

. . . I understand perfectly about the five cases [of paintings] left here and I will follow your instructions exactly. . . . Would it not be wise to open them up in order to air them out for several days? They are in the driest part of the house, but nonetheless last season was so humid that I found several things which I kept in cases completely mildewed. My sister can tell you how everything mildews in this climate, and if this were the case with the paintings, the [mildew] could eat the colors. Write me what you think about this. . . .

Your affectionate daughter,

Rosalie E. Calvert

1. Probably the Washington thorn, *Crataegus phaenopyrum*, a native small tree popular for hedging. David B. Warden reported hawthorn hedges at Riversdale in the 1811–1812 period (see Warden, *A Chorographical and Statistical Description of the District of Columbia* [Paris, 1816], p. 157).

2. The Gilbert Stuart portraits of Rosalie and George Calvert are in the collection of the Maryland Historical Society, Baltimore. George Henry Calvert said that Stuart spent a fortnight at Riversdale doing the portraits (Calvert, *First Years in Europe* [Boston, 1866], p. 58).

To H. J. Stier

Riversdale, 13 June 1805

Dear Father,

. . . With the certainty of seeing you again next summer, I can now bear our separation with patience. . . . My husband enjoys traveling and would be almost as disappointed as I if [the trip] were thwarted. You know that once he has determined to do something and made his arrangements, he doesn't like encountering obstacles. I do hope nothing happens in Europe to hold us back. . . . I read an article about Antwerp in the newspaper yesterday which frightened me a lot. I worry about your safety. . . . The more I contemplate America and the more I know her, the more I realize the advantages she has over Europe.

You are mistaken in thinking that the general custom in this country is to spend all one's income and not give a thought to one's children. I agree that people here are much less thrifty than in Europe, but this business of spending everything boils down almost entirely to that class [of people] who have no capital, who live on their labor (often on their knavery), or to those who made a quick fortune through no merit on their part and who think that such luck will always favor them. But the class of really wealthy people and those who had [well-to-do] parents live with more moderation and prudence. In general, I find that economy is becoming more fashionable than before, and the frequent bankruptcies of those who gave themselves so many airs, while proclaiming as misers all who didn't ruin themselves, have contributed to a much different way of thinking about this matter. It is incredible how fortunes are exaggerated in this country. They say so-and-so has so much, another that much, etc., and when they die, one discovers they don't leave enough to pay their debts. . . .

Please tell me if my brother has finally become more temperate in his love. This sojourn in Paris has been quite long. It seems to me that if he had been to the moon, he would have found there a bottle with his name, like Astolph.[1] I hope he won't delay any longer presenting you with a grandson of his own making. Tell me in time so I can make a nice little outfit, American-style, which would give me much pleasure. The fashions here for children are charming now. . . .

My husband is undertaking to make as many meadows as possible. As you say, nothing in agriculture is more productive than good meadowland, there is not as much expense and risk, and it is much more pleasant. I wrote you that by a law he had passed, he has declared open warfare on your old enemies, the pigs, who cannot enter our grasslands on pain of death—without trial!

We hope to make a very good harvest this year—[enough] tobacco to make twenty hogsheads is already planted, the wheat seems quite promising, as does the maize. So if nothing unexpected happens, we will do very well this year and make up the losses of last year. . . . Experience continues to demonstrate how plaster [of paris] fertilizes the soil. . . . We still use ten tons of it annually and a great quantity of manure, too. My husband buys almost all [the manure] available in Bladensburg, as well as their old ashes for almost nothing. . . .

As for buying land, I admit that it is a more secure investment and my system always would be to have a certain proportion, but we already have so much and no stocks. I think it is better to use our savings to buy [stock] now, [but] for you, with already a lot in the banks, perhaps it would be advantageous to buy some land. . . . All of Tom Dick's land is going to be sold shortly. If it is sold low enough to yield six percent, I will buy it for you, if you approve. So write me fully about this matter. . . .

Land is rarely sold now for ready cash; generally, the terms are one/third at purchase, or within sixty days, one/third a year later, and the rest a year after that. However, if one has the means, it is always profitable to make all the payments at once, since then you get a considerable discount.

We just bought some annuities for our three children in a new establishment called a "tontine," which seems advantageous. A lot of people are taking them out on young negro children. They only begin to pay interest in [. . .] years and they make a division [of principal] among the survivors at the end of a number of years.[2]

. . . Please write me the price of tobacco in Antwerp. . . . We still have not sold our crops of 1803 and 1804, which amount to 102 hogsheads.

The current price [here] is only six and eight dollars a hundred-weight. . . . Caroline asks me to send you a kiss. Believe me with the most tender attachment,

> Your affectionate daughter,
>> Rosalie E. Calvert

1. Charles Stier was on an extended honeymoon with his new bride. Astolph was Orlando's cousin who journeyed to the moon to cure Orlando's madness by bringing back his lost wits in a bottle. From *Orlando Furioso,* by Ludovico Ariosto (1516).

2. An annuity scheme named after Lorenzo Tonti, a Neopolitan banker who introduced it in France about 1653. A common fund is subscribed and survivors' shares increase as subscribers die. Mrs. Calvert left blank the number of years before interest would begin to be paid.

To H. J. Stier

Riversdale, 21 June 1805

Dear Father,

. . . I am grateful that you are willing to serve as godfather to my little Louise and that you approve the names I have given her. My intention in naming her is exactly as you suppose, and I sometimes think I see in her features a resemblance which makes her even dearer to me. I am delighted to hear that my sister's baby is so tranquil and resembles the one she lost—that must make him even more cherished. But it is with great regret that I learn Charles still has no hope of an increase in his family, for he undoubtedly wants it very much. I think that if he lived more quietly out in the country, it might bring about this desired addition. . . . Please tell him that if he wants to come to Riversdale for a while, I am sure he would not return without a young American. However, I fear that his sojourn in Paris made him completely French. I hope he is not appointed to the Legion of Honor.

There has been a terrible uproar here about the Emperor's minister, General Thurreau, who proposed to introduce some customs and manners for which the national character, although quite degenerate, is not yet sufficiently corrupted. Among other things, he dared, even though his wife was in the house, to bring in his secretaries and some girls who amused themselves by dancing quadrilles without any clothes on. He beat Madame Thurreau, who had displeased him, very cruelly, as well as her brother, a young man of fifteen or sixteen. He then threw her out of the house. She is returning to France, which will not only damage Thurreau, whom everyone spurns, but the French in general. These kinds of things are not tolerated in America. . . .

I wrote you that we have not yet sold our tobacco crops of 1803 and 1804. There is no money here and the banks will only discount for their directors. . . .[1] I would be obliged if you would tell me who the best agent [in Amsterdam] is, and if he would allow us to [have an advance] of a half or a third of the value [of the tobacco] when we ship it. We have the prospect of making a very good crop this year in hay, tobacco, and wheat. My dairy is also producing well.

From your letters and my sister's, it appears that your situation is not as pleasant as I had hoped, and I often tremble when I see how precarious the peace you now enjoy is. . . . With what pleasure I would hear that you are returning. . . . The more I compare the situation of Europe with America the more I am convinced of the advantages the latter offers. Everything here is improving every day—land is increasing in price, society and entertainments becoming more refined, all the comforts of life easier to get, one is less subject to huge losses, and the government is stable and good, the justice impartial.

I believe myself—and it is the opinion of many—that the present ascendancy of the democratic spirit is a genuine good fortune for the country. It certainly has not caused any of the disorders which were feared. The multitude here is peaceful—never insolent. If the change of governmental officials had not taken place in 1801, we might have gone on gradually to an aristocratic government instead of Federal. Now [the Federalist] party is beginning to get the upper hand again and is being more prudent.[2] The taxes we pay are nothing. One wagon sent to Washington pays all those on Riversdale. . . .

Your affectionate daughter,

Rosalie E. Calvert

1. Early banks made short-term, nonrenewable loans called "discounts," deducting the interest from the loan at the beginning of the lending period and giving the borrower bank notes.

2. A Federalist herself, Mrs. Calvert seems here to be indulging in wishful thinking. After Jefferson's overwhelming reelection in 1804, the Federalists showed little sign of "getting the upper hand"; however, there was a decided increase in factionalism among the Jeffersonians in 1805.

To Isabelle van Havre

Riversdale, 8 August 1805

Dear Sister,

. . . There have been many changes since you left—luxury is increasing a good deal and European customs are becoming prevalent. It is only the planters who stay the same and preserve their old-fashioned ways of life and behavior. The Democratic party weakens day by day. People make fun of Jefferson.

I was quite surprised when you told me that your husband wants to return to America, since he seemed to be the one who was least happy here. . . . What a joy it would be to hear that he had persuaded you all to come back. . . . You are mistaken in thinking you wouldn't have the same advantages as I. You would soon learn the language, and besides . . . French is so fashionable that all the children are learning it in school as soon as they can read. I had a hard time persuading our two Stuart nieces when they visited last summer that I had neither the time, patience, nor competence to teach them French. They were so anxious to learn that they pursued me with a grammar like the apothecaries of Poursognac [Pourceaugnac].[1] Several married ladies in Washington studied French last winter and spoke it whether they could or no. . . . Rest assured that if you lived here on the same footing as you do in Antwerp, you would have a brilliant court. When Europeans are known to possess a certain rank and fortune, they enjoy greater consideration than those born here. You felt a disadvantage in not knowing all the usages and customs, but since I am now completely initiated into the most secret mysteries, this disability is removed. . . .

Your taxes are dreadful. . . . We pay only a single tax now—on lands and personal possessions. You'll have an idea of it when I tell you that for Riversdale, including the land, house, furnishings, negroes, etc., we only pay $20 a year.

The servants are somewhat better than before. Surely it would be impossible to have any worse than those Papa had. The old woman Sara, whom we sold to Ben Lowndes, is the worst I know of among all the servants of our friends, and she regrets every day of her life the change of masters since your departure. My cook Sam is also the most heedless and least tractable of all my servants. I have a little fourteen-year-old negress who is invaluable. I could let you have half a dozen young girls to mind the children, all very good for that job with a little supervision. If you do return, I will undertake to provide you with servants who won't be perfect but a hundred times better than the best you had when you were here. Cooks and coachmen are the most difficult to find, especially the latter. We have a very good [coachman], but I am afraid he won't last long, as he has a consumption which I think is killing him. In the large cities when one is entertaining, cooks can now be hired by the day, as well as caterers and French confectioners who will come to arrange a dinner, dessert, etc.

Do tell me about the current fashions there. The styles here are quite becoming, but change frequently and are much too splendid for the pocketbooks of many women who, nonetheless, follow them to the letter. This is especially true among the merchants' [wives], and as a consequence their husbands are going bankrupt, as several recently did and more are expected daily. . . . The shortage of money is unbelievable. . . . Our friend Richard Lowndes is in difficult straits because he lost fully half of his income this year after unwisely investing all of his money in one stock. . . .

Caroline asks me to thank you for the pretty little tea set you bought for her in Alexandria which, having remained at Gadsby's since your departure, I finally received a few days ago. She has already had three tea parties with it, but she is sorry that her cousins are no longer here. *Adieu,* dear Sister, embrace your children for me and believe me with the most sincere attachment,

Your affectionate,

R. E. C.

1. A reference to the doctors and their patient in Molière's *Monsieur de Pourceaugnac* (1669).

To H. J. Stier

Riversdale, 20 August 1805

. . . I see by your letters and the newspapers that talking about politics or government is not fashionable in your country. Here we talk of practically nothing else—men, women, and children—not only about what is going on in the United States, but in all the corners of the world. And as our ships go to all the ports, we are quite well-informed—frequently better than the inhabitants. I trust you are receiving the papers you subscribed to at your departure. . . . I put several [issues] in the box of seeds . . . to let you see how they abuse Jefferson and his government. Declaring war against the Spanish is now the cry of the day and the people's desire, but I don't think it will be done.[1] The lack of money is universal everywhere because it [is flowing?][2] from north to south. People attribute this to payments made for the acquisition of Louisiana which the Democrats celebrated last year and the Federalists [sang] songs against, but nonetheless all dined and danced together.

I believe, dear Father, that you have a lot of stock in the Bank of Alexandria. If [William] Herbert is your correspondent in that city, you should be aware that if there were danger for this stock or it should depreciate, since he is president [of the bank] he would not tell you the real state of affairs but would put things in the best light. I say this not because I have heard anything detrimental to this bank's credit, but because you are so far away that you can't be vigilant and make sales in time. I would want to have only public bonds and stock in the Bank of the United States.

I don't think you need have any fear about M——n [McEwen]. Some time ago when my husband was in Baltimore, [he inquired and found] him considered very secure, with a reputation for having greatly increased his capital. . . . There have been several bankruptcies in Philadelphia, [William] Crammond's mercantile house among others, and several in Baltimore, such as Andrew Buchanan who is Ben Lowndes' brother-in-law, and more are imminent.[3] In Baltimore, Georgetown, and Alexandria, banks will only discount for their directors, and I believe they often can't pay when the notes are due. All this can't go on—I don't see how it has gone on so long. It must end in "a general breaking" (you undoubtedly recall this word), and perhaps that will be a benefit. . . .

The season has not been as favorable as the spring promised. I hope, however, that we will make between 60 and 70 hogsheads, estimating 5 at Riversdale, 35 at the adjoining plantation, and the rest at Mount Albion. Our wheat, which we leased out in the neighborhood, made us about 500 bushels. We don't grow wheat at Riversdale, and in the future we won't grow tobacco—only meadows, oats, clover, and enough maize for the consumption of the negroes, horses, etc. . . . I accept with gratitude your offer to send us some [sheep]. If they really are the Spanish variety, they are very valuable. . . . At present we have the finest bull, the best donkey, and the finest male hog in the county, so if you could send us a male and some female sheep, our collection would be complete. . . .

I really thought the bill for the mantels could not be correct, because even at $94, I think they are very cheap. However, if you send us other items, always send the true price. In this country where taxes are so reasonable, one feels obliged in conscience to pay them. . . .

Your affectionate daughter,

R. E. Calvert

1. The breakdown in negotiations with the Spanish over West Florida led many to think that war with Spain was inevitable at this time.

2. Illegible, but probably a reference to the drain of silver to Latin America. The United States stopped coinage of silver dollars in 1806 because of this problem.

3. Andrew Buchanan (?–1811) was a Baltimore merchant and the son of General Andrew Buchanan (1734–1786). His sister was Dorothy (Buchanan) Lowndes of Bladensburg.

To H. J. Stier

Riversdale, 22 September 1805

Dear Father,

While I mean always to write you every fortnight, I find that time slips by unaccountably and I don't get to it. I really have so much to do that I can't manage, and at this season when the Bladensburg spa is most visited, we have to entertain all of our acquaintances who come there. A dinner in the country is more trouble than half a dozen in town. . . .

I am always delighted, dear Father, when you write me frankly and please don't be concerned that your observations about economy could offend me—quite the contrary. But I am at a loss about not being able to convince you that we are conducting our affairs with the greatest care. You must take into account when making a comparison between our expenses and yours that we are obliged to receive more people, which is very costly. We have to have more household goods, more bedding, etc.—things you already had. . . . Each of our dinner parties costs over $20 on the average. We have to keep four horses because in winter the roads are such that with my children, servants, baggage, etc., two would not be able to draw [the carriage]. We have to have two other [horses], one for my husband and the other for sending messages to the mill, etc. In calculating what we have spent since 1799, you have to take into account the construction of our house at Mount Albion and the purchase of furniture to set up housekeeping. During 1803, [there were] the expenses for horses, three negroes, wagons, carts, etc.—in short, all that we needed to start up the [Buck Lodge] plantation, which previously was leased out. Moreover, in 1803 we had to buy furniture to come and live at

Riversdale, along with the expense of finishing and furnishing two bed-rooms, and then the payments made for land—Allen's at Mount Albion, Belt's, etc.[1] The flood damages in 1804, which had to be repaired, have been incalculable and in addition forced us to buy—at a huge price—enough maize for the negroes and horses of two plantations.

I regret every day that from the beginning we did not keep an exact account of all our expenses. I would have great satisfaction in showing you [the accounts] we now keep, since then I would be able to convince you that we manage our affairs not only with all possible economy but also with system, and that our method accords exactly with the plans you have often advised us to follow.

We just shipped 102 hogsheads of tobacco, the harvest of two years, from Alexandria to Murdoch in London. . . .[2] By the way, I must not forget to tell you that I am also a dairymaid and make $7 a week from my butter at a quarter of a dollar a pound, over and above our own consump-tion. . . . Another of my diversions is to make cloth for the negroes, which lasts twice as long as what we can buy and, everything considered, is much cheaper. For summer I also make cloth from cotton (which grows well here) for my servants, and I am sending you two small sam-ples. Much of the manipulation is done by some little girls who in the future will become good maids for Caroline and Louise. You can see that my occupations are quite different from yours in Antwerp—plays, balls, concerts. . . .

The yellow fever has done terrible damage in Philadelphia and New York, but none at all in Baltimore. We and our children enjoy perfect health. . . . We are very close to Richard Lowndes and his wife who are quite estimable people and who improve upon acquaintance. He often tells me to give you his regards. Bishop Carroll dined here the other day and paid us the $83.76 for the books. He had forgotten it, said he.[3]

I see that you are going to live in your old house on the Rue de Venus, and I will be greatly pleased to come and live in the part you are so kindly preparing for me. I don't want to fix a time for this pleasant interlude because it seems to me that brings bad luck. According to our papers, which are always accurate in their European news, there is going to be general war again if B. [Bonaparte] really intends to make this long-planned invasion. I wish he would just go ahead so we could be free of the uncertainty.[4] I think I wrote you that the Democratic party in this coun-try is declining a lot, especially since the party chiefs made the mistake of quarreling among themselves and by so doing revealed their views and secrets to the people. . . .

I wish Mr. van Havre could persuade you all to come back here. You would find everything much improved—society, all the necessities of life abundant, especially in Baltimore and vicinity, and even Bladensburg which now has two butchers.

Please tell my sister that I am too busy to write her at present. . . . My husband sends his regards. . . .

Your affectionate daughter,

R. E. Calvert

P.S. . . . I am about to go on a short visit to Virginia to see my sister-in-law Stuart, and I have much to do to arrange my household and everything for my departure.

1. In 1802 George Calvert bought 160 acres near his Mount Albion plantation from the sons of Joseph Allen and 119 acres adjacent to his Buck Lodge plantation from the trustee of Benjamin Belt, Jr. (Prince George's County Land Records, Liber J. R. M. 9, fols. 282, 301).

2. William Murdoch was the Calverts' agent in London.

3. When Stier left Baltimore in 1803, Bishop John Carroll asked him to send him some liturgical books from Europe.

4. Napoleon's plan to invade England ended when the French fleet was defeated by Horatio Nelson in the Battle of Trafalgar, October 2, 1805.

To H. J. Stier

Riversdale, 7 October 1805

Dear Father,

. . . I have not written you as often as I wanted this summer, nor as often as I intended, but I have had so many different occupations that I couldn't manage. I have been to Washington only twice since November 1804. My carriage horses and my coachman plowed all summer long, and now they are carrying the hay to W[ashington]. The Bladensburg meadow produced a better crop this year than it ever has, but hay fetches only a dollar this year; last year when we didn't have any, it was two dollars. We are having a superb autumn, after an extremely dry summer. . . .

I was delighted to see in your last letter that you still amuse yourself with agriculture and that you have some sheep. Undoubtedly you keep them at the Mick. Do you also have cows? I am willing to wager that you don't make anything like as good butter as mine. I am now making 25 pounds a week, and at the height of the season was making 40 pounds. It is quite renowned for its quality. . . .

Mrs. Peter has bought Frank Lowndes' country-house in Georgetown.[1] I don't know if you remember, but we went around it one day when we were taking a walk together. It has a beautiful location. A pretty little piece of land near Alexandria has been bought for Mrs. Law, but I am afraid she won't enjoy it. She has almost completely lost heart. Mr. Law, I fear, is one of the most dissembling of men, [something] which was not known until now. Mrs. Lewis has also built a lovely house on their land near Mount Vernon.[2] All these people inquire often about you and ask me to pay their respects, as did Richard Lowndes where we dined yesterday on venison. We did not lose anything in losing Dr. Mitchel. Dr. Baker, who replaced him, is an infinitely better doctor.[3] He is about fifty, very intelligent, well-read, quite amiable and attentive to his patients. . . .

Your affectionate daughter,

R. E. C.

1. Francis Lowndes (1751–1815) was the second son of Christopher Lowndes of Bladensburg. This was the original purchase by the Peter family of what became Tudor Place in Georgetown.

2. Eleanor (Custis) Lewis and her husband, Lawrence, built Woodlawn on two thousand acres given them by George Washington.

3. Dr. William Baker (?–1812) was one of only five Prince George's County doctors who had been a member of the Maryland Medical and Chirurgical Society since its inception in 1799 (R. Lee Van Horn, *Out of the Past: Prince Georgeans and Their Land* [Riverdale, 1976], pp. 230–31).

To Isabelle van Havre

Riversdale, 7 October 1805

Dear Sister,

. . . According to all reports, your child is as beautiful as Cupid, so it becomes essential for the purpose of perfecting the beauty of the human race that we plan to make a match, because surely there is nothing as pretty as my little Louise. She grows more interesting each day. My first two cried so much that they never gave me a moment's rest, but this one seldom cries. I have often been astonished at how people play with small children, but I never tire of playing with her—she is so good and cheerful.

> In her chin is a delicate dimple,
> By the finger of Cupid impressed;

There softness bewitchingly simple,
Has chosen her innocent nest.[1]

When I wrote you that I was afraid I would have to wean her, it was a false alarm which didn't last long. I am still nursing her and will continue until she is eighteen months or two years old, for as you observed, it is a pleasure to nurse a good child.

I was surprised to hear that your servants have become worse. As for myself, I have a pretty good set now. Several are quite young, but I find these the best—they are the most attentive and docile. . . .

We had Mrs. Harper in Bladensburg for a fortnight; she came to drink the waters, [but] I don't think she will live long.[2] She is just the same as before her marriage, and she had a Frenchman and his sister with her. . . . They all dined here, and the [French] boor presumed to find the elevation and the doors of the room too high, the mantel too low, and said a hundred other offensive things. After the women had left the table, the men made him shut up, but never again will another Frenchman enter my house at my invitation. Between Mrs. Harper and myself it was like a grand farce of politeness and nothing more. I know she likes me no better than she did in Annapolis.

I am sending the two recipes you asked for. . . . Embrace your children for me and believe me, dear Sister, there is no one with more affection for you than your,

R. E. Calvert

1. Verse from Mme Anne Dacier's (1654–1720) translation of Anacreon, cited in a footnote in Thomas Moore's *Odes of Anacreon* (London, 1800), which Mrs. Calvert later sent to her brother, Charles.

2. Catherine (Carroll) Harper (ca. 1778–1861), daughter of Charles Carroll of Carrollton, married Robert Goodloe Harper in 1801. Mrs. Harper, who lived on into her eighties, always considered her health precarious.

To H. J. Stier

Riversdale, 18 October 1805

Dear Father,

. . . Please accept my thanks . . . for the cask of red wine. . . . It is of a most superior quality and was perfectly clear up to the last bottle. We invited all our neighbors, your old friends R[ichard] and Benj. Lowndes, Cramphin, etc., to come and taste it and drink to your health. . . . This wine is becoming more fashionable every day and during the summer is preferred to madeira. However, it is difficult to get a good one here, and they charge an exorbitant price.

I am very grateful for the $150 [$1,500] you were so kind as to give my children.[1] I am going to invest it in stock of [the Bank of] the United States. I don't like the private banks—even though they pay more interest, I don't think they are as safe. . . .

I will take advantage of this assistance for a month or two, which is extremely helpful to us at this time. It prevents us from having to draw immediately on the tobacco we sent to Murdoch in London, which would oblige him to sell right away at whatever price was offered. Instead, this sum you were good enough to send will give us the advantage of being able to wait until the [rate of] exchange, which is beginning to increase, is more favorable. Then I will pay [the children] back and will continue to add the interest to the capital.

We intended to send the tobacco to Holland, but the situation of that country made us afraid to risk it. Your fears of a general war are going to be realized, so once again we won't be able to undertake this voyage, so long planned and so deeply desired. . . . It is horrible to see the excessive ambition of one man upsetting the whole world. . . .

At the moment I am busy planting my flower [bulbs]. I think I understand this culture now almost as well as you, and a resource you don't have, which I prefer to all types of manure, is old tobacco stalks. We cover the bulb beds with them in the winter, instead of straw, and it is amazing how it makes them grow. . . . The fancy for flowers of all kinds is really increasing; everyone takes an interest, and it is a great honor to have the most beautiful. . . . We have four or five flower-lovers in Bladensburg. I regret that I didn't have time to learn all your gardening secrets, for I often feel myself lacking.

I thank you, dear Father, for keeping a place for me in your theatre box, [and] I wish I could enjoy it this winter. It has been a long time since I have been to a play. We have a troupe of sorts here in Washington, but nursing my little Louise has kept me from going. I believe when I do attend a play again, I will have the same sensation of pleasure I had when I went for the first time. I often feel the loss of these pleasures. . . .

I am astonished to learn that Charles still does not expect an increase in his family. It is time now, after two years of marriage. In America one expects better than that—two women of our acquaintance came to their confinements after only seven months of marriage! It seems, dear Father, that there is little hope we will be able to come and see you next summer, [so] we plan on finishing the house. I would be much obliged if you could get me a mantelpiece for the drawing room. We think the one in the dining room is very pretty, but I would prefer this one to be a little taller. . . . I imagine that for $200, perhaps less, we could get a rather handsome one. Please also send a small ordinary [mantel] for my bedroom. . . .

Your affectionate daughter,

R. E. Calvert

1. Stier had written that he was setting up a fund for the three Calvert children to which he was initially contributing fifteen hundred dollars, to be divided equally among them. Recognizing the Calverts' need for ready cash, he authorized them to use the funds until their tobacco could be sold (HJS to RC, 24 July 1805, Stier-MHS). In her acknowledgment above, Mrs. Calvert erred in writing the amount by again omitting a zero.

To H. J. Stier

Riversdale, 24 November 1805

Dear Father,

. . . The latest news from Europe leaves no doubt that there is going to be a general war.[1] I hope that [Belgium] will not be the theatre of this war. I regret more and more every day that you returned there. Our plan of coming to see you next June will have to be deferred again. . . .

This morning I went to Georgetown and used a portion of your gift to buy an outfit to go to a dinner at Mr. Merry's. He is the English Ambassador who has shown us much courtesy. They live in a very grand style. . . . Mrs. Peter has left Georgetown to go live nearby in Frank Lowndes' house, which they have bought. This house is extremely small so when I want to go to the balls, I will have to go to a hotel [to spend the night]. That costs $7 every time, so I won't go often.

I see by your letter that there are a lot of marriages in Antwerp, but among those you name I see several who have very little wealth. How do they live? I suppose they have discovered the same secret a number of people here have—how to live splendidly without having a sou, whereas those who have a fortune barely manage to get by, even with great thrift. A Carroll, a Lloyd, a Tayloe, etc., often complains of lack of money, but those who are not reputed to have any money never lack. It really is tiresome how wealth is magnified here, and then when people die, they don't have enough money to pay their debts. . . .

I wrote you about the paintings. They have always been kept in the very place you put them. I opened one of the cases to check and found that they were not damp, but nonetheless they had white spots in some places, like mildew. Don't worry that I would ever wash them, because I didn't even want to wipe them. I know nothing at all about how to treat them myself, and I will not let anyone else touch them without your order. After airing them for two days, I put them back exactly as they had been. If they were mine, I would open and air them for several days, but since you don't think it is necessary, I won't do it.

I am afraid you don't correctly judge this country's situation from the newspapers you take. You know how each party always exaggerates, one against the other. These papers are written for the crowd—they have to shout very loudly in order to be heard. You need not have the slightest worry about the public bonds, nor, I think, about the banks. Land has been high for some time and bonds low. . . . Everything here is prospering greatly, politics is improving, the Democratic party is weakening, society is becoming more pleasant, manners more polite—in short, everything is getting better. Even Europe's wars and quarrels are advantageous for America, which is enriching itself on the spoils. By the way, [William] Bingham's house in Philadelphia has just been sold to an Englishman for $100,000; all the furnishings were sold, too. . . .

We are all well. . . . I have never enjoyed such good health. . . . I wish my dear little Louise were stronger. She has never been sick, but she has not yet started to walk, or even to sit up, although she is now a year old. She is still as pretty as an angel, and I continue to nurse her. . . .

As we have little hope that it would be prudent to come to Europe next summer, we are going to begin finishing the house. I wish my brother would send me a drawing of your staircase with the column and the plans for the Riversdale house. . . . My husband sends his regards. He complains as much as I about having too much to do. At the moment he is busy dismissing all his overseers in order to take on new ones who will, I trust, be better than the one at Mount Albion. He let six to eight hogsheads of tobacco be ruined in two days. If they had all been as industrious as [our overseer here], we would have made 100 hogsheads this year. Now I suppose we will make between 70 and 80. . . . Mr. [William Russell] Birch is here now and is busy making plans for the grounds of the house. I think he is very good at it and he is doing them with an eye to economy. . . .

Your affectionate daughter,

R. E. C.

1. The British victory at Trafalgar (October 1805) and Napoleon's simultaneous success against the Austrian army virtually assured a protracted and widening war.

Completing the American Château

WAR IN EUROPE AND THE DEMANDS of a growing young family
in America made Rosalie Calvert's prospects of a return to
Belgium increasingly remote. Accepting the reality of a permanent residence in the United States, Mrs. Calvert turned her efforts to finishing
the house and grounds of her Riversdale plantation. It was a large undertaking and occupied her for most of 1806 and 1807. The enterprise was
helped along by a distinct improvement in the Calvert family's fortunes—a spurt of prosperity during a period in which, Mrs. Calvert
remarked, America was profiting from Europe's wars.

Rosalie's European family provided advice and material aid for her
completion of Riversdale, and the results were gratifying. She took pride
in imprinting a European style on her fine home and exulted in the
admiration it attracted. She became a naturalized citizen of the United
States, primarily in order to hold this property in her name, and she
urged her father to transfer the title.

She hired artist William Russell Birch of Philadelphia to design a
landscape plan for her grounds. Decorative gardening was much in
vogue in the United States, and Mrs. Calvert and members of her social
class vied with each other in their "fancy for flowers of all kinds." A
mutual interest in horticulture also kept Rosalie and her father close
despite the passing years that separated them.

Mrs. Calvert became acquainted with British minister Anthony Merry
and his wife, whose splendid way of life at first intimidated her, but she

quickly gained confidence and ended by entertaining them at Riversdale and lamenting their departure. Inclusion in the Merrys' social circle provided opportunities to meet other members of the diplomatic corps, the Irish poet Thomas Moore, and young Augustus John Foster, Mr. Merry's secretary who was soon himself to be England's minister to the United States. Rosalie amused herself by conducting a flirtation with the well-bred and much-traveled Mr. Foster. She reassured her sister, however, that contrary to the practice in Europe, the better class of women in America did not have affairs, although all the young men kept mistresses.

Aside from the exciting diplomatic circle, she found the society of Thomas Jefferson's Washington "wretched," composed mostly of Democrats of low origin. The Calverts, however, had a nice circle of immediate neighbors whom they saw frequently and without ceremony. Their favorites were the Richard Lowndeses of Bladensburg, who lived in a fine house called Blenheim on a hilltop overlooking the town. Mrs. Lowndes filled a particularly significant void in Rosalie Calvert's life. Here, finally, was a friend, a woman she liked and respected, someone in whom to confide and share experiences, someone to dispel the loneliness and lack of female companionship she had felt since her family left. Scarcely a day passed without communication between Rosalie and Anne Lowndes, and their friendship lasted until Rosalie's death.

The Calvert family was increasing. Rosalie Eugenia, born in 1806, brought the total to four children, but Mrs. Calvert said she was no longer upset at the prospect of a large family, although she had feared it when she was younger. Part of the reason for her changed attitude may have been the ease with which she now delivered her babies—Eugenia's birth had been no worse than a migraine, Rosalie assured her sister. Everyone was remarkably well, except poor little Louise, who was not developing as she should. Rosalie blamed herself because she had gone horseback riding and sustained a fall just three months before Louise's birth. With the increase in her family and her household, Mrs. Calvert's work load mounted, too. She added schoolmistress to her other duties, teaching Caroline and George to read, but she felt "ill-suited" to the task and frequently expressed impatience about the demands of four young children. She confided to her sister that she worked "without respite" at Riversdale, adding that she was often so tired at night that she fell asleep during tea. Her day was spent "trotting from one end of the house to the other, in the morning giving directions about what has to be done and then after dinner, seeing that my instructions have been carried out."

A huge array of tasks was now performed at Riversdale—making cloth, candles, soap, jams, sausages, pickles, clothes for family and servants, draperies and slipcovers for the house—in addition to the normal daily food preparation, housekeeping, washing, and ironing. As mistress, all of these tasks fell within Mrs. Calvert's domain, and she was responsible for seeing that they were performed. She rarely did the sewing, but she cut and pieced all the clothes for the family and the curtains and covers for the house. As keeper of the keys to the food supplies, she was on call at all times to measure out what was needed.

Mrs. Calvert described her household at this time as consisting of twenty-one persons. Six were Calvert family members, and there were three white servants: a chambermaid, a gardener, and the overseer. A black man served her as chamberlain, or major-domo, heading a staff of eleven other slave servants. Field hands were not included in Mrs. Calvert's definition of her household, as they were on some plantations, and it is not clear what responsibilities she had for them. Most of the Calvert hands were based at Mount Albion, and responsibility for their food and clothing may have been delegated to the overseer and his wife.

Although proud of the work she accomplished, Rosalie Calvert did not want it generally known that she labored so much. In "lady of the manor" tradition, she ceased her frenetic activities when guests came, enlisted her white chambermaid to act as her housekeeper, and affected a leisure she rarely enjoyed.

To Isabelle van Havre

Riversdale, [? January ?] 1806[1]

. . . You are wrong, dear Sister, to accuse Mr. C of too much activity—that was only a false alarm, but for a short time it concerned me very much. I am still nursing my interesting little Louise. She is quite frail. I think I pampered her too much at the beginning. Children generally do better if they are not treated too delicately. . . .

The prospect of our trip prevented us from making any improvements here this past summer, but we are going to start as soon as the weather permits. The second wing is still just as it was when you left, and I am somewhat afraid I can hear your exclamation and your disapproval when I tell you that we plan to make it into a carriage house and a stable for our carriage horses. Of course, that won't be as pretty as a gallery for paintings—[Papa's] original intention. We will plant lots of trees around the entry so that no one will notice it's a stable.

I'll send you the plan we intend to follow for the promenades. We are also going to finish the rest of the house, having done nothing since 1802 except the dining room. All the grounds of the house are just as you left them also, but they are busy filling and leveling the large holes to the north right now. It will require a lot of time and work. . . .

I dined the other day at the home of the English Ambassador, Mr. Merry. It was a superb dinner [and] the dishes were exactly like those at elegant dinners in Antwerp—in three courses, the vegetables, ragoûts, etc., with everything arranged, served, and cut in the same way. We were seated about five o'clock. In the center of a single long table stood elegant plateaux with handsome groupings of white marble and bouquets of flowers, interspersed with beautiful silver candelabra. The dessert [service] far surpassed anything I've ever seen, as did the plate which was abundant, including three superb silver-gilt cabarets of different sizes. The spoons and forks were silver-gilt, too. Believe me when I tell you that I found the forks as disagreeable (being unaccustomed to them) as we found those steel ones on our arrival in Philadelphia. The porcelain was from France.

Mr. Merry enjoys speaking French, but I am so completely out of practice that I couldn't do it, which I really regretted since I was seated between two very pleasant young men, both of whom spoke French. [One was] Mr. Foster, a young man from one of the best families in England, who is Mr. Merry's secretary and has traveled virtually all over the world (and I am almost in love with him). . . .[2]

Mr. Merry did me the honor of escorting me to table first, a preference which earned me the envy of all the other women present. The Tunisian Ambassador was also there, wearing a magnificent Turkish outfit.[3] In short, it was a delightful evening. Mr. Merry was most gracious to us, but their way of life is so superior to ours that it makes me hesitate to cultivate their friendship, as much as I would like to do so. . . .

Your affectionate sister,

R. E. C.

1. Both the day and the month of this letter are illegible.

2. Augustus John Foster (1780–1848), after serving as Merry's secretary, became British minister to the United States, 1811–1812.

3. Sidi Suleyman Mellimelni was a special envoy who was in the United States during the period 1805–1806 to negotiate the return of three ships captured by the United States during its war with Tripoli.

To H. J. Stier

Riversdale, 3 February 1806

Dear Father,

. . . If you still receive the Philadelphia papers, you will see how we squabble here and the government's shameful conduct. I honestly don't know where it will end. The Democrats are now in possession of all the patronage—the majority [of their appointments] are incompetents and rogues, [and] the judges frequently tilt the scales [of justice] in favor of members of their own party. To fill the place of the late Mr. Hanson, they recently appointed Mr. Kilty to be Chancellor of Maryland, a man who is both ignorant and, it is said, a bit corrupt.[1] This is the most important position of the state so you can imagine what consequences this could have.

I hope that your country won't become the theatre of war—it is far away at the moment. Apparently nobody but England is able to withstand the Emperor Bonaparte—those two Emperors of Russia and Germany cut a poor figure. . . .[2]

We had a letter from Louvrex and van Lennep the other day offering to sell our tobacco. We plan to send a small portion to them and to sell the rest here, unless the price is not good, in which case we will send them the whole crop. I am surprised, dear Father, that you don't make your business agent [Louvrex] into a secretary to copy your letters and make duplicates of your accounts. It would spare you a lot of work. . . .[3]

Your affectionate daughter,

R. E. Calvert

1. Alexander Contee Hanson (1749–1806) served as Maryland chancellor and judge of the Land Office from 1789 to 1806. On Hanson's death, William Kilty (1757–1821), a physician and attorney, was appointed. Kilty became the author of the first complete codification of Maryland's laws and served as chancellor until his death in 1821.

2. Mrs. Calvert is reacting to Napoleon's overwhelming victory over the Austrians and Russians at Austerlitz in December 1805, and the haste of their Prussian ally Frederick William III to sue for peace.

3. Making copies of four- and five-page letters along with duplicates of several pages of accounts became an increasing chore for both Stier and Mrs. Calvert. However, as war and ship seizures made the mails more unreliable, it was a necessary precaution.

To H. J. Stier

Riversdale, 1 March 1806

Dear Father,

. . . I see that you have a considerable army in Brabant to oppose the English and the Prussians. This piece of news causes me much anxiety and its consequences frighten me. . . . It seems to me the war cannot go on much longer, and I hope [Belgium] will not suffer. Whichever way it goes, all the countries will be so weakened that they will have to remain at peace for a long time. . . .

The other day I met General Miranda who took the Citadel of Antwerp in 1792, and I had a long conversation with him. I don't know exactly what he came to this country for—they say he surely is employed against the Spaniards in South America.[1]

I see by your letters and those of my sister that you are busy embellishing the Mick. The countryside must be delightful now. Why can't I be there with you! Although your circle is already so pleasant, I am sure our little family would augment that pleasure, and since we can't come next summer, I am going make it, I think, even more numerous! You see, dear Father, that I bear this philosophically. I often dreaded having a large family, but now I deem it a source of happiness if they behave well and that generally depends on the way they are reared. My children seem quite promising and are a double satisfaction in my situation, so far from my own family. . . .

Knowing the high esteem you always had for the great General Washington's talents and judgment, I am sending you an article from the paper which shows how he anticipated the [current] superiority of the English navy. . . .

Your affectionate daughter,

R. E. Calvert

1. Francisco de Miranda (1750–1816), Venezuelan revolutionary and soldier of fortune, served as a general with the French northern army under Dumouriez in 1792 during the first French revolutionary incursions into Belgium. He became an apostle of Venezuelan liberty and was in the United States in 1806 to enlist aid for an expedition to that country.

To H. J. Stier

Riversdale, 19 April 1806

It has been a long time , dear Father, since I have heard from you. . . . We are all in good health except my little Louise who is extremely frail. I worry about her a great deal. Although no one says it, I often sense that people don't think I will be able to bring her up. You can imagine how sad this makes me. She is so dear.

At the moment we are quite busy with workers finishing the house. I think I wrote you that we plan to make a stable of the second wing. The house is spacious enough, and the wing will make a good stable and carriage house without anyone being aware that it is one.

My hyacinths are in bloom now and are quite beautiful. I plan to import some new ones from Haarlem next year. I regret not having preserved the names of those I have, but it is a lot of trouble to sort the colors and find a place for them. Richard Lowndes has a fine collection now, too, and each year we exchange some. I wish you would send me some offshoots of your tulips, and above all, some rose bushes. Winter would be the best time to ship the latter.

Your affectionate daughter.

[no signature]

To Isabelle van Havre

Riversdale, 20 April 1806

I see with infinite regret, dear Sister, that our correspondence is becoming less frequent day by day. This is almost always the case when people are so far apart, but I had hoped we would be an exception. . . . It seems to me that if I were in your place and you in mine, I would write you almost every day—all the subjects about which you can write are interesting to me. It is not the same for me. I cannot amuse you with anecdotes of society here, because you must long since have forgotten all the people, or at least they cannot interest you. You know precisely our way of living and our occupations, which are still the same. . . .

I strongly approve of your plan that we should all be together at the Mick—that will be delightful. You could make small bedchambers in the attic for our little monkeys. I hope my number will not exceed four. Although I don't trust my sensations, I am afraid of having two this time. I am so uncomfortable and so sick every morning that I don't know what to do, and I can't eat anything. I hope this won't continue for long, because it is most unpleasant and makes me good for nothing. Tell me if you will keep me company again this time.

I suppose you will soon think of going to live in your house. . . .[1] I want you to write me exactly how you are furnishing it. Have you bought many pretty things? I asked you to send me a detailed account of one of your large dinners—don't forget that, and also please tell me how much a service of French porcelain for dinner and dessert would cost. I don't want the first quality, as long as it is pretty. . . .

Has Charles still no hope of having a family? Mrs. Lowndes dined here and asked me to tell him that he should not despair, as she had been married for eight years before having a child and now has several. . . . I am waiting with impatience for your news, and every day finds me disappointed. . . . Caroline speaks often of her cousins. . . .

Your affectionate

R. E. C.

1. The van Havres had not been able to return to their former home in Antwerp as it had been sold and leased in their absence, but they had recently repurchased it (HJS to RC, 24 July 1805, Stier-MHS).

To Mrs. Rosalie Calvert from Henri J. Stier[1]

[Antwerp], 1 May 1806

My dear,

. . . I see from your last letter that you will not be coming this year. It certainly would have been a great happiness for me to have you here for a while, but . . . I defer to your reasoning. . . .

I am glad to learn that you are using the architect Birch. You must not concern yourself about the cost of the plans. Copy them and send them to me. I'll give you my observations. Believe me that water in the landscape, like mirrors in a suite of rooms, forms the principal ornament. The section to the north of your house is ideally suited to this embellishment, since you have a stream of water at your disposal and you only need to deepen the land by one or two feet. The water must always be at the level of the land.

You need to plant the surroundings and you don't have a nursery. You also have little choice of trees at your place, so don't fail to pay close attention to this advice: collect all kinds of seeds this autumn, both from your area and elsewhere, omitting none—spruce, holly, beech, elm, thorn, tulip-poplar, yew, birch, oak, willow. Try to get some larch—they create a majestic effect. In the fall I will send you all of these seeds. You should plant them in good soil, tend them well, and manure them for the first few years.

I close by embracing you most tenderly, as well as your husband and your children. I am your affectionate

H: J: Stier d'Aertselaer[2]

1. Stier-MHS.
2. Stier varied his signature, especially his spelling of Aartselaar.

To H. J. Stier

Riversdale, 22 May 1806

Dear Father,

. . . I hope that you have found some mantelpieces. When I mentioned the price of $200, I only wanted to let you know that I didn't want <u>to exceed</u> this price. Apparently those costing $100 or even less are as good as I want. I will always be satisfied with whatever you send me.[1]

I went to Marlboro the other day to be naturalized.[2] The transfer of Riversdale which you <u>previously</u> had executed is not valid. I consulted several lawyers on this matter and here is the result: no transfer of this property to my name will be valid here unless a deed exactly like that which my brother received is given [me], and which his wife must now join in signing. This deed must be signed in the presence of some person coming to this country, and this person must <u>witness</u> the transfer there and then take an oath here that he saw the parties <u>sign, seal</u>, and deliver the deed at your place. . . . You know, dear Father, that this deed must be in English since it will only be used in this country; you just have to copy the one Steuart gave you. You must also see that it is executed only a short time before sending it, since if it is not recorded here within ten months of its date [of execution], it is not valid.

I would be much obliged if you could send me [all] the papers relating to the land by the first good ship coming from Antwerp to Philadelphia. We have needed them two or three times, and it is both difficult and expensive to make copies from the records. The survey, for instance, will have to be redone unless you send it to us. . . .

We are finding it difficult to finish the salon, not having any of the plans. I don't know what [your] intention was.

I am curious to know if it is becoming fashionable in your country to become horticulturists. Here we occupy ourselves with that more every day and we are getting much better. Your old friend from Annapolis, the lawyer Key, is now one of the best gardeners in the neighborhood.[3] Two days ago, the Ambassador of England, Mr. Merry, and his wife dined here. They have been extremely civil to us and I greatly regret that he has been recalled. Lord Selkirk is coming to take his place.[4] [Merry] tells us that in England everyone is taking up horticulture. It is the most highly esteemed of all amusements, and nothing contributes more to a good and virtuous citizenry than the occupations of the countryside and the study of nature. . . .

Your affectionate daughter,

R. E. Calvert

1. Stier wrote that because of the war no Italian marble was available, "so they make mantels out of colored marble with ornaments and beads of white marble," and these cost only $40 to $50. He complained that "the style of the day is so peculiar, a mixture of Egyptian and *antique,* which is a motley combination," but that he would keep looking (HJS to RC, 24 January 1806, Stier-MHS).

2. Rosalie Eugenia Calvert was naturalized on April 16, 1806, after renouncing allegiance to any foreign prince and swearing to uphold the Constitution of the United States (Minutes of the Prince George's County Circuit Court, 1806, fol. 32).

3. Philip Barton Key (1757–1815), attorney, legislator, and congressman, was the uncle of Francis Scott Key.

4. Thomas Douglas, fifth earl of Selkirk (1771–1820), did not replace Anthony Merry as British minister. David Montagu Erskine (1776–1855) did.

To Isabelle van Havre

Riversdale, 20 July 1806

. . . I am glad to learn that all your little family is doing so well, but I am surprised at what you tell me about vaccinations. I have never heard of a single case here which caused the slightest trouble. My three children have all been vaccinated without the least eruption or indisposition. . . . Even my little Louise, who has always been frail, was vaccinated without any of the bad consequences you mentioned.

You say that your children require so much of your time making them do their lessons. How is it that you don't have a tutor? I guess you don't plan on giving them a private education, which does seem to me to have a lot of disadvantages. As soon as George is old enough, I shall send him to a college. I will keep my daughters at home until age fourteen or fifteen because the primary schools are so bad.

I have little time to write you now, dear Sister, being swamped with tasks, and we have a lot of laborers here which takes up a great deal of my time. I hope that our house will be finished before winter. Which reminds me, could you send me a plaster statue similar to the one on top of the staircase column in Papa's house? Our [statue] needs to stand upright, however, since our staircase column is only one foot in diameter, so she can't be seated like [Papa's]. It seems to me, too, that it would be a good way to <u>illuminate</u> the stairway if the statue holds a candelabrum with some candles or a lamp. If you can <u>easily</u> procure such a thing, I would be much obliged and trust entirely to your taste in selecting the statue, but please send it as soon as you can.

You are correct that there is a lot of talk about our house, but not because it is so splendid, since many in the Baltimore area greatly surpass it and even more beautiful ones are being built every year. The reason people talk about our house is because of its distinctive style, and people always much admire anything done by Europeans. A little while ago, Jefferson sounded out if he might come to see the house, having heard that it was in the Chinese style, which is as far-fetched as calling it Egyptian. Every day I discover what a singular advantage it is to be a European in this country!

[no signature]

To H. J. Stier

Riversdale, 6 September 1806

Dear Father,

. . . I am mindful, dear Father, of the many gifts you have showered on me, and I appreciate your invitation to comment on the silver service you have offered me, so I am going to speak frankly.[1] You ask if I have the accessories to go with such a service. So far we have no silver except an assortment of large and small spoons, all matched, which we imported from London this summer. With a service of silver plates it would be necessary to have a great number of pieces which we don't yet have. Therefore, I would much prefer it if you would substitute instead the [silver] serving pieces we need to accompany a set of porcelain which I plan to import as soon as our finances permit. I have asked my sister to send me the prices. You can see, dear Father, that I count a lot on the indulgence you have always shown me, since I have the effrontery to send you a list of the silver items I most want. . . . I put the items I want most first on the list, continuing so that the last are those least needed. . . .

I agree entirely with you about the system you suggest for setting up our house and the choice of furniture. I have learned from experience, the best of teachers, that spending on whim is ruinous . . . and how those kinds of expenditures leave no lasting satisfaction. Later one always says to oneself that if I had not bought this inanity, which gave me only momentary pleasure, I could have gotten something which would bring me joy every day. I have committed only a few follies of this kind, and I don't regret them because they reformed me and perhaps kept me from committing more serious ones.

I am convinced that you would approve the way we are furnishing the house—everything will be as unified as possible but quite different from the style here. People talk about [the house] a lot, and with great exaggeration, which amuses us immensely.

The salon will inevitably be more expensive than I wanted because all of the work is circular, for example, the three round doors and the moldings of the arches, for which they are charging quadruple. As soon as it is finished, I will send you the drawing of it.

The staircase makes a very handsome effect. We placed a column there, in imitation of yours, but only a foot in diameter, and I have asked my sister to send me a plaster figure to put there. . . .

In the second wing of the building we have made a stable housing six horses—where the kitchen and corridor are in the [first] wing—and we have a coach house for two carriages in the comparable space occupied by the pantry and small room in the old wing. Above the stables it would have been too dangerous [to store] hay on account of fire, so there is a large room for storing wool, cotton, bulbs, etc., and above the coach house is a little room for the coachman. Another, better room, corresponding to the room where you ate, is my husband's study and above that is a bedchamber. There is a small staircase in the corridor rising above the door.

I hope that the house will be completely finished on the inside before winter; then we will continue outside. It is frightening to see the amount of soil which must be carted to [fill in] around this wing in order to have the terrain level with the other [wing]. I will send you the plan shortly. . . .

Last year we made and are now ready to sell 71 hogsheads [of to-

Riversdale, 1827. Lithograph by B. King from watercolor by Anthony St. John Baker.
Henry E. Huntington Library, San Marino, California

bacco]; this year I am afraid there will only be 50. We lost half the crop at the two principal plantations due to a drought which was without precedent in this country. If you read the papers, you undoubtedly saw the details. People in some places had to send their grain 20 to 30 miles away to find a mill with enough water to grind it. . . . Even here I was obliged to send to the Eastern Branch for two months in order to wash laundry. . . .

Your affectionate daughter,
Rosalie E. Calvert

List of Silverplate[2]
2 pairs of candlesticks
2 pairs of candlesticks having 3 branches if possible, or else 2
6 salt cellars
1 vinegar caddy
4 butter and sauce boats

4 wine "coolers" like the ones placed at the four corners of the table
   with a bottle of wine inside (having forgotten the French word, I've
   done it in English)
1 bread basket
2 small cabarets, 9 inches long, 7 inches wide, or approximately
1 large cabaret, 34 inches long, 36 inches wide, or approximately
2 soup tureens

    1. Stier proposed giving each of his children a silver dinner service consisting of
"twelve to fourteen oval-shaped plates and an equal number of round ones, which
you can use to give a dinner in one or two courses by intermixing them with small
porcelain dishes, as is done here" (HJS to RC, 1 May 1806, Stier-MHS).
    2. Tax records confirm that the Calverts did not own much silver for most of their
married life. Rosalie was probably unable to secure the silver items she wanted until
after the end of the War of 1812. At Mount Albion in 1800 the Calverts were
recorded as owning 12 ounces of silver. From 1806 through 1812 at Riversdale they
had 45 ounces, and only by 1820 did they own a substantial amount, 196 ounces (see
Prince George's County Assessments, Personal Property, 1800, fol. 28; 1806, fol. 39;
1812, fol. 28; and 1820, fol. 29).

To H. J. Stier

Riversdale, 26 September 1806

Dear Father,
   . . . Our house comes along rapidly. At the moment we have brick-
makers, masons, carpenters, plasterers—we lack only painters to have all
the crafts represented, and we expect one tomorrow. The masonry of the
wing will be finished this week, but in addition to what has to be done to
the house and the porticoes, we also have to build a small house, a smoke
house, a dairy, and an orangerie. We are also going to build a wall to the
north and west of the garden, beginning at the wash-house and going
alongside the orchard. I thought I could send you the plans today, but I
didn't have time to copy them—that will be for my next letter. We also
need a house for the cattle. We won't stop making bricks until we have
170,000. You can see that we don't lack for work, which takes all my time.
   Birch drew us a plan for the grounds. He thinks an artificial lake would
be better on the south [side] of the house than on the north, since the
terrain is better adapted and it would be easier to make there. . . .
   I recall that you often imported plaster figures copied from classical
models, [and] I would be obliged if you could tell me their price. If I
remember correctly, it was not very much. They would be much admired
here—everything new makes a big impression. I am sure that our house

will be greatly admired and supposed to cost three times its real cost solely because everything about it is different from American houses.

We are going to wallpaper the staircase hall and the drawing room. The middle salon [will be] painted in imitation of marble with the pilasters and ornamentation white. The walls of the entry to the north are to be painted yellow and blue. The doors of the drawing room, salon, and dining room are of mahogany.

I completely agree with you about the choice and solidity of furnishings, [but] I don't know whether we will be able to finish furnishing the entire house this year. That will depend on our finances. We will have only a poor harvest of tobacco this year—the weather has been extremely unfavorable—and building is always more expensive than one had reckoned.

Peggy Adams' small plantation, which you recall is in the middle of ours, is going to be sold shortly. If it goes at a reasonable price, we ought to buy it because it is completely surrounded by our land. Besides, it is a continual source of problems from the cattle and negroes of its tenants, which frequently cause us a good deal of damage. . . .

I will send you a good number of tulip poplar seeds as soon as they are dry enough to pack, and also two views of Niagara Falls which I am sure will please you. . . . We have a tree here whose French name I don't know: it is a species of acacia which bears lots of yellow flowers, has long thorns, and becomes a large and beautiful tree.[1] There was one at Strawberry Hill near the well in the valley of the cherry trees. We planted a lot of them this spring. . . .

You will find Mr. Calvert has become completely European—they give him all sorts of names, such as "My Lord" and "Aristocrat." . . .

My sister wrote me that she is becoming lazy and doesn't see many people. As for me, I become more active every day, and I find that, like the *philosophes,* the more I learn, the more I am convinced that I know nothing. My children employ much of my time. I must exercise all of my patience in order to teach Caroline and George to read—it is so difficult to hold their attention. My little Louise is the prettiest child ever, but extremely delicate. She is beginning now to strengthen a little. At the beginning of November I am expecting another addition to my small family. . . .

Your affectionate daughter,

R. E. Calvert

1. Stier identified this tree as the honey locust *(Gleditsia triacanthos)* (HJS to RC, [1?] November 1806, Stier-MHS).

To Isabelle van Havre

Riversdale, 5 November 1806

Dear Sister,

Yesterday I received your letter . . . which cured the low spirits that being confined to my room for a fortnight had given me. I am pleased to announce the birth of a big baby girl who is in excellent health, as am I. I would have left my room long ago, but with all the lower level of the house being newly plastered, I thought it more prudent not to come down too soon. I was even more fortunate this time than last. I went to church in the morning and barely had time to return home to prepare to welcome her. I miscalculated by one month, not expecting the baby until November.[1]

Unless you plan to take your pick, tell Charles I'll send him a couple of nieces if he wants. Joking aside, I have greatly altered my way of thinking. Always before, I feared having too many children, [but] now I consider them a blessing.

I am delighted to learn that Louise likes music so much and plays the clavecin well enough to perform at a concert. . . . I plan to send her several tunes they play here which will be new in Antwerp. I rarely play anymore. I have so many other occupations, but even more because there is no one in my circle who is musical. Still, here as there, music is an indispensable talent for a young lady. Dancing is even more essential. We start children dancing here at age five. When it comes to educating children, living in the country is a real disadvantage. We shall be forced to hire a tutor next year for our two eldest. I teach them reading, but the role of school mistress ill suits me. I lack the patience necessary for it. . . .

I have told you of Mr. and Mrs. Merry's repeated kindness to us. They are leaving this country and recently put all their furniture up for sale. We bought several pieces, including a sofa and armchairs for our drawing room. We also bought some of their kitchen utensils. . . .

You made me laugh, dear Sister, with your portrayal of the humdrum life you lead. We can't complain about that here. Americans like variety so much that people become immensely wealthy in the space of just a few years and then six months later have nothing. As for what you say about the flirtations of your gentlemen and ladies, we are not yet so advanced. Quite contrary to Europe, the women of our better class are generally the most virtuous. All of our young men have mistresses, as do some of our married men, but the latter not publicly. . . .

Extend my greetings to Jeanneke—her attachment gives me real gratification.[2] Tell me if the style of clothing is still the same as before; I would like to send her a small gift, but I hesitate because what is worn here might be of no use there. My chambermaid (a stout, pretty girl) dresses as well as I do—her hair style [is] exactly like mine.

We just lost Mr. Cramphin of Bladensburg whom you knew. Old Mr. Peter of Georgetown also died recently and left a sizable fortune to his children. . . .[3]

I am surprised that our sister-in-law [Eugénie] fears the ocean. I thought she loved to travel, and it is the fashion now for ladies not to fear anything. You asked me to send you my portrait—I'll do it eventually when I find a good painter. Stuart did not succeed as well with mine as with my husband's. His, in fact, is quite good. You would find me little changed, perhaps a bit stouter.

I will live very quietly this winter. I often regret, dear Sister, the total absence of all the pleasures you enjoy. Washington society is regarded as very poor, without theatre, without concerts, very few balls, dances, or dinners, but lots of insipid tea parties where people perform. Living in the country is very pleasant in the summer, but extremely dreary in winter. . . .

Your affectionate,

R. E. C.

P.S. I must ask you again, dear Friend, to consent to be godmother to my little one whom we have named Rosalie Eugenia. I find myself in a rather unique situation in this regard—all my husband's family, being of a different religion, are barred from being godparents to my children. However, I must insist that you not send them any more New Year's [gifts], because in that case I would not dare ask you another time. Besides, it is not the custom in this country.

1. Rosalie Eugenia Calvert was born on October 19, 1806.
2. Jeanneke had been Mrs. Calvert's chambermaid in Belgium.
3. Richard Pottinger Cramphin (1760–1806) was the Calverts' friend and neighbor. Robert Peter (ca. 1716–1806) was the father of Thomas Peter of Georgetown, husband of the Calverts' niece Martha (Custis) Peter.

To H. J. Stier

Riversdale, 17 November 1806

. . . I will be mindful of what you tell me about the paintings.[1] It does not seem to me that there is the least likelihood of a lasting general peace in Europe, [so] if I were you, I would send them to England and sell them. You could buy [back] all the ones you wanted to keep. I don't think they are damaged yet, but during the course of the eight years they have been packed up and never opened, they <u>must</u>, I think, have suffered somewhat.

You ask me for details of their condition. I wrote you last year when we opened one of the cases that they smelled strongly of paint. We took some of them out and there were some white spots like mold. I took a fine silk cloth and wiped each painting, and put them back in the case in the same order as they had been (having numbered them as they came out). They have not been opened since. I will remove some boards from one of the cases, [and] if they seem to be in danger, I will unpack them and write to you in detail.

I have just learned that a ship from Antwerp has arrived at Philadelphia. I hope that it brings me more of your letters and the mantelpieces, because the drawing room is ready for [the mantel] to be placed. We are not yet rid of the workers, but I trust the house will be finished soon. Then we will start the grounds. We have made the columns of the portico out of stone; those [made] of brick with plaster tend to crack at the base from freezing [weather]. These porticoes with their steps are most pleasing. . . .

I almost forgot to announce the birth of a big baby girl who came into the world on the 19th of October, and for whom I hope you will be godfather once again. My husband wants to call her Rosalie Eugenia. I was even more fortunate this time than last, and I felt so well that three weeks later I went for a walk in the garden. There is nothing to having children in this country. . . .

Your affectionate daughter,

R. E. Calvert

P.S. In my letter I asked you to please send me a pair of candelabra to place on the mantel in the drawing room in the same style as the ones you had here, with bronze figures (those are the nicest I have ever seen). I also want some lustres to go with them. I am sorry, dear Father, to cause you so much trouble, but these are things which have to be chosen by a person of taste.

1. Stier was alarmed by Mrs. Calvert's last communications concerning the paintings and the possibility of mildew. He told her to "open the cases, take the paintings out, see how they are packed, and number them so you can repack them in the same way. If there are moldy spots, take a very dry muslin handkerchief, even warmed a little, and try it on each picture. Put them in a closed room where you can make a fire

in damp weather. Touch them as little as possible. . . . I strongly urge you to take good care of them—they are of great value and I have a large responsibility [for them]" (HJS to RC, 1 July 1806, Stier-MHS).

To Charles J. Stier[1]

Riversdale, 1 December 1806

My dear Brother,

. . . I thank you heartily for the information you sent me about furniture and dinners, but by your good nature in taking upon yourself the task my indolent Sister van Havre had no time to perform, you have brought on more trouble than you bargained for, because I shall take advantage of your patience still further and ask you to write me of what stuff the most fashionable curtains are made. You are keeping house then? That will clip your wings, dear Brother, for it seems to me that since your marriage you have only flown from one place to fly to another! How much I would give to be as frivolous. I would take a trial flight, too, but I have four fledglings here to make me stay at home and furnish me with amusement there which leaves a more satisfying impression than that produced by *le grand monde*. . . .

I see that the manner of serving your dinners has not changed, and I prefer it greatly to the American mode of serving all the meats and vegetables together. One doesn't have time to eat enough before half the dishes are cold, so one must hurry to swallow everything as if one had not dined for a month. But although I approve so much of three courses, I should like to divide them differently: nothing cold should come on for the first [course], and the roast [should come] before the stews. Since in this country everyone does as he likes, I am going to introduce a quite new mode. I shall take the best fashions from the different countries.

Mr. and Mrs. Merry, whom we are going to lose, lived in the European style. They were extremely courteous to us, and I am so sorry they are recalled. Mr. Erskine, who takes their place, will not live so well. He married in Philadelphia and is very young for an Ambassador.[2]

You are going to have still another general war in Europe whose outcome is impossible to foresee—in spite of the Paris *Moniteur*. That little island [England] gives Bonaparte enough work to do! For my part, I admire that nation more and more every day. In what does she not hold supremacy at this time: her government, her laws and the impartiality with which justice is administered, her ministers and generals—nearly all men of distinguished talent and also of merit and virtue. With what heroism a Nelson, a Pitt, a Cornwallis, a Thurlow have so lately met their deaths, giving both examples of courage and integrity beyond proof during their lives and of true piety in their last hours.[3] What do you think, dear Brother, of the belief in predestination? I am rather of that persuasion. The education I received at Liège, my two trips to Spa, and several other circumstances contributed to give me this preference for the English, which a comparison with other nations only confirms more strongly from year to year. What then would have become of me if I had married a Frenchman, or even one of my fellow-countrymen? It would not have suited me, I think.

I must finish, dear Brother, for I am sure my letter is not coherent. My children annoy me so, one climbing on my chair and Caroline has begun to read to her doll. I hope you will not delay much longer giving me the pleasure of congratulating you also on the birth of a son or daughter. You must not be despondent. I know here several people who, having been married several years without having children, afterwards had several. . . . I regret so much not knowing your Eugénie. . . .

Your affectionate,

R. E. C.

1. Carter Trans-MHS.

2. David Montagu Erskine (1776–1855) served from 1806 to 1809 as British minister to the United States. Erskine was married to his cousin, Frances Cadwalader of Philadelphia, daughter of General John Cadwalader.

3. This quartet of eminent Englishmen had all died recently: Horatio Nelson and Charles Cornwallis in 1805, William Pitt the Younger and Edward Thurlow in 1806. Thurlow was lord chancellor of England from 1778 to 1792.

To H. J. Stier

Riversdale, 11 December 1806

Dear Father,

. . . I find myself in a rather peculiar situation: I must baptize all my children by proxy since no one in my husband's family or even among my acquaintance is of the same religion as I. . . . Rosalie Eugenia is much more robust than any of my other children at the same age.

Caroline and George have excellent constitutions and are never sick. I have never seen children in better health. I wish I could say the same about my little Louise, who I fear suffered because I had a fall from a horse three months before her birth. She has not yet started to walk or talk, and she does not seem to pay any attention to objects that she sees. The doctors don't know what the cause is. At the same time, she is as pretty as an angel, all her limbs are very well-formed, she seems to enjoy the best of health, and she is getting fat. You can imagine, dear Father, how much this affects me.

We recently had a loss in the person of Mr. Cramphin of Bladensburg—it is a diminution in our little coterie which we feel deeply. To lose a good neighbor is an irreparable casualty in the country. He has not managed his affairs very well since he left almost as much debt as property, so they are going to sell everything. If the land which adjoins ours is sold at a reasonable price, that is to say, will produce six percent by leasing it out, we plan to buy it. . . .

I am afraid we are going to have a hard winter because it started earlier than usual. I went sleighing the other day. We will live very quietly this winter because the construction left us somewhat pinched. I don't think I am missing very much. The society of Washington and Georgetown is wretched—all the people employed there are Democrats and of low origin. . . . My children are not yet of an age to give me real companionship. It is, however, almost time to give them some teachers for their education. I don't know how we are going to do that—it isn't easy to find a good tutor. . . .

Your affectionate daughter,

R. E. Calvert

P.S. . . . If I remember well, there are often auctions of paintings in Antwerp. I would very much like to have some [paintings] of pleasant subjects, like hunting scenes or landscapes. I don't want them by the great masters—those would be too expensive. I don't want to exceed $25 or $30 apiece—as long as they are well-painted. If you could send me four, I would be obliged, but perhaps by limiting the price so low I have insulted the art of painting, and you will laugh at my ignorance. . . .

I must also ask you to send a seal with the family coat-of-arms, so I can use it to seal my letters. I would like to have the same coat-of-arms painted in color, too.

To H. J. Stier

Riversdale, 19 January 1807

I am taking the opportunity offered by the *William Murdoch,* [sailing] from Washington to Amsterdam, to send a box with some tulip-poplar seeds for you, . . . a small packet of books for Charles, and a few baubles for my sister and for Louise. Please also accept from me two prints which are views of Niagara Falls, recognized to be the world's most beautiful waterfall. . . .[1]

We are having a very hard winter which upsets all of our operations. Since workers are always much slower than expected, our house is not yet finished; we still have the plasterers and the joiners. The four doors of the drawing room and the dining room are made of mahogany and are very beautiful. My husband also found, by chance and at a good price, some white marble for paving the two porticoes. The columns are of white stone; those made of plastered brick (like those of Mr. Custis and others) do not hold up at the base with freezing.

I made so much profit last summer from my butter (which has a fine reputation) that I am going to have a nice little dairy built under the stairs of the north portico, vaulted like your wine cellar at the Mick. The floor and shelves on which the basins are placed will be of white marble. Speaking of that, I don't think I ever told you that each year we make a cask of cider which is almost as good as champagne. Several people refused to believe it was just plain cider. Mr. Merry and some of the other English confessed that they had never had such a drink in England. It wouldn't stand the rough jolting of a voyage, otherwise I would send you a few bottles.

You have never told me, dear Father, if you still receive the Phila-delphia newspapers. If you do, I hope you are not alarmed by what is said about the separation of the western states. No one knows yet what Colonel Burr's real plan is, but whatever way it goes, we have nothing to fear here.[2] Nor does it appear likely that bonds will be affected.

Our 1805 tobacco crop, 72 hogsheads, is being loaded right now. We are sending it to London; Amsterdam looks too uncertain, the remit-tances difficult, and the exchange always disadvantageous. I hope next summer we will have a better harvest. We don't grow any [tobacco] at Riversdale, but we made a nice crop of hay and 1200 bushels of oats last summer. . . .

Your affectionate daughter,

Rosalie E. Calvert

P.S. In the box of seeds I put a small package for my old chambermaid Jeanneke, with her name written on it. It is a ribbon for her bonnet. Please give it to her and tell her I am sending this bauble as a proof of my remembrance and that I would have liked to send something nicer, but not knowing the fashion of her clothes, I didn't know what would be suitable.

1. The Stier family traditionally exchanged gifts at the New Year.
2. Former vice-president Aaron Burr was involved in a privately organized military expedition in the American West whose nature is still in dispute. Burr was arrested in February 1807 for forming an expedition against Spanish territory, and later in the year he was indicted for inciting disunion. He was tried and acquitted of the latter charge.

To Isabelle van Havre

Riversdale, 20 January 1807

. . . You write, dear Sister, that you plan to send Louise to Brussels for a couple of years. It seems to me that in general more bad than good is taught in all boarding [and] convent schools. I think a private education is better for a daughter. A mother who will take the trouble to win the confidence of and be a friend to her daughter can better mold her character and manners than any school mistress who treats all her young charges the same, even though each has a different disposition.

I am delighted to hear that Louise is musical. I am sending her two airs. . . . There is also a small box for her with cotton for embroidery or sewing. We hardly ever use any other thread here; the cotton is so much better for sewing muslin and even linen. Please accept with my best wishes, too, a pair of lace sleeves, which are in the same box I'm sending to Papa.

Tell me, dear Sister, what is Papa doing this winter? Is he tending his flowers at the Mick or in town? I often think it must be sad for him living alone, with you and Charles living at a distance. Do you go out much? Do you ever speak English? For myself, I live so out-of-touch here that I think I'm becoming completely idiotic—being always with children must have that effect. I am sure that my letters show it and lack common sense, don't they? Our house is in great disarray now; we still have several workers, but I trust it will all be in order next winter and then I can renew all my acquaintances.

Please tell me what a table service of French porcelain costs—I would appreciate your writing me in some detail on this matter. I have asked Papa to send me several things; if they haven't been shipped yet, would you buy me four of the prettiest coffee cups you can find—each cup should be of a different <u>color</u>, but of equal size and shape. I want to place them on a mantel, which is the style here. . . .

I am afraid that I may be causing [Papa] too much trouble with all these errands. If it is not taking too much advantage of your good nature, would you take charge of them . . . ?

Your affectionate sister,

Rosalie E. Calvert

To Charles J. Stier[1]

Riversdale, [n.d.] January 1807

My dear Brother,

. . . [I am sending you], in a box addressed to Papa, four books of poems by Thomas Moore, which I beg you to accept. I have often read them and with renewed pleasure each time. Mr. Moore is a young man who is as agreeable in his manner and conversation as he is talented as a poet, and that is saying a great deal! He is much admired in England. He made a tour through America two years ago and wrote several scathing articles on this country and its government. I hear my sister-in-law is learning English—a perfect knowledge of the language is needed to appreciate the delicacies of Moore's style. If you care for these volumes, I will send you the rest of his works. The name of "Little" under which his first essays were published is fictitious.[2]

You will observe that he does not spare this country, but what he says refers to the Democrats and is not exaggerated. I don't know what is thought in your country, but you may find some of these poems too freely expressed. I acknowledge that they would not be proper for a young girl. He has been accused of the tendency to pervert public morals in his writings, but if you have continued to read English since your return to Europe, you should be fascinated by the simplicity and elegance of his style and language.

I have turned down the corners of several leaves in the back—of odes and epistles I admire the most. Write me what you think of them. The "Fragments of a Journal," page 111, gives a charming description of a journey in a public stagecoach.

Society in Washington is very inferior just now . . . so I don't go there often and I employ my leisure hours reading. Tell me how your ladies pass their days. They do not need, I suppose, to direct the most minor details in the care of their households and children as we must here.

What is our brother van Havre doing? Does he still get up at eleven o'clock? It is rarely the case that the rising sun finds me in bed. Morning is the best part of the day, the mind is more active and everything is done with more ease, and I believe that nothing contributes so much to the preservation of the youthful faculties as early rising. . . .

Do you talk of America sometimes, and what do you think of this country? The greatest failing I perceive in Americans is their heartlessness. They do not seem to feel anything deeply and are too prudent and reasonable to be lovable. We have a very nice little circle of neighbors whom we see often and unceremoniously. Your friend John Herbert who married Miss Snowden has built a house six miles away.[3] I am sorry Papa did not leave us the plans you made of the house, which would have helped us greatly. We are still working at it.

I see my dear brother is still the philosopher. I thought the lovely Eugénie van Ertborn would have converted you from that sect. You say one is less merry in luxurious apartments, but I think just the contrary. A beautifully decorated salon, filled with well-dressed people and musicians performing, enlivens me and makes me happier. But it is not the same here as at home—[here] one must differentiate oneself a little from the mob in order to be respected by them. . . .

Your affectionate,

R. E. C.

1. Carter Trans-MHS.

2. The Irish poet Thomas Moore (1779–1852) had by 1807 published *Odes of Anacreon* (London, 1800); *The Poetical Works of the Late Thomas Little, Esq.*, which first appeared in London in 1801 and was later published in Philadelphia in 1804; and *Epistles, Odes, and Other Poems* (Philadelphia, 1806).

3. John Carlyle Herbert and his wife, Mary (Snowden), built Walnut Grange near modern-day Beltsville in Prince George's County.

To H. J. Stier

Riversdale, 26 March 1807

Dear Father,

It has been three months since I have heard from you! It was, therefore, with great pleasure that I received two of your letters yesterday . . . along with the business letter containing the checks on the various banks. . . . I am sure that you have nothing to fear about McEwen's integrity except in case of a general bankruptcy. It's a pity these letters were so long in passage because you have lost three months' interest. . . . [In the future] it would be wise always to send the checks four months before the quarterly payment. . . .[1]

You ask if I have kept accounts of the various sums you have given me since your departure, and if the Riversdale plantation returns us $1,600 a year. I have kept exact account of everything I have received since my marriage, both in gifts and allowance. . . . I will send you today, if I can—otherwise next time—a note of what Riversdale produced the past year, which I think you will see exceeds $1,600.

I will take the greatest care of the paintings. They are stored in a dry place where nothing can harm them; [they are] in the coach house in the second wing, corresponding to what you called "the brick room" [in the old wing]. . . .

Thank you for the drawings of the mantels.[2] I hope to receive the two colored ones soon—they seem very pretty. We will use one and sell the other, doubtless at a good profit. I must ask you please to send me the white marble [mantel], like the one in the pencil-drawing, because while the others are quite pretty, I think the one in the drawing room ought to be superior to the one in the dining room. We have finished the drawing room in a manner which will suit it. I have intended many times to send you the drawings, but I always lack time to copy them. . . .

Thank you, too, for the drawings of the salon at the Mick.[3] I think you will find many faults with ours, which is not so highly ornamented. . . .

You seem to fear, dear Father, that we are spending too much on farming. I would like to be able to clear this up, but it is such a difficult matter to handle by letter—actually impossible without sending you all the accounts. I must, therefore, be content with telling you that we hold fast to scientific procedure and make our experiments only on small plots. I am sorry to hear that your Spanish sheep were not more successful. I think your flock is too large—75 is too many to keep all together. . . . We keep ours in three flocks on different plantations and keep all the young ewes apart.

You advise me that if I have a taste for the arts to form a cabinet of paintings. This is unquestionably an interesting notion, especially in America where there are none, but it demands too much outlay of capital. You frighten me when you say that you have bought paintings at low prices, and [then] mention one of two feet having cost £100. And since I am a little like Louis XIV, the most beautiful painting would not please me if the subject were not agreeable. For example, I cannot admire the best Tenniers because all his figures are grotesque.[4] I would like very much to have two or three good paintings in order to show an appreciation and inspire it in my children, but I don't aspire to a collection. It is too expensive a diversion.

I see, dear Father, that you don't approve of my comments on a silver service, but you must consider the differences in our countries.[5] From my experience and that of others, I find that one cannot make do with silverplate on any object: first, because in this climate it is subject to tarnish and rust, and second, because the servants damage and wear it out in cleaning it. Another strong objection to plate is that its price generally is high compared to the same thing in [solid] silver, and then when the fashion changes or it is damaged in some way, you lose the entire value whereas silver always retains its value. . . . In this day and time when everything is so unsettled, here as well as there, it seems desirable to have a certain amount [of capital] in silver. For the rest, dear Father, I submit my taste to yours. We still don't have any silver except an assortment of spoons imported from London last year.

Your observation that the condition of Europe must affect this country is very true. If things continue, a huge number of people, especially merchants, are going to be ruined, and we probably won't be able to send our tobacco to London any more. We will have to send it to Amsterdam and I thank you for your offer to help in that case, but I believe you are mistaken in advising me to stop growing it. This is a commodity which cannot be dispensed with; its consumption will not diminish and its culture is a fact. We could not undertake any other crop with the same profits. . . .

Our little family is in good health except for my poor Louise. We have little hope for her recovery. She has been wasting away before our eyes for some time. I told you that she must have been injured when I took that fall from my horse some months before her birth. She is the prettiest of all my children. It is very unfortunate, but we must submit to the divine will. My little Eugénie is quite strong and happy. I agree with you that we will have a large family, but in America it is easier than in Europe to provide for children. Anyone who is thrifty and industrious can make a fortune here. Observation has convinced me, however, that [even] the greatest industry unaccompanied by thrift is ruinous, whereas a system of economy, well-maintained, is infallible. You will think me like the preceptor who says, "Follow my advice, not my example," but we aren't spending anything now except on our house. It was the best time to finish it, and once it is done and furnished, it is forever. . . .

Your affectionate daughter,

R. E. Calvert

1. Stier received quarterly interest and dividend payments from his American investments, which he wanted forwarded to his agent Thomas McEwen in Philadelphia for reinvestment. Mrs. Calvert served as a conduit for these funds and also as trustee for his stock certificates. Stier praised his daughter's handling of his affairs, saying that her last account was "as clear and well-calculated as anyone could want. You are completely accomplished at this work, and if it were not an imposition to burden you with business affairs . . . I would want no other manager than you" (HJS to RC, [n.d.] September 1806, Stier-MHS).

2. Stier apparently sent sketches of three mantels: two, which he had purchased for a total cost of $89.64, he described as made of red marble with white marble ornamentation; a third, made of white marble, had not been bought because it cost almost $200, a price Stier deemed "entirely too expensive" (HJS to RC, [n.d.] September 1806, Stier-MHS).

3. Stier sent the Mick plans because his efforts to locate the original plans for Riversdale had been fruitless. He had intended the Riversdale salon to be patterned on that of the Mick. However, by the time the Mick drawings arrived, as she indicates, Mrs. Calvert had virtually completed her rooms (HJS to RC, [n.d.] September 1806, Stier-MHS).

4. Mrs. Calvert is referring to David Teniers the Younger (1610–1690).

5. Stier had suggested that the silver serving pieces Mrs. Calvert wanted could now be procured in silverplate (HJS to RC, [1?] November 1806, Stier-MHS).

To Isabelle van Havre

Riversdale, 2 April 1807

Dear Sister,

. . . Many thanks for the information about furniture that you gave me. Charles sent me a *plan de dîner*. I was really surprised at what you told me about it becoming fashionable to have only one course as we do here. And I was hoping to convert America to three courses, which I find far nicer. . . .

The design of the vase lamp is quite nice—we have a similar type here. I infer from this that the gilt candelabra with bronze figures, like yours and Papa's, are out of fashion. What have you done with yours? I asked Papa to buy me a pair for our drawing room. . . .

You asked me, dear Sister, for a complete account of the birth of my little Eugénie. To give you the best idea, I can only say that if it were always so easy, it would be less feared than a migraine. I think that the climate of America is very favorable to such labor. I had engaged a lying-in nurse for one month, but due to my miscalculation she couldn't come as she was attending another woman. So I was obliged to send for an old negress and I had the doctor in the house in case of mishap. I have an

Château du Mick, The Stiers' eighteenth-century countryhouse. Artist unknown.
Collection of Baron Henry de Witte

excellent white chambermaid who is accomplished at dressing and caring for a baby and is a good nurse. From the beginning my little darling has been, and continues to be, so good and in such fine health that she causes me no trouble. She is so robust and happy, always in motion, and a delight to me. Of course I am nursing her—I would not want to deprive myself of such an interesting occupation. Miss [Ann] Stuart, my husband's amiable niece, was to have come for my confinement, but [could not]. I wasn't annoyed because I prefer being alone at these times, as long as I have good servants. Too many visitors tire me.

I am at a loss as to how to give you all the details of our house, but I intend to send the plans to Papa and will ask him to show them to you. It is virtually complete and will be entirely finished this summer, at which time we will begin the grounds and promenades. I would not have believed that there was so much to do to build a house. It has cost us much more than I anticipated. . . .

I have not gone out this winter except to our neighbors whom we visit often, especially Mr. and Mrs. Richard Lowndes. Those two individuals combine all the most worthwhile qualities.

I hope you received the trifles I sent. . . . There were some books for Charles which I urge you to read and tell me what you think of them, but don't give them to Louise. They are written by the most charming little *génie*—he is too small to be called a man. . . .[1]

Your affectionate sister,

Rosalie E. Calvert

1. The poet Thomas Moore was so small in stature and youthful in appearance that when he was introduced to Jefferson by Mr. Merry, the president, mistaking him for a boy, did not address him—a snub that Moore never forgot (see Augustus John Foster, *Jeffersonian America* [San Marino, Calif., 1954], pp. 10–11).

To Jean Michel van Havre

Riversdale, 25 April 1807

My dear Brother,

I received your letter of 9 January with the invoice and bill of lading for the two crates containing the mantels, and I am most grateful to you for your kindness in seeing to this shipment. . . .

I rather expected that Colonel Burr's activities, which the newspapers have greatly exaggerated, would have alarmed you. They still don't know exactly what his intention was, but the government has arrested him and he is now in Richmond where he is to be tried. From all appearances, he is not guilty, but he is a dangerous and devious man. I know him personally. When he was Vice President, he came out to see us several times and showed us many courtesies. His duel with General Hamilton and the circumstances surrounding it have made him loathsome to a great many people. They have greatly exaggerated the movements attributed to him. Instead of 600—some even said 6,000—who were supposed to be following him, it now appears that only a few friends [were] with him. . . .

I see from Papa's letters that a rumor is going around about a war between this country and England. No matter what is said, don't believe such news—this is something that will never take place. They may squabble a lot, especially when we have a President like Tommy Jeff, but whatever differences these two nations may have, they will always be settled amicably. As for the blockade the Emperor has declared against England, we can only be amused. . . .[1]

I see that in France there is a massive conscription of men for the armies—is the same not true for [Belgium]? Still, I haven't heard of any young people of our acquaintance being called up. Are you more favored than the French or is it easy to get a replacement? It must be dreadful to have to fight for a cause in which one has no interest. Besides, these Russian gentlemen don't know how to take a joke and don't let themselves be bribed like the Prussians.

I am quite moved by what you tell me about my long absence not effacing my memory from the hearts of my family and friends. . . . I hope that you will continue to write me from time to time. I am always delighted to hear from you, and please believe me,

Your affectionate sister,

R. E. C.

1. Both England and France were engaged in various measures to shut off the neutral carrying trade and deprive each other of the materials of war. Napoleon's Berlin Decree (November 1806) declared the British Isles in a state of blockade, forbidding all commerce and authorizing seizure of all vessels not in compliance. England's restrictions on neutral vessels, because of its navy's overwhelming superiority and ability to enforce its restrictions, made far the greater impact on American commerce, and despite Mrs. Calvert's conviction that it could never happen, led eventually to war between the United States and England.

To Charles J. Stier[1]

Riversdale, 26 April 1807

Dear Friend,

 . . . I thought I would be able to write you yesterday without any interruption. My husband had gone to Mount Albion, there was nothing to disturb me, the day would be dedicated to friendship, and hardly had I opened my desk before I was obliged to defer writing again due to the arrival of Mr. [Augustus John] Foster, a very attractive and cultured Englishman who has traveled all over Europe and Greece. He stayed to dinner with me. What do you say to your little sister passing the day tête-à-tête with one of the most charming young men she has ever seen?

Today I hope nothing will occur to disturb me. . . . What would I not give to hear news of that increase in your family which you seem to desire so ardently? [Children are] undoubtedly a great happiness, but look around you, dear Friend—do you see anyone enjoying perfect happiness. . . ? No, perfect happiness is not of this world, else we should unduly regret leaving it. . . .

It seems fashionable in Antwerp as it used to be in France for girls to marry men much older than themselves. I do not approve of such marriages. One does not think at fifty as at twenty, and that union of feeling and thought so essential for husband and wife cannot be welded. . . .

I have taken a vow not to meddle in politics. They put everybody in a bad—if not savage—temper, and I see so many women making themselves ridiculous by discussing politics at random without understanding the subject that I am disgusted with all controversy except about flowers! Their culture absorbs me more every day, for as I go out rarely, it is my chief amusement. . . .

We are very much occupied in improving Riversdale, but there is still so much to do that I despair of having it finished in less than ten years! You wrote that you could not find a statuette for such a small pedestal as the column of our staircase. I should be so annoyed for I do not think a lamp would be as effective. If, however, you can't find a statuette, will you please send me [the lamp] you think most suitable. The column is one foot three inches in diameter.[2] I should like so much to have two plaster casts for our north drawing room.[3] Papa writes that they are all too indecent, but [people] have changed on that subject here. I should like to have one of the Apollo Belvedere and my husband says he must have the Venus de Medici sent too. . . . At all events, if the statues are such that I cannot put them in the drawing room, I shall put them in my husband's study. . . .

Your affectionate,

R. E. C.

1. Carter Trans-MHS.
2. In the Carter translation, the diameter of the staircase column is erroneously given as five feet three inches.
3. Mrs. Calvert meant to place the two plaster statues in the entry hall, which is on the north of the house. Her father had suggested such a placement in a recent letter (HJS to RC, [n.d.] January 1807, Stier-MHS).

To H. J. Stier

Riversdale, 27 April 1807

Dear Father,

. . . I have sent your April checks to McEwen. . . . As soon as they send me the certificates, I will forward you a record of their numbers and of the purchase account. I have directed [McEwen] to buy 6 Pcts. because the government, far from offering new issues, is busy extending the old ones, and for that purpose is offering some advantages to owners of 3 Pcts. to induce them to convert into 6 Pcts. . . .[1]

You are doubtless aware that the prohibition on the importation of certain English merchandise was suspended.[2] There is no doubt that the United States and England will make an amicable treaty. These two countries should always be at peace—it is impossible to imagine the contrary. The intrigues of the French cause our Democratic President to make a lot of mistakes, but [then] he reverses himself at will. He must remain at peace with England—a couple of ships of 74 [cannon] and some frigates could destroy the principal cities of the United States in a moment. There is nothing to prevent them from doing it. . . .

I am eager to have the seeds you [packed] in the box [with the mantels], since this is the best time of year to plant them. . . .[3] I amuse myself more every day with the cultivation of flowers and shrubs of all types. It's been a bad year for hyacinths, but nonetheless I have had some beautiful ones. . . . We lose some immature ones each year—however, I have never lost a variety entirely. I think I have all the varieties you have, but they don't grow such large and beautiful flowers. . . . Another flower I really want is the double violet, the white and the blue. I am going to try to assemble a large number of flowers and shrubs of all types to plant around our country-house. It is so pleasant to see everything grow and embellish one's surroundings. You have a superb collection of double poppies at the Mick—would you send me some seed? It is such a small grain that you could slip it in a letter. . . .

We are having a very bad spring, extremely late and rain almost every day. The public roads are impassable by carriage. . . .

Your affectionate daughter.

1. Mrs. Calvert is referring to United States Treasury bonds paying 3 and 6 percent interest.

2. The Nicholson Act, or first Non-Importation Act, prohibiting certain British goods from entering the United States, was passed in April 1806, to take effect in November 1806. It was enforced for about five weeks, when Jefferson recommended its suspension. Congress did suspend it in December 1806, postponing its date of effect, first to the summer of 1807 and then to December 1807.

3. Stier wrote that he was sending Mrs. Calvert seeds of Weymouth pine, larch, and balm of Gilead, which he advised her to plant carefully, since they "will be handsome and make a grand effect for the portions of your property which should constitute the views." He also sent gorse seeds for enriching fallow land and fir seeds for the slopes or barren land (HJS to RC, 8 December 1806, Stier-MHS).

To Isabelle van Havre

Riversdale, 6 May 1807

Dear Sister,

. . . You probably cannot conceive of all the duties which conspire to prevent me from doing the one thing I most want to do—visit with you by means of a letter. . . . So what do I do all day? I get up at five o'clock and we breakfast at seven. Most of the day is spent continually trotting from one end of the house to the other, in the morning giving directions about what has to be done and then after dinner seeing that my instructions have been carried out.

You know more or less how people live in America and what a lot of trouble we have with servants, and you can visualize how I live. A family like ours is like a little kingdom—the ministers often fail to do their duty, and sometimes, too, the subjects become discontent and have to be replaced. We have three white servants—a chambermaid, a gardener, and an overseer. Then [there is] a black prime minister who serves as chamberlain, confidant, "housekeeper," in short, as man-of-all-work. Our household consists of 21 persons, including my children.[1] Besides that, there are always workmen about, sometimes one, two, three, even four at a time—all to be lodged and fed, of course. You can see that so large a household requires much care to manage, especially as things are not yet properly settled.

Since the house has been in such disarray for so long, we have not received guests for some time, except for neighbors with whom we are on familiar terms—the women to dinner and the men often in the mornings. We are fortunate in our neighbors. Both of the R[ichard] Lowndes possess many fine qualities.

The roads are so awful because of the continual rain that, although I have been wanting to go to Georgetown for the past fortnight to buy summer clothes for my children, who are literally in tatters, it is impossible. To go by carriage would be too dangerous for the horses.

I haven't seen our nieces, about whom you inquired, for some time. Mrs. Lewis is the most pleasant of them, [and] we see each other once or twice a year. I see Mrs. Peter more often. Mrs. Law is living in a pretty little country-house near Alexandria. I understand that her husband is going to leave for England, [but] no woman could miss a husband such as he. They are separated "forever." She is a woman who combines several faults with some very brilliant qualities.

Custis's young wife is a very amiable person, but the poor girl lost her first two babies—the first lived only a few moments and the second, a delightful little girl, just died recently. She also lost her mother and her only sister within the past year. Mrs. Stuart hasn't had any more children, and it is high time she stopped since she has eleven living. Her oldest daughter was married the other day to a wealthy Virginian of good reputation, but not renowned for his intelligence.[2] She is an exceptional person and I am upset that she will be living so far from us.

It is a shame that the wife of my brother-in-law Edward Calvert is, as they say in English, "so ill-contrived."[3] He is such a fine man, but he certainly cannot get any satisfaction at home. She is both narrow-minded and ill-natured, and no one can stand her. By contrast, everyone who knows him loves him. . . .

I must thank you for the shipment of anchovies and for the roll of designs you tell me are in the crate with the mantels. I am very curious to see [these designs] before furnishing several rooms this autumn. . . .

Your affectionate,

R. E. C.

1. The 1810 census listed twelve whites, sixty slaves, and no free blacks living at Riversdale. Family members could account for seven of the twelve whites at that time; the remaining five whites were three males and two females (Population Schedules of the Third Census of the United States, 1810, Prince George's County, Maryland, fol. 67).

2. Ann Calvert Stuart married William Robertson in 1807.

3. Edward Henry Calvert was married to Elizabeth Biscoe (1780–1857).

To H. J. Stier

Riversdale, 23 June 1807

Dear Father,

. . . I am sending you a list of all the certificates of 6 Pct. stock in your name that I have received from Messrs. McEwen, Hale & Davidson since December 1806. . . .[1]

I have received the mantels, which are very pretty, but unfortunately they were not packed well enough to survive the rude jolts of normal ship unloading without damage. They needed more straw packed between each part. The three main pieces are not damaged, but the others are all broken, some of the small parts in four pieces.

I am greatly obliged to you for the seeds and will follow your directions exactly. . . . I think that the gorse will be a most valuable acquisition here for our slopes, as well as the firs.

I thank you, dear Father, for your advice about farming.[2] There is no doubt that your system is the best, even more profitable in this country than in yours, since your labor costs for annual crops are not as enormous as ours. I believe I have written you that we no longer grow tobacco at Riversdale and are growing mostly grain. Next year nearly all the plantation will be in meadowland, which is preferable to all other kinds of culture here for several reasons: our land's location and its susceptibility to flooding, the higher profits of hay as a crop, and certainly nothing gives as much embellishment [to the land]. We also found that by closing off part of the woods three years ago in a way that keeps the animals out, young trees spring up in abundance and replace the old, decaying ones fourfold. I hope the fir seeds develop well and I'm delighted with the other tree seeds, especially the larch which I have wanted for a long time. . . .

My husband intends in the future to give up growing tobacco at [Buck Lodge]. The terrain is unsuitable and the costs high in proportion to the profits. We have to continue [growing] it on the Patuxent [Mount Albion], and this year we have fine prospects, barring mishap, of making a very good crop at that plantation. . . .

Your affectionate daughter,

R. E. C.

1. Mrs. Calvert listed five certificates totaling $33,044.09, representing Stier's purchase of United States Treasury bonds from October 1806 through May 1807.

2. Stier warned the Calverts: "You can ruin yourself in agriculture as surely as in a badly calculated business venture. . . . You use up all your energy each year on cultivation of annual crops such as tobacco, clover, and grains. . . . If you have the slightest loss, you can be ruined by yearly repetition. . . . I myself work on making forests, and I find there a great profit and even greater satisfaction." He advised the Calverts to lease out their crops to tenant farmers and to turn their efforts toward getting their woodlands in good condition and putting as much of Riversdale as possible into meadowland (HJS to RC, 8 December 1806, Stier-MHS).

To H. J. Stier

[Mid-July 1807]

Dear Father,

. . . I am beginning to fear that our correspondence will be interrupted because the conduct of our government is such that a war with England appears inevitable. You read our papers and consequently will have seen that this fracas between our frigate and an English ship has produced a great ferment in this country.[1] Despite all the newsmongers' clamor, however, and all the preparations for armaments, fortifications, etc., sensible people acknowledge that the fault is with the Americans. The British have acted with the utmost possible moderation. It is impossible to predict how it will turn out. Our rogue of a President will glory in a war with England. Good-bye, then, to all American trade, to all the merchants who conduct it, to all the banks that make their fortune on it. Good-bye, too, to the profit from our tobacco, grain, etc. With twenty ships of war the British will blockade all our ports from Savannah to Boston.

There is no danger to the public bonds, but there is fear that the banks will suffer greatly. I think you would have done well to have sold your Alexandria and Baltimore [bank] shares long ago. . . .

You say in your last letter that we should think about preparing a nice trousseau for our little Caroline. Long ago it wasn't necessary to give dower for young women here, if they were pretty, but since this country has become more civilized, a good dowry is considered the greatest of charms. So we will take care to provide for that time. She is almost seven years old and promises to be quite pretty. I will not neglect to give her a good education.

My poor Louise is still in the same condition I've described to you, seeming neither to progress nor to fail. The three others enjoy an excellent constitution and uninterrupted good health. Our Eugénie is a little Amazon. She hasn't had a moment's illness since she was born and gives her nurse lots of exercise by jumping, climbing, and never staying still for two minutes. Unlike my others, she has blue eyes and blond hair and looks like her father. . . .

My husband sends his best. He's busy with the hay harvest, which is very good this year, as is the grain, and the tobacco promises to do as well.

I will write you again soon. It will be most painful if our correspondence is interrupted, but I still hope it won't happen because receiving your letters is my greatest joy since our separation. Oh, why must we live so far from you! I have everything necessary for happiness. Only two things mar my happiness—the condition of one of my children and my separation from my family. However, dear Father, I must not trust my pen on a subject which affects us both, because what good are useless complaints. My destiny fixes me in America and Europe's condition would not make me regret this, if we could all be reunited here. Being persuaded that you are happier in Antwerp, I submit to the circumstances. . . .

Your affectionate daughter,

R. E. Calvert

1. On June 22, 1807, the United States frigate *Chesapeake* was stopped on the high seas by the British ship *Leopard,* whose commander demanded to search the American ship for British deserters. When the American commander refused, the British ship fired on the Chesapeake, killing three, wounding eighteen, and removing four alleged deserters. The incident aroused intense anti-British feeling, and on July 2, Jefferson issued a proclamation ordering British warships to leave United States territorial waters.

To H. J. Stier

Riversdale, 1 November 1807

Dear Father,

. . . I am really sorry that you haven't been able to send me some offshoots of your [tulips]. . . . Some new ones would greatly embellish my collection. This year I am going to plant them in front of the house on the south, as well as all the shrubs I can find. . . .

We have had wretched weather the entire summer—rain almost every day—but autumn is making us ample recompense. Indeed, it is always the most beautiful season here.

Recently we had three days of horse racing in Washington, [and] I was there for the first day—it was a grand concourse of society. Congress is also in session so our environs will be splendid. . . . Your old friend Dr. Scott wrote me the other day and asked to be remembered to you. He is doing well and at the age of 85 is more active and hard-working than any number of young people. His garden is in good shape but do. ; not extend to the culture of tulips. However, he had the most beautiful garden balsam this summer.

We have put the mantel you sent in the drawing room. It looks very nice, but is a bit damaged because it was packed in too large a box with too little straw around it. What toil and trouble it takes to build and furnish a house in this country! Nevertheless, I intend to continue without slackening until I have it completed, and then to rest and enjoy it. We have imported several pieces of furniture from London . . . and we just received a Greek lamp to hang in the middle of the salon, which is beautiful. It cost ten guineas. . . . I am in negotiation for a good porcelain service which has a quantity of dishes—they are asking $300.

I think we will continue to send our tobacco to London. The price here is low, but the exchange in London is also low. Right now my husband is in Baltimore to see if he can sell the bills of exchange without too great a disadvantage. . . .

Your affectionate daughter.

To H. J. Stier

Riversdale, 7 December 1807
Midnight

I have been three months without news from you, so you can imagine, dear Father, with what ecstasy I received your [three] letters of August and September this afternoon. I practically devoured them, and since I am a widow for two days with my husband away at Mount Albion, I cannot resist the desire to write you right away. Besides, during the day there is so much noise, the children interrupt me so frequently, that I often feel giddy and don't know what I'm writing.

I have so many things to tell you. I must start by thanking you for the New Year's gifts you gave us, as well as for the [tulip bulbs]. I am going to write McEwen to send them by stage without delay. This is a gift, dear Father, which will be most precious to me, and although the season is advanced, I don't think they will suffer. . . . I shall prepare their bed tomorrow with great care. You can't imagine the pleasure I will have in cultivating these flowers which you raised and which are offspring of yours. While watching them bloom, I will often dream that perhaps at the same moment I am admiring mine, you are busy with yours. . . .

Now I will have the most beautiful collection in America, and I assure you that my reputation is already quite exalted. Thank you so much for the directions you give me which I will follow exactly, but I am sorry the packing was such a bother. It really is a very complicated and difficult task to keep all the names, etc., but, dear Father, rather than going to so much trouble you could have just sent them without names or remarks. Poor Dr. Scott has gotten his in such disorder that I truly believe he does not have a single one now whose name he hasn't mixed up. When he came to see mine, he greatly admired the "Marshal of France," and as I had several large bulbs, I promised to send him one. Would you believe that the [following] year he sent me (under a different name and as a very rare flower that a captain had imported from London) the very same flower I had given him! I know it was the same bulb. He added to it three tulips which were so bad that I had to dig them up in order not to ruin the view of the collection. I have often regretted not having the names of the ones you left me. They have multiplied a lot, and the little book you gave me with your notes and comments attached has been a great help to me in growing them.

I have not gained a single new flower from the bulbs you left me. Every year there have been several that changed, but all were inferior with the exception of a single one in 1803, which was strong and which I tagged in order to send you an offshoot. But that was the year we had the deluges that almost carried away the entire plantation, and with the rest, my tulip. Aware that a change of soil makes them change color, I gave [some of] all of them to Ben Ogle, and reserved the increase of any new ones produced for myself. . . .

On 3 November I sent you . . . a box containing tulip-poplar seeds and acorns. There are also a few seeds of the fragrant white azalea (*Azalea viscosa*). It is the most beautiful wild shrub in Maryland, as much for its flower as for its fragrance, and I don't think you have any at the Mick. . . . Enclosed is a copy of a list which Mr. [Augustus John] Foster lent me for choosing plants. I will try to get you the catalogue of Bartram of Philadelphia, who every year gathers seeds of different plants and trees of this country for sale.[1] If I remember correctly, the price of oaks on that list [Bartram's] was $2 and the others $12, which will give you a rough idea of prices.

I see that you disapproved of my desire for the white marble mantel you sent the drawing of—and I am afraid that you consider me extravagant—but the reason I persisted was that I thought [this] one would not be as pretty as the one in the dining room and that the furnishings of the drawing room ought to be more beautiful in comparison. But now that it is in place, I am quite satisfied with it. It is very pretty, and we have put together the broken pieces and filled the cracks with plaster of the same color so that you can hardly see them. So it is not necessary to have the other made. . . .

Since there are no lustres or candelabra in Antwerp, I will have them sent from London. . . . One of our best friends, Mr. Foster, who is presently embassy secretary, is returning to London. He is a man of taste and someone to whom I can explain exactly what I want as well as at what price. . . .

Regarding the paintings, you are right that it is a difficult taste to acquire in this country because there are no good paintings—indeed, there are no old ones, either good or bad. You say that in order to expand my knowledge, I could study the beauties of [the paintings] you left here, which would be very pleasant. We could put them in the bedroom over the drawing room, which is spacious and can be kept closed and protected from the sun by shutters. However, there is such an enormous drawback to this that I would tremble to do it. I think it would be impossible to take them out of their cases without people finding out (you know how everything in this country is found out), and I fear it would bring everybody down on us if we refused to let them all see. . . .

You ask whether we have bought the land of Peggy [Adams] and the late Mr. Cramphin. We have not yet made these acquisitions. Of course, we ought to have Peggy Adams' [land] some day, but there is no dealing with that ill-natured shrew. I had a four-page letter from her the other day complaining to me that Mr. Calvert had offered her too low a price, and would you believe that he offered her $16 cash an acre—which is much more than any other land in the neighborhood. Mr. Cramphin's is very poor land. . . . You probably remember that it is almost all hilly and eroded. There is only one small section adjoining us which is good. . . .

[Letter left unfinished; resumed 1 January 1808]

1. William Bartram (1739–1823), son of the first native American botanist, John Bartram, operated the family botanical garden in Philadelphia in partnership with his brother John.

To Isabelle van Havre

Riversdale, 10 December 1807

Dear Sister,

. . . I share deeply your worry about your Charles.[1] You seem in your letter to have little hope and perhaps by the time you receive this, it will only bring back sorrows which time had somewhat healed. Yet the hope of possibly being of service makes me risk reopening the wound. In my family I have had little experience since George and Caroline are never sick and my poor Louise's condition is beyond the reach of medical help, but in the past year I have seen two miraculous cures of negro children who were at death's door from nothing more than worms and who were cured by the use of "Carolina Pinkroot."[2] I recall having seen you give it to your children. . . . I mention this herb to you because it probably is not commonly used in Antwerp, but it has a very high reputation here. My husband is almost as concerned as I, dear Sister, about your child.

You know that [Charles] was his favorite. . . . I do so hope that he has recovered, but if our prayers have been futile, even though these blows are hard to bear, the high opinion I have of your courage and piety assure me that you will endure it with resignation. At such times, only religion provides us any real comfort.

There is a great similarity in our situations, dear Friend, and perhaps mine is worse since I have not the slightest hope for my poor Louise. . . . My only consolation is that she does not suffer. She has a nurse who gives her very good care and is as attached to her as if she were her own. . . .

My little Eugénie is as strong and robust as a little savage, mischievous, and always in motion. Of all my children, she is the one who has given the least trouble and the most joy. She never looks at anyone without smiling and is loved by all. I would have liked, this time, a longer interval of repose, but I find myself once again "in an increasing way."

You are quite right in saying that I live an isolated life—I imagine few women live as solitary a life as I. The only people I am close to are our neighbors the Lowndes, especially Mrs. Richard Lowndes. She is an excellent woman and few days pass without communication between us. Sometimes we write each other notes twice a day, but aside from her I don't have a single friend.[3]

You say that I tell you little about my husband's family. I didn't think it would interest you, but since you asked I will write <u>freely</u>. However, this must remain strictly confidential—I hope you will burn my letters.

Our brother-in-law Edward Calvert is an excellent man, and for him I have all the affection and esteem that he deserves. He comes to see us sometimes. His wife, however, is a wicked shrew—I don't think she has a single good quality. If my husband did not frequently advise his brother and very often conduct and manage his affairs for him, I think she would ruin him, despite the fact that he has 10,000 acres of land, which brings in at least $6,000, and no great expenses. She makes him, I think, very unhappy. The neighbors can't stand her. She fabricates lies about all the families she knows and does all she can to stir up trouble between the two brothers. . . .

The eldest of the Stuart girls is a very nice girl, but she now lives quite far away in Virginia. Her father, whom I am sure you remember as an extremely austere and tedious man—completely respectable, but more knowledgeable about the customs of the Greeks and Romans than of today—forced her against her will to marry a man who does not have enough intelligence to make a woman such as she happy. Although she writes me that she is perfectly [content], I do not believe it.

I would have proposed that she come and live with me and that would have prevented her marriage, but it would have forced me out into a wider social circle that I don't want to enter until my own daughters are old enough to be introduced. Another obstacle was that it is not easy to always have a third person around, especially when a wife and husband get along well together. They want to be alone sometimes. Mrs. Law lived with us for a year, and although she is very considerate and a woman of great intelligence, I was delighted when she left to live in her own home.

Of all that family, Mrs. Lewis is the one whom I prefer, but she has four children and lives so far from us that we rarely see each other. I see Mrs. Peter often, but she also has four children and a great defect in this country is that it is the fashion to take all one's children when one goes to visit for several days, and four naughty children like those spoil any pleasure I would have in her company. In any case, she has such a high opinion of herself and everything concerning her that it doesn't make her any more appealing.

My husband is chief adviser to the family and whenever one of them behaves badly, the others come to beseech him to intervene. He is feared and loved at the same time, which I find very odd. He often sends them all to the devil, saying he wishes he didn't have "a relation in America." I reply that apparently he thinks himself lucky that I don't have any, but he always pays me the compliment of telling me that my relatives are of a quite different sort with whom he would not have the same complaints.

I was quite surprised at what you told me about Papa not keeping his houses in good order. I would have thought that could be managed without difficulty, but there is no reason for him to worry about it. At his age, rest is what he most needs, and besides, he has other interests. We are not as indifferent here and we work without respite. Sometimes I am so tired by evening that I fall asleep while taking tea. We go to bed at 9 o'clock and rise with the dawn—it is rare that the rising sun finds me in bed. I have been very busy all this week making curtains for my bedroom. I have cut them all myself, as I have all the others in the house, as well as all the covers, etc. I am always my own upholsterer. I rarely do the sewing, but I cut and piece all my clothes and bonnets, all the children's clothes and linens, and all my husband's linen and even his waistcoats. Besides that, all my servants are dressed in a very pretty cloth of my own manufacture. I never buy candles or soap. I am always present during the making of my sausages, jams, pickles, etc. At this point I'll wager that you think I am exaggerating, but I assure you it is the pure truth, and I ask you at the same time to keep these proofs of my industry between us. I am more active than I want to be known, and I give you these details to provide you with an idea of the way I spend my time. When I have guests, all my functions cease and are performed by a white woman who is really my chambermaid but on occasion my "housekeeper."

However, by now I think that you are completely exhausted by my scribblings, but it's your own fault since I am only trying to answer your questions. . . .

Your devoted sister.

P.S. . . . By the way, I never received the anchovies you reported sending. . . . I fear the captain may have eaten them. Would you send me at the first opportunity three or four barrels of one thousand each, more or less—the quantity doesn't matter as they greatly improve with keeping—and also a dozen pounds of anise sugar.

1. Charles Jean van Havre (1799–1807) died from an illness that his grandfather described as baffling to the doctors, but that Stier himself thought was caused by worms (HJS to RC, 1 July 1807, Stier-MHS).

2. The root of *Spigelia marilandica* taken as an infusion was considered useful as a vermifuge, or destroyer of intestinal worms.

3. Mrs. Calvert's eldest son, George Henry, also remembered Mrs. Lowndes fondly: "Her gracious image with her sweet motherly welcome; her household sceptre, a bunch of keys, hanging at her side" (See George Henry Calvert's privately printed *Autobiographic Study* [Boston, 1885], p. 78).

Tommy Jeff's Embargo

THE PROHIBITION ON AMERICAN exports, designed by the Jeffersonians to keep the United States out of the war between France and England, had disastrous internal effects on the country. With no export markets for American commodities, prices collapsed, trade stagnated, and merchants failed. Political unrest followed the economic stagnation, with the northeastern states, who lived by trade, leading the clamor.

Rosalie Calvert, alarmed by the adverse effects of the hated embargo, stated her views forcefully. She thought that the country's situation was critical and that the president's course was wrong-headed, and she feared civil war if the policy continued. The Calverts were directly affected by the embargo, since they could not ship their tobacco, but Mrs. Calvert's comments were not grounded solely on self-interest. Having witnessed revolution in Europe, which had driven her from her homeland, she feared the economic and political turmoil taking place in her adopted land. Stability and peace were, understandably, values on which she placed a high priority. She wholeheartedly embraced the intense Federalist criticisms aimed at the Jeffersonians.

The election of President James Madison in 1808 promised little improvement. The scorned "Tommy Jeff" was out, but Mrs. Calvert believed that the country would only go from bad to worse under his "wavering, weak" successor. She warned her European family about a break-up of the Union, perhaps within a few years, with a republic in the north and a monarchy in the south. This, of course, was New England

Federalist rhetoric relayed by Mrs. Calvert, and in fact she appeared more interested in the monarchy than in the republic that her Federalist friends promoted. She confided to her sister that it was "high time we had a king." The Constitution had worked well under the venerable Washington, but constant elections merely appealed to the lowest elements in society. She worried, too, about the effects of disunion on the public debt, cautioning her father about his large investments in United States bonds.

But while politics and talk of politics became a much larger element in everyone's life, most of Rosalie's time was still devoted to the needs of her rapidly growing family and household. She was pregnant again—with her fifth child in nine years—and this time she wrote no paeans in praise of large families. Charles Benedict was born in 1808, and Rosalie made it plain that she hoped he would be her last. She was still doing most of the teaching for Caroline and George Henry; tutors were hard to come by, and those hired turned out to be worthless. The Calverts' middle child was a source of constant concern—Louise still could not sit up, walk, or talk. In the spring of 1809, the pretty little four-year-old died, and Rosalie's grief was mingled with self-reproach for what she felt was her part in her child's brief and tragic life.

Rosalie found a measure of solace in her religion and its promise of an afterlife, but she remarked bitterly to her sister that she had to stifle herself in communicating such thoughts. She felt isolated in her Catholicism, with none of her husband's family or even any friends who shared her faith. She was embarrassed to have to call repeatedly on her European relatives to serve as godparents for her growing brood. Mrs. Calvert rarely talked about religion in her letters, and she later left the Catholic faith—something she never told her European family.

There were other comforts and pleasures. She still read each day; poetry and novels were her chief delight. She had no time for music, but riding was a passion and she had a fine new horse. Horseback riding, far from being just a diversion, was considered an excellent form of exercise, especially for women, and essential to good health. Early rising and taking cold baths were also regarded as healthful, and Rosalie regularly reported observing such practices.

Rosalie's garden was her greatest diversion, however, and with her house finished, she enthusiastically turned her attention to its grounds. Much of 1808 was spent making embellishments and improvements, utilizing the plan drawn up by William Russell Birch, and by year's end she could report a great deal accomplished. On the south side of the house there was a series of terraced falls culminating in a lake at its base, "which looks like a large river." The flower garden on the terrace was not yet completed, but she planned to plant heliotropes, geraniums, jasmine, and roses, along with her highly prized tulips and hyacinths.

Off to one side of the house, beyond the stables and surrounded by great fine trees, Rosalie looked out on a new ice-house and a slave cabin, each designed to look like rustic huts complete with quaint thatched roofs. She planned another slave cabin with columns, designed to look like a small temple. This fanciful use of slave cabins as part of the landscape design, reminiscent of Marie Antoinette's hamlet of peasant cottages, must have been one of Rosalie's European-inspired contributions to the grounds plan. One can hardly imagine George Calvert coming up with such a conceit.

The grounds to the north, the entrance side of the house, were simpler, featuring "the loveliest possible lawn." Rosalie wrote of a system of promenades or walkways in the gardens and of raising numerous varieties of trees, which would be planted in "clumps," to ornament the views. There is later evidence to suggest a straight, tree-lined avenue approach to the house from the road, culminating in an oval or circular driveway on the north side of the house. Mrs. Calvert repeatedly promised to send the landscape plan to her relatives but never found time to make a copy, and the original has been lost.

To H. J. Stier

Riversdale, 1 January 1808

Dear Father,

Please accept our warmest wishes for your happiness during the coming year. . . . This letter was started long ago, but couldn't be sent because of the embargo our government has placed on all ships.[1] I fear that the opportunities to write you will be quite scarce for some time, which will be a great privation for me.

At present this country is in the most critical situation. Our good-for-nothing President does all the harm he can but dares not declare [war] against England—it might cause a revolution if he did. There is a frightening stagnation in the towns—a number of merchants have gone bankrupt.

This year is bound to produce momentous events whose outcome is impossible to foresee. I think you would do well to send your checks well in advance when you can, but perhaps by the time you receive this, the embargo will be lifted and everything will be in order. The way things are going, however, I think that the best days of American commerce are past. Never again will it enjoy the many advantages it had during the last six years.

I also feel that when you send checks to McEwen, it would be wise <u>to send me the letter under cover</u>—not that I have any reason to doubt his honesty, but one must be concerned that unless things improve here, no agent can be trusted. I think the McEwen & Co. business is done on a commission basis and that is very safe. Nonetheless, I don't like the fact that it always takes him so long after he has received the dividends to buy the certificates. It appears that he makes use of the money up to the last minute. . . .

The other day we opened two of the cases of paintings. They seem to be in good condition, but I think that airing them for a few days will be beneficial. There were some which had spots of mildew, but when I wiped them with a silk handkerchief they disappeared. I viewed [the paintings] again with great pleasure.

I have just learned that a ship carrying government dispatches is leaving from Georgetown [and] will stop at Amsterdam. I will take advantage of this good opportunity to send you this letter. . . .

Your affectionate daughter,

R. E. Calvert

1. The Embargo Act, passed in December 1807, prohibited United States ships from sailing to foreign ports except on government business, so official vessels became an important avenue for private overseas correspondence. Foreign vessels were permitted to bring goods into the country but not to take them out.

To H. J. Stier

Riversdale, 16 April 1808

I have just learned, dear Father, that a ship sent by the government with dispatches will sail from Baltimore for Falmouth and Lorient. . . . The opportunities to write you are so rare now that I am really sorry no one informed me before this, because I have a lot to tell you and only a few minutes to do it. . . .

I thank you again for . . . the flower bulbs which arrived in the best possible condition. . . . I planted them myself with the greatest care, following your instructions exactly. I looked forward with so much anticipation to seeing them bloom and boasted to everyone that I now had the most beautiful collection in America. When they began to come up, I was surprised that many were missing, but I thought perhaps some were earlier than others. At the end of last week I went to examine them and found that they had been eaten by moles. The shoots in an adjoining bed were not touched, but they left me only 30 of the others. It is a mishap I could not have foreseen (but which annoys me greatly), because last year we didn't have any of these pests and this year the garden is full of them. I will try by all possible means to exterminate them, and in the future I will plant my best flowers in front of the house. I intend to make some tubs of planks two feet deep in the ground [to protect them]. . . .

If you could send me some more offshoots this year, I would be very pleased, but don't go to all the trouble of labeling them—just throw them pell-mell all in together.

Another flower which I want very much is the double yellow wallflower and some little double pinks, too. I think they are called *dubbele pluimkens* in Flemish—they make a very fine display. Also [I want] some poppies and the double violet—you had such beautiful ones at the Mick. My garden is my greatest diversion, and I want all the prettiest flowers and shrubs. I am going to build a small greenhouse this year.

Here it is four months since I have heard from you, and I fear you will have gone that long, too, without news from me. It is still not known how long the embargo will continue, but its effects in this country are terrible. We cannot sell the produce of our lands, and even if [the embargo] were lifted, I don't think we would have a market for our tobacco because it appears that a rupture with the French Emperor is inevitable. . . .

Our little family is doing well and will be increased again this summer—in August, I think. . . .

Your devoted daughter,

    R. E. C.

P.S. In my last letter I sent you a list of the certificates [of 6 Pct. bonds] which McEwen had purchased with your [July,] October and January dividends and sent to me.[1]

---

1. In a business letter dated 17 February 1808, Mrs. Calvert recorded five certificates totaling $31,119.71, which represented H. J. Stier's investment in United States treasury bonds from July 1807 through January 1808. The Calvert-Stier correspon-

dence never provides an overview of Stier's total investments or net worth, but Stier was receiving and reinvesting about $25,000 every six months. At a 6 percent rate of return, this would indicate a capital investment of about $800,000. See Mrs. Calvert's letter of 23 June 1807, above, for a similar pattern of reinvestment in 1807.

To H. J. Stier

Riversdale, 5 May 1808

Dear Father,

. . . It is impossible to predict what this year will bring forth—the whole world seems upside-down. The effects of the embargo here are quite ruinous. If it continues for much longer, all the merchants will fail. The farmers and planters can't sell their commodities—nobody pays and everything is expensive.

They tried hard in the Congress this winter to pass a resolution to move the government to Philadelphia, but fortunately it did not succeed. The eastern states complain loudly about the southern states. All this tends to make the condition of America as uncertain as that of Europe. For my part, I do not believe this government will long continue as it is now—the eastern and northern states will detach themselves and we will have a king in the south. That is my prophecy, which I think will be realized in a few years.[1]

I often think about how your investments could be affected by these and other changes, but it is a labyrinth from which one cannot find the escape. Everything considered, it would seem that [yours] at least are safer than any others.

I will take care of your paintings. We opened one of the small cases and they are in good condition. . . . I have hung those we unpacked in the drawing room which I always keep closed. . . .

Mr. Calvert and the children are in very good health. I myself have been continually indisposed for several months. The cause is not alarming, but this kind of indisposition makes me good for nothing. I hope this will be the last time I find myself in this situation—our family will be large enough for our happiness. . . .

Your affectionate daughter,

R. E. Calvert

1. Talk of the Union's impermanence was common from its inception, but Mrs. Calvert's remarks reflect a heightened awareness of this possibility in the period from 1808 through 1814.

To Charles J. Stier[1]

Riversdale, 5 May 1808

Dear Brother,

. . . I must thank you a thousand times for the portraits of our dear parents. They are indeed admirably executed. I showed them to several of their friends who all recognized them at the first glance. I look at them every day with renewed pleasure. . . . I am much obliged, too, for your execution of my commissions for the candelabra and lustres, and I am curious to see the statue. That will be new here. We should have two, since one is more difficult to place. . . .

I thank you for the offer to send me music, but I must confess, to my embarrassment, that I play very rarely and then I choose the simplest airs for songs or other easy little pieces. You tell me that you yourself have little time to read or to draw, etc. You can imagine then how much less I have. Your household does not occasion you half the trouble given by mine. . . . I hardly have time to read a little every day, which is more interesting and amusing than music and restores me to good humor when sordid household cares have irritated me. I never hear music—not even the violin our old servant plays—without a sigh for the pleasures of the theatre and balls which I have so long been denied. Music makes me more sociable, but good reading makes me happier and more content with our daily existence. . . .

I am reading Gesner's works just now, which are well-translated from German into English.[2] I never admired him as much. What a fine style, so simple and touching! I was sure you would like [Thomas] Moore. Was there ever anything grander than his "Love and Reason," or the "Dismal Swamp," or Anacreon's description of his mistress, "Ode XVI"?[3] Moore is not liked here, as he is rather severe about the people of this country, but what he says is true enough, which I suppose makes it still more offensive. But though he is my favorite, I cannot pardon him for the way he speaks of the immortal Washington.[4] It was not Apollo but Midas who inspired him when he attempted to portray that great man ·

There is a very good theatre now in Philadelphia, much superior to what it was when you saw it. In the spring the same company plays in Baltimore and disperses in the summer, going to Alexandria and Washington sometimes and to other small towns. . . .

But are you not a little romantic, dear Friend, in your ideas on the education of children? You would like to carry out Rousseau's plan, but I hope that you would have the foresight to steal a mate for each one of your children to be educated in the same way as their future companions.

Charles Jean Stier. Miniature, artist unknown.
Copyright Bureau d'Iconographie de Belgique (ANRB), Brussels

Else after all your trouble, they might be the most unhappy of mortals all their life because of their greater degree of perfection! Believe me, these private educations which have been followed out with so much care and method often miss their purpose. Even here there are several examples of it, among others, my charming niece Miss Stuart in whom are united all the most lovable traits with the most solid virtues, fitted to adorn the highest position. And because her father had no fortune to give her, she has married a Virginia bonhomme who loves her *à sa façon,* and that is all. Her sisters, who are really her opposites, will perhaps be happier. Do we not also often see the greatest care and attention only produce imbeciles? What was Lord Chesterfield's son? [Or] the Duke of Hamilton, educated by Doctor Moore, the Duke of Tuscany by—I forget whom—

while we see the greatest men having risen without any particular trouble having been taken with their education. I am determined to spare neither trouble nor expense to bring up our children well, but if they are not born with talents, believe me, they will never acquire them. George seems to have a great deal of talent and application and as soon as he is old enough I shall send him to college. . . .

It is difficult to see clearly in political matters at present. We are perfectly informed as to what goes on in Europe. What a singular situation for all the Continent just now. It seems to me that it cannot last long. It is like Rome and Carthage, as Papa says. . . .

Your affectionate sister,

R. E. Calvert

1. Carter Trans-MHS.

2. Salomon Gessner (1730–1788), Swiss poet. There were several eighteenth- and nineteenth-century translations of his work, one published in 1802.

3. "Love and Reason" appeared in *The Poetical Works of the Late Thomas Little, Esq.* (Philadelphia, 1804), the only work that Thomas Moore published under a pseudonym; "A Ballad: The Lake of the Dismal Swamp" appeared in Moore's *Epistles, Odes, and Other Poems* (Philadelphia, 1806); "Ode XVI," Moore's translation in verse of the sixth-century B.C. Greek lyric poet Anacreon's description of his mistress, appears in *Odes of Anacreon* (London, 1800).

4. In "To Thomas Hume, Esq. M.D." in *Epistles, Odes, and Other Poems,* Moore wrote, in part, of Washington:

> How shall we rank thee upon glory's page?
> Thou more than soldier and just less than sage
> Of peace too fond to act the conqueror's part,
> Too long in camps to learn a statesman's art,
> Nature design'd thee for a hero's mould,
> But, ere she cast thee, let the stuff grow cold.

To Isabelle van Havre

Riversdale, 5 May 1808

. . . It is with the most sincere regret that I learned today of the death of your Charles. Your earlier letters made me fear this outcome, which surely has been a boundless grief to you as he was so promising. This is one of those sorrows that only time can soften but can never efface. I hope those [children] who remain with you will help to make up for the two losses you have had to bear, dear Sister. . . .

You are so right that the less often we write each other, the less we have to say. Why can't we see each other once in a while, especially now that our children are growing up? It would be so interesting to be together. You ask me if my husband turns a deaf ear when I talk about going to Europe. No, not at all, but you must realize that despite a great desire to go, I cannot even think of making the trip at present. . . .

I don't find your plan of taking Louise to Paris in the least extraordinary. French manners and deportment are everywhere admired, and as you observe, there is no danger that she would adopt their principles or their character. The best schools for girls here are run by the French. Caroline still hasn't been to school. I am teaching her to read and write myself, along with George, but I am about at the point of hiring a tutor, if I can find a suitable one. It will be better than sending them so far away; George is only five and Caroline not yet eight—they are still too young. If I can have a good tutor for two years, then I will send them both to a public school. . . .

Mrs. Peter spent last week here and sends her regards. You asked about Custis's wife; she is a very pleasant woman and quite well-bred, despite the fact, as you noted, that her mother was a woman without education and her sister a fool.[1] I regret not being able to see her more often, but she cannot leave her father who has become feeble in health, and even more in mind. If she did not stay with him, he would be in great danger of marrying an old maid who lives in the house. The young Fitzhugh is not such a good match as you think; his father has dissipated a large part of his fortune in standing surety for his friends.[2] However, the young man will have a fine fortune in land in Virginia which will produce a nice interest, if he manages it well—but everything depends on that.

Mrs. Peter does not live any more lavishly now than she did before the death of her father-in-law. Her husband is exactly like his father—he thinks only about accumulating property, which he manages to do solely through strict economy, because he manages his properties very badly. Still, he has an insatiable desire to acquire new ones, rather than buying stock. He also has adopted his father's plan of always being in debt so as not to have to make expenditures, and at the moment he owes more than $14,000 to the bank. Can you imagine anything more disagreeable for a wealthy man than to owe such a sum? . . .

And why do you think that the age of your *philosophe* will keep me from thinking malicious thoughts? Quite the contrary, that can make him more dangerous. It is when one doesn't expect any danger that it is often closest. Joking aside, a man so intelligent, so amiable, must be a marvelous resource in the countryside. I wish you could send me such a man, but I can do without the fifty-and-even-more-than-five years he seems to have. As for me, I am completely "in love" with a man who is as few men are, but unfortunately he is half the age of your swain.[3] Now I can see you take on your severe expression, which I have always so loved to see, but never fear—the ocean separates us now!

You can see that I am in good spirits despite our tribulations. If this state of affairs continues or gets worse, if we cannot sell our tobacco, I will go live in our little cabin at Mount Albion where I will sing the pretty little song I have almost forgotten: *dans ma chaumière me portant toujours bien, je ris de la sottise du pauvre genre humain. . . .*

Your affectionate sister,

R. E. Calvert

1. Mary Lee Custis's mother was Anne (Randolph) Fitzhugh and her older sister, Anne, was the wife of Judge William Craik of Maryland. Both women had recently died.

2. William Henry Fitzhugh was the only son of William Fitzhugh of Chatham and Anne (Randolph). The younger Fitzhugh married in 1814.

3. Mrs. Calvert is again referring to Augustus John Foster, the twenty-eight-year-old Englishman about whom she has hinted previously of a casual flirtation and who had recently returned to England. Foster evidently admired Rosalie Calvert, describing the Calverts as hospitable neighbors and remarking that Mr. Calvert was "married to a very distinguished looking Dutch lady" (Foster, *Jeffersonian America,* p. 17).

To H. J. Stier

[Riversdale], 12 May [1808]

. . . Did you think that the emigration of the Braganza family to Brazil caused a big sensation here?[1] Not in the least—it doesn't appear to affect us one way or another, at least for the present. Perhaps in the future it will have some influence on the United States, [but] it is the English who will reap all the fruits of this new branch of commerce at present.

We are so occupied with our own affairs at the moment that we are not worrying much about those of our neighbors. Our differences with England seem to be adjusted, but that, I strongly fear, will cause an open break with the French. We are caught between two fires. Independently of our quarrels with these powers, we squabble among ourselves here at home. The time for the election of the President approaches, along with that for members of the Congress. Jefferson is definitely out, but it is still undecided whether we will have a Democratic President or not. The Federalists have gained a lot this year, especially in New York where elections have [already] taken place.

You ask me if I can become acquainted with Galatin [Gallatin,] and if it would be advantageous to be on close terms with some members of the Treasury.[2] Nothing is easier. Our situation, rank, and connections here make it quite convenient, and as soon as it could be of the least use to you, I will do it with pleasure. At the moment, however, I don't see that any advantage would come from it, especially since it is almost certain that Gallatin and all that party will be out of office shortly.

Up till now I have always avoided becoming acquainted with Washington society, but as soon as all our furnishing is complete and in good order we will make our selection of society and give some proper dinner parties from time to time. . . .

Your affectionate daughter,

R. E. Calvert

1. The Braganza family was the royal family of Portugal. When the French invaded Portugal in November 1807, the royal family fled to Brazil and ruled the Portuguese empire from Rio de Janeiro.

2. Albert Gallatin (1761–1849) was secretary of the treasury under both Jefferson and Madison from 1801 to 1814.

To H. J. Stier

Riversdale, 9 July 1808

Dear Father,

. . . The ship *Osage,* which had been sent from [the United States] with peace proposals—first to Bonaparte and then to England—just returned, and I think it will be decided soon now whether we will have war with the Emperor or not. . . .

At the moment we are in a very critical situation. This embargo is ruining a vast number of people. If it continues for some time yet, the consequences will be incalculable. On the other hand, it is going to be the means of effecting a total revolution in popular opinion and of destroying the Democratic party. . . .

As you noted, we are absorbed here in political discussions and at the same time managing our affairs as best we can, which requires a lot of attention and activity in these times when everything is so uncertain. Our tobacco crop looks very promising this year, but that is small consolation when it is predicted that there won't be any market. We must also, I think, start making our own fabrics to clothe our negroes. Our children are growing up and require more attention every day, and their number is increasing. All this gives me so much to do that I can scarcely manage, and it is so difficult in this country to get adequate help—so few people one can rely on.

I was very pleased to hear that you are enjoying such good health and are amusing yourself at the Mick. How handsome that delightful place must have become—it has been fifteen years since I have seen it! Our drawing room here is admired by everyone and it really is charming. But ever since the porticoes were finished, there is nothing as beautiful, as grand, in my opinion, as the columns. . . .

[no signature]

To H. J. Stier

Riversdale, 10 September 1808

. . . Today, dear Father, I have the pleasure of announcing the birth of a son who came into the world on the 23rd of August.[1] He is doing very well, as am I. I left my room a week later—truly, it is a mere trifle to have children in this country. . . .

On the first of August I sent your July checks from the banks to the Messrs. M., H. & D. [McEwen, Hale & Davidson], and they have acknowledged their receipt. . . . [The total] was $11,155.38. Not having heard from them since makes me fear that they have been unable to find any 6 Pcts. to buy. There haven't been any on the market for some time. . . . At the same time, there is no indication that a new bond issue is going to be passed. Following your instructions, I wrote McEwen to use $2,000 toward the purchase of 3 Pcts. [and] the rest in 6 Pcts. What would you do in the eventuality that it becomes necessary to take some other bond? You must write me full instructions on this matter. . . .

I wish you could see our little Eugénie—everyone thinks she is a marvel. She has a lily-white and rose complexion, big blue eyes with black lashes, and blond hair and eyebrows. She is delightfully vivacious and gay.

We are having such a dry summer that everything is, as they say, "burned up," so much so that we are having trouble serving two dishes of vegetables a day. Our tobacco crop will be superb, however, if nothing unforeseen develops, but I see no hope of selling it soon. At present the way to make a huge fortune, easily and without risk, is through buying tobacco. It can be bought for $4 and $3—even for $2.50 a hundred for ready cash. Our last, which we sent to Murdoch, brought an average of $12 a hundred net, after all expenses, etc. were paid. There hasn't been a year [recently] when you could fail to make a good speculation by buying tobacco from the small farmers at the beginning of the season.

It is unbelievable what harm this embargo is causing. Just the other day a nearby plantation was sold for debt at a tenth of what it was worth.

I hope to hear from you soon. . . . My husband sends his regards. . . .

Your affectionate daughter,

R. E. Calvert

1. Mrs. Calvert was announcing the birth of her second son, Charles Benedict Calvert (1808–1864).

To H. J. Stier

Riversdale, 13 November 1808

Dear Father,

. . . You tell me to buy some tobacco for your account. Tobacco is expected to be a very good speculation, but at the same time this country is in such turmoil, so buffeted from all sides, that I don't know what to believe. A month ago, in October, tobacco was at $3 and $5. Suddenly it went up and all the merchants were buying, but after a few days it was over and now there is no standard price. Everyone is waiting. If the embargo is lifted—which I do not expect—everyone will rush to ship theirs, [and] then the price could be very low in Europe. If the price [here] falls considerably and if it seems possible to ship it—in short, if it presents hope of a fairly safe profit—I will make the speculation. We have two crops on hand ourselves at present, totaling more than 180 hogsheads.

There is nothing we can cultivate with our negroes which produces as much profit [as tobacco], but if all commerce with Europe remains interdicted, we are going to have to become manufacturers. Neither flax nor hemp suit us as well as wool and cotton. The latter is cheaper than linen and substitutes for it very well. . . .

I announced in my last letter the birth of a son. . . . He is healthy, indeed couldn't be better, and is much bigger than my other children at this age. . . . We have christened him Charles Benedict. My little Eugénie

. . . is the most beautiful little scamp I have ever seen—everyone's friend, lively, playful, and with an excellent disposition. George is also a very good boy and shows a good deal of intelligence and application for his age. Caroline does not give me as much satisfaction. She is very ill-tempered and willful, and I fear she is going to cause us a lot of grief. On the other hand, she is capable of great affection and I still hope to be able to correct her faults. I think I know myself pretty well and I see with sorrow that Caroline is extremely like me. The education of my children occupies a large part of my time. I am looking for a tutor, but have not found a suitable one yet.

We are having a delightful autumn and are quite busy working on the grounds of the house. I amuse myself raising fir trees from the seeds you sent me and also a few cedars of Lebanon imported for Jefferson.[1] The evergreen trees will make a lovely effect mixed in with the others. We also have some English elms—a beautiful tree—and some mulberries from China.

At this point in my letter I see in the paper that a ship is sailing right away from New York to Falmouth . . . and I don't want to miss this chance. So *adieu,* dear Father, I am sorry to have to finish in such haste. . . .

Your devoted daughter.

1. Thomas Jefferson recorded that on March 2, 1808, he paid [Theophilus] Holt one dollar for four cones of cedar of Lebanon *(Cedrus libani).* Jefferson had tried in 1807 to grow this tree from seed, and he recorded subsequent efforts in 1811 and 1812 (Edwin Morris Betts, ed., *Thomas Jefferson's Garden Book, 1766–1824* [Philadelphia, 1944], pp. 333, 384, 453, 475).

To Charles J. Stier[1]

Riversdale, 3 December 1808

Thinking of you continually as I do, dear Brother, how is it that I write to you so seldom? One time Charles has to be soothed, which takes a half-hour. Then they come to ask for mustard for a ragoût or sugar for a pastry, for you are aware that we American ladies are, alas, our own housekeepers! Then Caroline must have a reading lesson and George must write. A new coat is brought from the tailor which must be tried on. No, it is not right and a note has to go back with it. The man is going to Georgetown and a long list of details for the household must be remembered. All these occupations seem trifling and still they prevent me from chatting with you. At present I can hardly hold a pen as I have violent rheumatism in my shoulder and a packet sails in three days. The opportunities are so rare now. . . . I am going to send you these few lines. . . .

I must say a few words about business. I received all your checks and the duplicates.[2] It is rumored that in case of war, interest on bonds will not be paid to Europeans; therefore, Papa's would not be paid, and perhaps yours also would be stopped. Be assured that I shall spare no pains to protect your citizenship.[3] *Adieu,* dear Brother, I cannot go on without risk of missing this ship. . . .

Yours,

R. E. C.

1. Carter Trans-MHS.
2. Mrs. Calvert was looking after her brother's and the van Havres' American investments, as well as those of her father.
3. Charles J. Stier had obtained United States citizenship while living in Virginia, but in 1802 he had sworn allegiance to the French Republic, an action that, if known, would have nullified his American citizenship.

To Isabelle van Havre

Riversdale, 3 December 1808

Dear Sister,

. . . My baby is a giant compared to the others. I haven't written you since his birth—he came into the world the 23rd of August. Five days later I came down in order to see my flowers and [rose] bushes, and after the eighth day I had all my dinners downstairs. Mrs. Law and two young ladies had come the night before [the baby's arrival]. I told them that they would have to retire early since I had not slept well for two nights. The next day they were exceedingly surprised to find me in bed with a big baby boy. I had with me a woman in whom I have the greatest confidence and an excellent doctor in the house (in case of mishap). . . .

This country is in a state of complete turmoil. Our imbecile government doesn't know which way to turn. It is very much feared that the French Emperor has already declared war, or at the least that he has confiscated all ships—which amounts to the same thing.[1] There is no doubt that Madison will be our President. If Pinkney [Pinckney] had been chosen, there would have been some hope that America would recover her losses and her reputation, but with Madison we can only go from bad to worse.[2]

Just between ourselves, it is high time we had a king. This constitution, which has been so much lauded, worked very well at the beginning and as long as Washington was at the head, but ever since, the people have become more corrupt and the executive power has become weaker. One can sense the lack of energy. Any elected government is bad, I think— those who aspire to govern have to flatter the people too much in order to get elected, and once in office they are too afraid of displeasing them. . . .

The embargo is distressing for us. It is impossible to dispose of the commodities which provide our income, the farmers cannot pay their rents, and everything is higgling and haggling. Ah well, we must be patient and hope for better things to come.

I fear, dear Sister, that you may have trouble reading my scribbles. I have some rheumatism in my right shoulder which hurts so much that it is painful to lift my arm. Aside from that, I am much better and have gained a good bit of weight since my confinement. . . .

Your devoted sister,

R. E. C.

1. Napoleon responded to the American embargo by issuing the Bayonne Decree (April 1808) ordering seizure of any United States vessels entering ports of France, Italy, or the Hanseatic towns. Enforcement of this decree in 1808–1809 cost the United States some $10 million in goods and vessels.

2. James Madison (1750/51–1836), Jefferson's designated successor, was elected to the presidency in 1808. Charles Cotesworth Pinckney (1746–1825) of South Carolina, the Federalist candidate, received 47 electoral votes to Madison's 122.

To Charles J. Stier[1]

Riversdale, 10 December 1808

Dear Brother,

. . . What a delightful trip you had with your wife. I do not know if is indolence or the impossibility of carrying it out, but the taste for traveling no longer tempts me. It is undoubtedly agreeable to see lovely land-scapes, above all in the society of loved ones, but the inconveniences to which one is subjected before reaching them, the bad beds and musty inns, etc., seem to me to counteract all the pleasure one gets, added to which there is the regret for the loss of charming acquaintances met on the journey never to be seen again! I would more willingly go fifty leagues to see a fine play than the most beautiful scenery.

I am much obliged to you for the execution of all my commissions. I regret infinitely that you could not send them to me before this aggravating embargo came on. We work here still without pause. A lake just finished, which looks like a large river on the southern side, gives a very beautiful effect and furnishes us at the same time with fish and ice for our ice-house. I have intended a hundred times to send you our plan, but when I am writing to you I always have too little time to copy it. The old ice-house near the house was not good, because it leaked. We have built a new one in the wood beyond the stables. It is covered with straw and surrounded with great fine trees and looks like a little hut. A little farther on, a negro cabin gives the same effect and another we intend to build supported by columns will look like a temple. Our flower garden on the terrace is not yet completed, but I am raising a quantity of heliotropes to transplant outdoors in the summertime with the geraniums, jasmine, rose bushes, etc. On the north side we have the loveliest possible lawn.

Have you read *Corinne,* by Madame Staël-Holstein, an extremely interesting new romance?[2] I should like to be able to send it to you. In such a retired life reading is a relaxation after my domestic cares. . . . Poems, books on travel, and lives of our contemporaries (formerly not obtainable until after their death) are my favorites. You know how books travel in this country (much to the detriment of their covers), but it is an excellent idea. The expense of a complete library would be too great, so everyone purchases several new volumes each year, and they are loaned around and their merits discussed, which clears up the estimates on both sides.

You write, dear Brother, that you don't understand how anyone could attach so much importance to the care of a tree, to an equipage, or to a piece of furniture. But you are very fortunate to be able to pass your time with friends at will, while I am far removed from all those dear to me in whose society I could freely give way to my impulses. I must confess that a visit, above all from women, seems often too long for me. There are so few really amusing people. We have added a Mr. Stoddert to our set. He is a very learned man who has ruined himself in speculations of all kinds.[3] His two daughters are extremely attractive and better bred than young American girls generally are. Having lost their mother when they were very young, their father has brought them up in a way which he should certainly reap the rewards of in comparing them with their companions.

I ride horseback sometimes, and I bought a very fine horse last year. A good lady's horse is difficult to find and as this one was perfect, my husband was induced to give $200 for him. We always have four fine carriage horses, [but] our old carriage is very dilapidated and with this embargo a new one is not to be thought of. Quite a small vehicle serves me to go shopping in Georgetown. But what I would like to describe to you is a pony of my husband's, named Savage, of the breed called Texas pony. He was caught quite young with his mother in Mexico and some time I will send you his portrait. Black as ebony with a white stripe beginning at the head and continuing over its quarters, with two more on each side joining at the neck—it is the most beautiful animal I have ever seen. Several people have wanted to buy it to send to England. We have two of its foals at present which promise to be beautiful too. . . .

I must confess, dear Friend, that you have alarmed me as to the state of our dear father's health. You tell me that he often has attacks of weakness. That must be a recent thing for certainly he was not subject to them here. When I think how little hope I have of ever seeing him again, I can hardly refrain from regretting my situation here. Perhaps I shall never see any of you again. . . . I had no intention of touching on so afflicting a subject, but a very sad loss we have just had has disposed me to melancholy. . . . Benjamin Lowndes was one of our best friends, and it was only last week he dined here and seemed in perfect health. A pleurisy carried him off in three days and left his family without support. My husband was appointed one of the executors which gives him a great deal to do at this time. . . .

Your affectionate,

R. E. C.

1. Carter Trans-MHS.

2. *Corinne,* published in 1807, one of two novels written by Madame de Staël (1766–1817), features an aristocratic heroine in conflict with society. Its author, born Anne Louise Germaine Necker, was a prominent French critic and novelist who was exiled by Napoleon several times for her political beliefs.

3. Benjamin Stoddert, secretary of the navy from 1798 to 1801, had moved from his fine Georgetown house to Bladensburg to inhabit Bostwick, the girlhood home of his late wife, Rebecca (Lowndes). Stoddert had been heavily involved in land speculation in the District of Columbia and had monetary difficulties up until his death in 1813.

To H. J. Stier

Riversdale, 12 December 1808

. . . Our political horizon becomes darker each day. People talk openly of dissolving the union of states and if, as we fear, they continue with the present political system, that time is not far away. What the outcome will be is impossible to predict, but I am greatly alarmed about the public bonds. (However, it seems that no one else has such fears because they are higher than they have been for a long time.) Jealousy between the states of the south and those of the east, which has always existed, increases daily because of the former's haughty and uncompromising conduct.

In case the states do separate, what will become of the public debt? The southern states are not interested in it and were always noted for not paying their own debts. Would the others have sufficient good faith to repay all by themselves a debt contracted when they were in partnership? Well, I don't know what to think, but if this embargo is not lifted soon, a civil war is inevitable. I'm sorry to be such a gloomy prophet, especially since I may be alarmed without reason. . . . If you read [the newspapers], you can judge for yourself America's present condition. . . . My opinion is that a separate republic of the northern states will be formed, and after a lot of turmoil, a monarchy in the south.

Everything is paralyzed here—there is a complete stagnation in business. At the moment there is only one way in which this country is improving—that is in its roads. They are making some very good ones. For some time [Charles] Carroll of Annapolis has been investing all his money in shares of these public roads, which we call "Turn Pikes." One is planned from Baltimore to Washington. Yesterday people came by here to survey and fix the right-of-way, and they dared to mark it all through this property, passing very close to the stables. We will oppose this and it is only by force that they will obtain my consent. If they would make it on the other side of the Eastern Branch, it would be a great benefit for us, giving us an excellent road to Washington and Baltimore which would greatly diminish the distance.[1]

[*continued January 1809*]

1. Despite Mrs. Calvert's vehemence about protecting her property, the Washington-Baltimore Turnpike was constructed on the Riversdale side of the Eastern Branch.

To H. J. Stier

[Riversdale], [n.d.] January 1809

My letter was started a long while ago and now will be sent—thanks to Mr. Madison—on a government ship which is going to set sail.[1] Please, dear Father, accept our earnest wishes for your happiness during the coming year. . . .

They just passed new laws to reinforce this detestable embargo.[2] In the

New England states there is great ferment, and we fear every day hearing news of a revolution. In Boston, New York, and all the cities north of Philadelphia, they have already called assemblies of the people (which our constitution permits) and have established committees of surveillance and of public safety. Several members in the Congress have solemnly declared that the people are not obliged to obey these new laws, since they are not constitutional. . . .

Enclosed you will find a certificate of life attested by the Swedish consul. . . . I am sorry I couldn't get you the tulip-poplar seeds, but it is forbidden to export the least thing. As soon as the embargo is lifted (if it ever is), I will get you some. . . .

Your affectionate daughter,

Rosalie E. Calvert

1. James Madison, although elected president, had not begun his term and was still serving as secretary of state.

2. The Enforcement Act, passed in January 1809, provided for strict enforcement of the embargo, with severe penalties for evasion.

To Isabelle van Havre

Riversdale, 20 January 1809

Dear Sister,

. . . You are perfectly right, dear Friend, it seems a whole century since I have seen you, and I feel that every year we are apart increases the distance between us. So many things have changed during these last six years. Here my little niece Louise is now a big girl, [old enough] to be married, and I picture her as amiable and very pretty.[1] But where will you be able to find her a good husband? I don't like the vogue you have there for a very young girl to marry a man old enough to be her father. It is unnatural, and it is impossible for such marriages to be happy. I wish you could bring her here—with the fortune she will have, she could have her choice of all the beaux. What a pleasure it would be for me to introduce Louise into society here!

Why didn't you all agree with your husband who wanted to come back to America? But what am I saying—we, too, may be on the brink of a revolution. I have written to Papa and Charles about my fears on this matter, so if you are curious about our political affairs, they can satisfy you. But I don't want to waste the little time I have to write you discussing (or even more, talking nonsense about) politics. . . .

You ask what we do at Riversdale. Well, we work, each at his own task, from morning till evening. We are content (even happy, as I forget for a moment that I am so far away from you). Everyone admires our house.

My Caroline is exactly like your little sister was, and with all her faults. Your godson George is an excellent boy and everybody's friend. My youngest is a large and very good baby, resembling his brother a lot, although much bigger and stronger than George was at that age. However, it is my little Eugénie I wish I could describe to you, but it is impossible and anyhow you would accuse me of partiality. She is so good, so lovable, so happy that she is everyone's favorite. It is impossible to see her without loving her. I continue still to be a schoolmistress (much against my inclination), but what can I do? We cannot find the kind of teacher I want. If I had nothing else to do, it wouldn't be a problem, but household duties frequently interrupt the lessons.

I gave your compliments to all your friends and they all send regards, especially Richard Lowndes. We just lost a valuable friend, his brother Benj[amin] Lowndes. The strange thing is that he predicted his own death a month beforehand, when he was in perfect health. My husband is strongly affected by this loss—he knew him intimately for thirty years. Benj[amin] L[owndes] appointed my husband executor of his estate—proof, doubtless, of his great confidence, which is flattering, but it also causes much work and worry. We have already been embroiled in this way in another person's affairs—it was for Mrs. Law when the separation between her and her husband took place. It was necessary to appoint two trustees and the choice fell on Thomas Peter and my husband. Consequently, they became guarantors for the payment of $5,000 for a small countryhouse near Alexandria. Mrs. Law, who should have received a considerable sum which General Washington left her, still hasn't been paid, and lo and behold, Peyton of Alexandria from whom the property was bought, has instituted a suit against Thomas Peter and Mr. C.[2] They say there is no better experience than that acquired at one's own expense, and surely this lesson will prevent us in the future from ever standing surety for anyone in this country.

Please, dear Sister, give me all the details about what you do, how you spend your day. Do you go out in society every night? Do you still speak English? . . .

Adieu, dear Friend, embrace all your dear children for me and believe me with the most tender affection,

Your,

R. E. C.

1. Louise van Havre was now eighteen years old.
2. Probably Francis H. Peyton (ca. 1766–1838).

To H. J. Stier

Riversdale, 1 April 1809

Dear Father,

. . . So the embargo is lifted at last, but they have substituted so many laws—all just as bad—that we are just where we were before.[1]

In January [since] the 6 Pcts. were so high and there was talk in the Congress about a new bond issue, Gallatin advised me to wait before buying. So while I was waiting, I [thought I] could do something in tobacco according to your plan, but nobody wanted to sell. Everyone was waiting for another change, so I was only able to buy 100 hogsheads at $5 and $3—and this sometimes one or two [hogsheads] at a time from people who had the sheriff at their heels. However, those 100 hogsheads are all of excellent quality, with even a few of yellow [tobacco], and if it were possible to ship it, you would make a considerable profit. My husband thinks there is a certainty of making a good profit, but if the speculation does not succeed, I will regret not having managed your affairs well. . . .

Now let us put business affairs aside—I must tell you a little about myself. We have lost our poor little Louise. I have described her condition to you; for some time she grew weaker and weaker and on the 23rd of March it pleased God to call her to Him. It is a terrible thing to lose a child, but I am trying to bear it as best I can, submitting to God's will and bearing in mind that she is happier now than she could be here.

The others enjoy good health and excellent constitutions. I wish I could send you my youngest—he is a fine, big boy, and everyone flatters me that he greatly resembles you. George is the most industrious child I have ever seen; he is always working and at the same time shows a great facility and care for learning, to which he adds a most amiable disposition. A schoolmaster now comes to give them lessons twice a week; the other days I do it myself, but that takes up much time. . . .

The winter has been very hard, and now spring is wretchedly bad. Here it is April and the peas are barely up. We had planned to build a gristmill this summer, but being unable to sell our tobacco, we have to postpone that. . . . These last two years, we have made a nice profit by buying some lean young steers in the spring at $11 to $14 each and selling them in the fall for $22 and $30 apiece. Similarly, we bought sheep for $3 and sold them for $5, sometimes $7.

You tell me in your letter that you have no doubt that we are now well-to-do and able to begin making acquisitions of property for our children. Perhaps, dear Father, when I answer you "No," you will accuse me of lack of economy, even of extravagance—but I am too honest to tell you "Yes," when this is not the case. We certainly would not spend our income on living expenses solely, and don't forget that every year since our marriage we have increased our capital. We have acquired almost 1,000 acres of land, one parcel at Mount Albion and a small tract here, and some negroes. Last year we built a mill at Mount Albion. Since our stay here, we have paid very large amounts annually to finish the house and now the grounds, to establish the cattle, etc., not to mention our furnishings, equipages, etc. We want to finish all the improvements and be able, finally, to rest. Not being able to sell our tobacco crops of 1807 and 1808 is particularly unfortunate for us. The land we have acquired is for our children; similarly, our negroes are increased by a third.

A property adjoining us here . . . of excellent quality, almost entirely in mature forest, [and with] soil infinitely more fertile than Riversdale, is a purchase we have wanted to make for a long time. . . . I think it could be had for ten pounds an acre, cash, and is it not, dear Father, for the benefit of our children? . . .

I often walk in the garden, contemplating the roses I saw you plant here (and which for that reason I will always keep at the same place). I also have a Seigneur pear tree which you grafted yourself in Annapolis, that I planted at Mount Albion and, from there, brought here. I hope it will bear fruit this summer. How many memories these things give rise to. I recall the times I walked with you and the lessons about gardening you gave me. It is sometimes comforting to reflect on the happy future that religion promises us—without that, we couldn't bear the sorrows and privations which surround us. . . .

Your affectionate daughter,

Rosalie E. Calvert

1. The embargo was repealed by passage of the Non-Intercourse Act, which Jefferson signed in March 1809. The new law reopened trade with all nations except France and Great Britain; in the event either of those two nations ceased their violations of neutral rights, the president was authorized to resume commercial relations.

To Charles J. Stier[1]

Riversdale, 1 April 1809

. . . Alas, we are only too well convinced that this government and the Federal Union cannot exist without a respectable navy, but our wretched President is, I fear, one of those wavering, weak characters and although in reality an honest man, he will do as much harm as his predecessor. This country has reached a very alarming crisis. Torn by two parties, the eastern states jealous of the South, Congress enacting laws it is unable to enforce and obliged to retract them afterwards only to substitute equally bad ones, our flag insulted at the same time by both England and France—and all this the result of the administration of the wretched Jefferson. . . .

I am entirely of your opinion as to the bringing up of children. Chance doubtless has much influence over their inclinations, and a clear-sighted and watchful mother can be most useful to them in keeping her eye on all their actions, and without antagonizing them she can imperceptibly instruct them how to think and act rightly. Observing and studying their inclinations, she may choose the career likely to make them most happy, for one lad brought up to be a lawyer might have been a second Linnaeus, while another following the plow murmurs to himself dreamily the verse he read in the last almanac.

I am much obliged to you for your offer to introduce George to your world when he shall have reached the suitable age. I think several colleges north of Philadelphia are excellent, among others, Princeton, Cambridge, etc. But I greatly regret the lack of young girls' schools. This is beginning to worry me so much. Caroline is now nine years old, and I know of no good school to which I could send her. I do not like the young girls' manners here. . . .

Adieu, dear Brother, I must finish although I intended writing you a long letter, but I will do so another time for I have a violent headache today. . . .

Your devoted sister,

Rosalie E. Calvert

1. Carter Trans-MHS.

To Isabelle van Havre

Riversdale, 1 April 1809

It has been a long time, dear Sister, since I have heard from you. . . . Papa told me that you were expecting an addition to your family, but he didn't say when. . . . I am busy embroidering a little bonnet that I can send you inside a letter. I am also going to undertake a child's frock . . . and hope for an opportunity to send it. . . .

We lost our poor little Louise the 23rd of March. . . . Although I should regard it as a blessed end that it pleased God to call her to Him, it still grieves me very much. It is most painful to lose a child, and I always reproach myself for my imprudence in riding horseback when I was pregnant. . . . She would have been extremely pretty—her features were the finest I have seen. We experience only pain in this sad sojourn here. It is fortunate that we have such a consoling future existence to look forward to, to aid us in bearing the obstacles and afflictions we encounter daily. You can imagine, dear Friend, how painful my situation often is. It is so sweet to be able to communicate these thoughts to one's friends— how it does comfort one! But I must stifle mine in silence. Write me often, I beg you, dear Sister. You can't imagine with what rapture I receive your letters. You, never having been in a country so far away from your entire family, can have no idea of what I suffer.

3 May [1809]

This letter was begun a long time ago and today I received yours of 22 September 1808. I think that you were in as low spirits [then] as I was when I began this one. So I am going to try to be cheerful now, because truly one is wrong to take the disappointments and difficulties we encounter daily too much to heart. Let us do all the good we can and submit ourselves with humility to the decrees of Providence, and we will probably be happy here, and certainly hereafter. I am rather of the opinion of Dr. Pangloss that all is for the best.[1]

Being subject to low spirits is a great nuisance. I often feel that if I weren't so far away from all of you, I would have more reason than most of my friends to be happy. My husband, you know, has a cheerful disposition, and although he loses his temper easily, it passes over immediately. Besides, he is as indulgent and obliging as could be and lets me do anything I wish.

Our poor niece, Mrs. Peter, is most unlucky with her children. She had a son the age of my Eugénie whom she lost last year. She came to dinner here just day before yesterday and when she returned home, she found her little daughter of seven months somewhat ill. She sent for the doctor and three hours later, the child was no more. Mrs. Lewis just lost one of her children, too.[2]

. . . You would be surprised to see the amount of work we have done here since your departure from America. At present we are still using two masons and two carpenters to make improvements, along with sixteen of our negroes since for [the past] two years we haven't made a [tobacco] crop at Riversdale. We have planted a quantity of fruit trees of all kinds, grafted for the most part by Mr. Calvert, as well as some walnuts, etc. . . .

Your devoted,

R. E. Calvert

1. Mrs. Calvert neglected to complete the quotation: "All is for the best in the best of all possible worlds," from Voltaire's *Candide* (1759).

2. The infant Peter children were Robert Thomas (1806–1807) and Martha Custis Castania (1808–1809). The Lewis child was Fielding Augustine (1807–1809).

To H. J. Stier

Riversdale, 9 June 1809

. . . I trust that opportunities to write will become more frequent, although I fear that the amicable settlement of differences we just made with England will bring forth a declaration of war from France as soon as they hear the news in Europe.[1] That would probably be more troublesome for our correspondence than the embargo we have complained about for so long.

In my last letter I told you I had bought about 100 hogsheads of tobacco for you at $5 and $6. Since then the price has increased by one dollar and apparently will go higher. . . .

You asked me for some more tulip-poplar seeds, but when they lifted the embargo, it was too late to do it. I will take care of it next fall. . . . Do you still admire this tree more than any other? We don't find it worthwhile to plant here. For wood for carpentry, [the tulip-poplar] is only good when it is in large forests; trees that have been exposed to the wind are worthless, and they are not beautiful when they are old, having few branches and fewer leaves. Another disadvantage is that grass never grows under tulip-poplars. I asked you to send me some larch seeds, which we want to plant in large tracts. . . .

The other day my husband went to a "sheep shearing" sponsored by Mr. Custis, who is still giving prizes. He is a singular man, but with all his fanciful schemes of industry he spends a lot of money to no gain and neglects his affairs and the supervision of his properties. There were more than 100 people present, [and] a very well-provisioned table set on the banks of the Potomac under a pretty tent 70 feet long, adorned on the inside with garlands of laurel. All the guests were asked to come dressed in American-made clothes. The wine had been made in Virginia, as were all the beverages—apple brandy, peach brandy, whiskey, etc. It was a completely patriotic fête.

I am sorry you couldn't send me some Merino sheep—it would be a wonderful acquisition for us. A few have been imported into New York, but they are not to be had [here]. I think I wrote you that I, too, am a manufacturer—all the women in my house are dressed in pretty cloth made right here. All told, it costs me about three shillings a yard for a one-yard width.

29 July [1809]

This letter, dear Father, was started a long time ago. I got your letter of April 1st the other day. . . . I don't think there will be sufficient funds at present to do all that you direct. McEwen bought some 6 Pcts. for the amount of your April 1809 checks. The remainder of your January checks, after deducting for the tobacco I bought for your account and the sum of $892 for me, also has been sent to McEwen, amounting to nearly $6,000. He wrote me the other day that because of the scarcity of bonds on the market, he had bought only two certificates, costing about $1,824. He received $5,480.89 from your July checks and $651 from the Bank of Alexandria, making about $10,307 that he now has on hand. This is not enough to buy the two certificates for Charles and one for you, so I instructed him to buy first the $1,653.46 [certificate] of nominal old 6 Pct. stock in your name [and] then the $5,774.25 certificate of permanent 6 Pct. stock in Charles' name. Then since there won't be enough left to make up the sum of $5,482.22, [I instructed him] to put the rest in Charles' name and I will use your October dividends to make up the balance and will also begin in October to use Charles' dividends in his name.

You mention being surprised that purchases are at 101 3/4. The certificates McEwen bought last April were at 102 and now they are 102 1/2. If there were a new issue, the bonds would go down, but otherwise I think they will continue to rise. The English buy a lot of American bonds.

We thought our differences with England were entirely settled, and now comes the news that Mr. Erskine went beyond his instructions and [England] will not ratify the arrangements he made.[2] I think there was a lot of connivance and bad faith on the part of our government in this affair. Once again this is bad for our tobacco. As for you, I think you can be sure of making a profit, but we cannot hold out for a long time. If this state of affairs continues, we will have to sell at a low price. . . .

Your affectionate daughter,

R. E. Calvert

1. Following passage of the Non-Intercourse Act opening trade with all nations except France and Britain, British minister David Erskine stated that Britain would repeal the 1807 orders in council, as they applied to the United States, effective June 10, 1809. Unaware that Erskine had not been so authorized to speak for his government, President Madison issued a proclamation (April 19, 1809) legalizing trade with Great Britain.

2. British minister David Erskine was recalled in 1809, and the arrangements that he had made for reopening trade between the two nations were disavowed by his government. President Madison revived the Non-Intercourse Act with Great Britain by proclamation (August 9, 1809).

To H. J. Stier

Riversdale, 1 September 1809

Dear Father,

. . . In your last letter of May 1st, you said that you were giving up the purchase of 6 Pcts. and 3 Pcts. as long as they were above par. I don't know whether you can invest your funds elsewhere as safely. All stocks are high. The Bank of Alexandria is below par, but I don't think it is a good stock. There is not a capitalist in that town—they are a collection of bankrupts and adventurers, so the bank couldn't have any good notes to discount. The [Bank] of Georgetown is above par. A bank is going to be established in the City of Washington, which seems well organized and which my husband will serve as a director.[1] You will see by the second article of incorporation that after six payments it will be optional to pay the remainder on the shares. So it will be advantageous to take a larger number of shares than the amount you want to invest. . . . I think, therefore, that it will be well to subscribe 500 shares for you which, following your instructions, I will take in my name. . . .[2] One reason the public bonds are so high is the number bought by the English. Several private individuals in England have the greater part of their fortune in American bonds. . . .

I hope you will find [the enclosed] accounts in order. If they are not, you must show a little indulgence for my lack of experience in these affairs. I told you I have stopped buying tobacco. Nonetheless, I think you will make a profit on what I have bought, but we still have to wait. It is all [stored] in the county warehouses. . . .

We are all quite well. My little Charles, whom I just weaned, is a robust and very pleasing young fellow. . . .

Your affectionate daughter,

Rosalie E. Calvert

1. The *National Intelligencer,* September 15, 1809, lists George Calvert among the directors of the newly formed Bank of Washington. The bank was capitalized at $1 million. Calvert remained a director and served as bank president from 1828 to 1830.

2. Investors only had to pay a portion of the value of the shares. Mrs. Calvert planned an initial investment of ten thousand dollars for her father in the Bank of Washington.

To Charles J. Stier[1]

Riversdale, 1 September 1809

Dear Brother,

. . . What unexpected news we are receiving from the banks of the Danube and what a formidable fleet they are arming in England, and what—but I think it is better for us not to talk politics at the distance we are from each other. One never knows what changes will have taken place before a three-month-old letter arrives. Let's talk about ourselves. You will hardly believe, in the light of my delay in replying, that I reread your letters often and each time with renewed pleasure. How I envy you who are able to divert yourself and turn your attention to your friends, while I am absorbed in business, in household squabbles, the worry of teaching children, etc.

All these vexations are doubled by the commercial obstacles which prevent our selling our harvests and consequently leave us without income. I was just about to engage a tutor who was quite what I wanted for my children, but I must put it off still for those reasons and continue to teach them myself, which not only bores me insufferably, but by confining me still more closely to the house is injurious to my health and confuses my brain so that I often reason falsely and don't have good common sense. Have you not remarked that schoolmasters are always stupid people, like wanderers from another world or from a dead and bygone century. . . .

Your affectionate sister,

Rosalie E. Calvert

1. Carter Trans-MHS.

To Charles J. Stier[1]

Riversdale, 30 October 1809

. . . Some time ago the public papers announced that the English were going to attack the island of Walcheren at the mouth of the Scheldt. That was quite dreadful for me, and today I see that an attack on Fort Lillo is planned and perhaps on Antwerp itself. Imagine what anxieties that is causing me, dear Friend. I had hoped amidst the extreme disorder prevailing over all Europe that the town which holds everything dear to me would be far enough away from the theatre of war to be out of danger. Surely you will not remain there! But so long a time must go by before I can have tidings of you. Then this immense horde of troops sent for your defense must be a great tax on our poor country, and will your country estates not suffer? I wish you had all remained here where we shall be safe, at least as long as England keeps her supremacy at sea.

However, we have our bickerings here too. The two parties—Democrats and Federals—grow more eager from day to day to know who will win. This year there will be a small majority against us in the Maryland legislature, but we triumphed in our county. My brother-in-law Edward C, being the most popular man, was obliged to enter the lists again for the public good and was elected, as well as your old friend and our neighbor, John C. Herbert. . . .[2] My husband took a very active part in this election. It becomes more and more important for landowners. It is absolutely necessary that we should smother party feuds which are formed here, or they would destroy us in the end. The other day you might have heard me giving orders for an entire ox to be roasted for the support of our cause. . . .

You ask me, dear Brother, if Mr. C is still as gay as when you knew him. I think not. He has generally more to attend to than he can possibly manage, which is not conducive to gaiety. He is still as affectionate and indulgent to me as he was. My four children are a boundless source of happiness to me. . . .

So you are living at Cleydael Castle in the summer.[3] I remember I was

Cleydael, Aartselaar, Belgium. Castle (with moat surrounding) dating to fourteenth century; girlhood home and dowry of Rosalie's mother, Marie Louise Peeters.
By permission of owner, Jean Francqis Leitner

always delighted when we went there to spend a week or two, and I have just described to Caroline the big doll which was there and which at her age I was always so happy to see again. Have you made any changes in the promenades? All those impenetrable hedges made them gloomy. If they were cut down, it would be a superb estate and I wouldn't exchange the house for a duchy! After you have read all the romances about apparitions and trap doors, don't you shudder passing by those towers and winding staircases in the dark? And when you sometimes hear the owls screeching, do you remember the day we climbed up together on a ladder to get the young [owls] on the roof of one of the towers, and they pecked your hand?

Do you still paint? I would like to send you a copy of the fine view I see from my window while I am writing. There is such a variety of autumn foliage in one of the clumps of trees on the right. A very young hickory seems gilded, beside it a maple is entirely of deep red and a young magnolia of tender green, while a half-dozen other trees of different tints are reflected in the water. It is the loveliest season in America. . . .

R. E. C.

1. Carter Trans-MHS.
2. Edward H. Calvert and John C. Herbert were two of the four delegates elected in 1809 to represent Prince George's County in the Maryland House of Delegates.
3. Cleydael [Kleidaal,] a fourteenth-century structure rebuilt in 1518, had come into the family through Mrs. Calvert's mother, Marie Louise Peeters. H. J. Stier had expressed the hope that when Charles married and settled down, he would take Cleydael as his residence. The castle, which still stands, is located at Aartselaar, about five miles south of Antwerp.

To Isabelle van Havre

[Riversdale], 30 October 1809

For quite some time, dear Sister, I have expected news from you each day and I always find myself disappointed. It was the beginning of May, was it not, that you should have been delivered, and since that date I have heard nothing. . . .[1]

I saw with much satisfaction that the expedition against Scheldt-Antwerp, which frightened me so, had been abandoned. . . .

I am surprised that your husband thinks eighteen too young an age to introduce Louise to society. At eighteen, a girl is at the peak of her beauty, which will only diminish after that, and a girl that age should not continue to be shut up in a convent.

I was so pleased to see by your letter that Papa is well and in good spirits.[2]

You write that I have enough children now and ought to close down the factory. . . . I agree with you that I have just the right number, and in spite of that I plan to increase it again in the spring.[3]

I would think myself extremely fortunate if I could procure for Caroline an education as fine as that I am sure she would receive under the supervision of Charles and our sister-in-law, but don't you think a girl should always be raised where she is going to establish herself? I feel that from my own experience. One always retains the impressions received in childhood and an attachment to the country where one's first years were spent which prevents being happy in another.

We have once again lost one of our best friends, Mr. Ogle of Annapolis. I would not be surprised if his widow remarries. . . .[4] I must ask your husband to do an errand for me—it is to send me, if the opportunity arises, three small casks of anchovies. In my last letter I asked you to send me two dozen darning needles, from the finest kind to those we use to mend stockings. I would be much obliged.

You are going to have quite a lot to do when Louise returns from the convent and makes her entrance into society. Do you often go out in society? Do you frequent the theatre regularly? Of all the public pleasures, that's the one I miss the most. And how does Papa spend his days . . . ? For some time now the letters he writes me are very short and generally almost entirely about business. . . .

Your affectionate,

R. E. C.

1. Jules van Havre was born in 1809. Isabelle had written that she was expecting in late May, and that "this little monkey was coming at a rather inopportune time," because she had planned to take her children to Paris for several months before presenting her daughter Louise to society (Letter-draft, IvH to RC, 20 March [1809], Cal S-V).

2. Mrs. van Havre reported that Stier had enjoyed the winter social season. "Everyone thinks he is young and gay for his age. Since Carnival time he has spent a lot of time in the country, going out on Monday and returning [to town] on Saturday. By Easter his flowers will be in bloom, [and since] his most beautiful plantings are in his town garden, he likes to stay there and usually doesn't move to the country until June" (Letter-draft, IvH to RC, 20 March [1809], Cal S-V).

3. This would be Mrs. Calvert's sixth child. She was thirty-one years old and had been married ten years.

4. Former governor Benjamin Ogle died on July 7, 1809, in Annapolis. His widow was Henrietta Margaret (Hill).

To H. J. Stier

Riversdale, 1 November [1809]

I honestly don't know what we are up to here—we remain always in the same situation—[caught] between two fires. One day it seems we will have a war with France, another day with England. Our government is weak and the nation divided over this matter, but no one who is not in the pay of France wants a break with England. Mr. Jackson, the new English Ambassador, is negotiating with our cabinet at the moment, and I hope he will succeed in settling everything.[1] He is a clever fellow—they won't find him as easy to dupe as that imbecile Erskine. The other day there were some horse races near Washington which were quite splendid, and Mr. Jackson's equipage surpassed everyone's. I did not attend this year since it increases expenses, and for us now it is the reign of economy. I don't see any hope of selling our tobacco for a long time. . . .

Do you still amuse yourself with your hyacinths and tulips, dear Father? I am busy planting mine. My display beds are in front of the windows of the house where they will make a handsome effect.

We plan to build an orangerie next summer. I have a small collection of plants in pots which are a marvelous source of entertainment for me—geraniums, heliotropes, jasmines, China rose bushes, etc. I don't have any aloes or any of those other plants whose only recommendation is their rarity and which lack beauty. Our neighbor Mr. Ogle always has a nice collection and we frequently exchange [plants].[2] Among the flower seeds you sent me three years ago, there were some mallows—some double yellow [ones] and others [of] puce—which are extremely beautiful and are admired by all.

My garden takes much of my time since I am totally in charge of it, [and] my children take the rest of my time. I employed a tutor for six months, but he didn't teach them half as much, and now I instruct them myself. Caroline and George read very well and are beginning to write well, too. I also teach them English grammar and arithmetic—they are in long division now. You can imagine, dear Father, how much time this takes, and having a large household to direct in addition leaves me few moments of leisure. I have, however, enough [such moments] to be able to daydream about being with you in the gardens at the Mick and in your pretty little dining chamber in town, where I spent so many happy days. . . .

I almost forgot to tell you that I am once again expecting an addition to our family, in the spring. We are all quite well. My little Charles is growing robustly, and he is the most pleasing boy you have ever seen. . . .

Your affectionate daughter,

R. E. Calvert

13 November [1809]

P.S. There has been no opportunity since I wrote this letter, so it has not yet been sent. I received your September letter, written when the

English were coming up to the city of Antwerp. This warlike preparation greatly frightened me, and it was with a great deal of pleasure that I saw they had not made any attack on our good city. Now it appears that they are going to sink several large ships in the Scheldt in order to ruin the navigation of that river. This is not, it seems to me, like their usual magnanimity and generosity and it is inexcusable, even against enemies. It seems like an act of vengeance because their expedition failed, and it is at the same time a base and cowardly act.

In your letter you tell me to buy land if possible. At present land in this county is very expensive—it seems that everyone thinks as you do. A few years ago there was very good land to be had for eight and ten pounds an acre; now very mediocre [land] is selling for $30 an acre. My husband has been trying for three years to buy a parcel of land adjoining Riversdale and cannot get it for ten pounds [an acre]. . . .[3] From time to time there are some good opportunities to buy land, but they are rare. Fortunes have increased a good deal here the past several years, and wealthy people want to have a good portion [of their fortune] in land. I will be watchful, however, and if there are good opportunities, I will not neglect them. . . .

1. Francis James Jackson (1770–1814) was British minister to the United States from 1809 to 1811.

2. Benjamin Ogle II lived at his Belair plantation in Prince George's County.

3. Mrs. Calvert was referring to Maryland pounds, which were rapidly disappearing from circulation but still being used in some land transactions. A Maryland pound was worth about $2.67 in 1809.

SEVEN

Caught in Europe's War

JEFFERSON'S UNPOPULAR EMBARGO on all American exports gave way to a new policy which only forbade trade with England and France, but these two combatants, engaged in a life-and-death struggle for dominance of the European continent, paid little heed to the American concern for trade. The French seized United States vessels in European ports and the British seized them on the high seas. America was being sucked into Europe's war.

Rosalie Calvert blamed Napoleon for the upheaval in her world and found it ironic that her European relatives were beginning to frequent his court. Her sister, Isabelle, was presented to the French emperor in 1810, and the following year Isabelle's husband, Jean Michel van Havre, was a member of a delegation from Antwerp to congratulate Napoleon on the birth of his long-awaited son. Van Havre, reported Isabelle, was also invited to attend "the little brat's christening."

Back in America, the Calverts' tobacco continued to pile up in the warehouses because of the endless European war. Due largely to their agricultural diversification, the Calverts were able to defray their expenses, but without any income from their tobacco crops, they had little cash profit. They were obliged to live frugally and had to defer new investments which could have generated income, such as building a long-desired gristmill.

Still, the Calverts were far better off than most. They had access to a growing urban market in the District of Columbia, which enabled them to sell their grain, hay, and livestock and thus make expenses on their extensive holdings. They also had access to Henri Stier's investment income and to his unfailing generosity, which averted any real hardship.

With foreign commerce so disrupted, the mails also became unreliable. Rosalie received fewer letters from her family, delivery was much slower, some letters were lost entirely, and others were opened and read. Rosalie was forced to make decisions on her own about her family's investments. She began to master the intricacies of investing in stocks and bonds, real estate, and commodities.

Previously she had mainly reinvested her father's dividends; now some of his major investments—treasury bonds and bank stock—were being redeemed, and she had to reinvest the principal. Seeking advice at the highest levels, she made major investments in tobacco, new bank stocks and treasury issues, and real estate.

Such financial dealings were highly unusual for a woman. The legal structure did not provide for a married woman to engage in financial transactions independent of her husband, and often she had to enlist her husband's name or bond to complete her transactions. Although she sought her husband's advice, he never dictated her choices or was the dominant figure in these matters. Rosalie viewed herself as her family's principal business agent, and the responsibility of taking care of their financial concerns weighed heavily upon her. She was proud of her growing competence in business matters, however, and she chided her brother and brother-in-law for their neglect of their affairs.

Two more Calvert babies made their appearance, Henry in 1810, and a daughter in 1812, for whom Rosalie again chose the name Marie Louise. Pregnant with her seventh child in twelve years of marriage, Mrs. Calvert asked her sister how she managed to keep from having more babies. Isabelle replied that abstaining from marital relations was the only effective method, later confessing with embarrassment that a recent "moment of folly" had been her undoing. Women of their day had few alternatives. Accurate knowledge of fertility cycles did not exist. Condoms, made from sheep bladders, and vaginal sponges were in use, but they were used for protection against venereal disease, not for contraception, and certainly not in marriage. They were devices used by prostitutes and men who frequented them, and women of the Calverts' and van Havres' social class probably knew nothing about them. The practice of coitus interruptus, another possible alternative, was proscribed by the Catholic church and was totally dependent upon male initiative and control. Discontinuance of sexual relations and menopause were women's only means of release from continual pregnancy during this period. Mrs.

Calvert confided that she was considering adopting Isabelle's method, but like her sister she found that it was not a realistic alternative.

To H. J. Stier

Riversdale, [n.d.] March 1810

Dear Father,

. . . You will see by the accounts that you now have 1,000 shares in the Bank of Washington. If I can still get some at par, I will buy more, but [the shares] have been going up for some time and I think they will continue to do so. It is one of the best stocks there is at present. I don't know if you are aware that the charter of the Bank of the United States expires this year, and it looks like Congress will not renew it.[1] This made its stock plummet by 30 percent in just a few days. People say Congress would grant a new charter on the condition that the main bank be located in Washington. If [this doesn't happen], then the Bank of Washington will become, in a way, the national bank. I plan to pay only $10 for each of your shares, which will amount to $10,000 invested in my name, and you will begin to receive interest on the first four payments next May 1st.

The 6 Pcts. fell by two points because of the new bond issue which is supposed to take place as soon as Congress adjourns. They will probably decline even further which causes me to wait to invest the rest of your money. It looks like this new issue will be advantageous. . . .

I didn't know you had any 8 Pcts. You should send me the certificates of that bond immediately, along with a power of attorney to transfer them to the United States. McEwen wrote me the other day that . . . $800 in your name and $8,500 in Charles' name in this bond became subject to redemption on 1 January 1809. It has borne no interest since that time, so you have already sustained a loss of one year's interest on $9,300. [McEwen says that] to obtain payment the certificates must be transferred to the United States. My husband will go to Gallatin day after tomorrow to see if it is possible to obtain reimbursement without the certificates, but I fear it is not and you will probably lose another year's interest.

It appears, dear Father, that the first speculation I made for you in tobacco will not be very profitable. Some [tobacco] is being shipped every day, but it doesn't seem quite safe to me at present. Dealers are buying now at 4 and 5 and at 4 1/2 and 5 1/2. If we could send yours to

Europe, you would make a good profit because all of it is of the best quality. My husband, who bought all of it himself, always rejected any that was not really good. We still have ours from three harvests on hand, too. . . .

We had a very hard winter and I am glad to see my hyacinths starting to show their heads. It has been raining enormous amounts for some time—the roads are almost impassable. Congress finally passed a law to make a new road from the Capitol to Bladensburg which will be a great boon to us.[2]

I am afraid that this country's situation is alarming, and I often worry about the stability of our government. Incredible as it seems, a French party has already formed in this country and by each ship a number of spies and intriguers arrive who do everything to stir up trouble. I don't like discussing politics with you—it can be dangerous for you, and our letters being so long en route contain outdated news. . . .

Your affectionate daughter,

R. E. Calvert

1. Actually, the charter of the first Bank of the United States was not due to expire until March 1811, but Congress considered and rejected a petition for the bank's recharter in 1810.

2. An act to incorporate a company for making certain turnpike roads in the District of Columbia, including one which would run from the Capitol to the Maryland line in the direction of Baltimore, was passed by the Eleventh Congress (*Annals of Congress,* 1810 [Washington, D.C.: Gates and Seaton, 1853], pp. 2530–40).

To H. J. Stier

Riversdale, 6 May 1810

Dear Father,

I just received your letter of 24 December 1809, which pleased me very much since it has been six months since I have heard from you.

I am delighted that you are taking so much interest in Louise's debut. Instead of making you feel old, having a pretty young girl to marry off again should rejuvenate you. I am sure she must be a most interesting young person.

In contemplating my children (with that partiality from which no mother is exempt), I frequently regret that you are unable to enjoy their company. You would love my sweet little Eugénie most of all. I am expecting another [baby] any time now and fearing that I will be unable to write you for some time, I must unfortunately now speak to you of business matters. . . .

I thank you very much, dear Father, for your generous offer to take our tobacco at $7, but it would be an abuse of your kindness. If I really find myself in financial straits in the future, I will take advantage of your proposal. . . .

[The following proposition] is only in case we were going to make some sizable land purchases: when good offers present themselves, tell me if you would approve if I bought them in my own name and paid you six percent interest for the amount invested. This is only a proposal since at present there is nothing interesting on the horizon.

[Letter continued 15 June 1810]

To Isabelle van Havre

Riversdale, 5 June 1810

Dear Sister,

It was with the utmost pleasure that I received two of your letters almost at the same time. . . . I have been without any news from you for over a year. I accept with pleasure the title of godmother to your little Jules and hope that he will continue to do well and that some day I will have the satisfaction of embracing him. . . .

I had a very good delivery.[1] Today is the fifteenth day—it's another boy. You say that I never told you the name of the last one—it's Charles Benedict. I named this one after our dear father, Henry Joseph Albert. He is doing very well. He has blue eyes and fair hair [and] is the first of my children to look like his father. I still haven't gone downstairs because it is so cold and damp; even though it is June, I have a big fire in my bedroom.

As of three days ago I have a tutor for my children—he is an Englishman between 50 and 55 years old.[2] This is a great relief to me. You ask me how I teach [the children] catechism. George and Caroline go over it with me regularly every Sunday, and afterwards I also have them read a chapter in either the New or the Old Testament. At present I am only teaching them one prayer, which I hear them repeat correctly every day—it is the Lord's Prayer. This is all that their age permits me to do up to now, since I think it is very important not to force too much discussion of religion on children before they are able to understand. A word too much on this subject can do a lot of harm. . . .

Your affectionate,

R. E. Calvert

1. Henry Joseph Albert, the Calverts' sixth child, was born on May 22, 1810.
2. George Henry Calvert, writing in his old age, recalled his tutor: "We had a tutor at home, an Englishman, lately come from the Old Country with his family, and who had begun by opening a small school in Georgetown—Mr. Gunston" (Calvert, *Autobiographic Study,* p. 41).

To H. J. Stier

[Riversdale], 15 June 1810

Today I have the pleasure of announcing to you the birth of a fine big boy who came into the world on the 22nd of May. He could not be in better condition, and I am fine too. I am enclosing a letter for my Uncle Albert, asking him to be godfather.[1] We will name him for you: Henry Joseph Albert. Caroline will be his godmother. . . .

Just the other day we thought [this country] was going to declare war on France, and there was talk of sequestering the properties of all the French here. In that case, I don't know whether the designation on your certificates, "inhabitant of Bladensburg," would save your investments. I think the best thing to do is just to keep quiet and not speak up, so perhaps they will forget about you. And I believe our government is too much under the influence of Napoleon to dare to offend him.

It is impossible for this country to go on long in our present condition. If the spirit of democracy persists, our government will not be able to maintain itself. It is impossible to predict how much time there is before this happens, but a change, probably accompanied by convulsions, seems to me certain. I don't like alarming you, dear Father—especially since I may be mistaken.

It is too bad that nearly all the public bonds are in the hands of the English.[2] A small proportion is held in the Eastern states, but I don't think there is a single certificate south of Philadelphia. Couldn't this influence the Americans (who grow more corrupt daily) in the event of a change of government (which can only take place by a general upheaval and a separation of the states)? Couldn't this consideration make them—how shall I put it—forget to pay their debts (which, as you know, is one of the traits of the national character)? On the other hand, even if this were certain to happen, I don't see any remedy or any other investment one could make, unless one took up English bonds which doesn't seem to have much to recommend it either.

. . . Following your instructions not to buy any 6 Pcts. above par, especially when a new bond issue was being contemplated, I did not invest your April interest or part of January's. It seemed certain that the new issue, which Congress authorized, would be advantageous. Finally, tired of waiting and with the July quarter approaching, I addressed Gallatin through the intermediary of Comptroller-General Duval [Duvall]. Gallatin had to go to Pennsylvania before answering, [but] at last I received from Duvall the letter enclosed here. This "different way" of which he speaks is, I fear, "a very bad way" for the government's credit. I think it will be the means by which they will take extreme advantage [of investors] in the future. . . .[3]

Your affectionate daughter,

R. E. Calvert

1. Albert Pierre Stier (1745–1816) was a younger brother of Henri J. Stier.
2. Foreigners, primarily the English, held approximately 70 percent of United States treasury bonds and a correspondingly high percentage of shares of the first Bank of the United States—a factor in the nonrenewal of its charter.
3. Gabriel Duvall (1752–1844) served as the first comptroller of the Treasury from 1802 until 1811, when he was appointed to the Supreme Court. The letter from Duvall to Mrs. Calvert is missing, but the gist of it was that the government was exploring means other than issuing bonds to raise money.

To Charles J. Stier[1]

[n.p.], 23 July 1810

Dear Brother,

. . . Your sermon on the employment of time and the faults we inherit is indeed excellent, and I said Amen with a sigh. I am going to take your advice and do nothing more myself. Then I shall lose my reputation as one of the best housekeepers of Maryland, but I shall console myself by imagining I deserve it much more. I have had a tutor for my children for some time, but in return I have lost my nurse and cannot find a suitable one. Here is my little Henry who requires all my care, but he is so good and dear that I cannot do enough for him.

My husband does not agree with you and says he cannot have anything done properly unless he looks after it himself, and I must allow that this is the last country in which to find good agents. [My husband] has numerous duties, especially when we have workmen. He is also director of the Bank of Washington, which takes a day every week, director of a manufacturing company in Georgetown, and principal agent of a road which is to be constructed between here and Washington. Then he has to direct the work of our different plantations, one of which is eighteen miles from here, which takes a day and a half every fortnight.

You have no idea how this country has improved since you left. We have all the luxury of Europe and have lost that simplicity which was worth far more. In the towns the change is astonishing. An excellent bridge has been made over the Potomac facing the Capitol, which shortens the distance to Alexandria considerably. That town does not prosper. Still, the Bank [of Alexandria] gave a dividend this month of a half percent more than last time. A cabal was formed to deprive the worthy Herbert of the presidency and give his place to that parvenu Scott, but happily it did not succeed.[2] Casenove [Cazenove] is a furious Democrat, I believe—a great French partisan and "up to anything."[3] John Herbert, who married a rich heiress, comes to see us sometimes and asks about you. . . .

Your affectionate,

R. E. Calvert

1. Carter Trans-MHS.

2. William Herbert (1745–1819) had been president of the Bank of Alexandria since 1801; he was the father of Charles Stier's friend John Carlyle Herbert. Richard Scott was a director of the bank.

3. Antoine Charles Cazenove was an Alexandria merchant. Charles Stier and the van Havres had business dealings with Cazenove when they lived in Alexandria and after they returned to Europe.

To H. J. Stier

Riversdale, 2 August 1810

Dear Father,

. . . Congress authorized a new bond issue, but the government has since decided that it would endanger its popularity [so] it will procure the money necessary (probably more than 3 to 5 million) by other means. All this is a mysterious affair, and I fear it will result in great abuses.

I think it will become increasingly difficult to make a good investment of money in this country. Everything seems so uncertain, especially if our weak and wretched government remains under the influence of France. Land is also expensive in Maryland because all the large property owners buy continually.

Presently there is a parcel of land which I hear is going to be sold for debt and which would suit you. It is on the banks of the Patuxent River, eight to ten miles from Mount Albion. It is very level and fertile land, and I think you could rent it out profitably. I have some information about it, and if it is sold [at a price] which would produce six percent, or at least not less than five percent, I will buy it for you. . . .

In my last letter I proposed that if opportunities like this arise and if you approve, I would buy them in my own name and pay you six percent interest. I have thought a lot about this, and I think it is better to give land rather than stocks to my children—especially to my daughters—and although that time is far removed, opportunities to make good purchases could become even scarcer. Besides, it would be a great advantage to have [the properties] in the same county in which we live. Our negroes are multiplying and within a few years could cultivate these properties, which in the meantime could be leased out although they wouldn't produce that much interest. Give me your advice on this matter, dear Father. Like you, I think that mediocre lands are always a bad acquisition.

It is unfortunate that tobacco doesn't bring much of a price these days. We are harvesting one hundred [hogsheads] now and this will increase annually as the negroes increase.[1] Last year we had a superb harvest of all kinds at Mount Albion: 90 [hogsheads] of tobacco, which made four [hogsheads] for each negro who works there, including the women, besides enough wheat, pigs, beef, etc. to defray all expenses of the plantation, salary of two overseers, etc. And please note that we did not cut one branch of the forest—it was the farmer who produced [all this]. . . .

Your affectionate daughter,

R. E. Calvert

1. In 1809 the Calverts owned ninety-one slaves, up from the seventy-six they had owned when they married ten years before. There were more slaves at the Mount Albion plantation, which had fifty-eight, than at Riversdale, with thirty-three at this time; this, of course, was due to the more labor-intensive demands of tobacco cultivation, the principal crop at Mount Albion. Less than half of these slaves, however, were of optimum working and reproductive age, considered to be from age fourteen to forty-five for men and fourteen to thirty-six for women. Mount Albion

had twenty-six and Riversdale had sixteen slaves in the optimum category (Prince George's County Tax Assessments, Personal Property, 1809, fols. 25, 29).

To Isabelle van Havre

Riversdale, 12 August 1810

Dear Sister,

. . . This morning I had a violent headache which your letters have almost completely cured. I believe you, dear Friend, when you tell me that you don't write more often for lack of time, because it is the same with me. Although I think of you constantly, I rarely write for the same reason. . . . The English packets (the only way I can trust for mail now) are ordinarily advertised in the newspapers just three days before they are to leave New York. I don't get this notice until a day after it appears, which leaves me only a few hours to write to you as well as Papa.

I recently acquired a tutor for my children which relieves me a lot, but he can only stay on for two years at most because he is unable to teach them French, which I very much want them to learn. Caroline and George also take dancing lessons twice a week. This is merely to give them an idea as they are still too young for intensive instruction, but during the winter I plan to make them practice every evening.

You are right to forget your grudge against ————[1] in order to give Louise the diversions she would otherwise be deprived of. As you know, we are quite passionate in our political opinions here, but I would sacrifice them all if Caroline were of an age to go out into society and I could even—I think—pay court to our Queen Dolla lolla—a sobriquet given to Mrs. Madison. Happily, our children are still so young that we don't have to do anything except attend to their education. This is fortunate since it would be embarrassing if they were older now—all our sources of income are strained at present and will, I fear, continue so for a long while.

Caroline is improving a lot and I am very happy with her, but I wish you could know my little Eugénie. If I should have her portrait done for you, you would think it exaggerated. I often contemplate her with a pleasure mingled with anxiety—such a child is too precious a treasure not to fear losing her. . . .

We still live very much to ourselves. Except for Mrs. Richard Lowndes whom I visit frequently, I hardly ever go out. However, I am going to take a short trip to visit several members of my husband's family whom I haven't seen in several years. I will take my two daughters and the baby with me. George and Charles will stay at home with their father. It is inconvenient traveling with children—it takes so much preparation. . . .

I greatly admire the changes you have made to your house—it must be charming. It did cause great amazement here that you have large card parties on the Sabbath, and as a matter of fact, I do not approve of it. This only day of repose could be better used. We speak of you often and my children never tire of asking questions. They are constantly surprised at the big difference between the city of Antwerp and the plantation of Riversdale.

You must embrace my little godson Jules for me. I do hope someday I can have the joy of seeing him. Would you give the letter and enclosed papers to your husband? You are all, it seems to me, quite negligent of your business affairs. There is Charles who has already lost two years' interest on $8,000 worth of 8 Pcts. because he forgot they were to be redeemed, and here is your husband who . . . always leaves a balance in the bank of between two and three thousand dollars.

Adieu, my very dear Sister. Many kisses to all your children. Mine send you a million, and I remain with the most sincere friendship,

Your affectionate,

R. E. Calvert

23 November [1810]

[P.S.] . . . Many thanks for the needles which I received in good order. I would be much obliged if (when you have an opportunity to send them) you would buy me a tea set in nice porcelain of 18 teacups and saucers and 18 coffee cups and saucers. I would prefer not to have the teapot, sugar bowl, etc., but if they don't sell them without, you can take them.

1. Left blank in the original.

To Charles J. Stier[1]

Riversdale, [n.d.] August 1810

Dear Brother,

I was agreeably surprised to see Mr. Calvert come in with a fat letter from you, dated the 30th of January. I read with regret that you were so annoyed with contributions to be paid, soldiers quartered with you, etc., but you seem to bear it like a true philosopher. Half by choice and half through economy we live much more retired than you do since the French have taken possession of your houses. Our children are a great resource in this solitude. My youngest, aged three months, is the most charming little plaything you can imagine. I have a tutor for the two oldest, but I am not satisfied with his attainments so he cannot stay much longer.

You tell me my letters are often despondent. I am not surprised, for I am often low-spirited and my epistolary style reflects it. You should feel how often I regret the absence of all my relatives. In five or six years when Caroline begins to go out, I hope I shall become more gay.

You ask me if I often look at the paintings. It would undoubtedly be a great diversion for me, but if they were unpacked a number of curious, troublesome people would be drawn here, for the reputation of these paintings is extreme from one end of America to the other, and then I am afraid of their getting spoiled. One can never be sure that sometime the door key might not be forgotten in the lock. So they are still in the cases in which you packed them, with the exception of a dozen small ones which were in the hall at Annapolis and which Papa packed separately. We have hung them in the drawing room, which is always shut up unless we give large dinners and that doesn't happen often.

The cases are kept in the coach house. . . . I had a platform made over the carriages where they are safe from any accident and in the north [part] of the house. It seems to me, however, a great shame to keep such a collection without deriving any benefit from it. Papa does not want it, I believe, nor does any other member of the family apparently. Wouldn't it be better then to send them to England, where one could sell them at a good price? I often see advertisements of sales of paintings in the London papers, and several days ago I read of one in which a Rembrandt went for £5,000 sterling and two others for £4,000 with many others for lesser sums, but all for very high prices.

[continued]

[n.d.] November [1810]

This letter has not been sent as there was no opportunity, but Mr. Francis Lowndes who is sailing to Europe has kindly offered to take charge of my letters. . . . If you happen to meet him you would oblige me if you would be kind to him. He is a worthy young man and very charming and is, besides, the nephew of our best friends.[2]

We received your letter to Mr. Calvert dated 24 July, Paris, with the power of attorney and the copy of the certificates of $8,500 [worth of] 8

Pct. stock. He will go to Washington tomorrow to attend to the matter. I fear a copy will not be accepted unless there are proofs that the originals have been lost. You should have sent the originals. When you send the warrants for refunding your converted 6 Pct. stock . . . it would be well to mention in the warrant that you empower Mr. Calvert to substitute another person. That would obviate the necessity of his going personally to Philadelphia. . . . He will wait until January to go to Philadelphia in the hope that we shall receive the powers of attorney for your converted 6 Pcts., as well as those of Papa and van Havre, and then one journey will do for all. Do not think, dear Brother, he grudges going to Philadelphia for you—on the contrary he tells me he is delighted to have a good excuse to go there.

The national bonds become scarcer every day. The reason is that they are nearly all owned by Europeans and the government buys a certain amount of them annually for their sinking fund. . . .

I shall try to see Mr. Warden who is now in Washington. As he has been with you, he is certain to interest me.[3] I should be greatly obliged if you would send me a deed for the land of Riversdale by the first person who comes over to us. Several years ago Papa sent me one, but it would not be valid here. . . .[4]

I am sorry to give you so much trouble. . . . We have gone to great expense over Riversdale and shall be obliged to continue doing so; therefore, it is very important for me to have an indisputably clear title. . . .

> [no signature]

1. Carter Trans-MHS.
2. Francis Lowndes II was the nephew of Richard Lowndes of Bladensburg. Mrs. Calvert wrote her sister that young Lowndes was going to England to visit a distant relative who would leave him a fortune (RC to IvH, 23 November 1810, Cal S-V).
3. David Baile Warden (1772–1845), diplomat and author, had served as consul *pro tempore* at Paris since 1808 and was back in the United States to secure his position. Charles Stier had been in Paris in June–July 1810.
4. The deed sent by H. J. Stier had been in Flemish.

To H. J. Stier

Riversdale, 30 August 1810

Dear Father,

. . . Bonds are still very high, and McEwen writes [that there are] hardly any for sale. Since Gallatin's report in October 1809, everyone expected a new issue any day and it was supposed to be for at least $3 million.[1] In April Congress authorized an issue without determining the amount. . . . I spoke with some high government officials to find out when [the issue] would take place, and they all agreed that it would certainly be done before July. . . . Finally, in July it was announced that the Secretary of the Treasury would obtain the money needed by other means. I wrote you previously that last winter Congress did not renew the charter of the Bank of the United States—there were endless intrigues during the entire session on this matter. Finally, it was refused, but now they think that the Bank, in order to obtain a charter, will lend the government the money they need and will get a new charter in return. . . .

I had intentions of buying [stock] in some private banks, but I don't know if this would be desirable. Banks are springing up everywhere and it is impossible to know which ones are safe. I don't have a lot of confidence in the Bank of Alexandria. At the last election they wanted to dismiss good old Herbert as president and put that wastrel Scott in his place. Fortunately, that has been prevented. The Bank of Columbia, I think, is very bad, and there are so many [banks] in Baltimore that they are bound to destroy each other—there are seven or eight banks there. I wanted to buy more in the Bank of Washington—with my husband a director, we know exactly what degree of confidence it merits. I would not have hesitated for myself as I believe it is one of the best . . . but since you already have $15,000 [invested], I was afraid you might not approve. . . .

This summer several companies were formed to construct public roads, canals, factories, etc., but since you don't seem to want this type of stock, I didn't take any, and I agree with you completely on this matter.

There are several wealthy people in Baltimore, such as Oliver or Thompson or Carroll, who lend their money to private individuals at six percent interest and hold lands for the mortgage.[2] The other day my husband proposed doing that with your funds for his brother, Edward Calvert, but not knowing if you would approve, I did not want to.[3] My brother-in-law (this must remain between us) was on the way to ruin, [even] with 10,000 acres of land and making 100 [hogsheads] of tobacco a year (including what he receives from his tenants). Several years ago my husband tried to convince him that if he continued to be negligent (for he seems to make no extraordinary expenditures), he would be ruined. He refused to believe any of this. His wife persuaded him to take a house in Annapolis, where she ran up all kinds of expenses. Finally, he had a quarrel with my husband who, with tears in his eyes, predicted to him that the patrimony he had inherited would be sold, but he stubbornly disregarded his advice. Now he finds himself overwhelmed by debts—I think he owes at least $20,000. He is in despair, and when it was too late, he opened his eyes and resolved to go back to his plantation to work and live with the greatest economy and not to undertake anything without consulting his brother. He also gave [my husband] charge of all the tobacco he had growing [and] voluntarily put himself under his guardianship. He is a completely honest man, but he is weak and [has] a shrew of a wife—she makes him quite miserable. My husband doesn't know where to start to pay his [brother's] debts because his land is a compact parcel and none of his neighbors are in a position to buy it. He is going to Baltimore soon to try and borrow $12,000, putting up 6,000 acres of land for mortgage.[4]

In your last letter you ask to what degree present conditions are affecting us here. You can imagine how much when I tell you that we cannot sell our tobacco for more than $5 and $3. We would prefer to keep it than to sacrifice it for that price, especially since it could increase quite suddenly. This would happen in a minute if the ports of Holland were to open—then we would be sorry for having given it away. However, this situation causes us troublesome delays and privations of all sorts. It is even more vexing because we are making more than 100 [hogsheads] of tobacco a year now, and we have 300 in storage, with 100 more in the barns waiting to be packed. We grow some grain, and we also make a small profit from the sale of pigs and cattle, though profit from [our cattle] is greatly diminished by the general lack of commerce. But all this together only defrays the expenses of farming—tools, overseers' salaries, etc. Our tobacco crop was net income.

We cannot substitute anything for this crop which comes close to it. Our land is not suitable for growing wheat. We are improving our forests and seeding new ones, but this is a far-distant profit. This summer we made bricks to build a [grist]mill, which would be extremely profitable, but since it is impossible to sell our tobacco we will have to give it up. We rented an acre of land near Spa Spring to build a tannery. The man who undertook it is quite industrious and a good manager, but he doesn't have enough capital. In leasing him the site for a term of 23 years, I planned on lending him half of the necessary capital and on taking half of the profits. Being so nearby, it could be easily supervised. Then all of our operations are thwarted by the Emperor of the French, and I see no good ending. For a long time it seemed impossible to us that this state of affairs could continue—that our government would be obliged to decide for

France or for England—and yet still we are at the same point. It is impossible to foresee the outcome of all this—the most clear-sighted do not understand anything any more. Everyone awaits in a sort of stupor what tomorrow will bring. It is like a recurring fever—you think each attack is the last and each attack renders all hope more feeble. So you can see, dear Father, that we are strongly impeded not only in our pleasures but also in our plans for improvements.

[*continued*]

[n.d.] November [1810]

It has been a long time, dear Father, since this letter was begun. . . . Here at last is an opportunity to send it, and you will receive your accounts up to this date. You will note that I now have 2,000 shares of Washington Bank stock for you. I don't think there will be any more available at par for the present. All the last shares I bought were from people who had the sheriff at their heels. Since it was the first year, when the expenses of establishing a business are always more, the bank only paid six percent, [but] in the future it is expected to pay eight. . . .

I don't know, dear Father, if I am using your money as you intend, but I always act as I think you would prefer. The 6 Pcts. are high and so are the 3 Pcts. . . . I greatly regret that I cannot have your instructions before [re]investing the bonds which will be redeemed in January.

You have told me to buy land, but good properties in Maryland are so expensive that you have to cultivate them yourself—you cannot get a five percent [return] from leasing them out. Land in Maryland is more expensive than in any other state, except near big cities like Philadelphia. [However] everyone I have consulted advises against stock and in favor of land, [so] I will get all the information I can on this subject in order to be ready to seize whatever opportunities present themselves. . . .

Your affectionate daughter,

R. E. Calvert

23 November [1810]

P.S.—I will be much obliged if you would send me a power of attorney to vote your shares for the directors of the Bank of Alexandria in order to destroy the plot of this Richard Scott against our good old friend Herbert. . . .

8 January [1811]

P.S.—After making me finish my letter in a big hurry in November, the young man who was going to convey it has postponed his departure from one day to the next. . . . I cannot let him leave without asking you to accept the wishes we make for your happiness during the New Year. In the past I have always added the wish of seeing you again, but that hope is now extinguished. I will not cross the Atlantic any more.[5] All that is left to me, therefore, is the prospect of hearing from you often, and I hope, dear Father, that you will make this wish a reality. . . .

1. Gallatin submitted a report to Congress in December 1809 in which he said that a new loan would be necessary to carry the government through the coming year (*The Debates and Proceedings of the Congress of the United States,* Eleventh Congress, First and Second Sessions [Washington, D.C.: Gales and Seaton, 1853], pp. 2186–90).

2. In addition to Charles Carroll of Carrollton, Mrs. Calvert was referring to Baltimore merchants Robert Oliver (1757–1834) and Hugh Thompson (1760–1826).

3. Mrs. Calvert correctly anticipated her father's reaction to her husband's proposal. Stier replied in no uncertain terms: "Don't have business affairs with your relatives—it can bring disunion" (H. J. Stier Letterbook, hereafter HJS Letterbook, [n.d.] June 1811, Cal S-V).

4. On March 2, 1811, George Calvert recorded a debt of $17,000 owed to him by his brother Edward Henry and secured by a mortgage of 6,650 acres of land in a tract called His Lordship's Kindness (Prince George's County Land Records, Liber J. R. M. 14, fols. 336–41).

5. Difficult economic times, escalating hostilities in Europe, and concern for the safety and interests of her growing young family led Mrs. Calvert to this somewhat dramatic, but prescient, pronouncement.

To Isabelle van Havre

Riversdale, 2 February 1811

Dear Sister,

I wrote you a very hasty note in January because at the time my little Henry was extremely sick with a severe cold and I thought I was about to lose him. But by the grace of God he is completely recovered. . . . I received your February and July [1810] letters—all very pleasant and [they] cured me of an attack of low spirits which was tormenting me greatly. I was very surprised to learn that Charles had gone to Switzerland. . . .[1] Many, many thanks for all the details you give me, especially those concerning Papa's pursuits. So you are determined not to have any more children—this method you have taken is certainly effective.[2]

So you have been presented to their majesties.[3] I am very glad you gave me a description of that, but good Heavens, dear Sister, you talk so much of republican pride that you would make a good American! Believe me, republics are a hell for people of wealth. We are completely weary of it here, and (just between us) they say it won't last for long. I too think a new monarchy—or rather a newly fabricated monarchy—and an overnight nobility a sorry affair, but everything must have a beginning.

I very much fear that we are on the eve of a revolution here. This government cannot continue on the present track—it is upsetting everything. . . . [Members] talk publicly in Congress of dissolving the union of the states. [Congress] turned down a new charter for the Bank of the United States. However, there is some hope that this question will be revived and that they will grant the Bank at least three years to settle its affairs. If not, the consequences will be many and it could bring about the ruin of a vast number, perhaps all, of the banks. . . .

You will see by the enclosed account that Cazenove did not send me any of [your] July dividends. . . . On 10 January 1811, he sent us $300 . . . [but] you ought to receive $320 [because of the increase in the dividend]. My husband immediately wrote to acknowledge receipt and ask him [about this]. . . . I think Cazenove lost a lot in speculations and in shipping tobacco to Holland.

Enough of business! Read these items to your husband, but do not show him my letters. They are too badly written to be seen by any other than those whose affection will excuse their faults. I have completely forgotten French and cannot spell two words out of a dozen correctly, and I don't have time to do it carefully. Besides, my children speak English all around me as I write—I often think my letters don't make good sense.

23 February [1811]

I am obliged to write you as in a diary because often after a long time with no opportunity to send letters, one comes up quite unexpectedly and leaves me with only a few hours notice. Mr. Calvert received an answer from Cazenove the other day, a copy of which I am attaching here along with a copy of your husband's account with the Bank of the United States. . . .

Congress definitely refused a new charter to the Bank of the U.S. I am afraid that there will be various annoying consequences from this. I advised you for the past year that this outcome was expected. It will complicate your affairs, too, because the [interest on the] 6 Pcts. and 3 Pcts. won't be paid into this bank any more, so your checks will no longer be valid. I fear myself that I won't be able to get this April's [income]. I can't tell you how to remedy this situation without getting more information—it was only yesterday that this matter was settled. Mr. Calvert will go to the Secretary of the Treasury to find out what must be done. In any case, you will have to send a power of attorney to receive redemption of the shares you held in this bank. . . .

I am sorry to learn that there are so few good prospects in sight for your sweet Louise. You complain about the morals of your young people, but I think you have an advantage over us. It seems to me that among our [young people] good conduct is almost considered a fault. Yes, and even among the married there are few who are faithful to their spouses—I believe you were not aware of that. I speak the truth when I assure you that in my entire circle of friends I am unable to find one whose conduct I could call above reproach.

I was just told that Mr. David Bailie Warden, who is appointed Consul General in Paris, will sail immediately and will take care of my letters.[4] So I just have time to assure you of the most sincere friendship with which I remain

Your affectionate sister,

R. E. Calvert

P.S. If you want to send your letters to Mr. D. B. Warden in Paris, he kindly told my husband that he will send them to me with the dispatches he sends to the Secretary of State. It will be an excellent opportunity to write me as often as you wish. Just be careful never to talk about politics which would compromise him, because in France they frequently open the letters.[5]

1. Charles Stier and his wife spent over a year traveling in Europe from June 1810 until September 1811, going from Paris to Switzerland, on to Rome, and ending in Vienna (HJS Letterbook, entries for 25 August 1810, [n.d.] January 1811, 7 July 1811, and 5 October 1811, Cal S-V).

2. Mrs. van Havre's method of birth control did not prove effective. In the spring of 1812, an embarrassed Isabelle reported to Mrs. Calvert that she was again pregnant: "In your last letter, dear Sister, you mentioned that you were afraid you were pregnant again and you asked me how we were managing not to have any more babies. Alas, that is one of those decisions that a moment of folly can do in. I've had experience and I am sorry to have to confide that I am five months pregnant. I am extremely downcast and rather ashamed. No one knows except Papa—Louise doesn't suspect a thing. I fear that another little brother may cut down on the number of her suitors—that is always a problem for girls. Ah, well, one can only be patient. I shall never again take a trip—each one unfailingly results in a baby" (IvH to RC, undated letter-draft, [Spring 1812] Cal S-V).

3. Isabelle van Havre was presented to the emperor Napoleon and his empress, Marie Louise, during their post-wedding tour of the northern provinces in 1810, but her letter describing this event has been lost.

4. Warden did not leave until August 1811, when he and Minister Joel Barlow embarked together for France (see "Warden, Journal of a Voyage from Annapolis to Cherbourg on Board the Frigate *Constitution,* 1 August to 6 September 1811," *Maryland Historical Magazine* 11 [1916], 127–41, 204–17).

5. Warden visited Riversdale, probably on several occasions, and left one of the earliest descriptions of the house in an account of a summer visit in *A Chorographical and Statistical Description of the District of Columbia* (Paris, 1816), p. 156:

"The establishment of George Calvert, Esq. at Bladensburg, attracts attention. His mansion, consisting of two stories, seventy feet in length, and thirty-six in breadth, is admirably adapted to the American climate. On each side there is a large portico, which shelters from the sun, rain, or snow. The hall is ornamented with lemon-trees, geraniums, polianthusses, heliotropes, and other plants, which in the summer evenings, invite the hummingbirds to taste of their sweetness; and afterwards struggling to escape, they fly incessantly backwards and forwards near the cieling [*sic*], until from fatigue they perch on a stick or rod, when they are easily taken by the hand. In the saloon there are some fine paintings particularly Noah's Ark by Velvet Brueghell; the Judgment of Paris, and the portrait of Rubens, by this great master, of whom Mrs. Calvert is a relation." (Editor's note: Warden's measurements of the mansion apparently were of the central block only and excluded the wings. The room Warden called the "hall" was Mrs. Calvert's salon, and the room he called the "saloon" was her drawing room. According to the 1817 sale catalogue, there was no self-portrait of Peter Paul Rubens in the Peeters collection, but there was a portrait by Rubens of his brother Philippe to which Warden may refer.)

To H. J. Stier

[n.p.], [n.d.] February 1811

Dear Father,

. . . You will find the continuation of your account enclosed. You may be surprised that I invested so much in the Bank of Washington, but here are my reasons which I hope you will approve. My husband was in Philadelphia on the 20th of January to receive the repayment of Charles' 8 Pcts. We had a lot of difficulty obtaining payment of this redemption because Charles had sent a copy of the certificates instead of the originals. . . . Secretary of the Treasury Gallatin assured my husband that it had never been done without the originals. Finally, by Mr. Calvert giving his bond that he would be responsible for the amount of $8,500 and promising that the originals would be delivered to the office, he obtained from Gallatin an order for the payment. When he presented [this order] at Philadelphia, however, they were astonished and said it had never been done, but that they would follow the Secretary's orders. I do hope you can send me those certificates as soon as possible (as I understand that Charles is away traveling). . . . My husband also tried to redeem your converted 6 Pcts., but this cannot be done without a power of attorney. Gallatin laughingly observed that it was passing strange to have certificates without power of attorney in the one case and power of attorney without certificates in the other, but that the latter definitely was preferable. . . .

But back to Philadelphia and my investment of your money. McEwen had gone to Lancaster, but my husband spent a lot of time with his partners Hale and Davidson who advised him not to invest in the Philadelphia banks because all are quite precarious, except for [the Bank] of North America (whose shares are exorbitant and not for sale). [They said] that if the charter of the Bank of the United States is not renewed, it is possible all banks might fail. There were no old 6 Pcts. on the market, and 3 Pcts. were selling at 66.

Several things made me buy in the Bank of Washington. This bank is better managed and has a number of advantages over the others, such as [receiving] the government's deposits. Being one of the directors, my husband can know precisely what degree of confidence it merits, [and] even if the other banks fail, I think this one could sustain itself. Another advantage is that in case of a general upheaval in this country, with [this bank] being so nearby and with the certificates in my name, I could convert them more easily if it became necessary. So you now have $30,000 there and all the payments made, that is to say, at $10 a share. Congress granted this bank a ten-year charter and the Bank of Alexandria a continuation for [a like period]. . . .

I haven't received any of your letters since that of 29 January 1810, which I regret very much because if you have gotten mine, you could have given me instructions on the use of your money. . . .[1]

Your affectionate daughter,

R. E. Calvert

1. The mails were becoming increasingly unreliable. Stier complained that Mrs. Calvert's letters took much longer to reach him, that his letters had to be sent open, and that he no longer had access to news from America which would enable him to give instructions about his investments. He told his daughter to use her judgment and that in general he favored purchase of land and of United States treasury bonds (HJS Letterbook, 20 April 1811, and [n.d.] June 1811, Cal S-V).

To Charles J. Stier[1]

[n.p.], [n.d.] April 1811

. . . I have received your letters of 27 December and 17 January sent from Rome. I am quite vain that Mr. Calvert resembles as great a man as Titus! What an agreeable journey it must have been—I read your descriptions with much pleasure. Now that you are in the mood for traveling, why do you not come to see us? There is no more danger in crossing the Atlantic than in crossing the Alps, and you would not be away from home any longer. Some ships cross in thirty and even in twenty-one days from England. What a joy it would be to see you here, for I no longer have any hopes of coming to you. Our family is now so large that it would be impossible. You can imagine, dear Friend, how much it cost me to give up this project. It often makes me very sad. My position here is so isolated that I would willingly sacrifice half of my allotted years in this world to be able to pass the other half with my family.

Since your last letter you will have seen our Ambassador Mr. Barlow who planned to go to Antwerp.[2] He undoubtedly will have given you long accounts of this country and of the great improvements which have been made during the last few years. You know he is of the party in power, so as to the government—! But if he is sincere he can nonetheless give you many details about everything concerning America and especially financial matters which he understands very well. . . .

I hope you will find the accounts of my transactions for you in good order. . . . The books open for the new loan on the first of May, and I shall put your name down. . . . It was expected that the government would give eight percent, but Congress limited the interest on the loan to six percent. For my part, I would prefer banks to national bonds, especially as they give so much better interest. However, you say that you have no confidence in those south of Philadelphia, and the Philadelphia banks are so much above par—not necessarily because they deserve more confidence than the others but because in the Southern states there are few capitalists who invest their money in bank stock.

I am very sorry your money was so long uninvested, but that was caused by the advice of the best people. . . . In the future I shall always invest in whatever stocks seem best immediately after receipt of your dividends, as one often loses as much interest waiting as one otherwise gains. You cannot conceive to what extent everything is in confusion in this country. The most clear-sighted people are bewildered. I fear it will end badly, for we are going from bad to worse . . .

Your affectionate sister,

R. E. C.

1. Carter Trans-MHS.
2. Joel Barlow (1754–1812) was appointed minister to France by Madison in 1811 and served until his death in 1812.

To H. J. Stier

[n.p.], 1 June 1811

Dear Father,

Yesterday I received two of your letters which came by the same ship even though their dates were very far apart—12 March [1810] and 25 August [1810]. They had been opened and each of them numbered. . . .

You speak of being surprised that we are unable to find land to buy, but the reason is that all the wealthy people think as you do that no other investment is safe. [John] Addison's plantation near Washington has been bought by his brother-in-law, Dr. Shaaff, and the transaction has rendered the doctor quite odious since there is no doubt he took advantage of Addison's good nature and the pecuniary distress to which his lack of thrift had reduced him. The adjoining property belonging to another Addison could be had and would be a good acquisition, but it is offered with a lease for its owner's lifetime. For the past year I have continually kept myself informed about all properties which might be sold, but up to now I have found none which would produce a good return. Cramphin's [land] is [being] ruined by his nephew, but it has dreadful soil even for growing pines because it is all clay. . . . This year my husband bought the best part of the late Thomas Dick's plantation, which adjoins ours.[1] Peggy Adams' little farm is going to be sold; if it is cheap enough that we could make some interest, we will buy it and cover it with fruit trees—the soil is too worn out and poor to continue cultivating it.

24 June [1811]

. . . I thank you, dear Father, for your permission to buy properties for my account when any are offered which could become valuable for my children, and I announce to you with pleasure having made a purchase which seems extremely advantageous. And instead of the five percent you said would satisfy you, the income will be eight percent! I am enclosing the advertisement. The purchase price is $20,000 for 400 acres, which is $50 an acre. [The property] now produces $1,450 a year for one parcel which is rented to a Mr. McCoy for a seven-year term, and two other parcels are producing $150, making altogether eight percent on the purchase price. There is sufficient forest on the land and 60 acres of good meadowland. . . . The soil ought to become more fertile with each passing day as the tenant is obliged by the terms of his lease to utilize on the farm all manure produced there. Since 156 bushels of oats are consumed there daily, you can imagine the quantity of manure being produced. There are regularly 40 horses [there], and frequently up to 80, belonging to the different stages [stagecoaches] which converge on this route. . . .[2] [The property] is twenty miles from here. I think it is a valuable acquisition. The title will be transferred into my name, and you will see by the advertisement that there are three payments, for which my husband gave me his bonds. . . . We made the condition that we may, if we wish, pay the bonds before the term is up. So since there are no stocks worth buying at the moment, I will use the money from the redemption of your exchanged 6 Pcts. and your 8 Pcts. for the payment of these bonds, as soon as the Chancellor of Maryland has ratified the sale. . . .

You must, dear Father, give me ample instructions about the future use of your money and about [the total amount] you would approve of my [investing in] land. You will see by my accounts that you now have a large amount in the Bank of Washington. This stock continues to increase and is very hard to come by. . . . I think it will soon be one of the best stocks here. The government bought a number of shares the other day for the establishment of the navy and gives this bank some big advantages, such as payment of the droves of public employees and even some preferences over the Philadelphia banks. In the future I will use your money to buy some North American Bank stock if it can be obtained. . . .

Adieu, dear Father, I fear you are quite tired of reading my scrawl. We are all in good health. I learned with much pleasure that you enjoy such good health that you were not too tired to hunt for an entire day with Mr. van Havre. . . .

Your affectionate daughter,

R. E. C.

1. In 1810 George Calvert purchased thirty-seven acres of land on the Eastern Branch for thirty dollars an acre (Prince George's County Land Records, Liber J. R. M. 14, fols. 24–26).

2. This was the initial purchase by Rosalie Calvert of a property which included Spurrier's Tavern, a stagecoach stop in Anne Arundel County (in the present-day town of Waterloo in Howard County). The property was from the estate of the late John Spurrier, and it was sold in June 1811 at a public auction ordered by the Maryland Chancery Court. Due to complications with the title and negligence on the Calverts' part, the land was not recorded until 1832, at which time it was recorded in George Calvert's name (Anne Arundel County Land Records, Liber W. S. G. 17, fols. 193–95).

To Isabelle van Havre[1]

Riversdale, 15 July 1811

It seems to me, dear Sister, ages since I have received news from you. . . . You grow daily more indolent, I observe. I wish you had persisted in the desire you say you had at one time to return to America. Indeed I believe you will be obliged to do so for your [financial] interests, and I must confess that I do not like to have so great a responsibility resting on my shoulders as the management of such revenues entails, and especially because I foresee it will steadily become more difficult to do so creditably. If I were sure of succeeding, it would be a great pleasure, but I cannot conceal from you that my fears as to the stability of our constitution augment every moment.

I foresee an [in]evitable revolution and I fear its near approach. Do not think these idle crotchets—the best informed and most weighty people are of my opinion, and it is that of the most prominent Senators and members of Congress. A war with England, which our government will provoke, will be the prelude, and it is anticipated that the Eastern states will put themselves under the protection of that power. What then will become of the Southern states? They will either be torn asunder by anarchy or fall prey to Napoleon. In whatever way one regards the situation, it presents an alarming aspect. Any revolution would annul the public debt, but I fear that even if it were possible for the present state of affairs to continue, the debt would be endangered because the party now governing would not hesitate to pass the sponge over all their debts. But I will cease to act as ill-foreboding prophet!

I learned with much pleasure from your husband's letters that all your children are well. Tell me all about your two youngest boys, particularly my godson Jules. What a joy it would be to kiss him. If there are no good schools near you, send him to me and I will take care of him as my own child. All our little ones enjoy excellent health. The tutor I had was so worthless I had to dismiss him, and I have none at present. My little Henry is the most amusing little oddity possible. He runs all over the house and is never quiet a minute. I have just weaned him, which I did with much regret, but I was obliged to. It is a prospect which does not please me as I want no more children, and after this I believe I will adopt your way of not having any more. . . .

You ask me to give you all the news here. My sister-in-law Mrs. Stuart is very ill. They fear she has consumption and will not recover.[2] Custis' wife is also in very bad health, and I do not think she will live long. It is a great pity, for she is a woman in a thousand. She has only one little girl left, after losing three children, but the remaining one is charming.[3] Our niece Mrs. Law has secured a divorce and resumed her own name. She behaves very imprudently and is quite intimate with Mrs. Madison and the party we call in derision, "the Court." Mrs. Law has just left me after having spent a week here.[4]

They are making an excellent road from Bladensburg to Washington which decreases the distance considerably. A splendid bridge has been built over the Potomac opposite the Capitol, and it is nothing now to go from here to Alexandria. One is there in a few hours. . . .

Adieu, my dear Friend, I must finish. This will reach you through the courtesy of Mr. Barlow who is going as Ambassador to Paris. . . .

Your affectionate sister,

R. E. C.

1. Carter Trans-MHS.

2. Eleanor (Calvert) Custis Stuart died in September 1811 at Tudor Place, the home of her daughter Martha Peter.

3. Mary Lee (Fitzhugh) Custis did not die until 1853 at age sixty-five, outliving Mrs. Calvert by many years. Her only surviving child was Mary Ann Randolph Custis (1808–1873), who married Robert E. Lee in 1831. Two infant daughters had died in 1805 and 1807, and an infant son in 1810.

4. After living under a separation agreement for several years, Thomas Law established legal residence in Vermont in 1810 and filed for an absolute divorce from Eliza Custis Law. She did not contest, and the divorce was granted in 1811 (see Allen G. Clarke, *Greenleaf and Law in the Federal City,* p. 287).

Even before her divorce, Eliza Law "imprudently" began an open affair with a young French military officer whom she proposed to marry. The young man returned to France, a move probably arranged by Eliza's own family, who were scandalized at the idea of a remarriage, which neither church nor society would recognize as valid. During 1814 and 1815, a lovesick Eliza addressed numerous letters to the American consul in Paris, seeking news of her lost love (see correspondence from Eliza Parke

Custis to David Baile Warden [July 1, 1814, to July 14, 1815] in the David Baile Warden Papers, Maryland Historical Society, Baltimore).

To H. J. Stier

Riversdale, 7 December 1811

Dear Father,

. . . Today I have only a little time to write you because the [U.S.S.] *Hornet,* the ship by which my letter is going, is about to leave. They are only waiting for the Secretary of State's dispatches, which could be sent within an hour or not until a week from now. . . .

In your last letter you mention that there are some errors in the last accounts. . . . I believe that you are mistaken. The extracts which you sent me with that letter—transcriptions of my accounts—are not the same as mine. I think you made the error by forgetting the 400 Washington [Bank] shares purchased in March 1810, and marked on the enclosed account with an X in red pencil. If I am wrong and there are still points which are not clear, write me and I will do my best to correct them. I thought I had acquired an assistant to keep my accounts in my children's new tutor—he told me he had kept book for several years.[1] I don't know whether it is my manner or my not following the rules of the art or what, but we cannot come to an understanding. I had a hundred times more trouble getting him to copy this account out of my book than if I had done it myself. He is so slow to understand and even slower to get it done that I lose patience. He is occupied now with copying out and adding up the account of the tobacco bought for you in January 1809, but I don't think he will finish in time for it to go with this letter. . . . The public bonds are much lower and continue to fall. There is going to be a new loan. . . .

Your affectionate daughter,

R. E. Calvert

P.S. In your last letter you asked me to write you about the paintings. We opened them recently to see if they were being damaged. In the packing-case where you had put all [the paintings] of inferior quality, some are completely detached and thus are a little damaged, but as for the rest, they are in good shape. I didn't know that your portrait painted by Peale was in that case. I thought that Charles had taken it with him. You can imagine my joy when, opening the case, I first saw it. I have framed it and everyone thinks the likeness striking, but not flatter-ing. . . .[2]

[*Letter continued in March 1812*]

1. George Henry Calvert reported that the successor to Mr. Gunton, who lasted two years as the children's tutor, was another Englishman, a Mr. Bradley (Calvert, *Autobiographic Study,* p. 41).

2. Rembrandt Peale (1778–1860) painted H. J. Stier's portrait in 1799, while the Stier family was living at the Paca House in Annapolis. Peale wrote about seeing a part of Stier's collection of paintings at the time:

"[Stier] proposed to sit in his own house, as he wished to place before me three excellent portraits by Titian, Rubens and Vandyke, as objects of inspiration for a young artist. . . . The old gentleman was so well pleased with the effort I made that he volunteered to show me the greater part of his collection—and on the appointed evening, by the imperfect light of a single candle, and both of us shivering with cold, he carefully displayed to me his hoarded treasures. It was in vain I afterwards tried to induce him to show his entire collection to me in company with Chancellor Hanson, the only person in Annapolis of reputed taste in the Fine Arts" (Peale, "Reminis-cences," *The Crayon,* September 19, 1855).

Peale's portrait of Stier is in the United States in the private collection of a descendant of Rosalie Stier Calvert (1989).

To Isabelle van Havre

Riversdale, 12 December 1811

Dear Sister,

The opportunities to write you are quite rare now, and I just missed an excellent one last week for want of being informed in time. I can only write—with any certainty that my letters will reach you—by the public ships which the government uses to send its dispatches. My last letter of 15 July was entrusted to Mr. Barlow and I have no doubt that you received it. . . . I also think he could manage it so that I could get the candelabra, etc., that you bought for me. A large number of articles always come in these government ships—several ladies in Washington recently received a number of things that Mr. Warden sent them. . . .

I read [your last] letters with a great deal of pleasure for all the details of society you give me and especially those items about my dear Louise whose happiness interests me greatly. Surely you have determined be-forehand that if she should become attached to a certain person, you would not raise any obstacle. Otherwise, it would be cruel to let her be exposed for such a long time to the attentions and pleasing qualities of her Adonis. . . . I have often thought that when my daughter is out in

Henri Joseph Stier. Portrait by Rembrandt Peale, 1799.
Private collection, U.S.A.

society that as soon as a man makes the least advances to her, I will ask myself the question: "Is this a desirable match?" If the answer is no, I will tell her frankly and will convince her of the wisdom of discouraging every advance from the start.

These dancing parties in the country must be very pleasant for the young people, and I suppose often provide opportunities for the older ones to arrange some marriages. But how do you do it with this law of the Emperor that a girl of wealth cannot marry without his permission, which is probably granted only to marry his generals and minions? Please write me about that. I must give my compliments to your husband for the honor he had to be present at the christening. What a singular idea to revive the procession of the old Giant—that must have pleased the people. . . .[1]

My children are all well. We had a wedding in the neighborhood recently . . . which brought on several dancing parties. I took Caroline to one of these where there were going to be several children her age, which entertained her greatly, and she made her first assay. You will say that I am a very foolish mother, but I couldn't help thinking (while watching her dance for the first time with the best dancer there) that it was a good omen for her future success. She is, however, quite lazy about learning— everything that costs some effort fatigues her. George is much more energetic. He is the best dancer in the school, he applies himself, and he succeeds in everything he undertakes. He is also very cheerful and completely manageable—I am not aware of a single fault. He enjoys good health and a constitution proof against everything. Last summer he learned to swim in a very short time and he rides quite well. When I go to Washington, he often accompanies us and opens all the barriers.

I don't know if I wrote you that my sister-in-law Mrs. Stuart is dead. She left two boys and four unmarried daughters who are neither very pretty nor likable, so they will probably all become old maids. . . .

1. Jean Michel van Havre was one of a four-person delegation dispatched from the city of Antwerp to congratulate Napoleon on the birth of his long-awaited son in 1811. Isabelle van Havre reported this honor to her sister, adding that he would also attend "the little brat's" christening.

Isabelle went on to describe preparations in Antwerp for celebrating the little King of Rome's birth: "All classes of citizens, from the richest to the poorest, have been assessed for contributions to the celebrations. Dinners are to be given at the town hall and the whole city will be superbly illuminated. The famous giant called *groot Reus* [great Giant] will parade through the streets, accompanied by perhaps thirty floats like we used to see at Carnival, representing allegories, etc. All the cities are in great turmoil getting ready and the townsmen are weeping privately on all sides, but of course are obligated to pretend to be overcome with joy and join in the general rejoicing" (Letter-draft, IvH to RC, [April or May] 1811, Cal S-V).

The Giant of Antwerp, according to legend, had ruled the River Scheldt and cut off the hands of sailors who refused to pay him tribute.

To Isabelle van Havre

[March or April 1812][1]

. . . I am annoyed not to be able to write anything interesting about our society here, but all the people who compose it are absolute strangers to you, and besides I live as retired as a hermit.

Nevertheless, we often see the Lowndes and recently had a wedding in that family—Stoddert's daughter with Thomas Gantt who was in Antwerp some years ago.[2] Dr. Shaaff lost his wife and took another 18 months later. Betsy Chase, my old enemy, finally behaved so badly that she had to leave Annapolis. She had an affair with a married man (and with several others, I believe).[3] Mrs. Caton still has three of her daughters unmarried, in spite of common knowledge that they will each have $30,000 the day they marry.[4] Her brother Charles Carroll lives in Baltimore and they say he thinks of nothing but eating and food.[5]

I am vexed that you didn't write me any more about Colonel Burr's visit to you.[6] Did he say nothing of us? He was at Riversdale while he was Vice-President, and sometime after his duel with Colonel Hamilton he proposed to come here again, but my husband declined all familiarity with him. You say that he has the air of a rogue. He is certainly not a man one can esteem, but he does have some superior talents, and I wouldn't be surprised to see him at the head of the government in a few years (if we continue the present system). He is an intimate friend of another important ———,[7] who presently is plotting to become the next president and who might succeed. If these two ever get to that point, they won't stop there, but will try to establish a monarchy. Our poor President Madison is at the end of his maneuvers. He doesn't know where to turn anymore and loses supporters every day.

Since my last letter our family has increased again by a daughter who is doing very well.[8] Our factory does not grow feeble—it seems to me that each child is more perfect than the last. I hope, however, that we won't have any more now. . . .

[Mrs. Calvert was unable to mail this letter until July 1813.]

1. This is a continuation of Mrs. Calvert's letter of 12 December 1811. It is undated, but from the mention of Marie Louise's birth (6 March 1812), it was probably written in late March or early April 1812.

2. Nancy (Ann) Stoddert, daughter of Benjamin and Rebecca (Lowndes) Stoddert, married her cousin Thomas Gantt, son of Levi and Harriot (Lowndes) Gantt, in 1811.

3. Probably Elizabeth Chase (after 1784–?), daughter of Samuel Chase. Elizabeth

married George Dugan in 1804 and later married someone named Cole; her first husband remarried in 1806, so there must have been a divorce.

4. Mary (Carroll) Caton (1770–1846), daughter of Charles Carroll of Carrollton and wife of Richard Caton, had four daughters: Elizabeth, Marianne, Louisa, and Emily. In 1812, the girls ranged from nineteen to twenty-five years of age and only Marianne had married, although all eventually did.

5. Charles Carroll of Homewood (1775–1825) was the only son of Charles Carroll of Carrollton.

6. After his trial for treason and his acquittal, Aaron Burr resided in Europe from 1808 to 1812.

7. Left blank in the original.

8. Marie Louise Calvert was born on March 6, 1812. This is the second child to bear the name of Mrs. Calvert's mother; the first Marie Louise died on March 23, 1809.

America at War

THE FORMAL DECLARATION OF WAR between the United States
and Great Britain in June of 1812 came almost as a relief after the
long years of unsuccessful accommodation to an impossible situation.
The British blockaded the American coast and sealed off the Chesapeake
Bay. Communication between Europe and America became more difficult than ever. Shortly after war was declared, Rosalie's old friend British
minister Augustus John Foster stopped by Riversdale to pay his respects
before leaving the country, and Rosalie enlisted his aid to get a letter to
her father. Correspondence could only go by official means, and the
number of letters exchanged by Mrs. Calvert and her family dropped
sharply.

Rosalie Calvert, with considerable insight, feared civil war within
America more than she feared the British. Particularly alarming was mob
action in nearby Baltimore where a dozen prominent Federalists were
brutally beaten and one killed for their antiwar stand. Federalist disaffec-
tion with the war, especially in New England, raised new concerns about
the preservation of the Union.

Investment decisions in such a climate became increasingly difficult,
and Mrs. Calvert, fearful of the safety of the public debt, channeled more
of her father's money into real estate. She made four major land purchases totaling just over seventeen hundred acres. One of her new properties included Spurrier's Tavern, the bustling stagecoach stop, later
known as Waterloo, on the road from Baltimore to Washington. She
invested heavily in the Bank of Washington, where her husband served as

a director and provided her with information about the institution's financial condition. George Calvert also became president of the newly formed Baltimore-Washington Turnpike Company in 1813, and Mrs. Calvert recommended similar companies to her family as safe investments.

Illness and war made dramatic appearances at Riversdale during these years. An outbreak of typhoid fever in the summer of 1813 ravaged the plantation, striking first at the slave population and spreading to the family. Three house servants died, including the children's nurse. The Calverts' baby, seventeen-month-old Louise, died after a month-long struggle with the disease. Two of the other children came down with it, and Rosalie, who was pregnant and the principal nurse for her sick children, contracted it, too. Convinced that they had to leave Riversdale if they were to survive, an ailing Rosalie took her two sick children, Eugénie and Charles, to Washington where all eventually recovered. George Calvert stayed behind at Riversdale to care for his sick slaves. Typhoid struck again the following summer, and Rosalie almost died.

The two oldest children, Caroline and George Henry, at school in Philadelphia, were spared the terrible summers at Riversdale. Rosalie especially missed her twelve-year-old daughter, who had become a real companion, but the Calverts' unsatisfactory experience with two tutors at home made boarding school necessary. Tutors were especially deficient in providing extra refinements like French, drawing, music, and dancing, which demonstrated one's educational attainments to the world. Rosalie naturally wanted her children to learn French, and both of the schools she chose were run by natives of France.

Private boarding schools were expensive, but even during these relatively austere times for the Calvert family, both sons and daughters received an equal educational advantage. In earlier and in later times, the son's education would have taken precedence. Caroline, however, was the clear beneficiary of a late eighteenth- and early nineteenth-century attitude that stressed the importance of women's education. A woman needed a full education in order to be a worthy companion to her husband, a competent domestic manager, and a suitable teacher for her children during their early years. Rosalie herself had benefited from the improved education given upper- and middle-class women in the late eighteenth century, and she intended for her daughters to receive the same advantage. As she lay near death during her second bout with typhoid in 1814, she gave instructions for the education of her daughters.

All the Calvert daughters attended Madame Grelaud's Philadelphia school.

Mrs. Calvert rejoiced over Napoleon's overthrow in the spring of 1814 and the promise of peace it brought to Europe. The French defeat, however, allowed the British to intensify their efforts in America, and war came virtually to the Calverts' doorstep. In August 1814, even as peace discussions were beginning in Ghent, the Battle of Bladensburg, the greatest American disaster of the war, was fought just two miles from Riversdale. The American defeat left the road open for the victorious British to enter Washington, where they set fire to the Capitol, the President's House, and other public buildings. While Washington burned, Calvert slaves labored to bury the American and English dead who had fallen on the field of Bladensburg.

To H. J. Stier

[Riversdale], 17 March 1812

This letter was [begun] quite a long time ago, dear Father, and could not be sent for lack of opportunity.[1] Ever since you told me not to write by way of England, opportunities have been quite scarce, and unfortunately this one, which should have gone by the [U.S.S.] *Hornet,* arrived there a few hours too late and was sent back to me. So I have reopened it to add several particulars while waiting for another chance to send it.

Today I have the pleasure of announcing that you have another little granddaughter who came into the world on March 6. She is in perfect condition, and so am I although with the bad weather we have had, I have not left my chamber yet. We are going to name her Marie Louise in memory of my dear Mother. I hope that this will be our last child—we have enough now.[2]

My last boy, Henry, is the most pleasing and interesting child in the world—extremely lively and playful. Charles is more serious, but he is as handsome as an Adonis. Whenever I take him with me to Washington, everyone we meet stops to look at him and asks who this beautiful boy is. Eugénie is also very interesting and shows a lot of intelligence and understanding—I anticipate much pleasure from this child. I am not very happy with the tutor of my two eldest. He is so slow that they don't learn as much in a week as they should in a day. For the rest, he is a good man, but I cannot make him appreciate the value of wasted time.

My husband had a violent attack of rheumatism last month. A number of people had similar attacks this winter—some so intense that their lives were in danger. We recently had a great loss in the person of Dr. Baker, the physician we used and who was, I think, the best in Maryland.[3] I don't know what we are going to do if someone becomes ill, because although there are three doctors in Bladensburg, they are all young and I don't have confidence in any of them. Those in Washington and Georgetown are no better—they are all charlatans.

You ask me to give you many details about our way of life. For the sake of economy we are living a very retired life at present. I have not been in a house in Washington for four years, although I received several invitations this winter which greatly tempted me. We see our friends the Lowndes often—if it weren't for them, I think I would become a complete recluse. We have cut back on all possible expenses—instead of four beautiful horses, we have two who work every day. We still have all of our tobacco [on hand], and yours, too. I see little hope of ever selling it at a tolerable price, and what is even worse, there is nothing we can substitute for its culture that even approaches it. Our soil is too light for wheat at Riversdale, and on the adjoining plantation [Buck Lodge] we haven't grown tobacco for a long time and are working towards putting it entirely into meadowland for pasturing the cattle. However, this requires time and doesn't produce revenue right away.

Every day I regret that we still have not been able to build a mill. There is none in the neighborhood except for Digges' which earns $1,000 a year, and the mill and everything are not worth $5,000.[4] Besides, it is in such bad condition that it often breaks down completely. I am sure that a mill which cost $10,000 would earn a 15 percent return, not to mention the benefit of the manure produced by the animals one would fatten there.

I received your [letter] of 5 October [1811] the first of this month along with the powers of attorney to receive your interests, etc. They are quite in order and enable me to do all that is necessary in case of redemptions or any other changes. Everything is extremely unsettled here. The charter of the Bank of North America expires in two years, and people are saying it will not receive a new one. I have had the repayment of your exchanged 6 Pcts.—$13,464.01—on hand since August, and I still haven't invested it because every day we have expected the new loan which Congress authorized last session to open. I am afraid, dear Father, that all this may seem like negligence of your affairs, but I assure you that is not the case. I have done my best, and you have told me time and again that you prefer new loans. The State of Maryland has kept $60,000 uninvested since October 1810, besides $40,000 since January 1812, making $100,000 altogether, waiting to subscribe to a new loan—as have several agents for English investors in Philadelphia. The Comptroller of the Treasury himself assured my husband some months ago that the new loan would take place without delay, but that is how everything goes around here—you can't count on anything. Congress is still in session, and after having waited so long, I think we ought to wait a little longer. . . . So I will wait until April 15, and if [the loan] has not been offered by then, I'll tell McEwen to buy some old 6 Pcts. . . .

I am delighted that you approve of the purchase of the Spurrier property.[5] I regard it as an extremely valuable acquisition. It is only rarely that one encounters the opportunity to make such an advantageous purchase. We could have sold it a month afterwards with several thousand dollars profit. We still haven't made the first payment since the Chancellor wasn't able to make the transfer of the deed yet. I will continue to keep myself informed of all properties for sale, but although there are a good many, few possess favorable conditions or return a good interest unless you cultivate the land yourself. [The property] should have good soil and especially good forest which can be leased, as the tenant ruins your land, never fertilizing it, and cuts your woods without the slightest regard—if he does not take it to market! One of the causes for the high price of land is that lack of confidence in the government makes all the capitalists want to own land. Even Baltimore merchants, as soon as they make a little money, buy a few acres and become farmers. Also for some time, Pennsylvanians have been coming in to settle in Maryland, and more are coming each year. These farmers are a big asset for the state because they are an industrious and thrifty people, and their example is a great benefit. . . .

Since my last letter I have made another land purchase: 200 acres at $20 an acre. It was a parcel of land completely surrounded by our Mount Albion and a good acquisition for this reason, but it won't produce income equal to Spurrier's. . . .[6]

[n.d.] June 1812

Still no opportunity to send my letter. You will have heard that the Congress has put an embargo on all ships which is in effect until July. They also have declared war against England.[7] Our warships are going out, preparations are being made, etc. All this is nothing yet. The English can, with some fishing line, take all our frigates. They also can quite easily

Spurrier's Tavern, Waterloo, Maryland
Peale Museum, Baltimore

come to Annapolis to take the treasury, to New York for the banks, etc. But what I fear infinitely more is that it could produce a civil war— [something] much more to be feared than the English. In Baltimore the mob already governs the city, has demolished one house, and is threatening others.[8] This same mob only needs a leader like Burr, for example, to come to Washington, throw our poor President out the window, and take the government—nothing would prevent them from doing it.

22 July 1812

After waiting in vain for a good opportunity to send this letter to Mr. Barlow, I find myself forced to send it to London. Because of the declaration of war with England, there is no longer any means of sending letters to France without near certainty that they will be seized. So this one will come to you thanks to the kindness of Mr. Foster, the English Ambassador, who just left Washington for Halifax. . . .[9]

Your affectionate daughter.

1. This is a continuation of the 7 December 1811 letter, above.
2. Stier agreed that Mrs. Calvert had enough children. When informed of this birth, he wrote his daughter: "It is time to rest on your laurels!" Indeed, before Henry's birth in 1810, he had written that while he was looking forward to it with

pleasure, "tell your husband to spare you a little in the future" (HJS Letterbook, 3 January 1813, 9 March 1810, Cal S-V).

3. Dr. William Baker, who had been the Calverts' physician since 1805, died at Georgetown in 1812.

4. In 1812 the Digges' mill (now Adelphi Mill) was operated by Catherine (Brent) Digges and her son William Dudley Digges (1790–1830), who lived at Green Hill plantation in Prince George's County.

5. This was the 400-acre property discussed above (24 June 1811), which included John Spurrier's Tavern, hereafter referred to as Spurrier's.

6. Prince George's County Land Records (Liber J. R. M. 15, fol. 142) indicate that on February 15, 1812, George Calvert bought "all that part of the tract or parcel of land called Cool Spring Manor" from William White of Prince George's County for four thousand dollars. Mrs. Calvert clearly says that *she* made the purchase, and certainly with her father's money. It is unclear why she did not have the land recorded in her name.

7. A ninety-day general embargo had been passed by Congress in early April 1812 and was now drawing to a close, but because of England's seeming intransigence on negotiations, Madison asked Congress for a declaration of war, which passed on June 18, 1812. England had actually made an important concession by suspending the Orders in Council on June 16, but the president and Congress were unaware of this.

8. On June 22, 1812, a mob in Baltimore attacked and destroyed the offices of the *Federal Republican* and threatened the homes of the editor and several other persons. Two days before, the paper had printed a strong antiwar editorial. A more serious attack on this same newspaper occurred the following month, resulting in the killing of General James M. Lingan and the brutal beating of a dozen other prominent Federalists, including General Henry Lee (John Thomas Scharf, *History of Maryland* [Baltimore, 1879], vol. 3, pp. 3–24).

9. Augustus John Foster, whom Mrs. Calvert had met while he was secretary to Minister Anthony Merry from 1805 to 1807, was himself appointed minister to the United States in August 1811, serving until the rupture between the two countries in 1812. George Henry Calvert remembers Foster making a special stop at Riversdale to bid the Calverts farewell on his way out of Washington (Calvert, *Autobiographic Study,* p. 76).

To Charles J. Stier[1]

Riversdale, 24 February 1813

I have just received your letter of 12 September 1812, dear Brother, which gave me all the more pleasure because I had not received news from any one of you for a very long time. . . . At this time it is nearly impossible to send letters, and I begin this one without the least hope of being able to forward it for a long time. A fleet of two English ships of 74 cannon and six frigates close the entry to the Chesapeake and Delaware [bays] and do not allow the smallest boat to pass. Meanwhile the country is torn asunder by numerous factions, and in Congress there is open talk of dissolving the union of the states. In short, I do not know how it will all end. . . .

The moderation of the English is surprising. We have already taken three of their frigates, there is nothing to prevent their reducing all our ports to ashes (for there is no one to defend them), and still they are content to blockade us. I will send you some clippings from our newspapers on whose authenticity you may rely and which will give you some idea of our situation.

You have often complained of your childless state. Indeed, in such times as we are going through, it is better not to have any. They certainly give us many delightful moments, but what anxiety they cause. I often regard mine with much uneasiness as to their future lots, brought up in the expectation of a fine fortune of which they may be deprived. Sometimes I am sorry that they are not all boys, who—with a good education—can always carve their way in this country.

I don't know if I wrote you that my youngest is a girl . . . named after our dear departed mother, Marie Louise. She is very sweet, has begun to walk, and is very healthy. Eugénie, aged six-and-a half, is the most lovable child imaginable. If I had the power of the old fairies, I could find nothing to add to her person nor to her character. George and Caroline have been in Philadelphia at French schools since last November.[2] It is very expensive for us—over $1,000—but I think one can give nothing better to one's children than a good education, and I would rather economize on everything else but that. I had tried two different tutors for two years, who did not satisfy me. Besides, [the children] could not learn French or dancing or drawing here. Nonetheless, it was with great difficulty that I could part with Caroline who was a great companion to me in my loneliness, but I thought I should only consider her future welfare. They will return for the one-month vacation next September, and then we can tell what progress they have made and whether it is desirable to keep them there.[3]

Recently I have again resumed the <u>amusing</u> occupation of schoolmistress for Eugénie and Charles. This makes me waste much time and patience. I seldom go out and we see very few people which gives me the leisure to be constantly with my children, and finally I believe I shall become a child myself! Tell me, don't my letters already show it? All four are around my chair while I am writing, the smallest one is pulling my arm for me to take her and the others are making such a noise that I have to call them to order every minute. . . .

I heard with much sorrow that my sister was so ill, and I hope that this will be her last child.[4] After what she wrote me I did not think she would have this one—it is high time she yielded this right to Louise. . . .

11 April 1813

I have just learned that a cartel ship is to sail to carry ministers to St. Petersburg who are going to negotiate with England under the auspices of Alexander.[5] This gives me a good chance to send this. . . . I don't think our President was sincere in sending a minister to Russia; perhaps it was only a ruse to obtain money.

The [Treasury] loan which was opened at the beginning of March (paying 6 percent and an annuity of 1 percent for 13 years) had only a very moderate sum subscribed because it was evident that if the war kept on, the bonds' [value] would decrease to nothing. Now the Secretary of the Treasury has just contracted, in Philadelphia on April 6, for the entire loan at 6 percent and an annuity of 1 1/2 percent for 13 years. To obtain that he had to give his word, etc., etc., that negotiations are to be opened immediately to settle our differences with England.

Therefore a part of your January dividends and all your April ones will be invested, and I will send you the accounts at the first opportunity. I am acting according to your instructions, for it is my opinion, as well as that of most prudent people, that the national bonds are less advantageous than good banks or than bonds on the public roads. The latter are considered the safest of all, although yielding less interest than the banks. But as you seem to be prejudiced against these sorts of investment, I did not consider myself authorized to make them for you. . . .

I must finish, dear Brother. My sheet is nearly filled and I must still write to Papa. Give my love to your Eugénie and to my sister van Havre, and believe me, with the tenderest love,

Your affectionate,

Rosalie E. Calvert

1. Carter Trans-MHS.
2. Caroline was a student at Madame Grelaud's school for girls in Philadelphia from 1812 to 1817. George Henry was sent first to Clermont, a school run by the brothers Carré near the village of Frankfurt, Pennsylvania, where he stayed for a year and a half, and then was transferred to Mt. Airy, "a better school," run by another Frenchman, M. Constant, in Germantown where he remained for four to five years (see Lucy Leigh Bowie, "Madame Grelaud's French School," *Maryland Historical Magazine* 39 [June 1944], 141–48, and Calvert, *Autobiographic Study*, pp. 55–56).
3. The Philadelphia boarding schools attended by the Calvert children had an

eleven-month term with a month's vacation in autumn. Caroline was twelve years old when she went off to school, and George Henry was nine. He later recalled the intense homesickness he felt at this time: "I have hardly one pleasant memory of those school-days at Clermont. . . . To have numerous daily playmates was a new enjoyment, and was some easement of the heart-ache caused by being snatched from a warm partial home, and thrown suddenly among cold indifferent strangers. But there were hours when the wound of the affections would not be staunched, when I would quit the play-ground and go off to the southwest corner of the limited lot, the point nearest to my home, and there weep alone, looking wistfully down the road from Philadelphia for relief, as though my child's tears could work a miracle" (Calvert, *Autobiographic Study,* pp. 59–60).

4. Clementine van Havre, born in 1813, was the last of Isabelle van Havre's children.

5. Czar Alexander I offered to mediate the differences between the United States and England, and Madison sent James A. Bayard and Albert Gallatin to St. Petersburg as peace commissioners. By the time of their arrival in July 1813, however, England had refused the mediation. A cartel ship is a ship sailing under truce or diplomatic immunity.

To H. J. Stier

Riversdale, 12 April 1813

. . . You will see by the account sent [in January] that I bought shares in the Frederick road for you. I have since added enough shares at $17.50 [each] to round out the number. When my husband was in Philadelphia, McEwen told him that this kind of bond was considered the most secure against failure—that is also the advice of old Carroll, Mr. Cooke, and everyone whom he consulted.

The Maryland Assembly has passed a law authorizing a road from Baltimore to Washington, which is in the process of being laid out.[1] This will be highly advantageous for us, both for Riversdale and the Spurrier property (which we will name Antwerp eventually). I have subscribed $5,000, or 100 shares, in [the Baltimore-Washington] road for you. I have paid the first two installments of $2,000 each, and the interest will be payable in January. My husband was chosen president of the [road] company at an assembly of stockholders in Baltimore.[2] This will require him to go to Baltimore from time to time, but since he already has to go to Spurrier's at times, it will be only a few miles more. . . .

You don't seem to have as high an opinion of the Bank of Washington as it deserves. I wrote you in great detail in one of my letters the advantages this bank has. When Congress granted its charter, it reduced the capital required from the [one] million originally demanded to $500,000. It is rare that shares are sold—until just the other day my husband had $12,000 belonging to a man who wanted to buy this stock, and he had not been able to find anyone willing to sell for the past eight months.

It is a very long time, dear Father, since I have received a letter from you—the last was [dated] 18 March 1812. I regret, as you do, that we cannot enjoy those beautiful paintings, but I have been so afraid that they would suffer damage that I have not unpacked them.[3] They are in a place on the north side of the house where they are protected against the humidity and heat. When we unpacked them two years ago, following your wishes, I kept a few of the small ones out of the cases; these I have hung in the drawing room which is always closed except when we have visitors. Don't you want to have them back if peace is made? They could be sent to England then very easily. And isn't there a risk that staying packed up so long might ruin their colors?

I don't know whether I've ever told you about my lemon trees. I have four superb specimens which in winter we place in the four corners of the salon, where they make a lovely effect. Last November one of them produced 87 large lemons. The others didn't bear as many, but all are going to produce a good crop this year. As I write you, I can see the hyacinths from my window—they are quite beautiful this year. I haven't been able to enjoy the tulips because the deer come and eat them every night. We have eleven of these beautiful animals, so tame that they come all around the house and when we walk in the woods they allow us to come very close to them. However, they do a lot of damage to the young fruit trees, and I am afraid we shall have to kill all of them this fall.

I am delighted, dear Father, to enclose a letter that Caroline sent from Philadelphia. It is her first attempt, and she begs your indulgence. She is very happy at her school and is making good use of her time. Educating one's children is enormously expensive—would you believe that it costs us more than $1,000 a year to keep them in Philadelphia? All our little family are wonderfully well. My husband sends his best wishes, and I ask you to believe me, dear Father, with the most tender attachment,

Your affectionate daughter,

R. E. Calvert

1. An act passed on December 17, 1812 (*Acts of Maryland, 1812,* chap. 78), laid the foundation for the turnpike from Washington to Baltimore. It incorporated a company with a capital stock of $100,000, divided into shares of $50 each, to build the road and named twelve persons, including George Calvert, to be responsible for the

direction and supervision of the road building. Stockholders were to choose officers of the company. The road was to be sixty feet wide, and the tolls to be charged for each ten miles were specified, for example:

> One horse and rider—1/16 of a dollar (6 1/4¢)
> A chaise with 1 horse, 2 wheels—1/8 of a dollar (12 1/2¢)
> A coach with 2 horses, 4 wheels—1/4 of a dollar (25¢)
> A coach with 4 horses, 4 wheels—3/8's of a dollar (37 1/2¢)

2. The stockholders' election was advertised to be held on March 12, 1813, at Gadsby's Hotel in Baltimore (*Baltimore American and Commercial Daily Advertiser,* March 11, 1813).

3. In his last letter Stier expressed regret that Mrs. Calvert was not getting more pleasure from the painting collection. He told her that she had there "an inestimable treasure" and urged her, despite the inconveniences of showing the paintings, to use the collection to her advantage in these difficult times "to make contacts with important people" by showing them on special occasions (HJS Letterbook, 18 March 1812, Cal S-V).

To H. J. Stier

Riversdale, 23 November 1813

My dear Father,

It is several months since I have written to you or had a letter from you. Since my last letter I have suffered more than I can express. I lost my youngest child, the delightful and lovable little Louise. Two of the other children have been very ill. I myself was at death's door and escaped only by a miracle, or rather by the grace of God who restored me to life when I thought I had only a few hours left in this world. Our neighborhood was stricken by an extremely malignant bilious disease which began its ravages in June and continued until November.[1] All of our negroes were attacked at about the same time. We lost several, in addition to three of our house servants, among them an excellent children's nurse who can never be replaced. My little one was stricken towards the middle of July. Having no faith in the young doctor in Bladensburg, I employed one from Georgetown in whom, unhappily, I placed a degree of confidence that he did not deserve. He charged enormous fees for each visit and, even so, was rarely willing to come out. My little angel died on the 18th of August—it was a blow, dear Father, from which I shall never recover. Two days later Eugénie fell ill. The doctors kept telling us that the fever was not contagious, but being convinced otherwise, I decided to go to Washington with my children where Eugénie recovered in a fortnight.

When I left Riversdale, I thought I should never see it again since I felt that I had already gotten the poison, and two days later I fell ill, as did Charles. Henry was sent to Mrs. Peter's and escaped all danger.

Charles and I were sufficiently recovered after a month and returned here in October. Caroline and George, fortunately, were in Philadelphia, and my husband's good constitution protected him from the danger to which he was constantly exposed. Since we employed a doctor from Washington who could only come out every two or three days, [my husband] was obliged to go and see the sick negroes and had to bleed them nearly every day, often six to eight of them each morning—for that was the principal treatment.

I hope that we shall never again experience another summer or illness so terrible. We thought seriously of abandoning Riversdale and going to live in Philadelphia or Washington. But as long as the Democratic party remains in power, the latter is not a desirable place for us. We have to send our children to Philadelphia to be educated, which is very expensive, not to mention the unhappiness of being separated from them. I don't know what we will decide to do, but I do not want—for all the world—to spend another month as I have spent the last ones. The yellow fever in Philadelphia did not make any more of an impression. It is only recently that I have really begun to regain my strength. I don't know how I was able to stand a fatigue so continual and for such a long time. Since the dread of getting the sickness was so great, we could not hire anyone to care for the ill, and I went entire weeks without sleeping more than a half-hour at a time. You will not be surprised, dear Father, that during all this time I neglected your business affairs. The last letter I received from you was [dated] 3 January [1813], and I thank you for the gift of 100 Louis that you were so kind to give me.[2]

19 December 1813

Enclosed, dear Father, you will find your account where you will see a large amount of uninvested cash [on hand], and I am really at a loss about how to deal with it. In April I felt I should keep it in reserve since it was assumed that the new loan authorized by Congress would pay 8 percent. In July since I could do nothing myself, I instructed the cashier at the Bank [of Washington] to subscribe to that loan, [then] offering 7 1/2 percent, for you, Charles, and van Havre, which he did, and also for the Bank the sum of $70,000. After some time, it was discovered that some Philadelphia speculators had made an offer to the government for the entire loan, so we failed to get our subscription. Somewhat later the bonds went up three points which, added to my condition at the time, made me refrain from investing your funds. Now I think this same issue could be obtained at par, but I feel it would be very unwise to take it.

I have been writing you for some time that this government might not last. If it dissolves, the public debt goes for naught. I am quite certain that if the war with England continues for another two years, the government will be brought down, and we will have a civil war whose outcome is impossible to predict. But in any case, [investments in] the bonds would be lost. This is not my opinion alone, but that of the most knowledgeable people here in the Eastern states and of the most enlightened members of Congress and the Senate. Therefore, would it not be most unwise to further increase the already large amount you have in public bonds?

On the other hand, investment in land presents some problems. Prices have risen greatly in recent years, so that it is rarely possible to purchase land that will bring in an income without cultivating it oneself. You mention the "Back lands."[3] I think this would be most profitable, but it demands a lot of caution in order not to be cheated. Some people have made large fortunes by buying these lands while others have been ruined. And the only way is to go and see them in person. It is from waiting for my husband to be able to do that that I have postponed investing your money. However, he is so busy that I don't know when he will be able to do it, and in the meantime you are losing the interest. I have made up my mind to devote myself entirely to this matter for the next two weeks. Congress is in session which causes a number of informed people from all corners of America to assemble in Washington. I shall gather all the information I can on this subject in order to be able to make a determination. The President, in a communication to Congress, is asking for a loan of 30 millions. . . .

The children are all well, as is their father. I have recovered my health almost completely, but I cannot seem to get over the loss I have suffered. Oh, dear Father, you have no idea what a delightful little girl she was and how intelligent for her age.

Caroline and George have been here recently for a month but have gone back to Philadelphia. I am very pleased with their schools, but the price is exorbitant. They cost us between $1,100 and $1,200 a year. Being separated from Caroline is a great sacrifice for me, though Eugénie is a wonderful companion. I regret so much that you are unable to see her— she is very pretty and sprightly and has a most affectionate nature. I know she is going to be a joy to me. At the beginning of February I expect another addition to my family, and I do hope that, finally, this will be the last.

Please, dear Father, give a thousand compliments to my Sister, her children, to Charles, and to all who remember me. . . .

Your affectionate daughter,

Rosalie E. Calvert

P.S. I see that they have passed a decree in France, dated 23 August, requiring all subjects who have been naturalized in other countries to obtain ratification from Paris. Please tell me if it is necessary for me to do this, and by what means. You know that I was naturalized here in order to be able to hold in my own name the properties of Spurrier, etc.

1. Malignant bilous fever was typhoid fever, a disease caused by a bacillus parasitic to man. Transmitted through the feces and urine of infected persons, the typhoid bacillus contaminated water and food supplies.

2. In his last letter Stier expressed regret at Mrs. Calvert's report that it had been four years since she had enjoyed the social life of Washington, and he raised his New Year's gift by 100 Louis (approximately $375) "for her wardrobe," and "to help her again enjoy these pleasures" (HJS Letterbook, 3 January 1813, Cal S-V).

3. Stier wanted to buy more land, even the unclaimed western land which the government sold for $2 an acre (HJS Letterbook, 3 January 1813, Cal S-V).

To Charles J. Stier[1]

Riversdale, 18 February 1814

After not having had news of you for several months, you can imagine what pleasure your letter of 15 October 1813 gave me. I received it yesterday and I hasten to reply to it in the hope of sending it off soon, but opportunities are very rare and precarious at present. . . . I am going to reply to what you write to me about business on a separate sheet, which I beg you to communicate to Papa and to Monsieur van Havre. . . .[2]

You ask me if my husband continues to make improvements in farming and I in my gardens, etc. It is with much regret that we have abandoned all work of that description for the last two years, which will not surprise you when you consider that we have the tobacco harvest of several years in store, and that since this abominable war with England everything is double and triple the price, so that we must exercise the most scrupulous economy.

Caroline and George are still in Philadelphia where they will remain. We chose these schools after the most careful examination of their references, and they seem to be very good. George will not come back here, except during vacation months, until he has completed his education.

You must pass your time very agreeably between Paris and your lovely estates. I wish I could do the same. I am sorry to learn that our dear Louise is so hard to please as to the choice of a companion for life's journey. However, the estate of "old maid," which your sex endeavors to turn to ridicule, is, I think, more desirable than many others and also has no great anxieties. Here young men are so dissipated and corrupt—in short, all that is bad—that I very much doubt if I will ever allow my daughters to marry.

Apropos, I almost forgot to tell you that I have another little girl who came into the world on the 31st of last month, and to whom I hope you will be good enough to become godfather.[3] You doubtless know, dear Friend, that last summer I lost my youngest, aged 17 months, who was named after our dear departed mother. It is a blow from which I shall never be healed and whose memory will fill with bitterness the rest of my life.

Like you, I am very subject to headaches, which cause me to lose much time, as I am absolutely incapable of doing anything when a headache overtakes me. . . .

Your devoted sister,

Rosalie E. Calvert

1. Carter Trans-MHS.
2. A separate document entitled "Observations on Stocks, Lands, Etc." was attached to this letter and also to a letter to H. J. Stier of 31 March 1814. This document, which follows this letter, is from the French original and is not part of the Carter Translation.
3. Julia, the Calverts' eighth child, was born on January 31, 1814. Julia's date of birth in the Carter Translation is incorrectly given as January 30.

Enclosure to Charles J. Stier

18 February 1814

Observations on Stocks, Lands, Etc.

You say that the Bank of Washington would not be the best kind of investment if the union of the states should dissolve, but if that should occur, surely all stocks would be lost and most banks would fail. . . .

Not one dollar of the Bank of Washington has been invested in construction—a portion of their capital is in public bonds, the rest in discounts. At present I think this bank is one of the better, but since you don't seem to want it, I shall not increase your holdings in it.

For several months my husband has had considerable sums to invest in this stock (especially from planters), and it was not until just the other day that he was able to—obtaining it at a ten percent markup.

The bonds issued for the public highways are considered the safest investments, although they don't yield as much interest. I bought some for Papa rather advantageously. I consulted McEwen on the matter, along with several others. All agreed that it was these bonds whose safety they could count on the most in case of a revolution, which everyone thinks may not be far off. So I am sorry that you reject this investment also. The only alternative left to me then is more of the government bonds, the old 6 Pcts. and the 3 Pcts., which are difficult to obtain.

For quite some time I have not for one minute lost sight of the need to buy some land for Papa, but you have no idea how many difficulties this presents. Since your departure, land has doubled, in some places tripled, in value. And then, how to manage it? I could buy some land of middling quality, say at $20 an acre, and lease it out at five or six percent return, but it would deteriorate in value every year because the tenant isn't interested in improving it but rather in getting all he can out of it. . . .

If I buy fertile land located in an area which is increasing in value, the price is exorbitant [and] consequently the rent will bring only a small return. You know that we have 1,100 acres in Montgomery County, twelve miles from Georgetown, for which a few years ago my husband would have accepted $20 [an acre].[1] Now if he wanted to sell, he could easily get $40, and the land is not even very fertile.

The other day I bought a superb farm between here and Mount Albion called Oatland, comprised of 600 acres, at $40.25 an acre.[2] I have rented it for the coming year at a rate which will give me a three percent return, but I doubt whether that can continue. Every foot of the land is of the greatest fertility; 80 acres are in woods of the best quality, and there is plenty of pasture. I consider this a most fortunate purchase. The poor man who was obliged to sell it [at public auction] in order to pay his debts is an old bachelor who is always drunk. He has 700 adjoining acres where he lives in a fine brick house. He can't live long, and at his death the part which he has kept will probably also be sold.

If I could make some more purchases of this sort, it would certainly be better than investing Papa's income in public bonds which can be reduced to nothing in the wink of an eye. Everything depends on the government. If it makes peace with England, we are saved. If not, I tremble for the consequences.

Madison has just appointed Mr. Campbell, a rabid Democrat, as Secretary of the Treasury—a man no more capable of that job than I would be. He married one of my best friends, Mr. Stoddert's daughter.[3]

(As Mr. van Havre has not lost his taste for sea voyages, it would not cost him too much to make a little visit here to see for himself how we are getting on. . . . It would be a great comfort to have him share with me the heavy responsibility of investing such large amounts of money.)[4]

1. Mrs. Calvert is referring to her husband's Montgomery County holding in a tract known as the Hermitage. Tax records for the period, however, show Calvert's property to be 873³/₄ acres rather than 1,100, as cited by Mrs. Calvert (Montgomery County Tax Assessments, Real Property, 1798, 1813, 1820, fols. 106, 280, 272).

2. This purchase is recorded in 1815 under George Calvert's name and comprised a total of 595 acres in two tracts, Collington Manor and Partnership, bought from Henry S. Hall and William A. Hall of Prince George's County for $25,960. The property was located west of Collington Branch near present-day Bowie. The name Oatland is not mentioned in the land records, and Mrs. Calvert later referred to it more often as "the Hall purchase" (Prince George's County Land Records, Liber J. R. M. 16, fol. 353).

3. George Washington Campbell (1769–1848), United States senator from Tennessee, was appointed secretary of the treasury by Madison when Albert Gallatin was named to the Ghent peace commission. Campbell served only briefly, resigning to return to the Senate. He married Harriet Stoddert in 1812.

4. This final paragraph was not included in the version sent to Charles Stier, but was added to the copy Mrs. Calvert sent to her father.

To H. J. Stier

Riversdale, 31 March 1814

My dear Father,

As I had been so long without news from you, your October letter gave me great pleasure—the more so since by my brother's letter I learned that you enjoy such good health. Opportunities to send letters have been quite scarce here for some time, but now that communication between Holland and England is opened, they should become more frequent, I trust. I will send this [letter] through the courtesy of Colonel Barclay who for the moment is our neighbor, occupying the late Mr. Stoddert's house. [Barclay] is a former English officer and agent for the exchange of prisoners—an extremely cultivated and agreeable gentleman. He has the kindness to send my letter to you under cover to his son who is presently at the court of the Prince of Orange at The Hague. If [Barclay's son] comes to Antwerp, I hope you will extend all possible courtesies to him. . . .[1]

You asked where we stand with our tobacco. We have continued to grow some each year in the hope of being able to sell it. It is the same with the 100 hogsheads bought for you [which are] in storage and [which] I hope will soon bring us a good price. At present [tobacco] is being sold at $5 and $7, and I have no doubt that it will go higher.

I thank you very much, dear Father, for the New Year's gift of 100 Louis which you were so kind to give me.

I hope that you have received my December [1813] letter which included your account up to that date. Since then I have purchased a very valuable property (whose description you will find in my observations). The owner of the [adjoining] property is so weighed down with debt that I believe we could acquire that one, too, which would be most desirable. He offered to sell my husband 200 acres the other day, but we turned it down unless he would sell us the entire farm of 700 acres with a good brick house.

I am informing myself about all land sales because I dare not buy public bonds. I assure you that I am quite apprehensive that they will become worthless if the war continues and that this is the opinion of all knowledgeable people. I have been writing you this for a long time, but you don't seem to have great faith in my prophecies. I hope I will prove to be a false prophet, for it would be terrible if this should come to pass. . . .

There is such a general stagnation prevailing here that it is difficult to do anything just now. Everyone seems to be awaiting the results of the great events occurring so rapidly in Europe. . . .

I have to announce to you the birth of another little daughter who came into the world on the 31st of January. She is extremely pretty and has not had a moment's illness since her birth. My husband joins me in sending his affectionate greetings.

Your devoted daughter,

R. E. Calvert

1. Colonel Thomas Barclay was living at Bostwick in Bladensburg, the home of the late Benjamin Stoddert, who had died in December 1813. Barclay's son was aide-de-camp to the Duke of York who was with the Prince of Orange at The Hague.

To Isabelle van Havre

Riversdale, 24 May 1814

It seems to me, dear Sister, that it has been an age since I had a letter from you—the last was [dated] 9 August 1811! Is it possible, dear Friend, that you have been all that time without writing me? You say that opportunities [to send mail] have been infrequent; I agree and acknowledge that I, too, have neglected several [opportunities] for want of being informed in time. Now we can write each other every fortnight, since after the momentous events which have just taken place in Europe, I trust that our government will not be so foolish as to continue the war with England. We just received news of the Allies' entry into Paris and the restoration of the Bourbons.[1]

Yesterday [Colonel Barclay] showed me a letter from his son who accompanied the Prince of Orange when he left London for The Hague and later was with the English troops that attacked Antwerp under General Graham.[2] His letter was dated from Lounhout [Loenhout]. You can imagine with what emotion I read it—written so near our dear Mick which I fear has suffered greatly from the continual passage of troops. He also mentioned the destruction of Merxham [Merksem] and [said] that they [the English] aimed their fire several times on different parts of Antwerp. Imagine, then, with what impatience I am awaiting your news. I cannot believe, surely, that you would have remained in a city menaced by a long siege. Please give me all the details about our family. Has Louise finally made a choice from among her many suitors? We are all well. My little four-month-old Julie is quite pretty and looks very like the little angel I had the misfortune to lose last summer. How is your Clementine? You know quite well that you have not written me since her birth, which my brother informed me of. I shared most sincerely in the joy this event brought you, my dear Sister, for I have no other joy than my children. All the happiness I expect in this world depends on them and on their conduct. Caroline and George are still in Philadelphia. I think [their] schools are very good, but you have no idea of the extravagance of schools in this country—it costs me between $600 and $700 a year for Caroline. Eugénie never leaves my side; if I go out she goes with me, except when I go out to dinners which is not often.

[Letter continues 24 June 1814]

1. Allied troops took Paris on March 31, 1814, and proclaimed Louis XVIII king of France. Napoleon signed the abdication drafted by the Allied powers on April 13, 1814, and shortly thereafter left for the island of Elba.

2. In the Netherlands, a domestic revolt aided by a Prussian division overthrew French rule in November 1813, and William Frederick (1772–1843), Prince of Orange, later William I, was restored as Sovereign Prince of the Low Countries. General Sir Thomas Graham (1748–1843) commanded the British force sent to Holland in 1814.

To H. J. Stier

Riversdale, 10 June 1814

. . . Because of the recent changes in Europe I trust we will be spared the misery and civil strife that threatened this country. I am sure that our imbecile government will now make peace with England, since it is impossible for them to continue the war without money, without credit, without soldiers or ships. It must be hoped that everything will return to normal, as it undoubtedly already has in Europe.

We are all well here. Caroline and George are still in Philadelphia. My little Julie is growing and becomes more interesting every day. She is very like the little angel I had the sorrow of losing last summer. I often think the Good Lord sent her to console me for that loss which I felt so deeply. No day passes, indeed no hour, that I don't think of her.

I don't know whether I told you of the death of our good friend Dr. Scott of Annapolis at the age of 92. He left most of his fortune, after Mrs. Scott's death, to a nephew who came here from Ireland a few years ago and only a very modest sum to that good Miss Read who had been such a help to him for so many years.[1]

Another of our old friends, the venerable Carroll, is quite unhappy. His son-in-law Caton has gone bankrupt for the second time and in a manner so dishonorable that he is generally scorned. [Caton's] eldest daughter married badly; the other three are not likely to [marry] at all, I think, since they are so widely held in contempt—as much for their own conduct as for that of their father and mother—that no one wants such an alliance.[2] Charles Carroll [of Homewood] has become a "Sot"—he is drunk from morning to evening. He has treated his wife in the most impossible way, beating her almost daily and on one occasion almost strangling her. The poor woman, with four children, was obliged to return to her parents in Philadelphia.[3] Carroll's friends have tried to remonstrate against his conduct, but he responded that he was incapable of doing anything about his drinking habit since he had inherited it from his grandfather. I don't know if you knew that the older Carroll is an

Mt. Airy, Prince George's County, Maryland. George Calvert's birthplace.
Library of Congress

illegitimate son, and when he returned from Europe at the age of twenty, he refused to return to his father's house unless his father would marry his mother, who was a woman of the lowest class.[4] What an idea to say that the nobility is an imaginary good!

While I am on the subject, I cannot resist telling you something which I know will please you. I have discovered that the mother of my husband's father was of the highest rank in England, and he [my husband's father] was sent over to Maryland by order of Frederick, then Prince of Wales, who sent a frigate commanded by Admiral Vernon expressly to escort him.[5] You know that it was through a notary's mistake in Lord Baltimore's will that Mr. [Benedict] Calvert lost a very considerable fortune.[6]

Now that I have written more nonsense than you have patience to read, I must speak of your business affairs. On the first of May, I subscribed $25,000 in the new loan, $12,000 of which was for Charles, $10,000 for Mr. van Havre, and the rest for you. You will see by the attached account that in February I made the first payment for the property of Henry Hall, [and] for the two others my husband has given two interest-paying bonds, the first payable in February 1815, and the second in 1816. Since I feel that any investment is better than public bonds at this time, I have continued to buy (with Mr. Hall's consent) several bonds (which pay interest) which he will receive at par when the payments on the lands come due. This gives you the advantage of investing your money immediately in a secure bond and you receive six percent interest. We are buying the notes and bonds from his [Hall's] creditors [at] a little below par, but since that would complicate my accounts I have simply pocketed the profit. Please tell me if I have your permission to do this—it will be my commission.

I am not sure I am making myself clear—if you don't understand me, please say so. In a few days I can get still more of these notes, and I will continue to buy them until I reach the sum of $24,000 and then obtain title to the land. We have leased it for one year to the former owner at five percent interest on the purchase [price]. I don't know whether he will want to continue this arrangement.

I wrote you that the Dorsey tract, adjoining Spurrier's and bought for $7,000, only rented for $60.[7] The two tenants who are staying there have not paid their rent so you won't earn any return this year, as you see from my account. Perhaps some new [tenants] would do better. Most of this land is wooded and since it is only thirteen miles from Baltimore and on a good road, it will increase in value daily. If, despite that, you do not approve of this property without receiving interest, let me know and I can sell it right away at a good profit. . . .

Your affectionate daughter,

R. E. Calvert

1. Dr. Upton Scott died on February 23, 1814, in Annapolis. Miss Read [or Reid] was his niece.

2. Richard Caton (1763–1845), an Englishman, married Mary Carroll in 1787. Despite his father-in-law's fortune, Caton was plagued by debt throughout his life. The Catons had four daughters: Elizabeth, Marianne, Louisa, and Emily. It was Marianne, the second daughter—not the eldest—who was married at this time, having wed Robert Patterson in 1806.

3. Harriet (Chew) Carroll (1775–1861), daughter of Benjamin Chew, chief justice of Pennsylvania, married Charles Carroll of Homewood in 1800. She left her husband, taking their four children with her to Philadelphia, with the full support and approval of her father-in-law, Charles Carroll of Carrollton.

4. Charles Carroll of Carrollton was the only child of Charles Carroll, Sr., of Annapolis (1702–1782), and of Elizabeth Brooke (1709–1761). His father married his mother in 1757 when he was nineteen years old. Mrs. Calvert is mistaken about Elizabeth Brooke's low social status; she was descended from distinguished families in Calvert and Prince George's counties.

5. Benedict Calvert (ca. 1724–1788), George Calvert's father, was the illegitimate

but acknowledged son of Charles Calvert, fifth Lord Baltimore. His mother is unknown. It has been suggested that his mother was Petronille Melusina Schulenberg, countess of Walsingham (1693–1778), one of three natural daughters of George I and his morganic wife, the duchess of Kendall. Lady Walsingham married the earl of Chesterfield in 1733 (see S. H. Lee Washington, "The Royal Stuarts in America, " *New England Historical and Genealogical Register* [July 1950], 173–75). It should be noted, however, that the connection between Benedict Calvert and the countess of Walsingham in this article rests on "family letters" whose location is not given.

Benedict was sent to America by his father in 1742 and placed under the care of Dr. George Steuart (ca. 1700–1784) of Annapolis. The Prince of Wales in 1742 was Frederick Louis (1707–1751), son of George II and father of George III, but there is no independent confirmation of his role in this voyage. Charles Calvert, fifth Lord Baltimore, served as cofferer to the Prince of Wales and named his legitimate son and successor after him (see John Bailey Calvert Nicklin, "The Calvert Family," *Maryland Historical Magazine* 16 (1921), 313–18.

It seems unlikely that Admiral Vernon escorted the young Benedict to America; Admiral Edward Vernon (1684–1757) was heavily engaged in fighting in the West Indies during the 1740–1742 period and did not return to England until 1743 (see Douglas Ford, *Admiral Vernon and the Navy* [London, 1907], pp. 166–73). Nicklin, p. 314, states that Benedict was sent to Maryland in charge of a *Captain* Vernon.

6. In a will made one year before his death, Charles Calvert, fifth Lord Baltimore (1699–1751), left a property called Anne Arundel Manor in Anne Arundel County, Maryland, to Benedict Calvert. After the fifth lord's death, his legitimate son Frederick challenged his father's will and successfully invalidated this bequest, along with others in the will, citing conflict with the marriage contract that the fifth lord had made with his mother. Cecilius Calvert (1702–1765), brother of the fifth lord and secretary of Maryland, informed Benedict Calvert that his legacy was invalid in a letter dated London, July 9, 1752 (Calvert Papers, MHS, reel 26, item 1147). The property of over ten thousand acres was at that time producing £288 per annum in rents. Mrs. Calvert's statement that the loss of the bequest was due to a notary's error is incorrect, but it is curious that the will bequeaths Anne Arundel Manor to "Benj[amin] Calvert, Esq.," instead of to Benedict, an error which could have been that of a notary (Calvert Papers, MHS, reel 2, item 472).

7. Mrs. Calvert purchased 503 1/2 acres on Elk Ridge in Anne Arundel County from Owen and Nicholas Dorsey in 1812, after she acquired the Spurrier tract. The Dorsey purchase was recorded under her name on September 6, 1817 (Anne Arundel County Land Records, Liber W. S. G. 5, fols. 209–13).

To Isabelle van Havre

[Riversdale], 24 June [1814][1]

. . Since I started this letter, we have received some very interesting news from Europe—the abdication of Bonaparte, the arrival of Louis XVIII in Paris, etc. However, not a word from Antwerp which interests me more than all the rest of the world put together. We have also learned that the English are going to send a considerable force here. Their ships are already in our Patuxent [River]. They have burned several houses and tobacco warehouses. I don't know how it will all end.

Please give my compliments to your husband. I would have sent him the continuation of his account today along with some purchases I have made for him, but it is not copied and this letter must leave this evening or it will arrive too late. Tell him I have invested all the money I have of his in the new loan. . . .

Your devoted sister.

1. This is a continuation of Mrs. Calvert's letter of 24 May 1814.

To Isabelle van Havre

Riversdale, 9 August 1814

My dear Sister,

. . . I sincerely share the happiness which you must all feel to be delivered from such a horrible tyranny, and I am sure that you are going to enjoy a long and sweet peace. I wish I could say the same for our unfortunate America, but I fear that the discord, in leaving you, has flown here and we will not be easily rid of it.

30 August 1814

Since I started this letter we have been in a state of continual alarm, and I now have time to write only two or three lines to ask you to tell Papa that we are all alive, in good health, and I hope safe from danger. I am sure that you have heard the news of the battle of Bladensburg where the English defeated the American troops with Madison "not at their head, but at their rear."[1]

From there they went to Washington where they burned the Capitol, the President's House, all the public offices, etc. During the battle I saw several cannonballs with my own eyes, and I will write all the details to your husband.[2] At the moment the English ships are at Alexandria which is also in their possession.

I don't know how all this will end, but I fear very badly for us. It is probable that it will also bring about a dissolution of the union of the states, and in that case, farewell to the public debt. You know I have predicted this outcome for a long time. Wouldn't it be wise to send your husband here without delay, in order to plan with me the best course to pursue for Papa's interests as well as yours?

This letter will go, I think, by a Dutch ship. If I have time with the confusion we are in, I will write again in a few days, perhaps by the same vessel. At present my house is full of people every day and at night my bedroom is full of rifles, pistols, sabers, etc. Many thanks to your husband for the information in his letter of 27 April, and tell him that I invested all his money in the May loan. Please give many greetings to my dear Father and to Charles. Embrace your children for me and believe me,

> Your affectionate sister,
>
> Rosalie E. Calvert

1. The Battle of Bladensburg took place on August 24, 1814. The encounter has been called "the Bladensburg Races" for the swiftness of the American retreat when British troops under General Robert Ross routed a numerically superior but untrained American force under General William H. Winder. Commodore Joshua Barney and his 400 sailors offered the only real opposition to the British advance, holding the road to Washington for a half-hour against 4,000 invaders. Casualties for the United States were 26 killed, 51 wounded; for the British, 64 killed, 185 wounded.

Young George Henry Calvert was in school in Philadelphia at the time of the battle, but returned to its aftermath soon after:

"In September, when I came home, the little village was alive with wounded British officers and men, all who were too badly hurt to be removed with the retiring army. General Ross, the British Commander, immediately after his bold, successful dash upon Washington, hastily returned to his ships in the Patuxent. With the wounded was left gold to pay for all their wants. The officers were Colonel Thornton, Colonel Wood, and Major Brown. I accompanied my father on his visits to these gentlemen; for my father, who, the day after the battle, had taken all his field hands to the battle-ground to bury the dead, continued his attentions to the living" (Calvert, *Autobiographic Study,* p. 77).

2. Unfortunately, no such account has been found.

To H. J. Stier

Riversdale, 22 October 1814

My dear Father,

I received your letter of 19 August 1814 yesterday. I have written several times recently, but it had been a very long time since I had heard from you so it was a great satisfaction to learn by so recent a date of your continued good health and that of my sister, Charles, and their families. I am so sorry that I have very little time today, because I have a volume to tell you. However, this letter must go with the dispatches of the Secretary of State, and I am told that the ship will sail soon. I am quite busy just now getting George and Caroline ready to leave for Philadelphia. They have been here for a month's vacation and are to go back this week. Therefore I must content myself with writing only a few lines.

It is only eight days since I went out for the first time after having been confined to my room for seven weeks and to my bed for four weeks, because, dear Father, I have once more had an inflammatory bilious disease—more severe than last year's. You will understand [how grave it was] when I tell you that in ten days I was bled seven times, took an enormous amount of medicine of all kinds, and had five vesications all at the same time—one on my chest, two on my arms, and two on my legs. I received the Holy Sacrament, gave instructions for the education of my daughters—in short, I did not believe it possible to recover. However, it pleased God to spare me once again and I am beginning to regain a little strength, although very slowly. The doctors advised me to leave Riversdale, and we often contemplate building a small house on the Dorsey property adjoining Spurrier's, about twelve miles from Baltimore.

Eugénie has also been ill with an intermitting fever, but she is better.[1] The other children, as well as my husband, enjoy good health, but some of our negroes and servants have been very sick.

It astonishes me that you don't think our public bonds and banks [are] in danger. All the banks have already made a common agreement to pay only in paper. The government can no longer raise money; they are producing treasury notes with which they will pay the interest [on the bonds]. [The treasury notes] will decline in value in a short while—one doesn't know at what point, since that depends on the number they put in circulation. Everyone is paying for everything with paper. We tear dollar notes in half and that makes a half-dollar, etc. There is no coin to be had.

I haven't time today to send you your account. I have all but completed the payments for the Hall property by buying up his own notes, as I explained in an earlier letter. . . .

Your affectionate daughter,

R. E. Calvert

P.S. I would be much obliged to Charles if (now that there are so many Americans at Ghent) he would carry out the transfer of the Riversdale property to my name. He may never again have such a good opportunity. We know Mr. Bayard very well; he has dined here.[2] For the rest, any of them would suffice, either Mr. Hughes, or Dodd, or any of the others.[3] Enclosed is an account of the Battle of Bladensburg written by Caroline.[4] I counted several cannonballs with my own eyes and all our windows rattled horribly.

1. Intermitting fever was malaria.

2. James Ashton Bayard (1767–1815), United States senator from Delaware, was envoy to the American Peace Commission at Ghent. Mrs. Calvert's father had written that with the commission meeting only a short distance away, the family would seek out the American delegates and "neglect nothing to receive them well and procure them all possible pleasures." He said he would use the opportunity of the delegates' return to send her many things (HJS Letterbook, [19] August 1814, Cal S-V).

3. Christopher Hughes (1786–1849), a Baltimorean and professional diplomat, served as secretary to the American Peace Commission at Ghent in 1814.

4. Caroline's account has not been found.

To Charles J. Stier[1]

Riversdale, 27 December 1814

Dear Brother,

I received several days ago your letters from London, dated 3, 12, and 14 October, with the powers of attorney. Before proceeding to business allow me to thank you for myself and for Caroline and George for the articles you were good enough to send us by Mr. Hughes. I am very grateful to you also for the care you took of the cases containing my candelabra, etc., and for the deed to Riversdale. . . .

I am extremely sorry, dear Brother, you did not send me the instructions contained in your last letters sooner, for at present it is not possible to do anything. There is a general stagnation in all business. Our President has refused to receive Mr. Gilbert Robinson as agent for the exchange of prisoners and has suspended the functions of Colonel Barclay so that there is momentarily no English agent in the United States and it is, I fear, impossible to draw on London. Three different merchants whom I approached, as I knew they had money in England, said they did not wish to draw because their money was safer in London than here. . . . I fear the sale of the bonds is also impossible without an immense loss. The nominal price is 76, but there is neither buying nor selling. Everyone is waiting. I am sorry you did not say at what price you authorized me to sell, in case I can make remittances. As for nuggets or specie, that is out of the question.

There is not a single dollar in circulation south of Boston, and the banks have agreed not to pay except in paper. A person traveling from here to Boston exchanges Washington notes for Baltimore notes at par, then Baltimore notes for Philadelphia notes at a 5 percent discount in Philadelphia, then buys New York notes at a 5 or 6 percent [further discount], and from there to Boston [for another] 8 to 10 percent discount.

At present I have thought it most prudent to take government treasury notes for the balance in my hands as well as for your October dividends. They give interest and are as good as the new loan. . . . One condition alone I must stipulate with you in the management of your interests is that when you are not satisfied with what I have done, or when my accounts do not seem straight to you, you must say so frankly and be assured it will not offend me. On the contrary, I would have more confidence in myself if I were sure you would blame me when I deserve it. It is impossible that I should not make mistakes, being so little experienced in business.

I am vexed you did not mention the name of the person who said he saw my husband the day of the Battle of Bladensburg. I suppose it was Captain Smith whom he met in the English agent's [Barclay's] house. Among the wounded in our village there were Colonel Wood, [Colonel Thornton], and a Major Brown, who stayed here two or three months and whose acquaintance we made.[2] If you should meet them, they could give you news of us.

I am pleased to hear that you are all in such good health. Wasn't your wife delighted with her journey to England? My husband and children are quite well, but I cannot completely recover from the terrible illness I underwent last August, which left me very weak. . . .

Your affectionate,

R. E. C.

1. Carter Trans-MHS.
2. These were the English officers whom George Henry Calvert recalled visiting with his father as they recuperated in the village of Bladensburg. Colonel Wood, afterwards General Sir William Wood, returned the kindness twelve years later when George Henry visited him in Scotland. The name of Colonel Thornton is left blank in the Carter translation, but is supplied from young Calvert's account (Calvert, *Autobiographic Study,* p. 77).

NINE

Peace and Returning Prosperity

IN DECEMBER 1814, THE UNITED STATES and Great Britain signed the Peace of Ghent, but it was three months before news of the agreement reached America. As Mrs. Calvert observed, it was fortunate that peace was finally concluded because the United States was facing financial ruin. There was no gold or silver in circulation, no uniform national currency, and prices fluctuated wildly. But the avenues of trade were open again, and slowly prosperity and confidence returned. Napoleon's return briefly shattered the new tranquillity, but Waterloo restored it, and people could turn from the high drama of European politics to more ordinary pursuits.

The Calverts counted their blessings. The war had not been particularly harsh for them. Even with fighting all around them, they had suffered no loss of people or property from Riversdale. The British stole a few hogsheads of their tobacco from a warehouse on the Patuxent, but the great bulk of it was safe in storage and soon fetched a handsome profit in Continental markets. Rosalie's speculation in tobacco for her father proved a stunning success, and Stier and her brothers begged her to buy more. This proved impossible because most farmers, cut off so long from foreign markets, had abandoned tobacco and the leaf was in short supply.

Mrs. Calvert's real estate ventures were less profitable because tenants, hit hard by the war, were unable to pay their rents. Rosalie stopped buying land for her father's account and put his money into shares of the newly chartered second Bank of the United States. For herself, confident of returning prosperity, she forged ahead with land improvements. In

1816 Rosalie finally became legal owner of the Riversdale plantation, although it took an act of the Maryland legislature to accomplish it.

Meanwhile, Maryland Federalists approached George Calvert about becoming governor of Maryland, but Rosalie persuaded him to refuse. He had enough to do, she said, especially with her new properties to manage. She did not seem particularly impressed with the offer made to her husband. Her own distaste for politics made Rosalie politically un-ambitious for her husband, and she wanted him, like her father, to devote his energies to the economic interests of his family. George Calvert, however, came from a family tradition of politics; his forebears had ruled the colony, he was a legislator when he met Rosalie, and his brother was still in the Assembly. He was an apt choice for governor, and the Federal-ist candidate chosen in his place won easily that year.

With peace restored, H. J. Stier wanted the Peeters art collection he had left in the United States returned, and he asked Rosalie to ship the paintings to Antwerp. Stier and his daughter had used about a dozen of the smaller paintings to ornament their homes in America, but at least fifty paintings remained in their original packing crates and had never been shown. American artists knew of the collection, for it was by far the finest collection of European art in America, and they begged to see it before its return. Feeling the pressure, the Calverts opened Riversdale for a week-long public showing in April 1816, and artists and people of fashion came from far and near to attend this extraordinary event.

Mrs. Calvert's health was a mounting concern during these years. Her bouts with typhoid had left her debilitated, and even after passage of a year she complained of being unable to recover her strength. She suffered recurrent headaches and fevers and was forced to cut back on her usual activities. Finally, pregnant with her ninth child, she went to Philadelphia in 1816 to seek help from renowned physician Philip Syng Physick. His ministrations, along with a two-month reprieve from her household labors during her stay in Philadelphia, enabled her to return home much im-proved. That fall she gave birth to a healthy baby girl, Amelia, her sixth daughter and her last child.

To Charles J. Stier[1]

Riversdale, 10 March 1815

I wrote to you, dear Brother, four days ago and [sent] a letter of exchange on the English government for £2,000 sterling which I could only obtain at par. Before the news of peace the exchange on London was at 5 percent above par; now it is likely to fall lower. . . . According to your instructions, I shall charge your account and [van Havre's] with one-fifth [of this amount] each and Papa's with three-fifths. This sum is a part of your dividends in hand, and I will send you the remainder as soon as I can procure some more bills. You are mistaken in thinking the bills on the government lower than those on merchants—it is just the contrary. They are always higher for they are considered more safe, and they are payable in thirty days instead of sixty.

It is very fortunate for this country that peace was concluded, as otherwise the national bonds, banks, etc. would have gone to nothing. Now if we could just get rid of our Democratic administration and have a President of the Federalist party, the United States would soon recover from the losses they have suffered. Meantime, we are taxed literally up to our eyes. We have been more fortunate, however, than many others.

You will have foreseen when you heard of the astonishing fall in prices that I would not sell your bonds. At the moment there is no stable price for anything. Everything is in a constant state of fluctuation. If I cannot secure bills on advantageous terms shortly, I shall invest the balance of your credit in public bonds until you give me further instructions. Mr. Hughes is expected daily and doubtless he will bring me your letters written after the peace was signed. . . . Although we are enjoying peace for the time being, I do not think it advantageous to increase your investments here, especially if you can put them to better advantage where you are. If the Democratic party continues to rule, a dissolution of the Union will be the result sooner or later. . . .

Please send me a description of your tour in England. Did you find that beautiful and wonderful island much improved? Our sister wrote that she was thinking of sending her son there. I am very curious to know whether he has gone and if she is satisfied. As soon as George is old enough and sufficiently advanced, I should very much like to send him to an English college. We were not satisfied with the school where he was and have placed him at another at Germantown near Philadelphia. Caroline is with Madame Grelaud with whom I am quite satisfied, [but] I fear I shall soon have to send Eugénie there too.[2] It is not possible to educate her here. It will be hard to part from this sweet child. I could more easily bear the absence of all the others. Imagine all that is perfect in figure and in countenance as well as character, and you have her portrait!

Please give many affectionate messages to your wife, to Papa, and to my sister from me. . . .

Your affectionate sister.

1. Carter Trans-MHS.

2. All three Calvert girls—Caroline, Eugénie, and Julia—attended Madame Grelaud's school, as did their cousins, Eliza Law, Columbia and America Peter, and Frances Parke and Eleanor Agnes Lewis. The Philadelphia school was located first at 105 Mulberry Street, moved during the War of 1812 to Germantown, and returned to 89 South Third Street after the war (Bowie, "Madame Grelaud's," *Maryland Historical Magazine* 39 [1944], 141–48).

To H. J. Stier

Riversdale, 20 March 1815

It has been a long time, dear Father, since I've had a letter from you. The last two were [dated] 17 August and 15 September [1814], the latter containing your power of attorney to sell your bonds. You will have learned a short time later (and before we did) that the peace was signed at Ghent, and consequently I sold nothing.[1]

. . . I am afraid that we shall enjoy only a precarious peace. As long as the Democratic party continues to manage America's destiny, we have everything to fear. During the three miserable years just past, we suffered less than many others. Of the 100 hogsheads of tobacco that I bought for you in 1810, seven were in one of the warehouses which the British partially looted; they took five and left two. I hope the price we can get for the remainder will compensate you for this loss. I am most anxious to sell yours as well as some of our accumulated crops, but at this point there is no stable price for anything. Everything is in a state of constant fluctuation. The price of bonds, which went up at the first news of peace, has once again fallen slightly. . . . You will have seen by the [newspaper] excerpts I sent in earlier letters to my brother that north of Baltimore the government could not pay the last dividends on the public bonds. As a result, McEwen had to take some drafts on Baltimore, consequently [incurring] a five percent loss. If our envoys had not signed the peace when they did, our government would not have been able to continue for six months.[2]

I still hope to be able to get more favorable terms for some bills of exchange on London for the balance of your dividends remaining in my hands, and you will see by the enclosed account that I have completed payment on Mr. Hall's property. I am sorry to have to tell you that you will not earn any interest on that purchase for the coming year because I have been unable to rent it. Aside from that, I believe it to be a very valuable acquisition. Acreage in that district is increasing in value, and the soil is very fertile. Please give me some instructions as to whether you prefer to rent this property and risk the tenant cutting down the fine forest to grow corn each year, thus impoverishing the soil, or on the other hand, lose the interest on a considerable investment. All our poor tenant farmers have been so hard hit by the war that it was impossible to rent this year, but I hope to be able to next year. You will also see that the land bought from Dorsey is in the same predicament. There are two wretched houses on that property, each rented for $35; one of the tenants defaulted, so for the year 1814, I have only received $35. I am delighted that I did not continue my land purchases because I fear you are not going to be as satisfied as I would wish with my efforts in that regard, although I am convinced you would have strongly approved had you been on the spot.[3]

The day before news of the peace reached us the 6 Pct. public bonds were at 75; they immediately went up to 95, but there were no sales or purchases. Now the nominal price is 90, but still no one is buying or selling. The reason is that it is still not known how much the government is in debt, or the amount of loans that will be made, or at what price. It has just been announced that there will be a loan of twelve million [dollars], and I will subscribe for you and my brothers the balance remaining in my hands unless I can get some bills of exchange on London before the opening of subscriptions, which will be the 1st of May.

I just received, dear Father, a letter from Mr. C[hristopher] Hughes who has returned home. He tells of seeing you in Antwerp before his departure and that you and all the family were in good health. I had hoped that he might bring a letter from you, and I am extremely impatient to see him so I can ask him a thousand questions. My husband has already been to Washington twice without finding him at home. He writes that the small package which my brother asked him to deliver is with his baggage aboard the *Neptune,* which is expected at the beginning of May.

Caroline and George thank you profusely, as do I, for the watches you so kindly sent them—you overwhelm us with your generosity, dear Father.[3]

I regret so much, more and more each passing day, that we cannot enjoy the happiness of being near you. I should so like to show you my last four children, and I know that you would be pleased with them. My little Julia, now 14 months old, is quite pretty—she is so like the little angel I lost that I have been more comforted than I would ever have thought possible after that delightful little one's death. . . .

Your most affectionate daughter.

1. The Peace of Ghent was signed on December 24, 1814, but news of the signing did not reach the United States until February 11, 1815. The Senate unanimously ratified the peace treaty on February 17, 1815, and President Madison proclaimed it the same day.

Stier had written his daughter in September 1814 expressing anxiety over the lack of progress at Ghent: "Do the English drag the affair on in order to have time to get rid of English merchandise at a good price, or have they sworn to totally ruin America? It's a problem for us, but we incline to the latter opinion. . . . We have gotten all the information possible here. Your brothers start today for London to get more information." Stier sent proxies to enable Mrs. Calvert to sell all his holdings, "even at a loss," if she thought it advisable. But he worried about how she could safeguard the proceeds, "since under the circumstances you are living in now, ready cash can offer great worries" (HJS Letterbook, 20 September 1814, Cal S-V).

2. The inability of the Congress throughout the fall of 1814 to agree on any legislation to finance the war for another year had brought the United States to a serious financial and political impasse (see J.C.A. Stagg, *Mr. Madison's War* [Princeton, 1983], pp. 419–68).

3. Caroline's watch was accompanied by a note from her grandfather describing the keepsake he was sending her: "It's a little watch with a chain to wear around your neck. I recommend that each time you wind it, you think of me and tell me the first time you write me what time it is in Antwerp when it is twelve noon in Philadelphia, for you know that the sun doesn't shine for us at the same time." Stier asked for a little drawing of her, saying: "I think of you often, my dear, and remember very well how you were when I left you, but now ten years have gone by and you are quite grown up. I like to believe that you are very pretty and especially a very good girl. . . . It would be even better if you came to see me in person to satisfy my curiosity and the interest you inspire in me. . . . I am writing about it to your Mama, so all you have to do is ask" (HJS Letterbook, 10 October 1814, Cal S-V).

To Isabelle van Havre

Riversdale, 6 May 1815

It has been a very long time, dear Sister, since I wrote you, but not for any lack of thinking of you. Not a day passes that I don't recall the time we were together and regret that it is no longer so. However, as soon as I learn that a ship is going to sail, I always have so many absolutely necessary details to write Papa and Charles about their affairs, and especially so many horrible accounts to calculate, copy, etc., etc., that my head becomes completely muddled and time slips by without my being able to find even an hour to repay myself for my labors by chatting with you. . . .

We had scarcely finished rejoicing about peace here when along comes the news of Napoleon's restoration.[1] This made a great sensation here, with the "Demos" celebrating outrageously. I am most uneasy about the effect this [restoration] could have on my friends at ———.[2] Once again our correspondence probably can no longer be entirely free or uninterrupted. . . .

We spent last summer in a state of continual alarm. The burning of the public buildings in Washington is the best thing that has happened in a long time, as far as we are concerned, since this has finally settled the question of whether the seat of government would stay here. In the future they will no longer keep trying to change it, and as long as the union of states stands, the government will remain in Washington, despite the jealousy of Philadelphia, New York, and Baltimore. They are busy rebuilding the Capitol and all the buildings which were destroyed. I was quite calm during the Battle of Bladensburg because the only thing I feared was foragers, but we hardly suffered at all.

I must tell you an amusing story [of what] happened to my husband when he was on his way to Philadelphia a month or so afterwards. The carriage was full of all sorts of people; they began to talk about events which had taken place in [our] general vicinity, when one man sitting across from Mr. C remarked that Bladensburg would certainly have been burned if it hadn't been for "that damned old Tory George Calvert." You can be sure they made him change his tune in a hurry—the poor fellow was really stupefied!

I see in the newspapers that there are 40,000 British in Belgium—perhaps Colonels Thornton, Brown, or Wood are among this number, and having spent two months in Bladensburg, they could give you news of us. If a bullet is not an obstacle, I am sure that Colonel Thornton will become one of the most important generals, and he is a very pleasant man. . . .

I am not surprised that your Louise should be so difficult to please in her choice of a husband. I confess that I couldn't help hoping she would choose someone suitable from among the Englishmen who were with you. I have such a good opinion of that nation which I believe to be superior to all others.

I am infinitely obliged to you for the trouble you went to over my candelabra, lustres, and cups. No one has ever written me how much these items cost, [although] I have beseeched my brother. Would you please inform me so I can finally make the reimbursement? They are on board the *Neptune,* which is expected here this month.

Don't you think, dear Sister, that I write French worse every day? I have completely forgotten it—truly, I will soon have to write you in English. My paper is full so I must finish. . . .

Your devoted sister.

1. Napoleon left the island of Elba in late February 1815. Arriving in Cannes he marched toward Paris, picking up support along the way. By March 20, 1815, Louis XVIII had fled and Napoleon was once again emperor of the French.

2. Left blank in the original.

To Isabelle van Havre

Riversdale, 14 August 1815

My dear Sister,

. . . We just heard the news of the Battle of Waterloo and of Bonaparte's complete defeat. With what rapture I received this assurance that you had nothing more to fear, for I had been quite worried about you and your properties. I trust that now you will finally enjoy an uninterrupted tranquillity.

How much we owe the English—because there is no doubt that without them the French once more would have taken possession of our beautiful country. I fear it must have suffered a lot from this continual passage of troops, and I am impatient to receive the particulars of these great events from you. We saw in the papers that the inhabitants of Brussels were quite frightened. . . .[1]

Please give me some information about the Prince of Orange and whether the people like his government. Will Antwerp become a commercial center once more?

I wrote you on 6 May and again by Mr. Lansdale who plans to come to Antwerp and is bringing with him a small box with some trifles Caroline made for you, Papa, Louise, Charles, and Eugénie. . . .[2] By the first opportunity I am going to send my dear Louise the poems of W[alter] Scott and of Lord Byron, who are much admired here. Tell her that since she is so hard to please in the choice of a husband, I plan to send her our most celebrated young men. I am sorry that Colonel Barclay stayed only one day in Antwerp. I fear that our silly Americans (so satisfied with themselves) will not be much admired after one has been accustomed to the far superior society of the English.

One of our foremost generals, General Scott, just left for Europe.[3] If I had been acquainted with him, I would have given him some letters for you so he could place his laurels at Louise's feet, but unfortunately he doesn't have a cent. With him is a young man whom we do know and who has been here often—Major Mercer.[4] He is from a very good family [and] is a grandson of Sprigg, the former owner of Strawberry Hill. It is a pity he is a little foppish. I am sure you have been pleased with Mr.

Lansdale—he is a nice man, educated, sensible, and without affectation.

My husband and my children are in very good health. I feel better than I have for some time, but I cannot completely recover my strength and I have to spare myself constantly—the least exertion or fatigue gives me a fever.

Please, dear Sister, give my greetings to Papa, Charles, and to your husband. I had intended to write him today and send him his account, but it is not yet copied. Tell him I have invested all his dividends in 6 Pcts. Embrace your dear children for me and believe me

Your affectionate sister,

R. E. C.

1. Stier wrote his daughter a brief account of his reaction to Napoleon's return: "It seemed as if we would enjoy a universal peace and then came an event more astonishing than anything before: Bonaparte's return to the government, and so the whole of Europe is in arms. Hostilities started today with a bloody action at the border of Belgium. I could hear the sound of guns at my country place. What the final outcome will be is difficult to foresee. In the meantime we are living in anxiety and without pleasure, with more quartering and billeting of troops, more taxes. . . . The entire family is well, although on the alert and ready to leave the country if there is an invasion" (HJS Letterbook, [n.d.] June 1815, Cal S-V).

2. William Lansdale (?–1831) was a prominent Baltimore tobacco merchant. He was the son of Isaac Lansdale of Prince George's County, a neighbor of the Calverts at Mount Albion (RC to CJS, Riversdale, 11 June 1815, Calvert, CU-NYC).

3. General Winfield Scott (1786–1866), who had become an overnight hero in the Battle of Lundy's Lane in 1814, was traveling to Europe in 1815 to study military methods.

4. John Mercer (1788–1848), son of former Maryland governor John Francis Mercer and grandson of Richard Sprigg of Strawberry Hill, served as aide to Winfield Scott on his European trip.

To H. J. Stier

Riversdale, 11 November 1815

Dear Father,

The ship carrying this letter has 104 [hogsheads] of your tobacco on board.[1] There are six more still here which will go by another vessel since the owner of the *General Lingan* decided to sail a month earlier than he had first said, and there wasn't time to get them out of storage.

I wanted to consign this tobacco to Louvrex, but if I had, I would not have been able to get such a good ship to send it in so soon. The ship's owner had more offers than he had room for and he is paid $1 a barrel by

Willink and Murdoch for all that he gets consigned to them. . . .

These 104 [hogsheads] ought to bring a very good price, being for the most part of a superior quality and even [having] some [barrels] of yellow tobacco among them. I could have sold it very well here, but I thought it would be better to ship it to you than to buy letters of exchange, particularly when [they are] above par.

There is another ship which will sail in a month with more than 70 barrels of ours on board, [and] still another leaving this week from the Patuxent for England with 410 barrels. That will make nearly 500—the yield of our harvests for seven years.

I gave Murdoch instructions to remit £100 sterling to you which I entreat you to use to pay my debts, along with interest, for those articles which have been bought for me, and to hold the remainder for my account.

I am extremely sorry, dear Father, that this letter must be solely about business, but I hope within a few days to have the leisure to write you again. . . .

Your affectionate and obedient daughter,

Rosalie Eugenia Calvert

1. Mrs. Calvert began using the French *boucaut* instead of the English "hogshead" she had previously employed, but "barrel" and "hogshead" were identical measures to her and will hereafter be used interchangeably.

To Charles J. Stier[1]

[Riversdale], 16 December [1815]

I have just received, dear Brother, the two cases which came over in the *Neptune* and which should have been here three months ago. But I have been deprived of them all this time, first through the death of Mr. Bayard, and then through the negligence of McEwen's partners.[2]

We are beginning to breathe naturally after our two days' ecstasy of admiration. Please accept, dear Brother, and pray express to your wife, our gratitude for the superb cups, the interesting architecture albums, and the annals of the *Musée*. It is impossible to decide which cup is the most beautiful, for one insists that it is the green one and another is sure of the blue—a third declares for the purple, another for the scarlet, and we cannot agree except that none of them could be more beautiful. The architectural drawings are very interesting for us, as they give us an idea of the masterpieces of all countries, and the annals of the *Musée* are still more interesting since that beautiful collection has again been dispersed in returning the paintings to those from whom they were taken.[3] These books should make the long evenings seem short.

My children beg me to thank you heartily for the magic lantern. I had entirely forgotten how to manage it and we could not succeed at first, but by dint of trials and endeavors to remember the time you used to be showman for me, I succeeded—to the great amusement of the children! Even little Julia never grows weary of seeing it and, while looking at the giants and monsters depicted, forgets that it is bedtime and she is sleepy.

I am very grateful to you for the trouble you took to procure the candelabra and lustres for me. They are very beautiful and arrived in perfect order. . . . I have asked [Papa] to reimburse you with interest for the things you were good enough to buy for me. I am quite ashamed it was not done before.

[*continued 6 February 1816*]

1. Carter Trans-MHS. This is a continuation of a brief letter begun on October 28, 1815, whose content is insignificant.

2. James A. Bayard died on August 6, 1815, shortly after returning from Europe. Charles Stier had met Bayard at Ghent and entrusted him with several cases to be delivered to Mrs. Calvert.

3. This is a reference to Napoleon's looting of art treasures from all over Europe, including Antwerp, for the benefit of France.

To Isabelle van Havre

Riversdale, 17 December 1815

My dear Sister,

. . . I am very grateful to you for the pretty chemisette—it is really charming. They don't know how to embroider like that here. I will wear it with considerable pleasure. The travel library looks like a most interesting work and one which will be very useful to George and Caroline, as is the Young People's Theatre, and the magazine for adolescents,[1] which we cannot find here. [Caroline] asks me to send many thanks to Louise for the pretty little work-basket.

I don't know how, without knowing the age and disposition of my children, you could guess so well what would please them most. For more than a week my little Julia had talked incessantly about a dog and amused herself every day by hiding under tables and behind chairs, laughing and exclaiming that a mad dog was attacking her. When I opened the largest box, the first object to appear was the little dog. I presented it to her, pretending to make it bark. She was in ecstasy, and the three other children danced all around her in delight at the present which suited her so well. She never parts with it and we have to let her sleep with it.

The next thing we found were the two toy rifles which Charles and Henry seized immediately, jumping for joy and admiring their locks. They fired them twenty times in one minute, until they had used up all the flints that made them fire, and we had to get more. Right now they are marching like soldiers with their muskets on their shoulders.

Upon finding the little portfolio in the second case, the unanimous judgment was that it should be for George who, being in Philadelphia, couldn't share the pleasure of his brothers and sisters in seeing all the pretty things.

The two little painted inkwells were too delicate and pretty for the boys, so I awarded one to Caroline and the other to Eugenia. How beautifully the tiny scenes are painted on them! As for the two small toilette sets with looking-glasses, I have given one to Eugenia and the other to Julia, to be kept for her until she is old enough to take care of it herself. The little boxes we assigned to Caroline and George, as well as the prayer books.

You must have had a lot of work packing these cases—I have never seen anything so well-packed. They could have made ten trips from China without suffering from it. Everything was in the most perfect condition—not a bit of damage.

Accept, dear Sister, our collective thanks for your pretty gifts and for all the trouble you have had over my candelabra and lustres. We are all well here. Please give my compliments to Papa and your husband. . . .

Your affectionate sister,

R. E. C.

1. Mrs. Calvert first wrote *enfans* here, but scratched it out and substituted *adolescens*.

To Charles J. Stier[1]

[Riversdale], 6 February [1816]

Time has slipped away imperceptibly since I began this letter [28 October 1815] and when I was on the point of sending it, the lawyer who drew up the certificate said that it would be more satisfactory for you to have it annexed to the law passed by the State of Maryland. So I had to wait again. I hope it is as you wished. If not, I beg you to send me a copy as you wish it to be, and I will sign it. I had to appeal to the Legislative Assembly to make the deed [to Riversdale] valid. I am sorry, dear Brother, that I have caused you so much trouble on this matter. . . .[2]

Your affectionate sister,

R. E. C.

1. Carter Trans-MHS.
2. Charles Stier had sent the deed to Riversdale back to America and had asked to be released from his bond on the property. As it turned out, Charles's bond had been given to his father and required no legal action in America.

The reasons for appealing to the state legislature to validate the Riversdale deed are not given by Mrs. Calvert, but she consulted several lawyers during a protracted validation process. The matter was complicated by several factors: transfer of real property from a foreign national to an American citizen; existence of a preceding transfer of the property from Charles Stier to H. J. Stier in 1801 (of questionable validity, but based on an act of the Maryland legislature); and the transfer of property to a married woman in her own right, apart from that of her husband. Whatever the reason, by an act passed on January 18, 1816, the Maryland legislature vested all rights to the 729 1/4-acre Riversdale plantation in Rosalie Eugenia Calvert, her heirs and assigns (*Laws of Maryland,* 1815–1816, chap. 110).

To H. J. Stier

[n.p.], 19 February 1816

Dear Father,

. . . I'm sorry not to have time today to write you a long letter. . . . My husband and my little family are all quite well. They wanted to make my husband Governor of Maryland this year, but I persuaded him to refuse this honor and it was conferred on General Ridgely who has a large fortune and nothing to do.[1]

My own health is better than it has been for the last two years, and I have regained a good deal of my strength. However, I am still subject to nervous disorders and headaches which make it impossible for me to accomplish anything half of the time.

I hope to have news from you soon. . . .

Your affectionate and obedient daughter,

R. E. Calvert

P.S. The mantel and the statues have reached Philadelphia. I hope Mr. Murdoch has sent you the £100 sterling. Please use it to reimburse yourself and Charles. . . .

1. The governor was elected by the legislature at this time; George Calvert was probably approached by the Federalist leadership of this body. Charles Carnan Ridgely (1760–1829), a Federalist, was elected governor by the Maryland General Assembly in December 1815, defeating Robert Bowie by a vote of 47 to 45. He served from 1816 to 1819. Ridgely was wealthy, having inherited a considerable estate from his uncle Charles Ridgely, which included Hampton in Baltimore County.

To Isabelle van Havre

[n.p.], 5 March 1816

. . . I still greatly regret not having seen any of the people who have been to Antwerp and have seen you. At the moment my husband is in Baltimore, and he promised me he would go and see Mr. Lansdale who just returned from Europe and to whom I entrusted a box from Caroline to you. She is still in Philadelphia at the same boarding school with which I am quite pleased. She will stay there for at least another year, perhaps two. She is quite small for her age and appears a lot younger than she really is, [so] I think it will be to her advantage not to introduce her into society before she is seventeen.

George is also still in a French boarding school at Germantown, where he will stay until he is sufficiently advanced to go to college. I think he is learning very well there. You told me you were surprised that my husband consented to placing his son with a Frenchman, [but] after much inquiry we judged that it was the best school we could place him in.

I am beginning to be quite perplexed as to what I will do with the [children] I have here. Eugénie especially ought to be at school or have a tutor, but we have been so little pleased with our last two that I don't know what to do. Meanwhile, I am once more obliged to resume my old profession of schoolmistress which I find not at all amusing. Charles and Henry are so young that they can wait.[1]

According to the description you give me of your Clementine, I think she must greatly resemble my Julie. [Julie], too, is quite delicate in appearance and small for her age, but extremely pretty, dexterous, sprightly, and intelligent. She is the favorite of all the other children and of the household.

Since last summer we have had an addition to our little Bladensburg colony—the Fitzgerald family from Alexandria whom you should re-member, at least the wife who is a very fine woman. She has one daughter, 20 years old, who is amiable and well-educated, and three sons, one of whom is a doctor and another a lawyer. Mr. Stoddert's house has been bought by a man from Baltimore who is quite insignificant and whom we do not count among our neighbors. The late Benjamin Lowndes' house is also going to be sold, his widow having died. I do hope it will be bought by a nice family with whom we can be sociable.

I don't know whether I wrote you that Mrs. Ogle of Annapolis is dead.[2] Her will made my husband her executor, jointly with her son, but knowing that it would entail a lot of trouble and unpleasantness, he refused the appointment—very fortunately, since her daughter Mary just married a common laborer and we would have had a lot of trouble with its administration. . . .[3]

Your affectionate sister.

P.S. . . . The ship by which I intended to send this letter changed its destination and now I don't know when it will go. Our ports are full of ships which remain idle because they can't get a cargo. Yesterday I had the pleasure of receiving your letter . . . as well as Papa's with the instruc-tions for shipping the paintings.[4] Please, dear Sister, kindly tell Papa that I am going to occupy myself immediately and completely with the best method of making this shipment as soon as possible. . . . I will comply with his instructions in every particular, and I will spare no pains to have them well-packed and everything arranged in the best possible manner.

I am not surprised, dear Sister, when you tell me you have so few moments of leisure. The active [social] life you lead must leave you little [time], and I understand that you cannot do otherwise since you have children to introduce into society (which will also be my case in another year and a half). For myself, although I live so quietly and see so few people, I nevertheless rarely have time to rest and am nearly always behind in everything that needs to be done. But this is partly due to having poor servants whom I must supervise constantly, and frequently I must be extremely sparing of myself because of poor health.

Going out in the carriage does me a lot of good, but walking wears me out. If I go up and down stairs four or five times a day, I am sure to have a fever at night. Sometimes I am even forced to spend half my time reclin-ing on a sofa. You can imagine how disagreeable this is, especially for someone like me who loves activity and directing and overseeing everything myself. I must also eat very sparingly and drink only plain water—even a single glass of wine gives me a violent headache. As soon as good weather comes, I plan to make some little excursions in order to try to completely regain my health.

I learned with great satisfaction that the French had to give up the masterpieces which they had pillaged everywhere, and I would love to see the celebrations held when Antwerp's are returned to their rightful places.[5]

I am waiting impatiently for the account of the Battle of Waterloo which you promise Edward is sending me. Is he, like his father, disposed to become a general?

I thank you very much for the welcome information you give me about Papa's good health. Write me what changes he has made at the Mick since his return, and I beg you, dear Sister, make him remember to write me, even if it is only a few lines. I receive letters from him very rarely now, and you know what pleasure they give me. . . .

1. When this was written, Eugenia was nine, Charles seven, and Henry almost six years old.

2. Henrietta Margaret (Hill) Ogle, widow of Benjamin Ogle I, died on August 14, 1815, in Annapolis.

3. Mary (Ogle) Bevans married James Connor of Frederick County on February 8, 1816; her first husband, George Bevans, had died in 1814.

4. In late December 1815, Stier wrote that with peace in Europe and America, he thought the time was favorable for the return of the paintings he had left in his daughter's care. He instructed her to ship them directly to Antwerp, Amsterdam, or Rotterdam. In January he wrote in triplicate full instructions for their packing and shipping but unfortunately left no copy in his letterbook (HJS Letterbook, 28 December 1815, 16 January 1816, Cal S-V).

5. Both Mrs. Calvert's father and brother played a role in the return of works of art that Napoleon had taken from Antwerp. Charles Stier was appointed a commissioner by King William I to claim the artworks in Paris, and H. J. Stier, as a member of the Academy of Fine Arts, was made a commissioner for their receipt in Antwerp (HJS Letterbook, [n.d.] May 1816, Cal S-V).

To H. J. Stier

[n.p.], 20 March 1816

Dear Father,

. . . I have learned that the *General Lingan,* carrying your 104 barrels [of tobacco], reached Holland at a time when the price was very high. I do hope this made you a good profit. We also have just received news of the *Oscar*'s arrival at Rotterdam with our 410 aboard. My husband had written Mr. Murdoch quite explicitly not to be in a rush to sell since there is very little tobacco on hand here and the price would certainly continue to rise. However, [Murdoch] sold it right away for 10 1/2 stuyvers, and a fortnight later the price went up to 11 1/2, which with the 20 percent higher exchange resulted in a $10,000 loss on this cargo.[1]

I would be delighted to hear that yours brought a far better price. I am quite sure Murdoch acted as he thought best. He feared an immediate decline because there was so much tobacco in England and Holland, and [he] couldn't believe that there was scarcely any here. The fact is, however, that all our planters have almost abandoned this culture in the last four years.

We have sold 39 hogsheads here at $13 and $15 [a hundredweight], including five of yours which were stored in the warehouse; the sixth is still here and will be sold with the rest of ours if we can get $20 for it before May. If not, we will ship it all to Amsterdam. . . .

Two days ago, dear Father, I received your letter of 16 January [1816] with the instructions for shipping the paintings, which I shall attend to as quickly as possible. I have not yet had a reply to the letters I wrote to Baltimore on the subject. If we can ship them from that port, my husband will go there himself to get information and take care of everything. He was at Georgetown yesterday. A very fine ship is expected about May 1st to pick up a cargo of tobacco at Alexandria bound for Amsterdam (I have little hope of finding an opportunity direct to Antwerp). If this ship proves to be in good condition, I think this will be an excellent opportunity because there could be no more favorable type of cargo [than tobacco]. It would be less risky than with other cargoes, and we could put all the packing cases on top of the barrels where they would be protected against moisture.

I will follow your instructions exactly and will spare no pains to arrange the matter in the best possible way. I will personally supervise everything so there is no possibility of error. Presently there are two painters in Washington—Wood and Vanderlyn—whom I could employ to help me with the packing.[2] I know the former, but I do not have a high opinion of his competence. Some time ago Rembrant [*sic*] Peale of Philadelphia offered to come here to help pack the paintings, if I needed him, so that he might have an opportunity to see them.[3] Colonel Trumbull of New York, whose paintings I feel sure you have seen, has made the same request through the intermediary of Mr. Cooke, as has Sully of Philadelphia.[4] I think [Sully] might be the best and most knowledgeable, but I shall make further inquiries before deciding.

The frames which you had put on some of the small paintings are so narrow that they won't take up much room, and they are of sufficient length to insert in the vises. So I think it will be best to leave them as they are. I will also unpack the large cases which have not been opened for so many years and put flannel between each [painting], and if the cases are not strong enough, I will have new ones made. You can rely on me and on my husband to do all in our power to carry out this task for you. The only thing I dread, and that with some consternation, is the huge number of curious people who will descend on us when they hear that the paintings have been unpacked. You simply have no idea how famous they are.

I am so grateful, dear Father, for your kindness in giving me the two pretty landscapes by Swaegers and Antunnissens [*sic*].[5] I shall prize them highly. . . .

Your obedient daughter,

R. E. Calvert

1. A stuyver or stuiver (Dutch) is 1/20 of a guilder. The tobacco was being sold by the pound rather than by the hundredweight. With 410 hogsheads (410,000 pounds) being sold, a one-stuyver difference proved costly, as Mrs. Calvert said. The total sale was probably somewhere around $85,000, but that does not take into account shipping costs, commissions, or exchange differentials.

2. Joseph Wood (ca. 1778–1830), a New York portrait and miniature painter, had moved to Washington in 1816, and John Vanderlyn (1775–1852), also a New York artist, was back in America after an extended stay in Europe.

3. Rembrandt Peale said that George Calvert consulted him about buying the painting collection at Stier's proffered price of seventy thousand dollars. Peale advised him that the paintings would only bring ten thousand dollars on the market, but he persuaded Calvert to show them before their return ("Reminiscences," *The Crayon,* 19 September 1855).

4. John Trumbull (1756–1843) was a New York artist whose many paintings depicting the American Revolution brought him great fame in his lifetime. Thomas Sully (1783–1872) was emerging as one of the country's foremost portrait painters and later painted the Calverts' daughter Julia at the time of her marriage to Dr. Richard Henry Stuart in 1833. The intermediary mentioned here is probably William Cooke of Baltimore.

5. Frans Swaegers or Swagers (1756–1836) was a Dutch landscape painter, and Henri-Joseph Antonissen (1737–1794) was a Flemish landscape painter born in Antwerp. The two paintings were probably bought for Mrs. Calvert in 1807 when Stier wrote about beginning a "cabinet" for her; opportunities for safe shipping in

the interval had been few (HJS Letterbook, undated entry for late August/early September 1807, and 25 September 1817, Cal S-V). The two landscapes are still in the United States in the private collection of a descendant of Rosalie Stier Calvert (1989).

To H. J. Stier

[n.p.], 8 April 1816

. . . I am afraid I am going to have difficulty getting a ship sailing from here or Baltimore underline directly to one of the three ports you call for before June 30th.[1]

Ships often sail from Philadelphia for Holland and even to Antwerp, but I don't think it is expedient to send the paintings from [Philadelphia] because they would have to go there from here by water, whereas we could transport them to Baltimore by wagons. However, since I still have two and a half months, I hope I can be successful. The misfortune is that there is no more tobacco here, or at any rate very little, and no other cargoes are being sent from ports here. Also all the ships bound for Holland with tobacco are nearly always routed to put in at Cowes and at Market [Margate], which would not suit you since then they could be ordered to Hamburg or Bremen. There is an excellent ship sailing from Georgetown with a cargo of tobacco May 1st, but the owner is not willing to contract to go directly to Amsterdam and insists on putting in at Cowes. It is the same with a ship sailing from Baltimore. Please be assured, dear Father, that I will spare nothing in order to accomplish this shipment and will follow your instructions in everything.

My husband went to Baltimore and Philadelphia two days ago. I expect him to return within a week. He is gathering all available information and will engage the painter Sully to come here the 16th of this month to help me unpack and recrate [the paintings].[2]

As soon as I am sure of a ship, I will notify you by several copies and by bills of lading in plenty of time so that you can arrange for the insurance. If it had been left up to me, I would have [insured] it here—it seems to me [to be] more advantageous for you. . . .

You will see by your account that we sold 500 of your shares in the Bank of Washington at a ten percent gain and invested the proceeds in 6 Pcts. I did this because you seemed to think you had too large an amount in this bank. You will also see that the dividends from the banks were not invested in January, but in March—this comes about from the negligence

of McEwen's partners. I have good reason to complain about them—
they are insufferably negligent and careless!

I am sending you the charter of the new national bank which the
Congress just established and which will be subscribed in July.[3] I don't
know whether it will be a worthwhile stock for you or not. Several articles
[of the charter] are bad. . . .

Your obedient and affectionate daughter,

R. E. Calvert

1. Stier had specified Antwerp, Amsterdam, or Rotterdam.
2. There is no evidence that Thomas Sully did indeed come to help with the
packing. Rembrandt Peale said that Charles Bird King (1785–1862) supervised the
repacking of the Riversdale paintings ("Reminiscences," *The Crayon,* September 19,
1855). Another account mentions the painters [Rembrandt] Peale, [Charles Bird]
King, and [Joseph] Wood as coming to view the paintings (see Charles Burr Todd,
The Story of Washington [New York, 1893], pp. 382–83).
3. The Second Bank of the United States was chartered by the Congress in March
1816. It began operations in January 1817.

To Charles J. Stier[1]

Riversdale, 8 April 1816

Dear Brother,

. . . I just received your letter of 29 January 1816, signed also by Papa
and Mr. van Havre, asking me to buy 400 barrels of tobacco and consign
them to Louvrex. I regret very much that I am so often unable to carry
out your instructions. . . . You always give me your instructions too late,
dear Brother. A year ago I could have bought tobacco which would have
given you a profit, or at least not a loss, but now I am afraid it cannot be
done. There is very little tobacco in this country at this time. The high
price in Europe caused all the buyers to ship it, and also since there is no
money here, it is advantageous to send it to Europe. We just turned down
$16 [a hundredweight] for our last year's crop (which is not even com-
pletely packed), and I am sure we will easily obtain $20. . . . I don't think
anything can be done right now, but I am going to look into it. I am
expecting Mr. Cooke of Baltimore toward the middle of the month, and I
will consult him about it. . . .[2]

Our shipment of 410 barrels on the *Oscar* has turned out badly, however, because of Murdoch's stupidity. Despite the fact that my husband
had written him in November that he wouldn't draw anything on him

before spring and that since there wasn't any tobacco left here, it would greatly increase in value, [Murdoch] persisted in thinking the opposite and sold the cargo before the ship had even arrived in Rotterdam. Two days later this same cargo sold for a profit of $10,000 to a second party, and since then to a third for $20,000—all, moreover, without even seeing the tobacco! If Murdoch had followed our instructions, which were explicit, we would have had $20,000 more, since two-thirds of the cargo belonged to us—which he caused us to lose by his timidity and obstinacy. . . .

In saying that there is no tobacco here now, I mean that it has all been bought up long since by the Baltimore merchants. On several occasions last summer they even bought crops while they were still growing in the fields, paying the planters a sum in advance to be sure. I must close, dear Brother, by embracing you. Many compliments to your wife and believe me,

Your affectionate sister.

1. Calvert, CU-NYC.

2. William Cooke was probably coming to Riversdale to see the famous collection of paintings which the Calverts were putting on display before returning them to Europe. Mrs. Calvert never mentioned the public showing in any of her letters, perhaps because she had misgivings about it. It certainly added to her already burdensome task of safely returning the masterpieces—a responsibility which weighed heavily on her at a time when she was again pregnant and in poor health.

In any event, three brief accounts tell of the public showing of the Riversdale paintings. Rembrandt Peale, writing thirty-nine years after the event, recalled that "for two weeks [Calvert's] mansion at Bladensburg was the hospitable rendezvous of numerous visitors of taste and education, from different cities. . . . It was a new and pleasant sight to witness such an animated assemblage of artists and amateurs—members of Congress from the different States, merchants, lawyers, and country gentlemen—all engaged in discussing the merits of pictures and paintings" ("Reminiscences," *The Crayon,* September 19, 1855).

Mary Bagot, wife of the British minister to the United States, wrote her impressions in her journal on April 24, 1816: "Went with Mrs. Peter to see a collection of pictures at a Mr. Calverts within about two miles of Bladensburg. . . . We found a very curious collection of pictures—a few very fine Vandykes & two or three magnificent Rubens besides several other undoubted pictures of old masters. Mrs. Calvert is a direct descendant from Vandyke [Editor's note: R.E.C. was descended from Rubens] & these pictures belong to her father & had for twenty years lain packed in cases in a garret unthought of untill the old gentleman who is retired into Holland sent for them a few months ago—& they were to be packed the next day. Everybody flocked to see them[,] a collection of pictures being almost unheard of in the United States" (taken from "Exile in Yankeeland: The Journal of Mary Bagot, 1816–1819," ed. David Hosford, *Records of the Columbia Historical Society* 51 [1984], p. 36).

The Prodigal Son. Peter Paul Rubens.
Koninklijk Museum voor Schone Kunsten, Antwerp

Romulus and Remus. Attributed to Peter Paul Rubens and
Huysmans de Malines.
Private collection, U.S.A.

Philippe Le Roy and his wife, Marie de Raedt. Portraits by Anthony Van Dyck.
By permission of the Trustees of the Wallace Collection, London

Sarah Gales Seaton wrote her sister in May 1816 of experiencing a real treat the previous week—"a view of some of the finest paintings ever in America." Mrs. Seaton, wife of the editor of Washington's *National Intelligencer*, reported that the Calverts had opened their house to all art lovers for a five-day showing prior to the collection's return to Belgium. She said that her high opinion of the collection was shared by the connoisseurs present—"Peale from Philadelphia, King and Wood from Baltimore were transported with admiration" (Josephine Seaton, *William Winston Seaton of the National Intelligencer* [Boston, 1871], pp. 134–35).

To Isabelle van Havre

[n.p.], 2 June 1816

Dear Sister,

How much I regret having only a few minutes to write you. For two weeks I had worked without respite packing the paintings in order to send them by a ship bound for Amsterdam, and just yesterday I had a letter from Mr. Cooke advising me that in five days the ship *Oscar* would be sent to Antwerp. This was an opportunity we could not miss and we worked, my husband and I, with two carpenters and several of our people until very late last night in order to have them ready to send this morning. At last, the wagons have just left and will arrive, I trust, without mishap in Baltimore. The paintings are packed, I dare say, as well as possible, but two of the outside cases are not as good as I would have had them if we had had a little more time to build them. The fact is that the cases were all packed a month ago because I had hired a painter to do it under my scrutiny, and I think they were perfectly fine and the same as when they came here, only more secure. But then I received Charles' letter with instructions to pack them differently, so I was obliged to reopen the cases and begin everything all over again. . . .

Please convey my greetings to Louise and Edward and ask them to accept the poetry of Walter Scott and of Lord Byron which I put in Case No. 3 of the paintings. I am very sorry that the trunk which I sent by Mr. Lansdale has been lost through his negligence. He is unable to say what happened to it. I hope to hear from you soon and that you are all well. Our little family is in good health. I wish I could show you my little Julie, aged 2 years and 4 months. She is the best child I have ever seen, extremely intelligent. I am planning to leave on a little trip in a fortnight to recover my health. To my great sorrow I find myself pregnant again—I had hoped to have no more children. . . .

Your affectionate sister,

R. E. C.

[P.S.] I would be most obliged to you if you could send me by any ship coming to Baltimore or Philadelphia the articles on the list attached here. They are things I cannot easily get here:

One half dozen bottles of anisette liqueur and 1/2 dozen of curaçao.
One small cask of anchovies.
Two d° [ditto] of herrings from Holland.
A small quantity of Carmine color and an assortment of brushes for painting.
Some seeds of brussels sprouts.
D° of the kind of carrot found in Antwerp in Flemish sugar carrots.
D° of scorzonera.[1]
15 aunes of lace of the width here attached.[2]
16 d° of the smallest [width lace] or next smallest for children's bonnets in four different pieces and designs.

8 ostrich feathers. Two muslin bonnets for me like those worn at
home in the morning or *en demie parure.*
Two embroidered handkerchiefs, dº, dº.
30 aunes of muslin trim embroidered in the way we trim dresses,
handkerchiefs, etc.
7 brass saucepans with covers, of the measure attached or nearly so.
6 or 8 dozen of champagne wine, if a very good quality can be had.
One cask of red wine (of the kind we call "claret" here), if a good
quality can be had. All that which is sold here is bad and often
sour.

1. Black salsify, a vegetable cultivated in Europe for its roots, which have an
oysterlike flavor.
2. An aune is an old unit of measurement equal to forty-five inches.

To H. J. Stier

Riversdale, 5 June 1816

. . . The paintings, packed in four cases, left here on [June] 2nd by
wagon. My husband accompanied them and is still in Baltimore to oversee their embarkation. He will take care that they are placed in the most
favorable location on board ship (the *Oscar,* Captain Will of Baltimore).
The cargo consists of leather from Buenos Aires, some tobacco, and
cotton—all dry goods.

We had planned to send them on the *Emperor of Russia* . . . and were
busy repacking the cases when I had a letter from Mr. Cooke saying the
Oscar was to sail directly to Antwerp in five days. So I was obliged to send
them to Baltimore right away—this is why Cases No. 3 and 4 are not as
strong as I would have wanted if we had had time to make new ones. But I
had to use the old ones which I did have reinforced. . . . I felt it was too
good an opportunity to miss—direct to Antwerp, on one of the best
ships out of Baltimore, and coming just at the most favorable season of
the year.

The only thing that worries me is that I was unable to follow your
instructions to arrange for insurance over there. There simply wasn't
time to forward all the papers. I was forced, therefore, to insure here,
which I did for a valuation of $20,000 at two percent. I do hope this
meets with your approval. I was most uncertain as to what amount to
insure them for—$20,000 seems to me much less than their actual value.
But according to instructions you gave me when you left here and then

later on in a letter, you said to insure them for $12,000 in peacetime; they are certainly more valuable now than then, so in the end, dear Father, I made what I thought was the best decision. I should be terribly distressed if I have done the wrong thing.

24 June 1816

. . . I recently had a long consultation with Mr. Cooke and he advises me not to invest any funds for you in the new Bank of the United States, but rather to continue the 6 Pcts. He also agrees with me that there is no way to remit in letters of exchange just now without a substantial loss and that it is necessary to wait until the exchange is lower, which will probably occur in six to eight months.

Our little family is well. . . .

Your affectionate and obedient daughter,

R. E. Calvert

··⫰[FOLLOWING IS THE DRAFT OF A letter from H. J. Stier to George Calvert reporting the safe arrival of the Peeters-Stier painting collection in Antwerp. The letter is interesting for Stier's direct appeal to his son-in-law to spare his daughter any more children. The draft is in English and not in Stier's handwriting, evidently written by a secretary. From HJS Letterbook, Cal S-V.

To George Calvert from H. J. Stier

Antwerp, 15 August 1816

By the arrival of the *Oscar* [in late July] I received . . . the paintings in perfect good order for whose safe return we are indebted to your particular care; I beg you to accept of mine and of the whole families kind thanks.[1]

Your letters afforded me infinite pleasure. By every word you say concerning your family I perceive the satisfaction it procures you and the enthusiasm of a good father which you feel for them. You wish I could see your six fine children. I undoubtedly wish it still more than you and it depends entirely of [sic] you to satisfy us all. Bring them here and I once more will embrace them tenderly. I am firmly persuaded they will procure you all possible satisfaction; it cannot be otherwise their being of such a good breed; but your works being brought to the greatest degree of perfection, stop there and leave the rest to my dear Caroline, whom I hope you will soon have an occasion of marrying. I recommend very much to your care the health of your wife, who stands in great need of your attention.

I also learn with pleasure the success of your cultivation and the affluence in which the produce of sale of your tobacco and other crops has placed you. I hope the happy situation in which you are will not be disturbed by any changes in the present governments. We are here in perfect tranquility; our government organizes itself dayly [*sic*] and promises us prospects of future happiness.

My whole family here is well and happy. We often speak of Bladensburg and even indulge the plan of going all together to see you, so contrive to find lodgings for us all. I wish such a fine dream could be realized. I tenderly embrace you, your wife, and all your family.

[no signature]

1. Stier also wrote his daughter, thanking her for her efforts and reassuring her about the condition of the paintings; only one painting was damaged, and it was not an important one. He said that the collection would now be put up for sale, since this was necessary to settle the Peeters estate, but that he expected to buy back the most valuable paintings himself (HJS Letterbook, [n.d.] May 1816 and [n.d.] July 1816, Cal S-V).

To Isabelle van Havre

Philadelphia, 29 August 1816

You will no doubt be surprised, my dear Sister, to receive a letter dated from here. The fact is that for the past three years I have suffered from a lingering illness and am subject to frequent, quite severe attacks of fever. Finding that the doctors in Washington could not cure me, I made the decision to come here to consult Dr. Physick, the foremost doctor in America.[1] I expected to stay for only a fortnight, but he says he cannot undertake to cure me unless I stay for at least a month.[2] So I am settled here for that time very much in spite of myself, for I have left my two little boys at Riversdale where my husband will return tomorrow, along with George who has a month's vacation. Caroline is still [here] at the same school, and Eugénie and Julia are with me. . . .

Please tell your husband that I sent him his April account, that all the

July dividends have been invested in 6 Pcts. at 97, and that since then I have subscribed for him in the new Bank of the United States for $25,000. Since I had invested all the dividends and didn't want to sell any stocks, I had to borrow the sum needed for payment at the time of subscription. . . . Please tell Charles that I have taken the same amount on the same terms for him, and for Papa $50,000.[3] It is expected that those who want to may receive the dividend payments in London, which will be quite advantageous for you. . . .

You wouldn't believe how much Philadelphia is changed and embellished since 1793 [*sic*]—you would no longer recognize it. Several people have accumulated immense fortunes. Yesterday I went to see a country house on the banks of the Schuylkill. Everything is done in the European style and is really delightful. The shops are full of the most elegant merchandise and adornments and surpass everything I had heard. . . .

Your affectionate sister,

R. E. Calvert

1. Philip Syng Physick (1768–1837), sometimes called "the father of American surgery," had studied medicine at Edinburgh, but returned to his native Philadelphia to practice. He was on the staff of Pennsylvania Hospital from 1794 until 1816 and also lectured on surgery at the University of Pennsylvania from 1801 to 1819.

2. In addition to being ill, Mrs. Calvert was seven months pregnant with her ninth child.

3. No reason is given for this change of heart about investing in the Second Bank of the United States. Stier wrote Mrs. Calvert in May 1816, wondering if it wouldn't be advantageous to make a large investment in the new bank, but he left it to her discretion (HJS Letterbook, [n.d.] May 1816, Cal S-V).

To Isabelle van Havre

[Riversdale], 25 October 1816

My dear Sister,

While I was in Philadelphia . . . your letters gave me much pleasure and at a time when I had great need of such consolation, being very sick, far from my home, and with little hope of completely recovering. Now I find myself much better—to take a trip did me a lot of good.

The ship *Prince of Orange* arrived while I was in Philadelphia. Accept our thanks, dear Sister, for the box it brought us. Caroline is enchanted with her little notebook of waltzes and asks you to be her spokesman to thank Louise. The other pieces of music are still too difficult for her, as she is not sufficiently advanced. Accept George's thanks also for the *Jerusalem Delivered*—on my departure I left him very busy reading it.[1] I have had so much to do since my return here that I have not yet had time to begin *Corinne* or Mme Lafayette, but [they] look most entertaining.[2] The "Baby house" [belonging to] Eugénie and her little sister Julie (who has one floor) is magnificently furnished by all your presents.

I have never seen anything as fine as these open-work stockings—surely one should wear very short skirts with these. Do you wear other stockings underneath? The embroidery designs and little samples are a real treasure to us. Some are entirely new to us, and I am much obliged to Louise for her industry in collecting them for me.

We did not have as detailed a work on the Battle of Waterloo as the one you sent with the map, which is most interesting. Since this famous day will long be the subject of conversation and different opinions, I will now be able to settle many disputes.

I had endless pleasure reading the accounts you gave of your children and of society. You ask if I sometimes play music—I must confess that I don't have time for that. You have no idea of the multiplicity of my tasks. My husband has so much to do outside that he troubles himself <u>literally with nothing</u> in the house, and you know what attentions a numerous family and a house as large as ours demand. Also our servants are not like yours—they have to be supervised constantly. If a cask of wine has to be bottled, it is I who must preside. I must inspect to see that my carriage and horses are taken care of as they ought to be. I must completely supervise my garden [because], up to now, I have had only an ordinary negro for a gardener. Now, however, we have a German who seems to be knowledgeable and this greatly relieves me. One <u>small</u> inconvenience, however, is that he doesn't understand a single word of English—I have to explain everything to him by signs.

We frequently have hired laborers, such as carpenters, painters, etc. [and] they have to be fed, lodged. We must provide clothing for a large number of [house] servants, besides those for the outside negroes. All this is much more difficult in the country than in the city, where one can be assisted by agents whom I cannot obtain at this distance from Washington. A household in the country is also much harder to direct. Instead of going to the market every morning to buy what you want, here we must eat veal when it is slaughtered, the same with beef, and we must plan a week in advance for everything we will need. To do all this well and economically requires much judgment and exertion.

I have left Caroline at school for one more year. She is learning to play the lyre—is this instrument familiar to you? It is a lot like a guitar. I plan on introducing her into society the winter after this one. She is very small for her age, but fully grown. I think she will be pretty enough, but quite variable, infinitely better one day than the next.

[*continued 5 November 1816*]

1. *La Gerusalemme Liberata* (1575), by Torquato Tasso, recounts the feats of Godfrey of Boulogne on the First Crusade.

2. *Corinne,* a novel by Madame de Staël, née Anne Louise Germaine Necker (1766–1817), was published in 1807. Madame de la Fayette, née Marie Madeleine Pioche de la Vergne (1634–1692), was also a novelist; her best-known work was *La Princesse de Clèves* (1678).

To H. J. Stier

Riversdale, 29 October 1816

Dear Father,

I wrote you two or three letters from Philadelphia where I spent two months. I feel much better for the change and am very hopeful that after my confinement, which will take place around mid-November, my health will be restored. I received your letter of 20 May, and just now your letter of 29 July also, brought by the *Oscar;* it gave me intense pleasure to learn that you are enjoying such good health, that the paintings had arrived, and that you were pleased with what we had done. . . .

Your April and July dividends were invested in 6 Pcts., and in September I subscribed $100,000 for you in the new Bank of the United States. The stock is just as safe as the 6 Pcts., will give higher interest and has other advantages, notably, the probability that they will pay your dividends at London if you so desire. I am enclosing the charter of establishment, in case you have not received the one I sent from Philadelphia, and I hope that you approve of this use of your assets. I hesitated and deliberated a long time before coming to this decision. You know that in a short while all the old 6 Pcts. will be redeemed; the Bank cannot give less interest and will surely give more—so it ought to be profitable to convert the 6 Pcts. to this stock.

You asked me to give you details on the land purchases from the Messrs. Hall and Dorsey. Let's begin with Mr. Hall's, which we call "Oatland" and which is situated half-way between Riversdale and

Mount Albion. . . . You will recall that this 595 acres was bought in February 1814, for $23,948.95, or $40.50 an acre. . . . The owner was heavily in debt, and it was necessary to buy up his debts to avoid having the land attached. . . . The final payment, and consequently acquisition of the property, was made in January 1815, for $25,960 including interest. You will recall that at the time of the sale Mr. Hall's nephew had his grain, etc. on the land, and he agreed to rent [the property] for the year for $500. . . . [However,] during the following two years he could not afford to rent it. I don't know, dear Father, if you will understand my explanation. In the future I hope you will receive a good return. A large number of trees [on that property] were felled by a hurricane in 1815, which did a great deal of damage in Maryland. The wood [was] rotten, so this summer we had to make 105,000 bricks in order to build houses for the negroes, barns, etc. We will buy three or four negroes before January, supplying four or five of our own negresses, in order to work the place with an overseer. I shall report the profit involved. We also transported 300 bushels of plaster of paris there, which we have found by experience does wonders for the soil.

The Dorsey property of 505 acres was bought in July 1812 for $7,000, or a little less than $14 an acre. . . . [The property] adjoins the Spurrier tract, has 200 acres in very fine forest, [but] the rest is quite poor soil. However, as it is only eleven miles from the flourishing city of Baltimore and the new turnpike road will pass through it, it will surely increase in value each year. Another advantage of [owning] this property is that it assures the stability of the tavern [on the Spurrier property] because if someone else owned it, they well might build a second [tavern], which would greatly decrease the value of the first. . . .

This year we built a new brick stable at Spurrier's tavern which will house sixteen horses; there wasn't enough stabling for the horses of the stagecoaches which all stop there. [We also built] two houses for the tenants and their families; the stable cost $1,000, and the houses [illegible]. Now we are building a cook-house for lodging the servants, since the old wooden one was completely rotten—that will cost about $1,500, and an additional stable for forty horses will cost about $3,000.

So you can see, dear Father, that besides the two percent rent we have to pay you, this property involves us in great expenses each year— expenses that are necessary but that do tend to empty our pockets. . . . Before long it will develop into an important holding, however, and will provide a handsome marriage portion for one of our children. The Patuxent property will provide for two, the Oatland property for another, the Montgomery County property for the fifth, and Riversdale I plan to leave to Henry since he bears your name. And when we have built a fine mill [at Riversdale] which brings in a regular income, we can detach the adjoining farm to provide for the seventh [child].[1] If some of [the children] show particular talents for being lawyers or [members of] some other profession, this will be so much the better. You see I'm like Perrette [*sic*]—I only hope I don't overturn my pitcher![2]

. . . You seem to think that we could have obtained an indemnity for the five casks of tobacco the British stole, but I assure you we did everything we could, with no success. Many people, Edward Calvert included, lost some of their negroes, and some lost all of theirs, plus all their tobacco, grain, etc., without being able to recover anything. These acts were authorized by Admiral Cockburn and for his profit, I think.[3]

You complain, dear Father, that you have received no interest yet on the $5,000 which I subscribed in your name for the new turnpike road from Baltimore to Washington. I can only say, as a consolation, that my husband subscribed $10,000. When the road is completed, it will pay 10 1/2 percent which the law authorizes, and payment will begin this winter, I hope. . . .

I really must stop, dear Father, and I fear that my long letter may have tired you out. . . .

Your affectionate daughter,

Rosalie E. Calvert

1. The Calverts had six children living at this time and were expecting another.
2. In French pantomime, Pierrette is the female counterpart of Pierrot.
3. Sir George Cockburn (1772–1853) was the British admiral in charge of the Chesapeake Bay expeditions and, with General Robert Ross, the burning of Washington in August 1814.

To Isabelle van Havre

[Riversdale], 5 November [1816]

. . . My husband has just returned from Baltimore; he shipped three of the boxes [you sent] by packet, but he brought box No. 3 back [with him] in his cabriolet. Allow me to reiterate my thanks for the preciseness with which you carried out my commissions and for your pretty presents. The flowers are quite beautiful and the drawing by my dear Louise is really charming. It's like an engraving—I shall greatly treasure it. I am also most grateful to her for the samples of silk and dress trimmings. You make no mention of a very pretty bodice that I found in one of the cartons which is exactly my size. I suppose it should be worn over a dress, like what we call here a "Spencer."[1]

All the various items are very pretty, some more expensive than I expected, but then others less so. I am delighted that you didn't send me the embroidered handkerchiefs that you mentioned; by *mouchoir,* I mean to say something which you wear at the neck, perhaps you call it *chemisette,* but I think they are always worn there fastened in the front. I would like something which adorns the neck a bit without covering it too much, but perhaps that is not fashionable. What do you wear at your neck when you are dressed up?[2]

I am quite satisfied with the plumes. The batiste is also just what I wanted, [and] the hemmed handkerchiefs are a good buy. I will take care to follow exactly your directions for washing the embroideries and the silk stockings. I am delighted you sent me those samples of your dress trimmings—it gives me the idea perfectly. Your shoe is much too narrow for me—I'll send you one that fits me well, as well as one of Caroline's. In my present condition I cannot try on the corset, but I will do so as soon as my figure is back to its usual form.

My husband has directed the Messrs. Crommelin of Amsterdam to send Papa $300, which I have asked him to transfer to you along with a balance left over from my allowance. Please, dear Sister, reimburse yourself for all the expenses of my commissions and keep what is left over for the next time. . . .

Your affectionate sister.

1. A Spencer was a long-sleeved, short-waisted, fitted jacket which first appeared about 1804.
2. What Mrs. Calvert is asking for is a kerchief, or *fichu.*

To Charles J. Stier[1]

Riversdale, 7 November 1816

I received your letters, dear Brother, by the *Oscar,* and please accept many thanks for the books you were so kind as to send me. They are very interesting to me and will be still more so for my children. I reread Racine and Corneille with much pleasure. I had never read Molière nor Delille, so I will have all the more pleasure in learning to know them.[2] I have heard several people here speak of Chateaubriand's work in terms of the highest eulogy.

Allow me to repeat my thanks for the charming statues which arrived in perfect order. The Olympian victor is a little too *déshabillé,* but what beautiful lines and expression! As I have never had the pleasure of meeting your amiable Eugénie I could not recognize her portrait if I had not been instructed beforehand. The impression *en blanc* is especially charming. Why do you not bring the lovely original to us, who are all prepared to love her? They write me that it is your fault—if that be true I shall not easily pardon you.

I was very surprised to hear that Papa wanted the paintings, as he already has such a fine collection. But since he wants them, I hope he will get them, although I am of your opinion that if you advertise them in London there will be many competitors.

I hear with great pleasure that you are improving Cleydael, and I often recall the happy days I spent there. It is a charming home. Do you remember the little boat we used to row around the house together?[3] I was sorry to learn of our uncle Albert's death, for he was a good man although a little eccentric.[4]

You ask me to tell you about our children. They are all as well as they can be. My youngest, Julie, is the most delightful, interesting little girl you can imagine—perfect in every respect. Colonel Thornton would have done Eugénie's portrait for you, but it is not in one day that all her merits can be appreciated.[5] My little boys behave very well and are not a whit alike. Charles loves farming, horses—in short, everything belonging to a farm. Henry is his little sister Julie's cavalier, and he is also a great musician. You would be astonished to hear him play, or rather blow, on the flute for he knows no air as yet, but his tones are perfect. Caroline and George are still at the same schools in Philadelphia, where George will remain until he is sufficiently advanced to go to the university. We have not yet decided upon the one to which we shall send him. He is talented in every direction, but a bit lacking in perseverance and application and does not like irksome tasks. I shall bring Caroline back in another year and introduce her into society the winter after that. She is very small in figure, but has an interesting face. She is a little too timid and succeeds better with drawing than with music, which she does not like so well, and I have difficulty in making her dance. . . .

Your affectionate sister.

1. Carter Trans-MHS.
2. Abbé Jacques Delille (1738–1813) was a poet and translator of poetry.
3. The castle at Cleydael was surrounded by a moat.

4. Albert Stier, H. J. Stier's younger, unmarried brother, died at age seventy in June 1816.

5. Probably the wounded British officer mentioned in earlier letters.

To Isabelle van Havre

[Riversdale], 3 December 1816

. . . Allow me again a hasty thank you for all the pretty things you sent us, and Caroline joins me in appreciation. Tell my dear Louise that I have never drunk better coffee than that made in her coffee pot, and so easily made that even while I have been confined to my room, I pour myself a small cup each morning for my breakfast.

I have the pleasure of announcing to you the birth of a little daughter, who came into the world on the 14th of November.[1] She is the strongest baby I have ever had, which is a most pleasant surprise. Since I was so sick during my entire pregnancy, I feared she would be frail and tiny—instead, she is in the best possible health. I myself feel much better than I had expected and suffered less than usual.

I am very sorry not to be able to write you a much longer letter, but my eyes are still weak and writing generally gives me a violent headache. Also the ship should sail from Baltimore in two days. My husband is going to Baltimore tomorrow morning and will put this letter on board. It is now 10 o'clock, so I must finish. . . .

Your affectionate sister,

R. E. Calvert

[P.S.] . . . Would you ask your husband, Charles, and Papa to send me a proxy to vote their shares for directors in the new Bank of the United States?

1. Amelia Isabella was the Calverts' ninth and last child.

A Washington Debut

THE YEARS FROM 1817 THROUGH 1819 were a high point in
Rosalie Calvert's life. A mature and respected woman, wealthy in her
own right and married to a successful planter, Rosalie had reached the
stage when, for her children's sake, she had to play a larger role in the
society around her. Her daughter Caroline, seventeen, was of marriage-
able age, and the time had come for her presentation to Washington
society. For both mother and daughter this was serious business, but it
was also marvelously diverting.

Rosalie expected no help from her husband in her social campaign and
merely hoped he would not be too much of a hindrance. The responsibilities for cultivating the right contacts, scheduling attendance at the
proper events, ordering suitable wardrobes, and arranging reciprocal
entertainment all fell on her shoulders. She complained that her husband
lived in their house as if he were not the master and concerned himself
with nothing except managing his farms. Fortunately, Rosalie now had a
housekeeper she could rely on, a white woman who also served her as a
dressmaker, and for awhile she had a governess and teacher for the
younger children.

Social life in the nation's capital city was much more to Mrs. Calvert's
liking than it had been during the Jeffersonian era. The partisanship of
the prewar years was replaced by an era of good feelings and social
harmony scarcely imagined before. James Monroe was president, the
country was prosperous, and old animosities between the Federalists and
the Democrats were almost gone. First Lady Eliza Monroe brought a

more formal style to the President's House than her predecessors—a change highly approved by Mrs. Calvert.

Rosalie began planning for Caroline's debut a year ahead, ordering quantities of clothing and adornments for herself and her daughter from Europe. Their clothes, carefully selected by Rosalie's sister, Isabelle, were a source of great pride to Mrs. Calvert. Few other Washington ladies had European gowns, certainly not entire wardrobes of them, and the Calvert women's finery was much admired and even envied.

Women's costume became more ornamented in the second decade of the century. The classical simplicity of the high-waisted chemise dress gave way to gowns bedecked with garlands of flowers, ruffles, and lace. White muslin, so long the basis of fashion, became supplemented by a richer array of fabrics and colors. Skirts were shorter, and fancy open-work stockings showed beneath them. Hats and toques erupted in cascades of ostrich plumes and aigrettes. Jewelry, recently out of style, reappeared but remained simple. Corsets, too, were back, but they were short and only lightly boned, designed more to enhance the bust than to constrict the waist.

The 1818 social season opened on New Year's Day when President and Mrs. Monroe gave Washington, including the Calverts, their first glimpse inside the newly rebuilt White House. A dizzying schedule of social events followed—dancing parties, dinners, tea parties, assemblies—sometimes two or three events scheduled for a single day. People had to send their invitations out a week to ten days ahead to be sure of their guests. There was an assembly at the President's House every fortnight, the British and French ambassadors gave regular weekly parties, with standing invitations to all people of quality, and the president's cabinet heads were beginning to entertain. There was theater, a circus, and concerts in Washington also, but the Calverts rarely had time to attend. The carriage journey from Riversdale into the city took almost two hours, and with hotel stays "disagreeable," they generally returned home the same night. Mrs. Calvert restricted her acceptances to two or three evenings a week.

Caroline's search for a suitable husband continued into the 1819 season with an even more arduous social schedule. In addition to the regular assemblies and tea parties, she attended thirteen dancing parties that season. Rosalie considered herself "on very good terms" with Mrs. Monroe and was pleased to be included in an elegant dinner at the President's House for the diplomatic corps. Caroline had gone to school with Maria Hester, the Monroes' younger daughter, and the two girls, who were being introduced to society at the same time, visited back and forth. Caroline had plenty of suitors, but both she and her mother were particular and handed out rejections freely. Rosalie, who had married at twenty-one, was in no hurry for her young daughter to marry, expressing the hope that she would wait until she was twenty-four. Caroline, a shy and modest young lady, did not mind being teased about becoming an "old maid," responding that she was happy with her state and did not wish to alter it. Both mother and daughter were enjoying themselves.

Having Caroline home was a boon to Mrs. Calvert. Caroline assisted with household duties and helped instruct the younger Calverts. Rosalie even put Caroline to work as her secretary, writing letters and copying accounts. All of this eased Rosalie's load, provided her with companionship, and furthered her daughter's practical education.

H. J. Stier sent grandfatherly advice from Antwerp, warning against doctors, lawyers, and government employees as "sad" prospective husbands; he favored a businessman or a planter. Stier offered to help with Caroline's dowry, but insisted that any property given Caroline be legally placed beyond her future husband's control. Rosalie had already thought of that and replied that the Calverts would give Caroline a marriage allowance at first and later a plantation near them.

The stimulation of an active social life agreed with Mrs. Calvert. Her health was better, her spirits were high. She had another very important reason for feeling good. Now age forty-one, she confided to her sister that finally she believed she was safe from the prospect of having any more children.

To H. J. Stier

Riversdale, 3 January 1817

My dear Father,

Mr. [William] Lansdale, who is about to sail for Amsterdam, will bring this to you, and [as he] offered to take a letter to you, I couldn't let such a good opportunity pass without sending you our warm wishes for your happiness in the New Year—may it be unmarred and without interruption.

I also have the pleasure to announce the birth of another pretty daughter, who came into the world the 14th of November [1816]. She has enjoyed excellent health since [her birth] and is the biggest and strongest of all my children at this age except Charles. We are going to name her Amelia Isabella. . . .

Please accept, dear Father, my thanks for the cask of Ocheimer [Hocheimer] wine which I received several weeks ago. We haven't tasted it yet, for I still haven't dared go down into the cellar to supervise putting it in bottles and haven't wished to trust that task to other hands. My husband also asks me to offer you his gratitude for the gift of $400, which you had the kindness to send him by your letter on the *Oscar*. . . .

My health is better since my stay in Philadelphia, especially since my confinement. I hope that with the regimen I am now following, I will recover my health altogether and I will try, if possible, to take a little trip next summer because traveling, according to the advice of all the doctors, is essential for me. . . . Caroline and George are in Philadelphia; the five others are all well. Believe me always, dear Father, with the most sincere affection,

Your devoted daughter,

Rosalie Eugenia Calvert

To Charles J. Stier[1]

Riversdale, 3 January 1817

My dear Brother,

. . . Allow me to thank you again for the books you had the kindness to send me. They will be very useful, especially for next winter when Caroline will be here. I have begun Chateaubriand—he is highly imaginative. Molière makes me laugh often, but I am nearly afraid of taking up Racine, for once begun, I <u>cannot</u> put him down. I prefer him to anything I have ever read in French. . . .

May I ask you, dear Brother, to become the godfather of my little girl whom I shall call Amelia Isabella? And pray accept for yourself and for your wife the sincere good wishes we make for your happiness during the coming year, and believe me,

Your affectionate sister,

Rosalie Eugenia Calvert

1. Carter Trans-MHS.

To Charles J. Stier[1]

Riversdale, 12 March 1817

I have just received your letter of 12 December [1816], dear Brother, and I hasten to respond.

I am extremely surprised at the decision you have made not to continue your money in American bonds which I think are better now from every point of view than any others. The animosities between Federalists and Democrats are almost gone. The recent war, which came close to utterly destroying the Democratic party, left such an impression that they will take care not to engage in another for a long time. The last Congress established a sinking fund which will wipe out the entire debt of the United States within 14 years. So the sole objection to my advice to keep money in American bonds is the depreciation of the [dollar], caused by the excess number of banks and by paper money.

I thought that it would be better to send you the certificates of all your 6 Pcts., since you ask it, than to sell them here at par and buy bills [of exchange], because in that case you would be a long time without interest. I will send you all the rest of your dividends in bills of exchange on London. The $25,000, which I bought in your name in the new Bank of the United States, will also be payable at London next year.

This [letter] will go by a ship out of Baltimore which is advertised as sailing in two days, so I don't have time to enclose the certificates. However, I am busy listing their numbers and having notarized copies made, and I will send the originals to the Messrs. Van Neck's address by the first ship that sails for England.[2]

Our little family is very well. My health is better than it was and I expect to recover completely this summer. My doctors, however, do not agree with the pleasant regimen which you advise me to follow—they order me a diet of vegetables, forbid me wine completely, even beer and cider, and [prohibit] all fatigue, physical or mental. . . .

Your affectionate sister,

R. E. C.

[P.S.] . . . Tell me if you want me to sell your shares in the Bank of Washington. This bank has a considerable surplus and you will receive ten percent [interest] in the next two payments.

1. Calvert, CU-NYC.
2. Shortly afterwards, Mrs. Calvert sent twenty-eight certificates of United States 6 Percent Treasury bonds, totaling $54,732.18, to her brother. She also sent him a certificate for 250 shares in the Bank of the United States, representing an investment

of $25,000. She reiterated her advice not to sell the bonds, saying that since the secretary of the treasury was authorized to buy $19 million for the sinking fund that year, the bonds could not fall below par (business letters of 14 and 29 April 1817, RC to CJS, Calvert, CU-NYC).

To H. J. Stier

Riversdale, 26 March 1817

Dear Father,

. . . I see that I completely forgot to carry out your order to purchase $3,000 [worth of] 3 Pcts. I shall do so in July since I have used up all your dividends to pay for 500 shares in the new Bank of the United States. . . . I want to send this letter on right away because it will include . . . the third of three bills of exchange . . . putting the income [of $9,775.06], which is the balance on hand as of January, at your disposal. . . .[1] The bills of exchange are "60-day sight" drafts because I could not obtain government bills which are quite scarce now. Tell me whether I should continue to send your dividend income in bills of exchange. If tobacco reaches your price, I will buy some for your account. Do you advise me to send our tobacco to Europe every year, no matter what the price here? That still seems to me to be the most profitable way to dispose of it.

My health is much improved since my confinement. My husband had a terrible fall from his cabriolet some time ago, when his horse became frightened. For some five to six minutes they thought that he was dead. He was unconscious, bleeding profusely, [but] now is almost completely recovered except for his arm which is still weak.

The children are all well. My little Amelie, now four months old, is a pretty, amiable child, quite strong and healthy, and gives me infinitely less trouble than any of the other children. Julia could not be prettier and has a most agreeable disposition—a delightful child. Her brothers Charles and Henry are good boys. Henry will be a fine musician; he already plays the flute extraordinarily well for his age. Charles loves farming and horses. Eugénie will be very pretty, I think, and is most affectionate and easily managed, [although] a bit too lively.

George is still at the same school in Germantown, near Philadelphia. He has real aptitude for learning and is also beginning to acquire more ability to apply himself. He has only one real fault—being inconstant and not staying with a task. I hope he will correct that and then I will be completely satisfied with him because he has an excellent disposition.

We shall send him over to you as soon as his education is completed, which I anticipate within three or four years.

Caroline is also still in school at Philadelphia, but will return home this autumn to make her entry into society. I anticipate this time with a degree of anxiety since her future happiness depends on it. She is quite small, and although not conventionally pretty, she has an interesting face. She is too shy in company. Well-educated for her age, she is not particularly fond of music but excels at drawing and painting. I'll send you some of her work at the first good opportunity to Antwerp. I really hope that she will not marry too young; within our circle I don't know of a single young man at the moment to whom I would want her to become attached. The young men here do nothing but dissipate their money, which they should be saving for the support of their families.

But I think that you are surely tired of my chatter, so I will bring this to a close and write you again soon, dear Father. . . .

Your devoted daughter,

R. E. Calvert

1. This was a combined balance for H. J. Stier, Charles Stier, and Jean Michel van Havre, but two-thirds of it was due the senior Stier.

To H. J. Stier

Riversdale, 12 May 1817

I fear, dear Father, that my long letter of 26 March [1817] may have bored you. Today I only have time for a business letter. . . . I have given [McEwen] an order to buy the $3,000 worth of 3 Pcts.

You will be surprised to hear that I have sold $24,600 worth of 6 Pcts. to pay for your [Bank of] Washington shares, but here is the explanation. I had always kept these shares uncompleted because I foresaw that this stock would increase in value. Being a director of this bank, my husband knew that there was a surplus of $80,000, which was to be divided among the stockholders this summer. [This] caused me to complete payment on [the shares] last November 1st when they were only $10—after which they went to $20 a share. You will receive [dividends of] five percent on May 1st, June 1st, August 1st, and November 1st, and there will still be a $20,000 surplus in the bank (but this is just between us). Since the $24,600 [invested in 6 Pcts.] had only been producing six percent and this way you would make twenty percent, I trust that you will approve of my speculation.

I was tempted to do the same thing for Charles and van Havre, but I was afraid they might not approve. If you wish, I can sell half of your shares after November 1st, so please write if you want it shifted out of your name. This bank is one of the best; it doesn't have bad debts like so many do. I sent you [its] charter in a small brochure a while ago, along with the report of the Secretary of State who, you will note, called it the best in the District.

I consider Frederick and Baltimore road stock infinitely preferable to the public bonds, which will soon be redeemed. [The road] stock is certain to increase in value in view of Baltimore's astonishing prosperity.

I hope that you approved my investing $50,000 for you in the new Bank of the United States.[1] I sent you its charter last summer from Philadelphia. It is undoubtedly just as safe as the public bonds, and it offers some advantages—it pays more interest, and you can receive the dividends in London besides. . . . The last Congress created what is called a "sinking fund" to retire the public debt, and the Secretary of the Treasury presently is authorized to purchase up to $10 million worth. Please write me if I should continue to invest in public bonds, or if instead I should send you your remittances in bills of exchange each quarter. I would advise you to invest. This country will be extremely prosperous (for several years at least). It no longer has the different parties which tore the government apart—it is unimpeded and its resources are immense. . . .

Let me thank you again for the excellent cask of Hochheimer wine. I drink two or three glasses daily and it seems to do me good. My health is certainly better.

My husband . . . is very busy at present making improvements, such as building a brick barn on the [Buck Lodge] plantation adjoining Riversdale [and] another at Oatland (the property bought from Hall). They also built two houses for the negroes [at Oatland] and one for the overseer, all of brick, plus a tobacco house.

I told you I will give you an account of [Oatland's] earnings for this year. We have put five of our negresses there and bought three negroes, four horses, four mules, etc., in order to operate this farm which we have been unable to rent out since it had no houses, etc. And [tenants] who have sufficient funds to undertake so large a farm prefer to buy a smaller one where they are their own master—or else they are off to Kentucky.

We are also going to build some stables on the Spurrier property; it needs accommodation for forty more horses this summer. In addition, my husband is going to build one or two houses on his Montgomery [County] property. As you can imagine, all this requires a lot of going around from one place to another supervising all the work. . . .

In your letter of 20 May 1816, you tell me I must charge you the expenses of the person who helps me prepare my accounts. I have never employed anyone for such work except once back in 1810. I do all of this work entirely by myself, without any assistance, and I must scold you a bit for having so little appreciated the talents of your former little secretary! Joking aside, if I lived in town, I would take on an agent for this work who could come once or twice a week, but I cannot get such a person out in the country. And I assure you that it gives me great pleasure to be of service to you. When Caroline returns next fall, I will install her as my clerk and private secretary.

But *adieu,* dear Father—in the beginning of this letter I said I would write only of business matters, and if I don't stop this minute I shall risk not having time to copy your accounts. However, whenever I begin writing to you, it seems to bring us closer and I never know when to stop.

Your affectionate and obedient daughter,

R. E. Calvert

1. Stier replied that he highly approved of his daughter's investment in the Second Bank of the United States and of her speculation in the Bank of Washington. He advised her to reinvest his income, preferably in treasury bonds (HJS Letterbook, 29 May 1817 and 14 July 1817, Cal S-V).

To Isabelle van Havre

Riversdale, 12 May 1817

Dear Sister,

. . . I am told that a ship is going to sail from Baltimore to Antwerp; this is the first opportunity I have had to send you the washing blue that you asked me for. I hope you will find it suitable and the kind you wanted. Inside the packing case you will also find a small box of handwork which I ask my dear Louise to accept and some books of poetry for Edward. There is also a toy for my godson Jules—to make [the dancer] dance, you must hold the house upside down for a minute so that the sand runs to the top and then put it on a table to make the dancer start moving; if he is not active enough, hit it with your hand on top, which will make the sand run down.

You will be surprised when you unpack this case to find an old ragged dress, but it was the only thing I had which could serve as a measure. The [dresses] I am wearing now are all so large that it would be impossible to guess my size. The corset is a good deal shorter than you wear them; it comes together completely at the bottom, but gaps a little at the top and nearly two inches in the middle of the waist. The one you sent me does very well now, but I had to cut it at the bottom; it was two inches too long and four [inches] too narrow, which I let out.

Caroline's corset fails to meet along its entire length by about two and one-half inches. Her *fourreau*[1] fits her well and is a good length right now, but since she will grow between now and winter, it would be better for the skirt to be a little longer and the bodice a bit wider. Here are the things I would like for you to send me:

For me, a winter hat like those they wear at home in the mornings to go calling (or *en demie parure*); three or four pairs of shoes, two white and two of color; a complete dress outfit topped off with a matching bonnet or turban for paying my first visit to our court, as I am on very good terms with Mrs. Monroe; a semi-dress or morning gown; a chemisette; two bouquets of flowers.

For Caroline, also a winter hat; six pairs of shoes, four white and two colored; a complete dress outfit for her first visit to our court; a dress for dancing; an [outfit], *demi-paré,* or like those they wear at home in the mornings; two or three bouquets of flowers; flower dress trimmings; two head-dresses such as young ladies of her age wear at home to match both her outfits.

I am afraid, dear Sister, that all this is going to give you much trouble. Don't spend a lot of time searching for just the right thing, but send me what you can find easily. The only thing that really matters to me is that I have them by November, or by the first of December at the latest. If there are no ships from Antwerp which will arrive here by then, please don't buy [the items], but notify me so that I would have time to find them here. It doesn't matter if you send the packages to Philadelphia, Norfolk, or Baltimore, although the latter is preferable. [Address it] to Jonas Clapham, Esq. at Baltimore; he is our agent, a very haughty man and Mr. Cooke's step-son.[2] If you ship to Norfolk, address it to my husband, "to be left at the Custom House till called for by his order." Since a packet sails between Washington and Norfolk regularly, we can easily get it here by sending the bill of lading and an invoice. . . .

Please give me more information about your children. Mine are quite well [and] my health continues to improve. . . . Tell your husband to continue writing me his letters which give me so much pleasure. I am sorry not to have time to write him a little note today, but if he takes a look at the fat packet of my writing which this ship brings to you, he will know that my fingers have to be tired from holding the pen. . . .

Your affectionate sister,

Rosalie E. Calvert

1. A tight-fitting dress.
2. Jonas Clapham (1762–1837) replaced William Cooke, who died in 1817, as the Calverts' business agent.

To H. J. Stier

Riversdale, 1 August 1817

Dear Father,

After having gone so many months since your last letter, you can imagine how much pleasure your letter of [15] April [1817] gave me when I received it this morning.[1] Eugénie, who was nearby while I was reading it, observed, "Is it possible, Mama, that it is Grandpapa who wrote this long letter? I thought that old people couldn't write very well and that their hands always shook, but Grandpapa writes better and in smaller script than many young people."

I was delighted to learn that you are enjoying yourself so much making improvements at the Mick—it must be an enchanting place to live now. I want to thank you on behalf of Caroline for your nice gift of [20] Louis, which I will give her on October 1st when she will be back here.[2] The daughters of Mr. Tayloe and Mrs. Lewis (my husband's niece) are returning home at the same time, so Mr. Tayloe will accompany my husband to escort home these three young ladies who all attend the same school.[3]

You ask how I am going to manage Caroline's introduction into society. To be quite honest, I am not too sure and anticipate the prospect with a bit of dread lest I not acquit myself as well as I might wish. It is a great disadvantage for me to have lived the last ten years in such seclusion. I cannot count on any help from my husband in this task, and I very much fear that instead of helping, he's more likely to hinder since he knows nothing whatever about such affairs. So I regard her debut with much anxiety. She is greatly loved by her schoolmates and is her teacher's favorite. It seems to me that she may be more pleasing to women than to men, which is a little strange. I'll write you in great detail what success she has.

I would be happy if I were as sure of her success as I am of George's. I don't know how the little rascal does it, but he charms everyone and I fear that when he is a little older, he is going to receive entirely too much admiration from the ladies. He has a great talent for learning of all sorts, but he lacks persistence and is extremely lazy. I just had a letter from him which I'm tempted to send you so you can judge his style and writing for yourself.

All of our little family are very well. Julia is the prettiest child you have ever seen and Amelia is the best. She is much stronger than any of my others at this age, which is all the more singular in view of the fact that I was so ill throughout my pregnancy. My husband is well except for the headaches to which he is so subject. My own health is almost completely restored, although I still lack the strength for physical exertion.

Now, dear Father, since I have gone on about my family enough to bore you, I will get down to business. . . . I am completely satisfied with my administration [of your affairs] for the last nine months. On the capital of $49,200 in the Bank of Washington, you will realize $9,840 in one year, or twenty percent. . . . As for the $50,000 subscription I made for you in the Bank of the United States . . . , you could get $67,000 for it at present if you chose to sell, which is 34 percent above par. I only regret that the amount was not $100,000 instead of $50,000, but I allowed myself to be guided in this by Mr. Cooke, Carroll, and others who were wrong. Thus since last October I have made up to $30,000 more for you than you expected.[4]

I hope eventually to be able to give you a good account on the Oatland, or Hall, property, whose name we have changed to Waterloo.[5] We were over there a few weeks ago with all the children who were much amused at dining in the woods on ham and a couple of cold chickens, with a tree trunk for our table and cushions from the carriage for chairs. We bought three negroes who are there with five of our negresses, and they have been busy building houses for the negroes, for the overseer, for tobacco, a barn, etc. Last year they made over 100,000 bricks there. The crop they are growing there looks very promising for a first season. The owner of the adjoining property of about 600 to 700 acres just died, and it will be sold this winter. There is a good house on the property, but he has freed two of his negroes and given each of them 150 acres, which would give it bad neighbors unless one could make them sell their land. . . .

It is vexing to have to tell you that the proxies you sent me are not the ones I requested. They are for voting only and are useless, since now no one is allowed vote by proxy for another person. So here is what I need for your shares of road stock, in approximately these terms and including a power of substitution:

"Know all men, etc. . . . do constitute and appoint Rosalie E. Calvert of Riversdale in the state of Maryland my true and lawful attorney for me and in my name to receive and give receipt for the same all interests, revenues, dividends and reimbursements which are now due or which may in future become due to me on any stock now standing in my name or which may hereafter stand in my name in the books of the Baltimore and Frederick Turnpike Company, etc. etc."

Lacking such a power of attorney, I left the stock in my name in order to receive the interest. I have a power of attorney under my husband's name to receive the dividends from the Bank of the United States, which includes all banks in the United States. Don't forget to tell me if I am to hold or sell your shares in the Bank of Washington which are also in my name. If you decide to keep them, I'll transfer them immediately to your name. . . .

Your affectionate daughter,

Rosalie E. Calvert

1. The date is missing from Mrs. Calvert's letter, but Stier recorded it in his letterbook. Stier apologized for being so long in writing, saying it was not from lack of thinking of his daughter, but because he was becoming "so old and lazy" and had much work at the Mick which tired him (HJS Letterbook, 15 April 1817, Cal S-V).

2. Stier sent the money—about seventy-five dollars—for Caroline to buy "some trinkets" for her upcoming debut. He stressed the importance of Mrs. Calvert arranging a good marriage for her daughter and urged her not to delay, since "you have to take advantage of the first bloom of youth and of the facility to adjust to a new way of life" (HJS Letterbook, 15 April 1817, Cal S-V).

3. Catherine Carter Tayloe (1799–?) and Frances Parke Lewis were Caroline's schoolmates. The girls often traveled back and forth together, escorted by one of their parents (correspondence of Eleanor Parke Custis Lewis to Elizabeth Bordley, July 23, 1815, and August 20, 1815, Archives of the Mount Vernon Ladies Association).

4. Although Mrs. Calvert had made two very successful investments, she was inflating the total she claimed credit for here. She was probably feeling defensive about the Oatland property, which Stier had pointed out was a $25,000 investment producing no return.

5. The name Waterloo did not stick to this property, which continued to be known as Oatland and eventually passed down to the Calverts' daughter Julia. The name Waterloo did, however, attach itself to the Spurrier tract, which eventually went to daughter Caroline and became the present-day town of Waterloo, Maryland.

To Charles J. Stier[1]

Riversdale, 8 November 1817

Dear Brother,

. . . I regret not having the leisure today to send you your account, but since Caroline's return on October 22nd, I have had visitors practically every day except for five or six when I was so sick with a cold that I couldn't do anything. . . .

Please accept Caroline's thanks and mine for the necklace and earrings you were so kind as to send her. She is most grateful for this proof of your affection and remembrance and for the good wishes you offer for her success in her debut.

What pleasure it would give us if your plan of coming here could be realized! You would be greatly surprised at the many changes which fifteen years have produced here—in the country, society, manners, etc.

You ask what George is doing. He spent the vacation month of September here. We are sparing nothing which could contribute to providing him with a gentlemanly education. He is completely proficient in the French language and is learning Spanish. He draws well and is studying music. He is very advanced in all branches of mathematics, astronomy, [and] mensuration besides making the usual progress in Latin and Greek. In short, he has the ability to succeed in everything he undertakes, but he is a little lazy and lacks perseverance. If he rectifies these defects as he grows older, he will be an outstanding man, but all depends on that.

I am sorry you have not given me a more detailed account of the sale of the paintings. I am most curious to know all those that Papa bought and at what price.[2] *Adieu,* dear Brother. I must close by embracing you and your Eugénie, and please believe me

Your affectionate sister,

R. E. Calvert

P.S. . . . I have left to my new secretary, Caroline, the care of transcribing this letter. It is her first endeavor—she will improve with practice. . . .

1. Calvert, CU-NYC. This letter, in French, is not in Mrs. Calvert's hand but was signed by her. As she indicates in her postscript, she had her daughter Caroline transcribe it.

2. The Peeters painting collection had to be sold to settle the estate of Rosalie's grandmother, Mathilde van den Cruyce Peeters, who had died in 1796 while the Stiers were in America. The sale took place in Antwerp on August 27, 1817. H. J.

Stier later wrote his daughter that he had bought "the best 20 of the 63 [put up for sale] at a price of 12 to 13 thousand dollars." He added that the paintings had been in the family since 1680 (HJS Letterbook, 25 September 1817, Cal S-V).

To H. J. Stier

Riversdale, 9 November 1817

My dear Father,

. . . Please accept Caroline's and my thanks for your beautiful gift of jewelry and for all the other lovely things with which you are overwhelming her. . . .[1] I am very aware, dear Father, of all your kindnesses to her and of the deep interest you take in all her concerns. I shall write you how her debut succeeds. I agree entirely with your advice that public employees are undesirable [as prospective husbands] since [their employment] is so precarious.[2] I don't know who will become my son-in-law; up to now I don't have my eye on anyone. My daughter looks much younger than she is; at first glance one might take her for only thirteen or fourteen years old. For her dowry we are presently thinking about giving her what is called here "real property," which is to say, lands or houses over which a husband has no power and which one can even entail over the liens. . . .[3]

Mr. Lansdale wrote us at the time of his arrival back in Baltimore that he had seen you on July 4th in excellent health and he regretted having so short a visit. I shall be taking this letter to Baltimore myself. We are going there tomorrow to go in the evening to the theatre, where a very fine singer has just arrived from London. This will be Caroline's first public appearance. As I cannot leave my small children for any length of time, we will return here the following day. I still must make some preparations, dear Father, so I will finish this by embracing you and I ask you to believe me

Your affectionate daughter,

R. E. Calvert

1. Stier had written that he was going to look for a necklace for Caroline; in the following letter to her sister, Mrs. Calvert sends him thanks for "the splendid set of amethyst" (HJS Letterbook, 29 May 1817 and 14 July 1817, Cal S-V).

2. Stier had definite ideas about a suitable match for his granddaughter. He ruled out doctors and lawyers as "sad professions" which "leave widows without resources," and objected to government employees on the same grounds. That left business and trade people, who would be acceptable "if the man has capital, energy,

and deportment." A planter would present even more advantages; "his widow can continue the management."

He also had some advice about preparing Caroline herself for marriage: "accustom her from the start to observe a great regularity in her daily habits, to keep her belongings well, to be very neat as to her person, more especially about her ordinary clothes than her fine garments. That's a sure way to please a husband. Let her take care of your household. [Knowledge of] orderly and economical household management gives a woman the opportunity to restore many losses a man lacking in foresight can bring about" (HJS Letterbook, 29 May 1817 and 14 July 1817, Cal S-V).

3. An entail limits the inheritance of property to a certain line of heirs so that it cannot be left to anyone else. Stier had cautioned Mrs. Calvert to make sure that Caroline's property went to her offspring, not to her husband, at her death.

To Isabelle van Havre

[Riversdale], 27 November [1817][1]

My dear Sister,

. . . We just unpacked the trunks [you sent], but don't assume that I can tell you everything we think about them today. . . . We have scarcely had time to admire it all—so many pretty things, as well as the way in which they were packed. I recognized at first glance the artfulness and care of my dear sister who, as a *commissionnaire excellent,* has no equal in all the world. My husband stood in front of the fireplace, and as we opened the boxes, made fun of my exclamations and outbursts of admiration, but he admitted that everything could not have been prettier or more splendid. When we had everything spread out on the beds and chairs all over the room and were busy each moment discovering some particularly attractive item we hadn't noticed before, he suddenly gave a long sigh, which made us burst out laughing, and he said, "I can see that all these beautiful things are going to cause me a lot of trouble. I will have to accompany you to numerous parties to show off all this finery."

Since you haven't sent me the bills, dear Sister, I cannot comment on the prices. I hope to receive them soon. You did tell me the embroidered percale dress cost 160 francs—I find that quite inexpensive, and it couldn't be more beautiful. The long-sleeved muslin bodice to wear over it is charming, as is the one with small pleats, but you should have sent me a washerwoman in the box. We don't know how to do up things like that here. I always iron our embroidered muslins and laces myself.

How pretty my muslin chemisette is—this embroidery of little roses is delightful. Since you asked me to tell you if anything was not the way I wanted it, I will say that I regret that my full-dress gown is trailing. I don't

Isabelle Stier van Havre. Portrait by Fred. van Engel.
Collection of Barons van Havre, List Schoten, copyright Bureau d'Iconographie de Belgique
(ANRB), Brussels

think anyone is wearing them like that here, so I will shorten it all around.
It is also much more splendid than was necessary for me—when I made
this observation, Mr. Calvert made fun of me, saying that was just false
humility. It is very pretty and I am sure will be greatly admired by Mrs.
Monroe. The cashmere dress is exactly what I wanted, and it is very
convenient to have two kinds of sleeves in order to be more or less
dressed-up. It makes two outfits out of one which suits me doubly. . . .

All of Caroline's gowns are charming, especially the one embroidered in chenille, and they fit her well. Tell Papa that the rose silk gown which he picked out is her favorite. Will you also, dear Sister, give him Caroline's thanks for the splendid set of amethyst and to my brother for his nice gift. She will write them herself at the first opportunity.

The white satin brocade embellished with roses is a superb dress, and the one with the geranium garland is quite pretty. Of the garlands for the hair, we prefer the one of daisies, but they are all nice. My toque is beautiful and wonderfully becoming. The hats are pretty, especially the feathers, but we find them rather large. Caroline's, however, suits her very well—she will wear it for the first time tomorrow to pay a morning call on Mrs. Bagot.[2] My lilac hat is lovely, but the brim is too large for me; I think that I can easily cut it smaller or turn it up in the front, and it will go well with my lilac dress. Please thank Louise for the doll which she outfitted by hand—the first time Caroline goes out she intends to have her hair arranged exactly like that.

You can't conceive, my dear Friend, how much more precious and meaningful all these things are to me for having been chosen by you, arranged by your own hands and those of my dear Louise. I cannot thank you enough for your kindness. . . .

Your affectionate and grateful sister,

R. E. Calvert

1. This letter is a continuation of one begun 8 November 1817, in Caroline Calvert's handwriting, but resumed here by Mrs. Calvert.

2. Mary Bagot (?–1845) was the wife of Sir Charles Bagot, British minister to the United States from 1816 to 1819. She was the eldest daughter of William Wesley Pole, Lord Marlboro, and the niece of the duke of Wellington. It was Mrs. Bagot who told of visiting Riversdale in 1816 to see the painting collection before it was returned to Antwerp.

To Isabelle van Havre

[Riversdale], 30 December 1817

My dear Sister,

I am quite astonished at the time which has slipped by since my last letter. . . . I was planning to write you again in a few days, and yet almost an entire month has gone by without my doing it. How can that be, when we speak of you every day and when all our pretty clothes constantly remind us of you?

The fact is I thought I would have more time when Caroline returned, but instead I have a good deal less. We have to go out much more often, receive callers, etc.—and even so, entertaining has not yet begun in Washington. Up to now, Mrs. Monroe has been confined to her room. Some say it is because her health does not permit her to receive company; others say it is because her house is still not furnished. Finally, the house will be opened next Thursday and we are going. Today we were supposed to go to the French minister's, Mr. Hyde de Neuville, and to the Spanish minister's, Don Onis, but it began to rain which kept us at home.[1] We are on good terms with the English minister [Sir Charles Bagot] who has dined here. Mrs. Bagot much admired the delightful embroidered muslin chemisette you sent me by Mr. Bayard. . . .

You are certainly the queen of *commissionnaires*. Permit me to convey again a thousand thanks for your kindness in carrying out my commissions in such an admirable manner. I can't imagine how you did it, getting everything into two trunks and not even the smallest pleat out of place. They are very reasonable at the custom[s] houses here, and they accepted the list for all the goods without wanting to open the trunks.

You ask me to write you frankly what we think of everything. . . . Since [the lilac hat] was too dressy for morning, I took the brim off and made a toque out of it, or what we call here a "turban," and now it is charming. Caroline's hat is most becoming to her. She has worn it two or three times and it has been much admired. The large blue [hat], though pretty, did not become me. I took it to my milliner who sold it for eight dollars—she is very accommodating about these matters.

My full-dress blue gown is quite beautiful. I only regret that it is somewhat long, but that is easily remedied. You did well to put the *blondes de fantaisie* on it instead of ordinary blond lace—I think they are very pretty.[2] I couldn't be happier with the lilac dress; it is just what I wanted and the two [sets of] sleeves are a great advantage since they make two different outfits. The embroidered muslin chemisette is really attractive—I have never seen anything prettier; [its] little border embroidered with tiny roses is enchanting. The shoes fit us perfectly.

All of Caroline's gowns are exactly her size, except for the percale *canezou* with little pleats which was too small.[3] I opened the bodice under the arm and inserted a small piece there as well as in the sleeve, and now it fits her quite well. It is very pretty, as is the long-sleeved muslin bodice which she will wear next Thursday, New Year's Day, to the President's morning reception. We think the percale petticoat which goes beneath is extremely elegant and pretty. The rose silk gown is her favorite. The one adorned with the two rose decorations is quite sumptuous and nice. The ball gown embroidered in blue chenille is lovely; she will wear it to the first ball, given either by the French or the English minister. For myself, I like the geranium garland very much and am delighted that you have placed it on more than one gown. All the flower trimmings are charming.

Thank you for your offer to have the *blondes* washed when they become soiled—I will send them to you. Caroline's corset fits her well, but mine is about three inches too small. When it is laced as tight as I can stand it, it is open four inches.

Tell my dear Louise that the doll is much admired. Eugenia carries it into the room when our friends come to call and, together with the little fashion designs, it has often helped the conversation along immensely. . . .

There, dear Sister, I have filled an entire page with talk of clothing! What would my husband say if he saw that? He makes fun of the importance we attach to our clothes, and we take our revenge by laughing at the importance he gives to his barn, etc. . . .

I was so sorry to learn that my dear Louise's health is not yet completely restored. I know too well from experience that one does not recover easily from such illnesses, because I am still feeling the effects of the one I had in 1814. Although my health is much better, it was not so for two years and until I had gained a lot of weight. I still can't bear fatigue or humidity, and a mere trifle can upset me no end. I don't think I will ever be as strong as before. I hope that Louise's good constitution and youth will restore her health soon.

1. Jean Guillaume, Baron Hyde de Neuville (1776–1847), served as French minister to the United States from 1816 to 1821. Luis de Onís (1769–1830?) was Spanish minister to the United States from 1815 to 1819.

2. Blond lace was made from unbleached, natural-colored thread; *blondes de fantaisie* were made of fine mesh with patterns worked in silk, producing a shiny, satin-like finish.

3. A *canezou* was a lightweight short wrap, often of lace.

To Isabelle van Havre

[Riversdale], 8 January [1818][1]

You asked me to give you a detailed account of Caroline's entry into society. The first time she appeared was New Year's Day when we went to the President's House in the morning. Everyone goes there on that day. There was such a crowd in the room where Mrs. Monroe was that we could hardly move, either forward or backward. She received us very graciously. Since it was morning, people were not very dressed up. Caroline wore the pretty rose hat you sent her, the embroidered percale petticoat with the long-sleeved muslin bodice, and a pretty white shawl of French merino wool with a border of flowers. Her attire was considered very pretty.

The Saturday afterwards, we were at the French Minister's *levée* which is held every Saturday evening. There were a lot of people there, but they were not very dressed up. We went in muslin. Caroline's hair was done like the doll's, with fresh flowers—geranium leaves, rosebuds, and camelia buds. Around her neck was a garniture of the pretty lace you sent me last year, and on the lower part of her gown was one of the embroidered muslin trimmings.

I had on the lilac turban, which is so pretty and was much admired, and the charming embroidered muslin chemisette that is open in the front and fits me wonderfully. M. and Madame de Neuville gave us the most flattering welcome and entreated us to come every Saturday, and at the dance M. de N[euville] presented his secretary to Caroline for her first partner.[2]

Since it was the first time that we had come out into society, we had to get acquainted with everyone so I cannot yet judge what success my daughter will have. Young Ogle, the late Mr. Cooke's grandson, has come here three times recently. I think that if he received any encouragement, he would become Caroline's suitor, but that would not suit me because his father has only his plantation and nine daughters, not one of whom is married yet, and two other sons. It is too bad because he is a handsome young man, although not very bright, but well-mannered, of excellent character, and from one of the best families in Maryland on both sides—something not easy to find here.[3]

You ask how we live in our house. As for me, my bedroom is the one above the dining room, and little Amelia sleeps beside my bed. My four other children have the adjoining room and with them stays a white woman who serves me both as housekeeper and dressmaker. Caroline has the little room where Papa used to do his writing; I have put a small closed stove in this room which gives out a little heat. The central bedroom and the one over the drawing room, as well as the small one, I reserve for guests. I would love to have you come and bring your whole family to use them, but let me know in advance. You know that surprises of great joy have sometimes been fatal, and I will not answer for what might happen if you arrive unexpectedly.

Please give my compliments to your husband. . . . The January account has still not been done—I will send it to him shortly. American bonds should continue to rise in value. There are no longer different parties within the country—we are all united. We learned our strength during the recent war which, although it was disastrous, made us realize the immense resources which the United States possesses. . . .

Your affectionate,

R. E. Calvert

1. Continuation of letter begun 30 December 1817.

2. Family reaction to Caroline's first dancing partner was one of unanimous opposition. Mrs. van Havre reported it to Rosalie: "The account you gave of your first social calls amused me. I read your letter to Louise, including the part where Caroline danced with the secretary of the French Embassy. Louise cried, 'Good heavens, Mama, write quickly to Aunt that she must guard against the French. They are such flatterers, they will turn my cousin's head since she doesn't know them like we do, and she will be most unhappy.' I reassured her by telling her that you did not like the French, but nevertheless I agree with her. Have as little communication as possible with individuals from that nation; the best of them are good-for-nothing, and they are still dangerous. Papa, Eugénie, and Charles in turn each made the same comment that Louise had" (IvH to RC, undated [March–April 1818] letter-draft, Cal S-V).

3. Benjamin Ogle III (1796–1839) was the son of Benjamin Ogle II of Belair and Anna Marie (Cooke) Ogle. William Cooke, prominent Baltimore attorney and merchant, was the young man's maternal grandfather, and both his paternal grandfather and great-grandfather had been governors of Maryland. Young Benjamin III, however, died by his own hand after a life of personal and financial failure (see Shirley Vlasak Baltz, *A Chronicle of Belair* [Bowie, Md., 1984], pp. 61–62).

To H. J. Stier

Riversdale, 9 April 1818

My dear Father,

Yesterday I received your letter of 10 January [1818] with a pleasure impossible to describe, and Caroline says to tell you that she would swear your letter to be that of a young beau and that few among her Washington swains could produce so delightful a letter or one so prettily written. . . .[1]

I am appalled to realize how long it has been since I last wrote. My daughter's return has so greatly increased the demands on my time that I often despair of completing half of what I have to do. It is quite difficult, I may even say laborious, to take an active part in Washington society at this distance. . . . Saturday next we are going to a dancing party at the French Minister's and on Monday one at the English Minister's. Madame la President's assemblies came to an end in March. Congress has to adjourn on the 20th of this month and with that the social season of the capital ends. . . .

I was delighted to learn that the paintings were such a great source of enjoyment for you and that you had bought 22 of the most valuable.[2] I want so much to know which ones these are. I know from my sister that you have *La Charité Romaine, L'Enfant prodigue,* and *M. & Madame Le Roi.*[3] Surely, you will not have missed *L'Admiral,* or *La Tête de Rubens,* or *Romulus et Remus,* or *L'Arche de Noé.*[4] You did not tell me whether it is the famous *Chapeau de Paille* or another portrait which you bought from the van Havre family. . . .[5]

Caroline and all the family join me in sending their love. I remain

Your devoted and dutiful daughter,

R. E. Calvert

1. Stier neglected to record the text of this "prettily written" letter in his letterbook, noting it only as an "insignificant letter" containing a request to Mrs. Calvert to ship him fifty hogsheads of tobacco if it seemed a good speculation (HJS Letterbook, 10 January 1818, Cal S-V).

2. Stier had earlier reported buying twenty of the best paintings in the collection (HJS Letterbook, 25 September 1817, Cal S-V).

3. The paintings listed by Mrs. Calvert are Peter Paul Rubens's *Roman Charity,* now in the Rijksmuseum, Amsterdam; Rubens's *The Prodigal Son,* or *The Stable,* now in the Koninklijk Museum, Antwerp; and Anthony Van Dyke's portraits, *Philippe Le Roy, Seigneur de Ravels,* and *Marie de Raedt* (Le Roy's wife), now in the Wallace Collection, London (see Soeur Gladys Guyot, "Un Milieu Rubenien à Anvers," *Le Parchemin,* no. 187 [January–February 1977], p. 22).

4. Stier had bought at least three of the four paintings Mrs. Calvert inquired about: *L'Admiral,* Anthony Van Dyke's portrait of François van der Borght, now in the Rijksmuseum, Amsterdam; *Romulus and Remus,* attributed to Rubens and Huysmans de Malines, now in the United States in the private collection of a Calvert descendant; and *The Animals Ready to Enter the Ark,* by Jan (Velvet) Brueghel. *La Tête de Rubens,* mentioned by Mrs. Calvert, may be a portrait of Philippe Rubens, brother of the artist, also purchased by Stier in 1817 (see *Catalogue d'une Précieuse Collection de Tableau,* public sale, 27 August 1817 [Anvers, G. J. Binken, 1817], and *Catalogue de la Collection de Tableaux,* sale, 29 July 1822 [Anvers, G. J. Binken, 1822]).

5. Stier had purchased the famous *Chapeau de Paille,* now in the National Gallery, London. Isabelle van Havre wrote that Stier had bought the painting for fifty thousand francs (about ten thousand dollars): "He now has the most beautiful collection

in the country. . . . No foreigner of note passes through Antwerp without asking to see the famous painting of Rubbens [*sic*] called the *Chapeau de Paille*" (IvH to RC, undated letter-draft [March/April 1818], Cal S-V).

To Isabelle van Havre

Riversdale, 26 April 1818

My dear Sister,

Once more three months have passed since I last wrote to you. I have found over the years that time slips by faster, but since Caroline's return it seems that the months are weeks and the weeks days. Indeed, at times the number and variety of my occupations, and the thought of all I have to do and not knowing where to begin, gives me a kind of fever.

My husband has become so lazy that I must exert myself even more, since I have to manage everything myself. He lives in our house as if he were not the master—not giving any instructions, not worrying about anything—and is content to manage his various farms. So you can imagine how overwhelmed with work I am at times.

We haven't gone out in society as much as, for Caroline's sake, I would have liked. The winter has been very harsh, the roads bad, and it really is a formidable enterprise to go from here to Washington on pleasure trips and return in the middle of the night—or rather at two or three in the morning. Twice we have spent the night in a hotel, but we found that even more disagreeable and tiring than coming back here. Sometimes, too, our coachman falls asleep and the other night he very nearly turned us over in a deep ditch.

You urge me to tell you what success Caroline has had this winter and especially how the presentation at Madame President's went. I scarcely know how to answer you. In the first place, the assemblies at Mrs. Monroe's are neither pleasant nor rewarding for young people. We have been three times and have been extremely well received—the President singled us out with special courtesy each time. One always finds all the Ambassadors there with their wives, secretaries, etc., consuls, all the foreigners who are in Washington, a large number of members of Congress, and sometimes the residents of Washington and Georgetown with their families. One goes at eight and leaves at ten o'clock. During Mrs. Madison's reign everybody went, even the shoemakers and their wives, but things are better managed now and one meets the best of society there.

During the entire winter season the English and French ministers each give an assembly on a regular day once a week, and you are invited to come there for the season, any time you find it agreeable. There is dancing, and these parties are very pleasant. In addition, there is a public ball each fortnight, [but] we, preferring the private parties, have not attended so I cannot describe these to you.

There are also a large number of tea parties and special dances during the winter, so that few days [pass] without one, and sometimes two are given on the same evening, even though invitations are sent out ten to twelve days in advance. I am not a good judge of Caroline's success. She seems pleasing enough and doesn't lack for dancing partners, but she has no avowed suitor up to now. The Congress this year was very well-composed—there were some young members who were quite nice, although none with a large fortune.

Mrs. Peter has a 21-year-old daughter who doesn't have the most amiable personality, and [Mrs. Peter] does not look with favor on the fact that Caroline is more attractive and sought after than [her daughter].[1] The eldest daughter of Mrs. Lewis, aged 18, has been at school with Caroline for three years, and they seemed to love each other like sisters.[2] My husband brought them back home together, they made their entry into society at the same time, but since then their friendship has completely cooled. I think Miss Lewis doesn't like it that her cousin is so much better dressed than she, and she, unfortunately, has the worst possible taste and dresses very badly. Her mother is a charming, amiable woman—the best friend I have. She does not, however, have my good fortune in having a sister and a niece who take such an interest in my daughter's success and who go to so much trouble to make her stand out by the taste and elegance of her apparel. I don't know, dear Friend, how we can ever thank you enough for all the trouble you have taken to furnish us so many attractive clothes. We admire them more each day.

At the moment Caroline is in Baltimore at the home of her cousin Mrs. Rogers, where she will stay for a week. [Mrs. Rogers] is Mrs. Law's daughter, who married a young Baltimore man of good family and fortune last year.[3] She and Caroline spent three years at school together and she is quite attached to Caroline. She is very well-educated and a nice girl—it is an advantageous connection for [Caroline]. Mr. Carroll's daughter, Mrs. Harper, sent her oldest daughter to France for her education. She just learned of her [child's] death and is going to leave for Europe for her health—perhaps she will come through Antwerp.[4]

One of the daughters of Mr. Stoddert, whose house you lived in in

Bladensburg, married Mr. Campbell, a member of the Senate, some years ago. He has just been appointed Ambassador to Russia.⁵ It is possible that on their return they will call on you. I would like that. She is one of my best friends and could tell you a lot about all of us.

My paper tells me that I must finish. My husband and Caroline join me in sending love. I remain

Your affectionate sister.

1. Columbia Washington Peter (1797–1820).
2. Frances Parke Lewis.
3. Eliza Law (1797–1822), daughter of Eliza (Custis) and Thomas Law, married Lloyd Nicholas Rogers (1787–1860) of Druid Hill, Baltimore, in 1817.
4. Mary Diana Harper (1803–1818), eldest daughter of Catherine (Carroll) and Robert Goodloe Harper, died at age fifteen in France.
5. George Washington Campbell served as minister to Russia from 1818 to 1820. He was married to Harriet (Stoddert).

To Charles J. Stier¹

[n.p.], 1 June 1818

Dear Brother,

. . . You remark, and I note, with obvious regret, that Caroline's first [dancing] partner was the secretary to the French minister. Is it possible, dear Brother, that you have forgotten the strong prejudices which Mr. C and I have against that nation—prejudices which our children inherit and which would be impossible to efface? We have been obliged to send our older children to schools where the headmaster and the headmistress are French, but since all the students were American, I have not feared that Caroline or George would acquire a partiality for that nation from which, fortunately, they are as much estranged as we. So have no fear that your niece could ever form an attachment to a Frenchman.

The Minister, Mr. Hyde de Neuville, and his wife are most gracious, however. They have more visitors and give more dances than anyone else in Washington. Theirs is a house which is pleasant to frequent, as is that of Mr. Bagot, the English Minister.

Up to now Caroline does not have a declared suitor. She has interesting features, but is not pretty, is very small of figure, and much too shy in company. . . .

Your affectionate sister.

1. Calvert, CU-NYC.

To H. J. Stier

Riversdale, 4 August 1818

My dear Father,

. . . We are all well. George will return for vacation in September—he comes and goes [by himself] now all the way from Philadelphia to here. We plan on sending Charles there, too. I am happy to learn from Mr. Lansdale that you are looking well and enjoying excellent health. He reported that you greatly enjoy your paintings and that the [Château du] Mick was truly lovely. Mr. Bagot, the English minister, says he thinks you got a great bargain when you bought the *Chapeau de Paille* for $10,000. [He called it] one of the most celebrated paintings in Europe, and he knows his paintings. Mr. Gilmore [Gilmor] has arrived in Baltimore. No doubt he has seen your collection, and I am very curious to see him. . . .[1]

I am very sorry, dear Father, not to be able once again to send your account today, and I fear you will think I am becoming lazy. Actually, however, it is all the fault of McEwen who still has not sent the July account. Your January and July dividends are all invested in 6 Pcts. at 103 1/2.

It's been a very long time since I have heard from you, my sister, or Charles. Please give them my compliments and my greetings to all of the family who remember me. My husband and Caroline join me in sending love.

Your very dutiful daughter,

R. E. Calvert

1. Robert Gilmor II (1773–1848), prominent Baltimore merchant, philanthropist, and art collector, had seen the Stier collection. Isabelle van Havre wrote that the family had "a visit from Mr. Gilmor of Baltimore a fortnight ago. It gave Papa great pleasure to show him his collection, first as a relative of his [late] friend Mr. Cooke, and second as a connoisseur of paintings. Papa said he has met few amateurs who knew so much about them. He is a pleasant man and his wife is quite pretty" (IvH to RC, undated letter-draft [March/April 1818], Cal S-V). Gilmor was married to his second wife, Sarah (Ladson), at the time; his relationship to William Cooke stemmed from his brief marriage to Cooke's daughter Elizabeth Susan, who died in 1803.

George Calvert to H. J. Stier[1]

Philadelphia, October 22, 1818

My Dear Sir,

Finding a Ship about sailing from this Port to Antwerp I could not let pass the opportunity of writing a few lines to inform you that my Dear wife and children are all well. I came here a few days ago with my sons George and Charles. George has been at a School at Germantown for three years and I am pleased with his advancement & I have now placed Charles there with him. This has been a good season for our Indian Corn and good for the Tobacco where it was planted in time. The Crop in Maryland will be short. I have made more than last year as most of mine was planted early. My last year's Crop [of] 96 Hogsheads is not yet sold. I am offered $16 [illegible] for it which I shall take if it does not get higher in a few Days. Maryland Tobacco will not decline, I think, a great deal as the Quantity made is not half what was made some years ago and the consumption in Europe has increased. U.S. Bank Stock has fallen from an advance of 56 to 11 and will no doubt go down lower. This is owing to the bad direction of this Bank.[2] [Six] Per Cts. are at 103 of the loan of 1815. I beg you to present my best Respects to your Son & Mr. and Mrs. Van Havre and family and remain

> With great Respect & Esteem

> Yours Geo: Calvert

1. Van Havre-S.

2. The inept management of the Second Bank of the United States by its first president, William Jones, brought about a congressional threat to repeal the bank's charter in January 1819. The bank survived this threat, but Jones was ousted.

To Jean Michel van Havre

Riversdale, 10 January 1819

My dear Brother,

I have just received your letter of 5 September and 15 October [1818], and since I have become such a complete business woman I hasten to reply (as you request, "as soon as possible") and to send you the law [pertaining] to alluvions. . . .[1]

Your letter gave me the greatest pleasure by bringing word that you are all well and by giving details about Papa. The amusing description you gave of your doctors does not tempt me to employ them, so I rejoice that you have attracted a good English doctor to Antwerp. If ever you have the misfortune to lose him, which I trust will not happen, have one sent from here. I know some excellent ones. For the past three years we have had one in Washington who never makes a mistake. There is no way to die in his care! As for me, I am convinced that when one has a family a good doctor is more important than a good table or any other good thing.

I must admit that we don't have husbands here who are as complacent as those you describe. That style will not catch on here, I think. I expect you will laugh at us when I tell you that it is really a pleasure to see how attentive husbands are to their wives in Washington society and with what courtesy and affection they treat them in public. Perhaps in some instances this is only for appearances and not at all sincere, but it is nevertheless agreeable to see. For a married woman to have a "gallant"—that is not done and would not be tolerated. She would be banished from society.

I wish I could say as much for the young men's conduct, which is far from what it should be, but at least they conceal their depravity as much as possible and do not flaunt it in public as is done in some European cities.

Neither you nor my sister tells me anything about Charles in your letters. How is he and what is he doing? They ask me in Philadelphia whether Charles lost a lot in the failure of the house of van Ertborn. I fear he is managing his affairs badly.

I hope that your project at the polder will be successful, but I don't like hearing that you and Edward went there and came down with a fever. My sister tells me that Edward loves to go hunting for snipe. I wish he could come here to hunt, as we have quantities of them. The other day my husband killed the most beautiful <u>wild</u> turkey I have ever seen. It weighed twenty pounds and was extremely fat. A few days before, he killed eleven partridges and seven doves, and three Englishmen who had come out to hunt with him got sixteen partridges and seven snipe—all in less than four hours.

By the way, do you know the Viscount of Quabeck or his family? He was sent here by your king as *chargé d'affaires.*[2] He dined here the other day and greatly admired our turkey.

But *adieu,* dear brother, I must close by asking you to believe me

Your affectionate sister,

Rosalie E. Calvert

1. Alluvion is the gradual increase of land along a shore or river bank from natural or artificial causes.

2. Alexandre Joseph, Vicomte Goupy de Quabeck (ca. 1782–1867), served as Belgian *chargé* in the United States from 1818 to 1825, when he was elevated to minister.

To Isabelle van Havre

[n.p.], 11 January 1819

Today when I received your letter of 1 October [1818], my dear Sister, I was completely dismayed to see how much time has passed since I last wrote you. I don't know how it happened because not a day has passed that I don't think of you. . . . The fact is that I have more work than I can do. My husband takes care of nothing regarding the household or the servants. I must manage everything—the wine, provisions, everything! You can [imagine], with a family as large as mine and in the country where we can't get the help which could be had in town, how overwhelmed with work I always am. When we entertain, Mr. C does nothing whatsoever—all the trouble, all the arrangements fall on me.

Day before yesterday, we had a full-scale dinner for twenty people. We were obliged to place the table from one corner of the room to the other, [since] the room was not long enough to position it as usual. We were expecting the English Minister, Mr. and Mrs. Bagot, but the previous day they learned of the death of the English Queen so they had to go into mourning and were unable to come.[1] However, we had the French Minister and his wife, the Prussian [Minister], and the Viscount of Quabeck, your King's *chargé d'affaires*.[2] How is it that you have never spoken of him in your letters? He is a very nice man, well-bred, and he knew—quite well—our Uncle Albert, Mr. De Rose of Antwerp, Madame Hovorst. He comes from near Brussels. Tell me if you know him or his family. As he is from my country, I greatly enjoyed seeing him and entertaining him. That one we had last year, Mr. Ter [Cato?] was an imbecile.

The social scene in Washington is quite sparkling this winter. We have been to three very splendid private balls, one at Mr. Tayloe's, the others at Mr. Bagot's and Mr. de Neuville's. Here at Riversdale we have had two dinners, and we are planning a fine luncheon where there will be dancing. At these elegant dinners we sit down to dine at 5 o'clock.

I believe that going out in society is good for my health because I am feeling a lot better now. Our whole family is in good health. George is still at Germantown where last October I also sent Charles, [who] is very happy there. [George] will go to college in the spring, I think, or certainly next fall. For the last year I have had a governess for Eugenia, Henry, and Julia, but I have not been satisfied so I am trying to get another. If I don't succeed, I will have to send Eugenia to Philadelphia. My little Amelia is two years old and a charming child. Don't you deem me most fortunate indeed to think that she is the last? I believe I am safe now from having any more children, and I am greatly delighted.

Caroline still has not made a choice. She is very reserved—too much so, I think. I never saw a girl so little the coquette.

I wrote you that the lovely outfits you sent us last year are as good as new, and we had two new ones of the same type made for this winter. For next [winter] I must ask you to send us one or two more [outfits] so as to give us an idea of the latest styles. I will also ask you to send both Caroline and me a cloak, or what I think you call a *douillette*.[3] We wear it here for morning visits or to church. We will each need a winter hat to wear with our *douillette* too.

If they get here by the end of December that would be in time, but since ships are always delayed it would be better to send them [to arrive] by December first. This is especially important if the ship is bound for Philadelphia, because we are always a fortnight—sometimes longer—getting things from there, as opposed to Baltimore where we can get delivery in a day. It is absolutely imperative to have our hats and *douillettes* before the first of January so we can go to the President's House in the morning. We have some old ones which are serviceable enough for nighttime or for when the weather is bad.

I hope you have kept our measurements. Would you please send eight pairs of dancing shoes for Caroline and four for me—those from last year fit perfectly. Please tell me the price of your Kashmir shawls, whether they are pretty, and whether you have any from France that are less expensive but still nice. The ones they are wearing here from India are outrageously expensive—from $400 to $600—and to me not attractive. I should point out something to you about Caroline's clothes: she has a lot of bosom and the dresses were a bit too revealing—she likes them to cover the neck.

I was very amused by all your description of last winter's social season, and I imagine the new season is just opening with some new recruits. I hope you will keep me informed. How is it that my dear Louise cannot make a choice from her many admirers? I think she must be too hard to please. And Edward—has he still not felt the power of Cupid, surrounded by so many belles? Is Papa complaining that he is not yet a great-grandfather? Don't count on us here. Caroline is so disdainful of suitors that she sent two away without permitting them to explain themselves, and I don't know anyone here whom I would want for a son-in-law. . . .

Your affectionate,

R. E. Calvert

1. Queen Charlotte, wife of George III, died on November 17, 1818.

2. The French minister was Hyde de Neuville; the Prussian minister was Friedrich Greuhm, who served from 1817 until his death in 1822.

3. A *douillette* was a warm, lined coat-dress, but one usually reserved for domestic wear; a pelisse was the type of coat-dress usually worn for morning calls in this period (see Millia Davenport, *The Book of Costume* [New York, 1966], vol. 1, pp. 793, 807).

To H. J. Stier

Riversdale, 13 March 1819

My dear Father,

It has been a long time since I have had the pleasure of writing to you or since I have received any letters from you. I am sending your account from November 1817 to March 1819 attached—it should have been sent earlier. The reason I converted a portion of your Bank of Washington shares into 6 Pcts. is that banks have become so numerous and the Bank of the United States does them so much harm that they cannot continue to give high dividends. Also, the charter of the Bank [of Washington] expires in three years and it is uncertain whether Congress will grant them a new one. Since this stock is presently selling at from nine to ten percent above par, it seemed advantageous to sell it. I would have sold even more, but it had to be done secretly and in small amounts because, with my husband a director of this bank, the value would have fallen considerably if we had offered all of your stock for sale. So I had to wait, but after next May 23rd I will sell the rest, especially if the government authorizes a new bond issue to pay for the province of Florida which they have bought from Spain. . . .[1]

I had the great pleasure the other day in Washington of meeting Mrs. Gilmor of Baltimore, who told me of being at your house and that you showed her your fine collection of paintings. You can imagine how I overwhelmed her with questions!

The social season is coming to an end along with the session of Congress; [the season] was quite lively this winter and Washington quite splendid. Caroline has gone to thirteen dancing parties, not to mention the dinners, the tea parties, and the assemblies at the President's every fortnight.

There has been a good company of actors [here], but we have not gone; nor have we been to the several concerts and we attended only one of the public balls. I have found that going out two or, at the most, three times a week is quite enough. There was something every day during

December, January, and February, and sometimes two assemblies on the same evening, but I don't think it is good for a young person to be constantly in society—a little spacing is better.

Up to now, Caroline has had no offers which we wished to accept. [There was] a lawyer, but unless such a person possesses superior talents, that is not too promising a position. [Another], a merchant, although apparently wealthy, [presents] an uncertain prospect. We therefore declined these two offers as well as one from Mr. Ogle's eldest son. At the moment Mr. Tayloe's third son, whom you should remember, is courting her.[2] He seems pleasant and industrious. His father has brought him up to be a planter and will give him a good start even though there are eleven other children. From the standpoint of family this match is advantageous, though not brilliant in other respects. The young man is about twenty years old, I think, and small in stature. Caroline seems to like him well enough. I don't know whether I want this to succeed or not, but since she is so young I think it would be better to wait at least a year.

She has been much sought after this winter. Her gowns have been quite the most beautiful in Washington, except for those of Mrs. Bagot and Mrs. Monroe's daughter.[3] [Caroline's] especially were in the best possible taste, thanks to all your efforts.

There is a great deal of diversity in Washington society. There are several young girls who are very pretty but without fortune or family, and several who are quite ordinary looking but very wealthy. No marriages have taken place in our circle. Luxurious living is so much on the rise that the young people are afraid to marry. . . .

I have just dismissed the governess whom I employed for the past year for Eugénie, Henry, and Julia. She did not have a good method of teaching. If I cannot find a better one, I shall have to send Eugénie to a school and teach the other two myself with Caroline's assistance. . . .

Our winter social season is over, but I have much to do to get my kitchen garden organized. [I] recently discharged my German gardener, whom we bought along with his wife off a ship.[4] He knew nothing at all and couldn't tell a carrot from a turnip, but he was very industrious and did more work in a day than three or four of our negroes.

Yesterday we dined at the President's House. I have never seen anything as splendid as the table—a superb gilt plateau in the center with gilt baskets filled with artificial flowers. All of the serving dishes were solid silver; the dessert spoons and forks and knives were silver-gilt. The plates were fine French porcelain. The guests were thirty in number—all the [foreign] Ministers with their wives and their secretaries. My hus-

band and I and General and Mrs. Mason were the only ones from here—
all the other guests were European (Caroline was not included as young
people are not invited to these dinners).[5] I was seated at the table between the English Minister, Mr. Bagot, and the Russian Minister, Mr.
D'Ashkof.[6] It was a great honor for us to be included in such a distinguished company, and both Mrs. Monroe and the President received us
with the most flattering kindness, in such a way that I spent a very
pleasant evening (as they dine at 6 o'clock).

But I really must close, dear Father. . . .

Your affectionate and dutiful daughter,

R. E. Calvert

1. The Adams-Onís Treaty between the United States and Spain was signed in
February 1819. By its provisions, Spain renounced all claims to West Florida and
ceded East Florida, and the United States assumed the claims of its own citizens
against Spain up to five million dollars.

2. William Henry Tayloe (1799–1871).

3. There were two Monroe daughters, both active in helping their mother with the
social responsibilities of the president's wife: Eliza, married to Judge George Hay of
Virginia, and Maria Hester, unmarried at this time and probably the daughter Mrs.
Calvert was referring to.

4. Mrs. Calvert means to say that she bought his contract or indenture. This
gardener was mentioned as recently employed in the letter to Isabelle van Havre of 25
October 1816, above.

5. General Mason was probably John Mason of Georgetown, who had been
Commissary General of Prisoners during the War of 1812 (*Niles Weekly Register* 4
[24 April 1813], 130).

6. Andrei Dashkof (?–1831) represented Russia in the United States, first as
consul general from 1808, then as minister from 1811.

To Charles J. Stier[1]

Riversdale, 24 March 1819

Dear Brother,

. . . According to your description, Cleydael must be greatly embellished by the changes you have made there. The other day I gave Caroline
a description of that beautiful castle, and now she has been seized with a
passionate desire to go and see it and the dear friends who live there. All
she talks about is going there to surprise you one day. . . .

How do you amuse yourself during the winter, dear Brother? And how
does my sister, your good Eugénie, occupy herself? I don't imagine you

have the large number of household tasks of which we complain so much here.

We have made only a few embellishments at Riversdale, but this summer we plan to make a lake to the south of the house, to clear and improve this piece of ground which is very poor and is now used merely for pasture.[2] I wish you could come and supervise our improvements and tell us where to plant the clumps of trees which I intend planting in great number this spring.

Please, dear Brother, give my compliments to your wife and accept those of Caroline and her father. They have gone out riding to our neighbor Mr. Lowndes' house. Believe me

Your affectionate,

R. E. Calvert

1. Calvert, CU-NYC.
2. This would have been the second time a lake was undertaken at this location. In 1808, Mrs. Calvert reported a lake "just finished" to the south of the house (see RC to CJS, 10 December 1808).

To Isabelle van Havre

Riversdale, 25 March 1819

. . . Thank you for all the details about your social life which greatly entertained me. I hope you will give me more information about what you are doing this winter. . . . Did you give another fine ball this season as you did last year?

You ask me which families do the most entertaining in Washington. The ministers of France and England give each week a large dinner on Monday evenings and a reception on Saturday evenings. Everyone who has previously been introduced to them may attend, and they extend an open invitation for the season to people of the first class. There is dancing and these parties are really quite pleasant. One goes to these events a little less dressed-up than for a ball. In addition, they give two or three grand balls where a really splendid cold supper is served, but where the guests, being more numerous, are a mixed lot—anywhere from 300 to 400 people.

Our three Secretaries—of State, War, and the Treasury—also give dinners and two or three large dancing parties, besides some tea parties where we do not dance. After the ministers and the secretaries, Mr.

Tayloe is one who does a great deal of entertaining. He has a dinner every week and has given a ball and some tea parties, too.[1] Our niece Mrs. Peter has not given a dinner, but [has given] three balls and several tea parties.

There is a public ball every fortnight and an assembly at the President's House every fortnight, also. People go [to the President's House] at 8 and leave at 10 o'clock; they entertain themselves by promenading from one room to another and conversing with their acquaintances. All the ambassadors and their families are obliged to go, as are all the military and public officials, etc. There are always a good many foreigners in Washington during the session of Congress, which makes society here very pleasant and diversified.

There is a theatre with a tolerably good troupe, but it is seldom frequented by the best people—we have never been. There is also a circus where the performance is extremely good and with beautiful horses. [This season] there were about a dozen concerts, recitations, etc., in short, not a day without something going on, [and] frequently two or three parties on the same evening. People have to send their invitations ten to twelve days in advance to be sure of their guests.

You seem surprised that we prefer coming back here in the middle of the night instead of taking rooms in town, but I am certain that if you tried it both ways, as we did, you would prefer returning here, too. We have a well-closed carriage, specially-made slippers which keep our feet as warm as possible, and large cloaks of silk lined with wadding and [worn] with a calash, which don't rumple either our clothes or our coiffures.[2] There is always a place to put the cloaks so that we are in less danger of catching cold going to a dancing party than in going from one room to another in our own house. Then, too, I don't like to leave either my children or my house [overnight] in the winter.

Caroline has only three dancing frocks which she has worn to fourteen dances, but they are almost as fresh as the first day she wore them. They are not at all bedraggled—only the satin petticoats are a little soiled at the bottom, but it wouldn't be noticed at night. We have made a dress exactly like the one with the geranium garland, but trimmed in rose instead of flame-color, and I have put one of the trimmings of roses on it, which made it a very pretty costume. Her white satin brocade gown is also still quite presentable, as is the blue chenille.

These clothes will be quite serviceable again next winter, but as I think there will be a lot of elegance next year and the session of Congress will be very long, I would like her to have something new. So please send a dancing frock for Caroline, which is not too expensive, and several of those little engraved sketches showing morning and evening dress, like the ones you sent before—with them we will be able to copy your styles. Would you also send us two wadded *capottes,* or *pelisses,* or *douillettes*— I don't know what you call them—one for me, another for Caroline. We wear them in the mornings to pay social calls. I don't want them to be too splendid, because we can only wear the same ones for two or three years.

Would you also send each of us three pairs of shoes to go with the *capottes,* besides two pairs of white [shoes] for me and six pairs of white dancing shoes for Caroline. [We also need] two hats to wear with the *capottes,* one with plumes for Caroline, but one without for me, since I have five sets of plumes which are all good. They clean them very well in Philadelphia, by the way, as well as the blond laces. The dressmaker must be told that Caroline has put on weight, so she has to make the bodice wider than the last measurement. She also wants her dancing frock to be a little less low-cut than they are wearing them in France. Since she has a rather large bosom, she prefers her dresses quite high on the neck.

Caroline's shoes fit her very well, but I would like mine a little wider and the bodice of my *capotte* not too short or too narrow. It would be a good idea if [the dressmaker] would send us a little of the [excess] material to use in case of mishap.

The corset you sent me stays open [3 1/4 inches].[3] I think I am much fatter than you are, especially in my hips.

I also would be much obliged if you would send us some embroidery patterns, and if by chance you find any more of these inexpensive and pretty trimmings, like the geranium garland on the bottom of the tulle dress, please send me three or four more. They would make nice presents for Caroline to give to her friends. We need to have these things by the first of December at the latest, and by mid-November if possible. If the ship gets to Baltimore by December first, it will be in time; but if it arrives in Philadelphia after the rivers are frozen, it can take a month for things to get here. In the summer there is no problem, because it only takes a week for the packets to get here.

I fear, dear Sister, that all these things will once again give you much work, but there it is—you did such a good job of executing our first commissions that you have brought on more. However, I beg you to make it easy on yourself. When you find something pretty, take it—don't tire yourself out trying to find something better.

We had a good laugh at Louise's and your fear that a Frenchman could turn Caroline's head. Don't worry about that. Caroline often dances with

Frenchmen, but she doesn't like them at all and thinks them much inferior to her fellow countrymen. She is American to the bottom of her soul and declares she is determined to marry only an American. She is very hard to please, and although she had several offers this winter, I don't have any hopes at present of getting her settled. No beau has made the least impression on her heart, and I am glad because I wouldn't like to have any of those who have pursued her for a son-in-law. I wouldn't be at all surprised if next winter turned out the same as this, and actually I don't want her to marry before she is twenty-four.

The other day we went to an extremely splendid state dinner at the President's House. All the foreign ministers were there. I was seated between the English and Russian Ambassadors. Mrs. Monroe gave me the most flattering reception; she does the honors with much grace and dignity. She is a charming woman, much superior to the last President's wife.[4] She is from one of the better families and received an excellent education. She spent several years in France and in England when Mr. Monroe was Ambassador. Her oldest daughter, who is married, was educated in Paris and couldn't be nicer. The younger [daughter] was at school with Caroline [and] returned home last month. She was here [at Riversdale] yesterday to see Caroline.[5] Mrs. Monroe, her daughters, and four or five other Washington women receive their clothes from Paris, but they are not in as good taste as ours.

We have every kind of social activity here except gambling parties, and I am very pleased about that. Sometimes at balls there are four or five gaming tables for the men, but none of the women play. We go to the dancing parties at 8 o'clock and leave at 11. It takes an hour and a quarter to return here, so we are in bed just before 1 A.M.

You say that you were surprised that I let Caroline spend a week with her cousin Mrs. Rogers without accompanying her myself, but I am sure you would not disapprove if you knew Mrs. Rogers—she is a woman such as few women are. She is extremely and genuinely attached to Caroline, has a great deal of discretion, and I can rely on her. . . .

I think, dear Sister, that you must be tired of all my nonsense, so I will finish by embracing you and Louise and all your children. My compliments to your husband and tell him he is very lazy for writing me so seldom.

Your affectionate sister,

R. E. Calvert

1. John Tayloe III.

2. A calash was a large bonnet-type hood designed to protect elaborate coiffures.

3. Mrs. Calvert marked off a space here on her paper which measures 3 1/4 inches.

4. Eliza (Kortright) Monroe (1766–1830) was the daughter of Lawrence Kortright, a New York merchant. Mrs. Monroe was being compared here with her immediate predecessor, Dolly Madison.

5. It was Maria Hester Monroe (1803–?) who visited Caroline at Riversdale.

To Isabelle van Havre

[Riversdale], 25 July 1819

My dear Sister,

. . . Our compliments to my dear Louise on her marriage, which I imagine has already taken place.[1] May she enjoy all the happiness which the state of matrimony is capable of conferring—that is the wish all of us here join in sending her. Her choice must be very satisfying to you since you know the young man so well and all his family is so respectable—that is a most important consideration in establishing our children. I hope that Caroline makes as good a choice as her cousin in three or four years—I don't want it any sooner. I am curious to know if you accompanied the young newlyweds on their trip. You must give me all the details of the wedding. If this wretched ocean did not separate us, I would have come to take part.

I thank you for the particulars you provide about the V[iscount] de Q[uabeck] and we certainly will not invite him here any more. But there was no reason for you to be alarmed. I was merely surprised you had not mentioned his coming to America before, and I wanted to know whether he was a man one could ask to see *en famille* or not. He dined here three or four times when we had large gatherings and before we knew of his conduct or character. He seemed pleasant enough to me then. However, there was never any danger to Caroline's heart. . . .

You don't seem, my dear Sister, to be completely aware of our nature and manner of life. You must ask questions about us when you meet people who come from Washington, and then I am sure you wouldn't have any fear for your niece or her mama—because it seems to me that you think neither of us knows how to escape the charms of the handsome V[iscount] who is over 40 years old and not in the least irresistible! I expect we err rather in the other direction of being too haughty, and you can rest assured that no man who is not highly thought of and also from a good family will succeed with Caroline. . . .

In my March 25th letter, I asked you to send me some articles of clothing, but I imagine that with Louise's marriage this could not be done, especially if you accompanied them on their trip. And, dear Sister, if it would cause you the least trouble, please don't do it—the more so as I think there will be very few social activities next winter. Everyone is so badly off because of the depression of the banks that a large number of people will have to make do with their old clothes instead of making new ones. . . .[2]

Your affectionate sister,

R. E. Calvert

1. Louise van Havre was married to John M. J. della Faille de Leverghem (1780–1848) in 1819.

2. The panic of 1819 brought numerous bank failures, a general contraction of credit, and great hardships for debtors.

To Isabelle van Havre

[Riversdale], 17 September 1819

My dear Sister,

I just received your letter of 9 and 10 June [1819], and I cannot imagine how it could be three months en route from Antwerp to Phila-delphia. It seems my letters are also very slow in reaching you. I suppose the ships are often detained in port after our letters are aboard. . . .

Undoubtedly our dear Louise is Madame De La Faille by now. May she find all the happiness which I am certain she deserves. I hope I will soon receive more information on how the wedding went—give me some description of her trousseau and also a plan of your dinner, which I imagine must have been brilliant. I approve your plan of going to spend the night at Cleydael and am interested to know if you went on the trip to Switzerland. I think that would do you a lot of good.

I am extremely obliged to you for the care you took with my commis-sions. If I had known about Louise's wedding, I would not have asked it of you because I am afraid I caused you a lot of work at a time when you already had too much.

I wrote you in my last letter that you had nothing to fear on the subject of a certain gentleman from your country. . . . As for having affairs with married women, it is unknown here (in the first circle) and would not be tolerated. So if he remains in Washington, he will have to continue to behave himself, whether he likes it or not. . . .

We are all well. George and Charles are here for a month's vacation, so

I have all my children at home. I will try to write more often in the future, especially to Papa, but you can't imagine how much I have to do. My servants are very negligent and my husband does absolutely nothing other than manage his lands. The wines, the provisions, the servants' work, horses, carriages, garden, dairy—I am in charge of all that. Besides which, all our clothes, linens, etc., from mine to Emily's[1] are made here at the house and I have to supervise everything, often cutting and fitting them myself. Since winter I haven't had a teacher for my three youngest children; Caroline gives them some lessons, but it takes up some of my time, too. And then I am not as strong as I once was and I have to take care of myself. When our servants are sick, we use a doctor from Washington, but he makes us prepare all the remedies, etc. It all takes a lot of time and you can well imagine that with such a large number of negroes, we have illnesses frequently. There are people who do more in an hour than others in a day, but I am not one of their number, and without being lazy, I am slow in everything I do. . . .

Your affectionate sister,

R. E. Calvert

1. Nickname for the Calverts' youngest, Amelia, now almost three.

To Charles J. Stier[1]

Riversdale, 19 September 1819

Dear Brother,

I received your letter of June 13th two days ago and I shall begin this by speaking of business interests. Enclosed are your accounts up to this date. The purchase of the [bill] of exchange [was] deferred until 5 September, because the United States Bank did not want to draw on London sooner because of the great bank panic, and for the same reason it was difficult to procure a bill about which we could be sure. The affairs of the good banks are on the road to mending, and I hope we will have no more of such difficulties.

I will send you as soon as possible a butt of the best Madeira, but you do not tell me if I should send it to Amsterdam or if it should be forwarded to Antwerp. It will be easy for me to send you some good wine from Baltimore, but it is seldom ships sail from that port to Antwerp and it will be more difficult to find good wine in Philadelphia. . . .

I must use the rest of this sheet in talking to you about us. I often imagine myself near you at Cleydael. How greatly that lovely estate must be beautified by the changes you have made! I often describe it to Caroline. I am delighted to hear your brother-in-law's affairs are on the high road to prosperity. We are all well. I have all my children with me now, but George will go to the University of Cambridge near Boston the 1st of November. He is as tall as you. Caroline is still [not] engaged. . . . We often tease her by saying she will certainly be an old maid and she answers that she thinks so, too, and is very happy and content with her state and does not wish to alter it. . . .

You ask me if we have improved Riversdale greatly. Indeed, not at all. My husband is a splendid farmer and planter and has fine cattle, cows, sheep, etc., but our place is only an American farm, and I fear very much it will continue such if you are not to aid us with your advice to beautify it. *Adieu,* dear Brother. . . .

Your affectionate sister,

R. E. Calvert

1. Carter Trans-MHS.

To H. J. Stier

Riversdale, 22 November 1819

Dear Father,

For quite some time I have intended each day to write you and still time has slipped past without my having done it. What a bad habit it is to put things off. Today I am making a firm resolve never to put anything off, since all one ever gains are regrets for having done so. Several days ago I received your letter[s] . . . which made me very ashamed of my long silence. [My negligence] probably has also been somewhat occasioned by the fact that recently I have met several people who have seen you and who have given me such good reports of your health and appearance that I have been content at hearing about you without stopping to think that you must be awaiting news of us. Mr. Harper, and most recently Mr. Tayloe, brought us the welcome news that you were in the best of health, quite cheerful, and "in excellent spirits."[1]

I thank you, dear Father, for your advice about Caroline and I am entirely in agreement with you concerning her eventual establishment. I am also most grateful for your kind offer to help us with her dowry, but that would be unreasonable on our part.[2] With seven children to provide for, you can imagine that we are as economical as our situation and position permit (I fear in the eyes of the public perhaps too much so), but I find real pleasure in economizing for my children. So whenever Caroline wishes to settle down, we will find the means to provide for her without availing ourselves of your generous offer. My plan is to give her an allowance to begin with—that is the best way in this country by all reports—or if she marries a planter, to buy her a tract of land in our vicinity. However, it is impossible to decide anything about this until we know what choice she has made. In your country everything is ordered, there is only one way of life, but here, as you know, it is quite different. At the moment she has no particular sweetheart, having rejected Mr. Tayloe's son.

You are mistaken, dear Father, about [Mr. Tayloe's] character—there are few people as frugal as he, and his wife is positively stingy. He has not been preoccupied with horseracing for some years now. They have handsome equipages and cut a fine figure in society, but they manage all this with the greatest thrift. The eldest son married—against his parents' wishes—a charming girl who didn't have a penny.[3] His father, nevertheless, gave him a fine plantation, but I fear [the son] prefers drinking to everything else, a bad habit he acquired in the navy where he served as a lieutenant during the recent war. [The Tayloes'] eldest daughter married a man of wealth.[4] I don't know what she received from her father, perhaps an allowance, or I think it more likely that he gives her gifts from time to time. There is another daughter, eighteen years old—an extremely nice, industrious, and sensible girl—and two other sons.[5] He has given each of these [sons] a fully-equipped plantation for which they pay their father an annual fee of two percent of its valuation.

This is a rather long story of a family which wants very much to be allied to ours, but I do not foresee that taking place. The father is a man who thinks very highly of himself, and I am afraid that several of his children take after him.

Caroline and I both thank you, dear Father, for the New Year's gift and also for your promise of a handsome wedding present. When I see the probability that she will settle down, I will let you know—at the moment I see none.

You asked if there were any jewelers in diamonds hereabouts. There are several in Philadelphia and one of them does especially fine work and is trustworthy. I had him reset a pair of amethyst and diamond earrings that my dear Mother had given me, and he did an excellent job. [But] unless my daughter marries an extremely wealthy man, I don't think it would be desirable to give her diamonds. I should prefer to give her a small service or some solid silver pieces, which would be more useful. Caroline is very sensible and quite moderate in her desires. She really does not like anything ostentatious.

You are quite right, dear Father, in saying that we have the reputation of being ten times as rich as in fact we are.[6] Fortunes here are always imagined to be double or even quadruple their real value—our own even more so because of the funds belonging to you which pass through my hands each quarter.

George has been at the University of Cambridge near Boston for a month now. I do hope he will cut a good figure there. He will have to remain there three years to complete all the classes. Cambridge is, according to everybody, the best university in America. . . .

We have had an extremely hot and dry summer—all our vegetables were completely burned up. We did make a good wheat crop and a large harvest of Indian corn, but because of the drought we were not able to plant the tobacco [in time] so this crop has not been as good.

We are sending our 1818 tobacco crop to Mr. Murdoch in London this week. I hope it will bring a good price. We did not find it advantageous to sell it here. Because of the general [financial] disorder, the banks are not discounting and all the merchants are in distress. On the first of November there was a general meeting of the stockholders of the Bank of the United States, and they appointed a committee to examine the conduct of the directors of the Bank. I am enclosing the committee's report. Due to the infamous conduct of the president and some directors, [the Bank] did not pay a dividend last July. Now it has a good president and I hope that payment will be honored in the future. . . .[7]

Your dutiful daughter,

R. E. Calvert

1. Robert Goodloe Harper (1765–1825) and John Tayloe III.

2. Stier had offered to provide a yearly allowance to Caroline after her marriage, but cautioned that it could only be during his lifetime (HJS Letterbook, 1 June 1819, Cal S-V).

3. John Tayloe IV (1793–1824) married Maria Forrest, daughter of Colonel Uriah Forrest.

4. Henrietta Hill Tayloe (1794–1832) married H.G S. Key, a brother of Francis Scott Key, in 1815.

5. Probably Catherine Carter Tayloe (1801–?), Benjamin Ogle Tayloe (1796–1868), and William Henry Tayloe (1799–1871).

6. Stier warned Mrs. Calvert to beware of fortune hunters and to exercise great caution in selecting a mate for Caroline. He expressed reservations about the Tayloe

alliance: "The father's character leads me to think he will sacrifice his [other] children to benefit his eldest son, *milord Anglais,* and [Caroline's] suitor is merely the third. Has he the ambition of the father? Is your daughter wise enough not to be dazzled by the glitter? Consider all of this well, and above all be sure about the young man's firm establishment now—don't gamble on the future" (HJS Letterbook, [n.d.] June 1819, Cal S-V).

7. Langdon Cheves (1776–1857) of South Carolina served as president of the United States Bank from 1819 to 1822 and restored it to sound financial condition.

Last Journeys

IN FEBRUARY 1820, THE CALVERTS suffered a cruel blow. Two of their children, nine-year-old Henry and three-year-old Amelia, became ill and died within a week of each other. The symptoms of their illness, a severe sore throat and high fever, and the rapidity of their death suggest that they had diphtheria, a leading killer of children under ten. Eugenia, fourteen years old, also came down with the disease, but survived. All social activity ceased, and the Calvert family went into deep mourning.

That summer George Calvert took Rosalie on an extended trip to help her recover from this devastating experience. Caroline, Eugenia, and Julia accompanied their parents on the two-month journey. George Henry was at Harvard but joined his family for a portion of the trip during his vacation, and Charles remained behind at a school near Baltimore. The Calverts traveled first to Bath in western Virginia, then through Baltimore and Philadelphia to the Jersey shore. On they went to New York City and up the Hudson River to Saratoga and Lake George. The trip was leisurely, with time for taking the waters at various spas along the way.

The journey fulfilled its purpose. Eugenia, who had still been weak from her illness at its inception, was strong enough to be left at Madame Grelaud's school in Philadelphia on the way home. The numerous changes of scenery and diverse experiences proved a tonic for Rosalie and did not permit her to brood over her lost children. She returned home claiming to feel ten years younger and making plans for another trip the following year.

It was the last pleasurable time Rosalie was to know. In late November 1820, she became bedridden, suffering from acute edema in the lower extremities. Suspecting that her condition was hereditary, she wrote urgently to Isabelle for information doctors in Antwerp might offer on treatment. At least seven doctors treated her, including Dr. Physick who had helped her once before, but to no avail. The edema, caused by congestive heart failure, spread to her vital organs, and on March 13, 1821, at age forty-three, Rosalie Calvert died.

To Isabelle van Havre

[Riversdale], 29 February 1820

My dear Sister,

Never have I written to you with such a heavy heart. Pity, my dear Sister, your poor friend—in one week I have just lost two of my children. On the 4th of this month, my dear Henri was suddenly stricken with a sore throat and a malignant fever, and he died on the 6th. Two days later my delightful little Amelie and her sister Eugénie came down with the same illness. It pleased the Almighty to spare Eugénie for me, but my dear Amelie was taken from me in three days. Only you, my dear friend, can possibly understand my sorrow. These two children were so promising. They were always in the best of health and were so lovable and engaging, and I had such expectations for them. But the will of God was done. He gave them to me to make me happy for a few years, and He has taken them back. My only consolation is the thought that they are much happier now than they could ever have been in this unhappy world. . . .

Please give Papa my best and tell him I'll write him soon, but I don't want to do it today since I would only grieve him. I hope he will continue to enjoy the excellent health and good spirits which everyone tells me he has. . . .

My husband and my five children are well, but, my dear Friend, out of nine children to have lost four—was there ever such misfortune? Please embrace yours for me, and that they will long continue to make you happy by their good conduct and prosperity is the most sincere wish of

Your affectionate sister,

R. E. Calvert

To H. J. Stier

[Riversdale], 17 April 1820

Dear Father,

I have not had the heart to write you for the last two months. You will have learned from my letter to my sister in February of the cruel losses I have sustained. In one week I saw two of my children, my dear Henri and my delightful little Amelie, torn from us by a malignant fever and sore throat. Eugénie was also in great danger, but it pleased Almighty God to spare her. . . .

My Eugénie, who was so ill in early February, has almost completely recovered, but is still weak and must be careful. I hope that the month of May will restore her strength, and in July we plan to take a short trip to the mineral springs of Pennsylvania or Virginia. The rest of my family is well. Caroline had begun her winter campaign with much brilliance, but our troubles put a stop to that and since the 6th of February we have been completely in seclusion. She had several admirers, the principal one being the English consul general.[1] He is about 30 years old and a man who conducts himself very well. He receives $10,000 a year from his government and is very sensible and thrifty, but this position can be taken away from him. I do not want any man for my son-in-law who is dependent on a position or on the favor of ministers or others in high place. Caroline's heart is still as free as when she first came out, and I am very glad for that.

George is still at the University of Cambridge. I believe that he will cut a fine figure in the world. He had a month's vacation in January, and I took him to several private balls where he acquitted himself quite well. I have a tutor for my other three children until next October, and then I hope to send Eugénie to Philadelphia to the same school that Caroline attended.

Dear Father, I hope to have letters from you soon, and I will write you again shortly. My husband and children ask to be remembered to you and please believe me

Your devoted and dutiful daughter,

R. E. Calvert

P.S. The Viscount of Quabeck just left Washington with the intention of sailing from Philadelphia to Antwerp. He came out to call on me and offered to take my letters to you, but from what you had said I thought you might not wish to make his acquaintance so I didn't give him any. He has behaved himself very well during his stay in Washington.

1. Anthony St. John Baker (1785–1854) was the British consul in Washington in 1820. He had been secretary to British minister Augustus J. Foster in 1811 and became consul after the war, probably arriving in 1816. He served in New York, Philadelphia, and Baltimore in addition to Washington. Baker made the earliest known pictorial representation of Riversdale, a watercolor probably painted while he was courting Caroline. The watercolor is lost, but a transfer lithograph dated 1827 was made from it by B. King of London. The lithograph is found in Baker's *Memoires d'un Voyageur qui Se Repose* (privately printed, London, 1850), opposite p. 232.

To Isabelle van Havre

[Riversdale], 11 May 1820

. . . I have frequently wanted to write you, dear Sister, and I just did not have the heart. I could not write to my best friend without talking to her about the terrible losses I had in that miserable month of February. It was in that month that both my husband and I were born and we have lost four of the nine children we have had, and now I regard the others in fear and trembling. It seems to me that they are all walking continuously along the edge of a precipice. . . .

Eugénie, who was also quite sick, still has not entirely regained her strength and this summer we plan to take a trip to restore her health. It will take us about two and a half months. I need it myself, too, because you cannot imagine, my dear Friend, how much these losses have crushed me. I will never get over it. Those children were so good, so lovable, they promised me so much happiness, and they were carried away from me in such a short time. . . .

Since we haven't been out in company since February, we haven't missed the things you were sending us at all. . . . [However,] I did think they would have arrived this spring by one of the many ships from Amsterdam. . . .

I am delighted to hear that Papa is doing so well. You must keep a close watch on the cook since she is so important to his health. I hope to hear some good news from my dear Louise and her husband and that soon you will become a grandmother. You tell me that you have had many vexations since your return from Switzerland—you wrote that on the 12th of February. Consider, dear Sister, how much happier you were then than your poor friend and acknowledge that your troubles were trifling. May you never experience losses such as I have had, and [may you] be fortunate in your children is my most sincere wish. . . .

Your devoted sister,

R. E. Calvert

P.S. I just this moment received a letter from McEwen who tells me that our boxes have arrived in New York, so we will have them here soon. My thanks again for all your trouble and I'll write again as soon as we receive them.

To H. J. Stier

Riversdale, 5 June 1820

. . . At present I am very busy getting ready for a two-month trip we are taking to complete Eugénie's recovery during the summer. In September I hope to place her in the school in Philadelphia that Caroline attended. You can well imagine that I have a lot of work to do to get ready for an absence of two months. George is still at the University in Cambridge, near Boston, and I am placing Charles at school and taking [Caroline, Eugenia, and Julia] with me.

We have had a very cool spring following a winter so cold that the oldest people could not remember its like. The freeze was so hard on the first of January that plants and shrubs were destroyed which never before had needed cover. Do you still have a fine orangerie at the Mick?

Do you remember the plain to the north of the house which you had sown in oats the first year of your residence at Riversdale? My husband replanted it as a meadow and for over ten years had good crops of hay, but as the grass there had begun to deteriorate, he has just had it cultivated in order to make a crop of tobacco there. He covered the entire area with manure and in October he will again seed it with grass.

We have bought a piece of Cramphin's land which lay between us and the road going to Baltimore and also the small plantation of Peggy Adams which our property surrounded.[1] My husband is more absorbed than ever in his farming, and this year he is going to build a large mill.

It has been a long time, dear Father, since I've had a letter from you—the last was 25 June [1819], exactly a year ago this month, so I hope you will write me more often.[2] You can't imagine what pleasure I experience when I do receive one of your letters. . . .

Your devoted daughter,

R. E. Calvert

1. The Adams farm was finally acquired by George Calvert, but not from Peggy Adams, who had refused his offer of sixteen dollars an acre in 1807. Calvert got the 102-acre farm in 1814 for one thousand dollars, buying from a third party (Prince George's County Land Records, Liber J. R. M. 16, fol. 126).

2. There was a long hiatus at this time in Stier's correspondence with his daughter, for he was aging and ill. His letterbook records the letter of June 1819 referred to here, and then the next and final entry is for a letter written in February 1821, which would not have reached Mrs. Calvert before her death.

To Isabelle van Havre

[Riversdale], 12 July 1820

Dear Sister,

We are about ready to leave on a trip to Bath, and from there we plan to go by way of Philadelphia and New York to Saratoga, and maybe to see Niagara Falls. I think this [itinerary] will take us up to the middle of September. I have only a little time to write you today, dear Sister, but I must thank you for the admirable way you have once again executed our commissions. We received the two boxes from New York last week.

The *pelisses* fit us very well, are quite pretty, and exactly what I wanted. The material is completely new here—I have never seen anything like it. It is strange that the clothes we have made here, even though we try them on several times, don't fit as well as the ones you send us. We are very pleased with the hats and the shoes, and the two ball gowns are charming, especially the rose-colored one which is most becoming to Caroline. Please, dear Sister, give Papa Caroline's thanks and mine for this pretty gown. The garlands are also exactly what I wanted—I intend to give them to four of our nieces. . . .

I am sorry, dear Friend, not to have time to write you a long letter today, but as we are leaving in a few days I have a lot to do to put everything in order for such a long absence. George, who is at the university at Cambridge, will have three weeks vacation around the end of August and will join us at Saratoga then. We are putting Charles in a school ten miles from Baltimore, and our three daughters are coming with us.[1] On the way home, I'll leave Eugénie in Philadelphia at [Madame Grelaud's] school. There, dear Sister, are all my plans, if it pleases God to allow me to carry them out. . . .

Your affectionate sister,

R. E. Calvert

1. Charles was probably being placed at St. Mary's College for Boys, a Catholic preparatory school located about eight miles from downtown Baltimore. St. Mary's educated the sons of many prominent Maryland families. By 1824, however, following the death of his Catholic mother, Charles was back in school in Philadelphia (see Thomas Willing Morris to CJS, December 4, 1824, Cal S-V).

To Isabelle van Havre

Riversdale, 24 September 1820

Here we are, dear Sister, back from our trip. We have been gone two months and in that time have traveled between 1,100 and 1,200 miles of the country. It did me good, even more than I had hoped for, and made me feel ten years younger. Eugénie also completely recovered her health, and Julia grew stronger and feels better then she ever did. It is a pity that traveling is so expensive in this country—even with the greatest economy and with only one servant, we spent more than $1,700.

We left here on the 15th of July and went to the new spa of Shanandale in Virginia, which has a delightful location on the banks of the Shenandoah River.[1] The waters there have great efficacy and I would have liked to drink them for a whole week, but all the houses were full. We would have had to go back the same day except for the courtesy of a gentleman who had dined at our home several years ago and who gave up his room to us. However, it was so uncomfortable that we only stayed for two days. From there we went to see Harpers Ferry at the junction of the Potomac and the Shenandoah—it is a most sublime and picturesque prospect.

Then we went on to Bath in the county of Berkeley in Virginia, where the baths are superior to any you can possibly imagine.[2] The water comes out of the ground at a moderate temperature and [is] extremely pleasant for bathing. After staying there for ten days and using the baths twice a day, we came back through Baltimore and Philadelphia to Long Branch, New Jersey on the seashore. I was expecting to receive much benefit from sea bathing, but it is so dangerous and disagreeable in every respect that we only stayed ten days. From there we went by New York to Ballston and Saratoga. The waters of this last place did me a lot of good, [and] it was there that George joined us since he had a four-week vacation.

From there we went on to see the beautiful Lake George and two superb waterfalls on the Hudson River which in beauty and grandeur of landscape surpass anything of this kind I have ever seen.

From there we went to the springs of Lebanon in Massachusetts, which are a lot like those of Bath in Virginia. A society of Shakers has settled there—a most peculiar sect.[3] They live in large houses owned as common property, the men and women in the same house in different apartments, and in a state of continual celibacy. They augment their society by adopting poor children whom they raise and who are free to leave if they choose when they come of age. They share all expenses, [and] everyone works for the common good. They are very charitable towards all those outside their society who are deserving. Their clothing is extremely simple, a lot like that of the Quakers. We saw them at their church; their service consists of an extremely high-pitched and very unpleasant chant, then dancing altogether in time, forward, backward, and returning again. It looks ridiculous—like a dance of dead people. There is much simplicity in their manners.

Since it was too late then to go to Niagara, we returned by way of New York, Philadelphia, and Baltimore to Riversdale. One portion of our journey was made by steamboat, a most rapid mode of travel. We embarked in New York at 10 o'clock in the morning and arrived in Albany the next day at the same hour—160 miles in 24 hours! The Hudson is a delightful river and its banks continually offer the most beautiful vistas.

I regret that we couldn't go to Niagara, but everyone told us that September was too late to go there and that we would risk catching the tertian fever. So we thought it best to postpone it until next summer when I do expect to go and see it. We will leave here about the middle of July and go straight to Niagara and from there down the lakes to Montreal and Quebec. I wish you would send Edward to accompany us; this trip would be very interesting for him, and I would look after him as if he were my own son. I felt so well traveling this year, and the months of August and September are so unhealthy at Riversdale that I think it is absolutely necessary to the preservation of my health not to remain here during those months.

[no signature]

1. Shannondale Springs, thirteen miles south of Harpers Ferry, was located in Jefferson County, Virginia, now part of West Virginia.

2. Bath is now Berkeley Springs, West Virginia.

3. New Lebanon is in New York State on the Massachusetts border. Founded in 1787, this was the oldest Shaker community in the United States.

To Isabelle van Havre

[Riversdale], 6 December [1820][1]

. . . For the past fortnight I have been confined to my bed, not from illness because my health is better than it has been for a long time, but because of a swollen stiff leg. Eighteen months ago I noticed a small swelling in my groin the size of a nut. Not knowing what it was, I consulted our doctor who gave me several remedies over a period of four months, which did me no good. Then I consulted the foremost doctor in Philadelphia, Dr. Physick, by letter. He responded that he could not advise me without making an examination. This, as you can guess, was not agreeable, and since I thought it was nothing dangerous and [I was] not suffering any inconvenience, I believed that the waters of Bath or of the sea would cure it. However, soon after I returned from the trip, the swelling in the groin increased considerably, and the thigh also swelled so much that it is now double the size of the other. On account of that I decided to go to Philadelphia, and Dr. Physick examined it.[2] He told me to apply leeches and vesicatories alternately and that I absolutely had to remain in bed and stay very quiet. Now I cannot walk without a lot of pain and am unable to even bend my knee, which is quite swollen as well as the thigh.

I recall that our Grandmother Peeters could not walk without support and pulled her one leg after the other exactly like me. I also remember having seen in the carriage-house cellar at Papa's a chair of singular construction, on wheels, and that I was told our great-grandfather used it because he couldn't walk. Would you gather all the information you can about that and write me the results <u>immediately</u>. I want to know, if possible, the reason they couldn't walk—perhaps my case is similar to theirs. It seems that here they don't have any precedents, and I have consulted four doctors, all with a great deal of experience. Maybe this is an illness peculiar to our family (but I entreat you that all this remain just between the two of us).

You asked me if the dresses, etc., in the last boxes were damaged—not in the least! They were so well-packed that I think they could have been thrown in the sea without moisture getting into them. All the things were as fresh as the day they were packed. You are absolutely the best of all agents, and please accept again our thanks for all your trouble.

I placed Eugénie at the same school in Philadelphia where Caroline was. She is very happy and most eager to learn and improve herself. The school which George attended is not as good anymore; they have too large a number of boys there now. This persuaded me to put Charles in a school ten miles from Baltimore which I think is much better, but he is not learning French there. You can see that three of my children are far away from me—I only have Caroline and Julia left at home. What a difference from last year! Oh, my dear Friend, I will never get over the loss of those two delightful children.

My compliments to your husband and tell him that I would have sent him his account today, but although I can easily write a letter lying in my bed, transcribing an account is more difficult. I will have Caroline do it tomorrow and will send it to you shortly. . . .

Your affectionate sister,

R. E. Calvert

P.S. Would you send me a half dozen of the latest fashion designs like those you sent in the boxes? [If you] cut off the white paper surrounding them, they could easily fit in a packet like a letter.

1. A belated continuation of the previous letter (24 September 1820) to Mrs. van Havre, which Mrs. Calvert said she forgot to mail.

2. The Calverts, accompanied by Caroline, were in Philadelphia in November 1820. When they returned, they brought their niece Frances Parke Lewis home from Madame Grelaud's school with them; Parke later wrote that her Aunt Calvert was suffering much from her disease at that time (C. M. Calvert to E. B. Gibson, November 11, 1820, and F. P. Lewis to E. B. Gibson, November 20, 1820, in the Correspondence of Eleanor Parke Custis Lewis with Elizabeth Bordley Gibson, Mount Vernon Archives).

··ᢞ[THIS WAS THE LAST LETTER Rosalie Stier Calvert wrote to her family in Belgium. On 13 March 1821, she died. The attending physician, Thomas Sim of Washington, D.C., certified that he had treated her for "general dropsy affecting the whole system," but that her illness originated from "a diseased state of the Heart and larger blood vessels ossification . . . of some standing." Treatment was ineffective, said the doctor, and the patient died "as is generally the case in such diseases, by a large accumulation of water in the cavity of the Heart and in the Chest also."[1] Rosalie's family in Belgium had to be informed, and George Calvert wrote first to his father-in-law to tell him of their loss:

To H. J. Stier[2]

Riversdale, March 18, 1821

My Dear Sir

The painfull task devolves upon me of informing you of the death of my beloved wife and your most valued Daughter, after an illness of four months confined to the bed the whole time, and Suffering much pain which She bore with the greatest fortitude and resignation. She left us on the 13 Instant at 1 O'Clock. My only consolation was that her last moments were easy and I think happy, for She Said to me, "Oh how mercifull God is to me, I never could have Supposed that I could die So easy." My dear Rosalie's health had been bad for Six years and upwards. I do not think in that time She enjoyed one week of good health at a time. We consulted the best Physicians that could be found in this Country, among them Doct. Physic [*sic*] who is the most eminent and Six others, but they could not reinstate her health. At the particular request of my much lamented wife I Shall write to Mrs. van Havre, and inclose her a description of her case drawn up by Doct. Sim who has attended Mrs. Calvert for many years and who was constantly with her in the latter part of her illness. Be assured, my dear Sir, that nothing has been omitted by her afflicted husband that could either relieve or comfort her in all her illness.

With esteem & Respect

Yours, Geo: Calvert

1. Quoted from a report of Mrs. Calvert's illness and death prepared by Thomas Sim, M.D., and dated Washington City, March 24, 1821 (Cal S-V). Mrs. Calvert had requested that such a report be sent to her sister. Dropsy was congestive heart failure, characterized by fluid retention and swelling, commencing in the lower extremities and progressing to the vital organs.

2. Van Havre-S.

··◦] IN A LETTER TO ROSALIE'S SISTER, Isabelle van Havre (March 18, 1821), Calvert reported that his wife had been attended in her final illness by her good friend and neighbor, Anne Lowndes, and by the Calverts' niece, Martha Peter, who took charge of the Riversdale household for the last two weeks. Martha Peter informed her sister, Eleanor Custis Lewis, about their aunt's demise, and Nelly shared the details with her friend Betsy Bordley Gibson. Nelly, who had been Rosalie's favorite niece, also paid loving tribute to her aunt.

Eleanor Custis Lewis to Elizabeth Bordley Gibson[1]

Woodlawn, March 22, 1821

. . . I heard yesterday from Riversdale, the family bear their loss as well as could possibly be expected—poor Uncle suffer'd excessively at first, & will, no doubt, long feel this irreparable loss, such a wife is not easily found. He will carry dear Caroline & Julia with him to Ph[iladelph]ia & stay a short time.

I heard, only a week before she died, that my kind Aunt was almost well; I had been prevented going to see her, by the roads, & the necessity of someone being with Mr. L[ewis]. . . . On Monday, I heard that she had relapsed, but did not credit it because I had no news from her family, & on Wednesday night, Patty [Martha Peter] wrote me that she died on Tuesday at 1 o'clock.

It will appear strange to you, but I really am ignorant what her disease was . . . you recollect that she was lame from a swelled knee. I believe that an imposthume was formed just above it, but I am not certain— some persons thought it was a cancer in the kidnies [sic], others, Schrophula [sic]. She had seven physicians, & no two of them agreed in opinion. Patty says that my poor Aunt's sufferings exceeded all she has ever witnessed. She bore her illness with great fortitude, & died with perfect resignation. She said that she no longer wished to live, she had made her peace & was resigned to the will of her Maker & Redeemer; perhaps should she live, she should be drawn away by worldly pleasures & not be so well prepared at another time.

I loved her as much as any connection I possessed—she was the most hospitable kind & generous of friends, & I shall long feel her loss. Her dear children are worthy of her. I wrote to my Uncle begging him to leave them with me whenever he left home (he will not part with them alto- gether), & assured him I would be a mother to them. I will always endeavor to prove my love to her by affection for them. . . .

1. Lewis–Bordley Gibson Correspondence, Mount Vernon Archives.

·❧ ONLY TWO OF ROSALIE'S CHILDREN were at Riversdale with her when she died, Caroline and Julia. George Henry, Eugenia, and Charles were all away at school. Caroline left her account of her mother's death in a letter to her uncle:

Caroline Calvert to Charles J. Stier[1]

Riversdale, July 27, 1821

My dear Uncle,

. . . You ask me for the details of the last illness and of the end of my dearly loved Mother. She was obliged to keep to her bed from the beginning of the winter on account of that lameness which I believe she described to my Aunt van Havre. At first we hoped she would be cured, but I think she herself felt her end was approaching, but this moment had no terrors for one who had for several years regulated her life by the laws of Holy Scripture.[2]

During the intervals of cessation of pain, she was busied in giving directions to her gardener, and even separated a quantity of seeds herself and said where and how she wished them to be planted. She instructed us in the most careful way in the management of the household.

The day before her death she gave something to everyone of her friends who surrounded her and to all her servants. She consigned her children to their father and to the care of the Almighty.

She was buried with her four children on an eminence not far from the house, and my father has ordered a beautiful white marble tombstone, which is nearly finished. On the head of the panel he had executed by an Italian sculptor the figure in low relief of my mother ascending to Heaven on a cloud, and a little higher, four angels, her children, are stretching out their arms to receive her into the Celestial City. . . .[3]

Your affectionate Niece.

1. Carter Trans-MHS.

2. Caroline did not address the question her uncle probably most wanted answered, i.e., whether Mrs. Calvert had received last rites from a Catholic priest before she died. In fact, Mrs. Calvert had left the Catholic church some years earlier, but she had kept this from her family in Belgium. George Henry Calvert said his mother became a Protestant Episcopalian, which was her husband's faith, from reading the New Testament (see Calvert, *Autobiographic Study,* pp. 32, 140–42).

3. The burial site, chosen by Mrs. Calvert, is located a quarter-mile northwest of the Riversdale mansion. The small, fenced cemetery contains the graves of Rosalie and George Calvert, their four infant children, and Charles Benedict Calvert and one of his infant children.

The Italian sculptor who executed the marble tombstone for Mrs. Calvert's grave was Giovanni Andrei (1770–1824), who lived and worked in the Washington-Baltimore area from 1806 until his death in 1824. Andrei was in charge of ornamental sculpture for the United States Capitol from 1815 to 1824.

Jonathan Elliot, editor of the *Washington Gazette,* visited the Riversdale cemetery with George Calvert in the late 1820s and described the resurrection panel of Mrs.

Detail of Rosalie Calvert's grave, Riversdale cemetery, Riverdale, Maryland. Rosalie is being received into heaven by her four dead children.

Photo by author

Calvert and her children as a work from "the masterly chisel of André." Elliot went on to say, "The principal figure is a good likeness of the original, and a fine specimen of Italian sculpture" (*Historical Sketches of the Ten Miles Square forming the District of Columbia* [Washington, 1830], p. 278).

The inscription on Mrs. Calvert's tomb is as follows:

Here rests the body of
ROSALIE EUGENIA CALVERT
Wife of George Calvert and Daughter of
Henry J. Stier Esquire of Antwerp
who died March 13, 1821 Aged 43.

May she be numbered among the Children
of GOD, and her lot be among the Saints.

———— · ————

We see the hand, we worship and adore
And justify the all disposing power.

⇥ MRS. CALVERT'S FAMILY IN BELGIUM received the news of her death in May 1821. Stier, who was seventy-eight years old, was inconsolable at the loss of his youngest child and did not long survive the news of her death. He died at his beloved Mick on June 22, 1821. Isabelle van Havre died the following year. Charles Stier lived on until 1848; he and his wife, Eugénie, childless themselves, took an active interest in their American nieces and nephews.

After Rosalie

I T HAD BEEN A GOOD MARRIAGE, and George Calvert was deeply affected by his wife's death: "I am as one lost, my home is no longer dear to me; I have improved Riversdale very much, yet have no pleasure in anything I have done, because I have no one to participate with me. I have lost my confidant, my ablest counselor," he grieved in a letter to his father-in-law.[1] He took comfort in his children, but they could not fill the void.

Rosalie's death left her husband with five children, ranging in age from twenty-year-old Caroline to little Julia, aged seven. George Henry, eighteen; Eugenia, fifteen; and Charles Benedict, thirteen, were all at school and would remain there for several years. Relatives offered to take Julia, but Calvert, wanting to keep his family together, refused. Caroline dutifully took over her mother's household responsibilities, including Julia's care, and did a creditable job, according to her father. Calvert privately lamented, however, that Eugenia, "who was the favorite of both Mother & Father," was not finished with her education and back at Riversdale, as she "would be a great source of pleasure to me."[2] Calvert, lonely at home, turned to his farming and business pursuits to fill his time and began to expand his already large holdings.

THE BELGIAN INHERITANCE

The death of Henri Stier in June 1821 brought pleas from Charles Stier and Jean Michel van Havre for their brother-in-law Calvert to come to Europe to help with the division of Stier's vast estate.[3] Faithful to his longstanding policy of treating his children equally, Stier had specified that his estate be divided into three portions, one of which would go to Rosalie's children. Stier's late wife, Marie Louise Peeters, had also left a large estate, and with his death this also could be distributed.[4]

Rosalie had died without leaving a will, relying on her 1799 marriage contract and on her husband to protect her children's interests. The marriage contract gave Calvert a life interest in Rosalie's estate and in Rosalie's share of her mother's estate, after which it would go to her children.[5] Since Rosalie had died before her father, George had no life interest in Stier's estate, and Rosalie's portion of her father's estate should have gone directly to her children as they came of age.[6] However, in the English and American tradition, George kept all of his children's inheritance under his firm control until he was ready for them to have it.

Calvert decided not to go to Belgium for settlement of the estate, citing his children's opposition to the trip and authorizing Charles Stier and Jean Michel van Havre to act for him.[7] Charles proposed that the Calverts retain all of Stier's American land and that the Belgian real estate, which was worth about twice the American, be divided between the van Havres and himself.[8] This arrangement was agreeable to George Calvert.

The remainder of the estate consisted of American and European securities, Stier's painting collection, and family jewels and furnishings. Charles asked Calvert to provide a listing of all Stier's American stocks and bonds. With the help of Thomas McEwen's Philadelphia brokerage house, this was done, and the final reckoning showed that Stier held American securities worth approximately $270,000 at the time of his death, divided about equally between United States Treasury bonds and stocks in American banks and road companies.[9] The value of these assets in 1988 dollars would be at least ten times as much.[10]

The equity assets were subject to easy division, but Stier's art collection, some eighty-nine paintings and seven pieces of sculpture, could hardly be divided without being sold. A sale was arranged for July 1822, and Charles wrote Calvert, asking if he wished to buy any of the paintings. Calvert requested three paintings but added, "I want none unless they can be purchased cheap."[11] Charles also suggested that Calvert advertise the sale in the United States and try to interest the government in it, since the collection was suitable for the formation of a national gallery, but Calvert apparently took no such action. After the sale Charles wrote that he had bought the *Romulus and Remus* for Calvert for $22.88, but that he had been unable to get *The Boar Hunt* for him, because its $66.88 selling price exceeded Calvert's limit.[12] Charles purchased fifteen of his father's paintings, and William I, king of the Netherlands, bought three pieces, but the proceeds of the sale—some $31,604—disappointed everyone.[13] Calvert later regretted not buying more of his father-in-law's famous collection.

In December 1822, the probated estates of both Marie Louise Peeters and Henri Joseph Stier were recorded in Antwerp. The four hundred-page document detailing the division is notable for the equal treatment accorded the three heirs: Charles Stier, the late Isabelle van Havre's husband and children, and Rosalie's husband and children. The properties and securities were divided into lots of equal value, and by prior agreement the Calvert children were given those lots containing the American lands. Marie Louise Peeters's will left bequests of 130,000 florins, or $52,000, to each of her three children; these bequests were the maternal part of their dotation or marriage settlement. The gift of Riversdale to Rosalie was considered part of this maternal bequest, and she was credited with already having received its value of 100,000 florins, or $40,000. The bequests, including the $12,000 difference owed to the Calvert heirs, were to be paid prior to the division of the estate. The Peeters estate was then divided into four lots, each worth about $50,000 in the currency of the day, one of which went to the Calverts.[14] The fourth Peeters lot went into the estate of H. J. Stier, where it was then redivided. Stier's estate was divided into three equal parts with the Calverts receiving as their share properties valued at $139,000. Thus, from the combined estates and including the value of Riversdale, the Belgian inheritance of the Calverts totaled about $241,000. Generally, however, this included properties rather than cash—land, stocks, treasury bonds, and turnpike stocks, along with forgiven debts.[15]

As the legal guardian of minor children, Calvert had great leeway in the use and control of their inheritances, and he did not hesitate to exercise it. Even before settlement of the estate, Calvert helped himself to dividends belonging to his late father-in-law in order to purchase over one thousand acres near Riversdale, including Ross's Tavern, and to build the gristmill at Bladensburg that he and Rosalie had so long desired.[16] When Charles questioned his use of these funds, Calvert passed it off, noting what "a great addition" he had made to the Riversdale estate and that while he had "found it necessary to take most of the dividends to enable me to make the payments . . . they have all been employed for the benefit of my children." In any case, said Calvert casually, he was sure he had acted properly.[17]

During the 1820s, Calvert lent large sums of money to his older brother Edward Henry, sums that he could hardly have raised without benefit of his children's inheritance. In return Calvert received mortgages on properties Edward Henry had inherited from their father, Benedict. As Edward Henry defaulted on the loans, George acquired more and more of the Calvert inheritance.[18] Even in 1828 George Calvert was by far the wealthiest man in the county, and by 1831 he had added almost half of his brother's holdings to his own.[19]

It is impossible to say how much of his children's inheritance and how much of his own funds went into these acquisitions. He was bound by law to maintain accounts of his guardianship and to deliver each child's portion undiminished in value, but in fact there was very little check on his actions, and as his wife had observed long ago, he was a most reluctant bookkeeper.

ESTABLISHING ROSALIE'S CHILDREN

In 1823 the Calverts' first-born, Caroline, was married to a Philadelphia lawyer, Thomas Willing Morris. An Episcopal minister performed the June ceremony at Riversdale. None of the Calvert children followed their mother's Catholic religion. Caroline's husband was descended from two long-established Philadelphia families. The Morris forebears were Quakers who had come to Philadelphia in the late seventeenth century, and Thomas was named for his great-uncle, Thomas Willing, president of the First Bank of the United States, on whom the Stiers had relied for financial advice when they first came to the United States in 1794. Calvert described his new son-in-law as "a man of good connections" and "respectable standing at the bar," but with "little property."[20]

Caroline and her husband made their home in Philadelphia, and Morris took over many of the American business and legal affairs of her Belgian relatives. At her marriage Calvert assured Caroline an annual income of fifteen hundred dollars on her inheritance, but did not turn over her capital.[21] Caroline's lawyer husband began to ask questions.

Meanwhile, that same year, Calvert's elder son, George Henry, was expelled for rebellion from Harvard College in May of his senior year. The rebellion was directed against a particularly unpopular faculty member, and George Henry played a moderate role, but he, along with forty-two classmates, was nonetheless expelled and denied his degree.[22] This must have disappointed Calvert, but degrees were less important then, and plans for his son to continue his studies abroad were not changed. George Henry became the first of the Calvert children to visit his mother's Belgian homeland. He spent the fall of 1823 with his Uncle Charles and Aunt Eugénie Stier before taking up studies at Göttingen University in 1824. He remained in Europe for over three years, becoming proficient in French and German and coming to know his Belgian relatives well.

The year before George Henry returned home, he was joined in Europe by his father and his sister Eugenia. With Julia safely enrolled at Madame Grelaud's school in Philadelphia under Caroline's watchful eye and Charles Benedict at the University of Virginia, George Calvert was free to treat nineteen-year-old Eugenia to the trip her mother had so wanted to take. Calvert and his son and daughter spent almost a year, from the summer of 1826 to the spring of 1827, touring together, first in England, then on to Belgium, where they tarried some weeks in Antwerp with Charles and Eugénie. Together the Calverts and the Stiers proceeded up the Rhine, through Switzerland to Lyons and then to Paris. Paris was a letdown to the Americans, "unsightly and dirty . . . gloomy and forbidding."[23] The senior Calvert became ill and wanted to go home.

The return to America witnessed the first real crisis in the Calvert family since Rosalie's death. Once back home, George Henry declared his intention of marrying a Baltimore woman, Elizabeth Steuart, and his father threatened to cut off all means of support to his son if he continued to see her. George Henry said his father's opposition was based solely on the young lady's lack of property, and this was probably true. Elizabeth was the youngest daughter of Dr. James Steuart, a family with whom the Calverts had long been friendly, and personally she was beyond reproach.[24]

The rift between father and son, however, was a sharp one. "I have left my father's house," George Henry wrote his Uncle Charles in November 1827, adding that he found himself "unexpectedly thrown upon my own resources after having been brought up with the expectation of having at least a sufficiency to live without any exertion on my part."[25] The young man inquired with urgency about his inheritance from his grandparents, saying his father professed to know nothing of anything due him. Charles replied that George Henry, being of age, was entitled to his portion of his

The Stier-Calvert Family

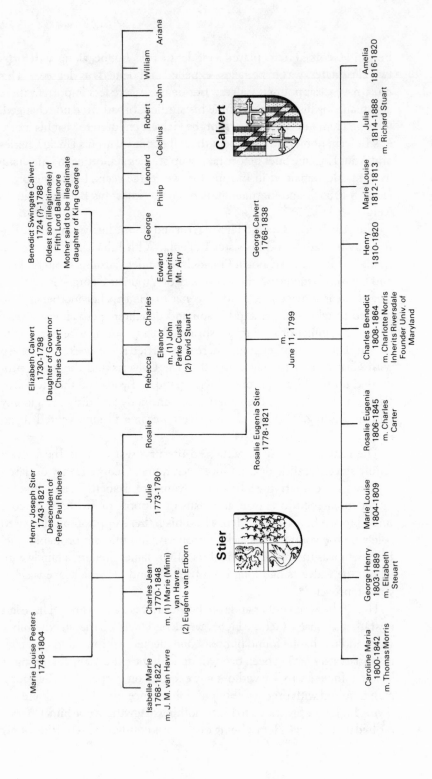

grandfather's estate, but that George Calvert had the use of both Rosalie's estate and Marie Louise Peeters's estate during his lifetime. He calculated that George Henry would have only about fifteen hundred dollars a year to live on from what was due him, and advised the boy to make peace with his father. "It seems to me that the eldest son of Mr. Calvert has a lot to lose if he breaks with his father," wrote Charles.[26]

Fortunately, the break between father and son was repaired shortly afterwards by compromise on both sides. Calvert withdrew his opposition to Elizabeth, and George Henry agreed to a waiting period before the marriage.[27] A year and a half later, in May 1829, the couple was married in the bride's home in Baltimore. A financial arrangement between George Henry and his father must have been part of the compromise, too, for George Henry was free to pursue the literary career he preferred, first in Baltimore and later in Newport, Rhode Island.

Eugenia—her father's avowed favorite—was the next to marry, but again George Calvert was displeased with his child's choice. Calvert wrote the Charles Stiers in April 1830 that his twenty-three-year-old daughter had a number of admirers, none of them suitable, and that she seemed to favor a particular one to whom he would never consent.[28] The gentleman in question was Charles Henry Carter, a member of the aristocratic Carter clan of Virginia and a grandson of the famous Revolutionary hero Henry (Light-Horse Harry) Lee.[29]

Calvert's disapproval of what would seem a promising alliance stemmed from a particularly malodorous scandal involving young Carter's uncle, Henry Lee II. Lee had seduced his wife's younger sister and stolen money from her while he was her guardian, and the whole affair became common knowledge in the spring of 1830, just when Eugenia was making known her wish to marry Carter. The scandal cast a shadow over the whole Lee family and everyone connected with them.[30] Calvert also may have been concerned about Carter's ability to provide for his daughter, for while the family was known to be well-off, they were extremely numerous. Young Carter's father was one of twenty-one children and not among the elder sons.[31]

Thwarted in her desires, Eugenia left Riversdale and went to Philadelphia to stay with Caroline and Thomas Morris. Pleading poor health, she stayed on there to consult the doctors. Perhaps these tactics caused Calvert to relent and give his favorite daughter his blessing, but there is reason to think not. Eugenia and Charles Henry Carter were married in November 1830, but in Philadelphia—not at the bride's home. Eugenia was the only one of the Calverts' three daughters not to be married at Riversdale.

A reconciliation between Calvert and his daughter was not long in coming, however. In January 1832, as Eugenia was expecting her first child, a marriage contract was drawn up for the couple.[32] This was a step George Calvert would insist on before turning over Eugenia's inheritance, although he was not ready to relinquish that yet. Meanwhile, Calvert gave Eugenia and Carter the use of his own first home, Mount Albion plantation, which they renamed Goodwood, and finally, four years later, he gave them actual control.[33]

Julia was the last of the three daughters to marry, but at nineteen she was the youngest to wed. Like Eugenia, she chose a Virginian for her husband, but unlike her sister, she encountered no paternal opposition. Julia and Dr. Richard Henry Stuart were married at Riversdale in May 1833, and went to live at Cedar Grove plantation on the Potomac River in King George County, Virginia. George Calvert must have thoroughly approved of Julia's doctor husband, for when he turned over Julia's inheritance, he transferred it directly to her husband without any of the trustee or contract arrangements with which he had protected his other two daughters.[34]

Calvert's younger son, Charles Benedict, was the only child still unmarried and living at home when Calvert died in 1838. Charles, age nineteen, had graduated from the University of Virginia in 1827 and returned to Riversdale. He spent the next ten years helping his father manage the family holdings. His older brother had renounced any interest in an agricultural career, and it came to be expected that Charles Benedict would follow in his father's footsteps and take over Riversdale. In 1839, a year after his father's death, Charles Benedict married Charlotte Augusta Norris of Baltimore and brought her to be the new mistress of Riversdale.

GEORGE CALVERT'S OTHER FAMILY

> Like the patriarchs of old our men live all in one house with
> their wives and their concubines, and the mulattoes one sees
> in every family exactly resemble the white children—and
> every lady tells you who is the father of all the mulatto chil-
> dren in everybody's household, but those in her own she
> seems to think drop from the clouds, or pretends so to think.
> MARY BOYKIN CHESNUT[35]

Like many other slaveowners, like some of his own ancestors, George Calvert had another family. We can be sure of at least one slave mistress, and he probably had others. There were children from his liaisons, and Calvert, a man not given to freeing his slaves, set them free. There is no evidence that Rosalie knew of his relationships with his female slaves; certainly she never mentioned anything of the sort in her letters. It is difficult to imagine, however, that she did not know. Her slaves knew, and for a number of years Calvert's wife and his mistress lived on the same plantation.

George Calvert's relationship with his slave mistress, Eleanor Beckett, began long before he met Rosalie Stier. After his father's death in 1788, George, age twenty, became master of Mount Albion plantation, and there he spent a long bachelorhood, not marrying Rosalie until he was thirty-one. At Mount Albion Calvert began his affair with Eleanor Beckett. Evidently the relationship became emotional as well as sexual, for eventually he freed her, his children by her, and other members of her family as well. After his own marriage, he arranged a suitable marriage for Eleanor. When she was widowed, he moved her and her family to Montgomery County and made costly arrangements for their well-being. Like his Lord Baltimore ancestors, he did not deny his illegitimate offspring or the woman who had borne them.

There are only fragments of information about Eleanor Beckett. Apparently she was an Indian-Negro mulatto belonging to the Calverts, and sometimes she was called Charlotte, sometimes Nellie. Her first child with George Calvert was probably Anne, born in 1790, and the second was Caroline, born in 1793. Both used the Calvert surname in later years. Three more children came along to Eleanor—Cyrus, Charlotte, and John. They were also probably George's children, but we cannot be sure, and we do not know what surname they used.

The legal record begins in 1801 when, two years after his marriage to Rosalie, George Calvert freed ten of his slaves, including "Charlotte" Beckett and her five children, Anne, Caroline, Cyrus, Charlotte, and John.[36] In 1822, soon after Rosalie died, George Calvert returned to court to clarify the record, explaining that the "Charlotte Beckett" he had freed twenty years before had been "christened" as "Eleanor Beckett" and reaffirming that she and all her children were forever free.[37]

It was difficult in Maryland for manumitted blacks to maintain their free status, and evidently people were raising questions, because Calvert kept returning to the court to reaffirm the freedom of Eleanor and her children. In 1824, Calvert thought it necessary to repeat the manumission of Eleanor Beckett's second daughter, Caroline, age 31, along with her seven children—his own grandchildren—George, age 11; Caroline Elizabeth, 9; John Henry, 8; Henrietta Maria, 6; Thomas Adolphus, 5; Marietta, 2; and Richard, one month.[38]

We can wonder about his thoughts as he freed the grandchild apparently named for him by his mulatto daughter who herself bore the same name as his first-born daughter by Rosalie. The following year he reaffirmed the manumission of Eleanor's first daughter, Anne, then age 35, and her six children: Theophilus, 11; Louisa, 10; Lucian, 8; John, 6; George Washington, 5; and Lucretia, 2.[39]

A remarkable family account, handed down through four generations and published in 1927 by Nellie Arnold Plummer, a black great-granddaughter of Eleanor Beckett, supplements the legal record. Nellie Arnold Plummer descended from one of Eleanor Beckett's later children, after Eleanor lived with an Englishman named William Norris. Nellie Arnold Plummer recounted the family memoir:

> Nellie [Eleanor] Beckett, an Indian-Negro mulatto, a slave of the Calverts, married William Norris, an Englishman, who had to serve Calvert for seven years for debt. On finding that his wife was bearing children for Calvert as well as his own, noting his helplessness to correct matters, he died of a broken heart. Norris, with Philip Brashears and two apprentices, made all the shoes worn on the Riverdale [*sic*] plantation. Norris had two sisters who accompanied him to America. The sisters went to Montgomery County, Maryland, while their brother's time was bought by George Calvert, Riverdale [*sic*], Prince George's County, Maryland. The Calvert children of Nellie Beckett-Norris were so white that they were sent to Pennsylvania to live. From there Caroline, who had become Mrs. Crompton [*sic*], took her children and her six sisters to Monrovia, Liberia, Africa, with other mulattos who wished to be free.[40]

No record remains of William Norris's bondage to George Calvert or his service at Riversdale, but a link between the two men exists in the record of George Calvert's manumissions. In 1822 Calvert freed two young mulatto women, Charlotte and Sophia Norris, both born about 1803.[41] Several years later, Calvert freed Matilda Norris, a "bright mulatto" born about 1805.[42] These could have been Eleanor Beckett's daughters by William Norris or by Calvert while she was living with Norris. In

1827 Calvert freed a mulatto male named William Beckett, about twenty-one, perhaps another of Eleanor's children.[43]

In all, George Calvert freed thirty-three slaves during his lifetime. Twenty-nine of these bore surnames or are identifiable by family group, and twenty-three were members of the Beckett-Norris family.[44]

As Nellie Plummer reported, Eleanor Beckett went to live in Montgomery County, probably after William Norris's death, and took her children with her. George Calvert owned almost 875 acres in Montgomery County, part of a tract called The Hermitage. Tax records show that he kept no slaves on this parcel of land from 1798 through 1812, land which he probably leased out. In 1813, however, a group of nine slaves is recorded there, headed by a female over age 36, accompanied by three females aged 14 to 36, two children from 8 to 14, and three children under 8.[45] This was the only time Calvert was recorded as owning slaves in Montgomery County. Eleanor would have been over 36 by this time if she began bearing children in 1790, and her daughters Anne and Caroline would have been 23 and 20. This record seems to show Calvert's relocation of his Beckett family after William Norris's death.

In 1820, the federal census showed Eleanor Beckett living as a free "colored" resident of Montgomery County and head of a household consisting of six persons: one female over 45, two females 14 to 26, two females 0 to 15, and one male 14 to 26.[46] Four of her household were engaged in agriculture, but none were property owners. In 1840, Eleanor Beckett was still living in Montgomery County with one other free black female, age 10–24, but by 1850 she was gone, probably dead by that time, as was her former master and lover.[47]

The Beckett family's move to Montgomery County had remarkable consequences for Eleanor's second daughter, who called herself Caroline Calvert. About 1812, Caroline, nineteen and in the full flower of her youth, met one of Montgomery County's foremost citizens, the elderly Thomas Cramphin, Jr. Cramphin, a planter and large landholder, was seventy-two years old and retired from a long career of public service which included three terms in the Maryland legislature and various judgeships. Part of his land was in the tract known as The Hermitage, where he maintained his dwelling plantation, adjacent to George Calvert's land.[48] Cramphin and Calvert surely knew each other; Rosalie wrote of Richard Cramphin, Thomas's half-brother, as a valued friend, although she never mentioned Thomas.[49]

In any event, Thomas Cramphin, who had never married, took

Caroline, the daughter of Eleanor Beckett and George Calvert, to live with him. They lived together for approximately nineteen years and had nine children.[50] Maryland law did not recognize their union, for the state had forbidden interracial marriage since the seventeenth century.[51]

Thomas Cramphin acknowledged Caroline and their children in a will he made in 1824, leaving them most of his substantial estate. The will describes his relationship with Caroline: "to the woman now living with me and by whom I have children, who calls herself Caroline Calvert the daughter of Eleanor Becket, I give and bequeath her choice of ten of my negroes . . . all my household and kitchen furniture, all my plate, all the stock of liquors, groceries and provisions . . . all the crops of every kind on hand . . . also my carriages and harness—also all my stock of horses, cattle, hogs and sheep . . . together with all the waggons, carts, ploughs, geers, and all farming utensils belonging [to my dwelling plantation]." He left his dwelling plantation, containing between eight hundred and one thousand acres of land, to Caroline "during the term of her single life."[52]

Aside from several small bequests, Cramphin left the rest of his estate to "my confidential friend George Calvert . . . in trust for the support, education and benefit" of his and Caroline's children. The seven children born by 1824 are named in the will: George, Caroline Elizabeth, John Henry, Henrietta Maria, Thomas Adolphus, Marietta, and Richard.[53] Cramphin seemed to anticipate that his will might be challenged by some of his kin. He left a bequest to his nephew, Dr. John Bowie, on condition that Bowie, in writing, relinquish all other claims to the estate.

Cramphin was a very wealthy man, and the estate he left was impressive. His worth at his death in 1831 was estimated at $68,140.86 current money, and included 245 slaves on five plantations, china, and paintings.[54] Seldom if ever in Maryland had a mulatto woman and her offspring received such an estate.

A few months after making this will, Cramphin had second thoughts about leaving so much of value directly to Caroline. Caroline's status as a mulatto woman, not legally wed to her benefactor, left her particularly vulnerable to challenges. So Cramphin amended his will, leaving everything in trust to George Calvert and directing him as trustee to furnish Caroline with an annuity of five hundred dollars for the rest of her life, and to allow her and the children use of his dwelling house, servants, carriages, and the rest. He also revoked the bequest to his nephew, Dr. Bowie, who would not agree to refrain from challenging the will.[55]

As Cramphin had expected, his will was challenged after he died, but by his niece, Elizabeth Bowie Davis, rather than his nephew. Elizabeth Davis and Dr. John Bowie were sister and brother, children of Thomas Cramphin's only sister, Ruth, and Ruth's husband, Allen Bowie. In 1835 Elizabeth Davis brought suit, questioning the will's validity and seeking a ruling that Cramphin had died intestate. The court appears to have presided over a compromise solution to the potentially thorny case, refusing to rule until an agreement had been worked out between Mrs. Davis and Calvert. For the sum of thirty thousand dollars, Mrs. Davis agreed to sell her interest in the Cramphin estate to Calvert, and in return she received a verdict from the court that Cramphin had died intestate. Calvert paid Mrs. Davis in January 1836, and she released all her rights in the estate.[56] Calvert was then free to execute the trust just as if the will had been upheld.

Calvert had the right to sell Cramphin's properties under the terms of the will, and he was entitled to reimburse himself from the estate for this extraordinary expense of settlement with Mrs. Davis. He served as trustee, provided for Caroline and her family, and began liquidating the holdings, but his death in 1838 put an end to his efforts. Caroline was left without a protector and the estate without a trustee.

Caroline petitioned the court to appoint a trustee who would carry out the provisions of Thomas Cramphin's will, stating that she was entitled to a five hundred-dollar annuity and a dwelling house and that her children were entitled to a portion of the estate when they came of age.[57] She argued that George Calvert had a large sum of money on hand from selling parts of the estate, mostly in the form of bonds from purchasers, which was now in the hands of his son Charles Benedict Calvert. She asked the court to subpoena Calvert to answer these matters. The court ruled for Caroline and her children and appointed Charles Benedict trustee for the Cramphin estate.[58]

That court ruling in the spring of 1838 is the last we know of Caroline Calvert and her children. The federal census does not show them as residents of Maryland in 1840, although Caroline's mother, Eleanor Beckett, was still living in Montgomery County at that time. Nellie Plummer's family memoir said that the Calvert children of Nellie Beckett-Norris were so white that they were sent to Pennsylvania to live, and that Caroline, who had become Mrs. Cramphin, took her children and her six sisters from there to Monrovia, Liberia. We know, however, that Caroline Calvert and Anne Calvert lived in Maryland until they were mature women and had children of their own, and a search of Pennsylvania census indexes for 1840 and 1850 fails to turn up any Caroline

Calvert, any Cramphins, or any name like Cramphin with the distinctive Christian names of Caroline's children.

Nor is there evidence for the family's migration to Liberia. An 1843 census of people living in Liberia contains no Calverts, Cramphins, Norrises, or any pattern of Christian names which would indicate Caroline and her children. Passenger lists of emigrants from the United States to Liberia from 1835 through 1857 yield the same disappointing result.[59]

Still, family legend may preserve more of what happened than the records, which are always incomplete. Caroline Calvert was only forty-five years old in 1838, when the record of her existence disappears, and there is every reason to think that she was a capable and attractive woman with some financial resources. Perhaps she married, this time relinquishing the Calvert name she had so proudly claimed. She and her children may have found their way into either culture, black or white.

DEATH OF GEORGE CALVERT

In 1835, when he was sixty-seven years old, George Calvert made his will and began to put his affairs in order. His will was remarkably short and simple, one paragraph in length, leaving "all the property real, personal, and mixed, that I may die possessed of" to be equally divided by his two sons, George Henry and Charles Benedict.[60] The will's simplicity was deceptive, however, and its key was the phrase, "that I may die possessed of." For George Calvert had several different types of property in his hands: property that belonged to him, property that had belonged to Rosalie, property that had belonged to the Stiers, and property that he had acquired since 1822 with a mixture of assets belonging to him and to his late wife and in-laws.

In 1836, he transferred property to each of his daughters, hoping to settle their claims to their inheritance from their grandfather and from their mother's marriage contract. Caroline got Waterloo, the Spurrier's Tavern property of 516 acres, in Anne Arundel County; Eugenia got Goodwood, 728 acres at Mount Albion on the Patuxent, along with forty-two slaves; and Julia got Oatland, 595 acres in Prince George's County, along with forty-two slaves.[61] Trusts were set up for both Caroline's and Eugenia's property, which gave them full use and disposition of the properties but protected them against their husbands' creditors. Julia's properties were not placed in trust but were transferred directly to her husband. The transfer to Eugenia specified that it was made in full payment of her claims against her grandfather's estate and her mother's marriage contract, but the transfers to Caroline and Julia did not include any such language.

The two properties with slaves given to Eugenia and Julia were roughly equal in value, but the property transferred to Caroline, which had once been quite valuable, was much depreciated by 1836. The Tavern, the property's main source of income, had burned in 1835, and Caroline's husband, Thomas Morris, complained that it was worth less than half what it had cost and that Caroline had received only a portion of what was due her.[62] There was justice in Morris's complaint. There was a sharp disparity in value in what was transferred to Caroline and to her sisters. Possibly George Calvert intended to make up the difference in a cash settlement to Caroline before his death, but in fact he did not do so, and this led to bitter lawsuits between Morris and Calvert's sons after Calvert's death.[63]

Probably because of Morris's discontent, Calvert executed a special agreement in 1837 giving his two sons all properties which he owned in his own right, including thirty-eight slaves listed by name. He said he did this in consideration of monies he owed them from their grandparents' inheritance and to aid them, as his executors, in settling claims against his estate from the other children. The key to this agreement was Calvert's statement that he wanted his sons to reimburse themselves for their own claims first and then settle with the other children.[64]

Calvert had been adding to his lands ever since Rosalie died, and his holdings were now immense. Excluding the properties he had settled on his daughters and that portion of Riversdale which was his wife's, Calvert owned almost 10,000 acres at the time of his death.[65] Riversdale, the original purchase of 729 1/4 acres, had never belonged to him; it had been his to use during his lifetime, but at his death it would go directly to Rosalie's children, each of whom had a one-fifth share.

The division of Calvert's own large estate between his two male heirs while his daughters received their inheritance solely from the maternal side showed a striking disregard for the principle of equity followed by Henri Stier and embraced by Calvert's wife. Calvert was, of course, adhering to the centuries-old English tradition of preserving an estate through male succession—a tradition so inbred that he probably gave it little conscious thought. He was doubtless satisfied that he had done his duty by his daughters, but the fact remained that he left them nothing of his own and that he had used their assets to build his own, which he then divided between their brothers. Rosalie's scrupulous bookkeeping for her father and brothers had been far different, and we can guess that the estate would have been divided more equitably had she survived her husband.

George Calvert died just days before his seventieth birthday in January 1838. His two sons were named co-executors of his estate, but George Henry asked to be excused, and the entire burden fell on Charles Benedict. In the fall of 1838, Thomas Morris brought suit on Caroline's behalf against Charles Benedict, as executor of the estate, for an accounting and settlement of Caroline's inheritance from her grandparents.[66] Morris, an attorney, knew better than most what records should have been kept, and he informed himself of the complexities of the Belgian inheritance through a long correspondence with Charles Stier.

Morris's lawsuit against the Calvert estate dragged on for years. The Morrises left Philadelphia in 1841 and moved to their Maryland property, which they now called Glenthorne. Caroline was in poor health but continually pregnant, and her last four babies had died as infants. The year after the move she died of consumption at age forty-two, leaving four surviving children. Morris and the children lived on at Glenthorne, and he pursued his lawsuit against the estate on behalf of his children.

After Caroline's death, her brothers and sisters joined in a countersuit against Thomas Morris, charging that certain land in his possession, called the Dorsey purchase, should be sold, since it was in fact part of Rosalie Calvert's estate and should be divided among her five children. Ironically, this was the only piece of real estate, besides Riversdale, recorded in Rosalie Calvert's name; she had bought the property in 1812 to protect Spurrier Tavern from possible competition.[67] Equity would have been better served by leaving this property in the hands of the Morrises, since that would have made the distribution of assets between the Calvert daughters more equal. The court, however, found that the property was part of Rosalie's estate and ordered that it be divided among her five children or their heirs.[68]

Finally in 1846, Thomas Morris got a favorable judgment in his suit against George Calvert's estate. The court ruled that the estate should pay Morris $11,260 with an annual interest of 6 percent dating from the year 1838, plus costs of the suit.[69] This did not satisfy all of Morris's claims, but it helped to equalize the settlements made to the Calvert daughters.

By the time the litigation was ended, another one of the Calvert daughters was dead. Eugenia, only thirty-nine years old, died, like her sister

Caroline, of consumption in 1845. Eugenia died at her Goodwood home, leaving seven children.

Julia was the only one of the Calvert women to attain old age; together with her doctor husband, she lived on into her seventies at her Virginia plantation, outliving four of her eight children.

George Henry resided in Baltimore until 1840, when he and Elizabeth undertook a three-year trip to Europe, visiting their Belgian relatives but spending most of their time in Italy. On their return they bought an estate in Newport, Rhode Island, which became their permanent home. George Henry even served a term as mayor of Newport, but his major energies were directed to his literary career. He produced several scholarly studies, notably works on Goethe, whom he had met while a student in Germany, and on the English Romantic poets. He also wrote a life of his famous ancestor, Peter Paul Rubens, along with numerous poems, essays, memoirs, and travel accounts.[70] The George Henry Calverts had no children. He died in Newport in 1889 at the age of eighty-six, surviving all of his siblings.

Charles Benedict took over Riversdale and most of his father's holdings. George Henry wanted cash or income-producing holdings for his share of the estate, and the two brothers worked out an informal division of the assets between them. George Henry would take the Rossborough farm in partial payment of his claim, and Charles Benedict would take the Buck Lodge land adjoining Riversdale and the huge tract of His Lordship's Kindness.[71] Charles Benedict had to buy Riversdale from the estate and reimburse each of his siblings for their one-fifth interest; he set the purchase price at $20,416.65 and paid $4,083 to each of his four siblings.[72] As $20,000 was the approximate price of the land alone in 1800, and an exceptionally fine house with other improvements had since been added, he made an excellent deal for himself.

Charles Benedict lived out his life at Riversdale and turned it into a showplace of progressive agricultural practices. He was a dedicated scientific agriculturist and took the lead in establishing first local, then state, and finally national agricultural societies. He served as first president of the Maryland State Agricultural Society, helped found the United States Agricultural Society, and was the moving force in the creation of a federal Department of Agriculture in 1862. He was the principal founder of the Maryland Agricultural College, which became the University of Maryland, and provided land for its campus from his vast holdings.[73] When the Civil War brought the dissolution of the Union that Rosalie had so

Contemporary Riversdale (1981), prior to restoration
Photo by John Walton, Jr.

feared, her son Charles Benedict established a peculiar place for himself as a slave-owning supporter of Lincoln. He was elected to Congress on a Unionist platform, serving from 1861 to 1863. He died at Riversdale in 1864, survived by his wife and five children.

After Charles Benedict's death, the Riversdale estate was divided among his heirs; the house and some three hundred acres went to his widow, Charlotte Augusta, and remained in the Calvert family until 1887, when it was sold to land developers. During the next hundred years, the house passed through a succession of owners and uses, serving alternately as a boardinghouse, a gentleman's club, and a residence for sundry political figures.[74] Finally in 1949, Riversdale, the fine house built by Henri Stier and his daughter Rosalie Calvert, passed into public ownership. In 1988, the Maryland-National Capital Park and Planning Commission, utilizing the unique record of life within the house left by its former mistress, undertook to restore Riversdale to the period when Rosalie and George Calvert lived there.

NOTES

1. GC to HJS, Riversdale, August 1, 1821, from R. Winder Johnson, *The Ancestry of Rosalie Morris Johnson,* vol. 2, p. 46. News of Stier's death in June 1821 had not yet reached Riversdale.

2. GC to IvH, Riversdale, August 1, 1821, Cal S-V. Calvert probably brought Eugenia home to take over Julia's care after Caroline's marriage in 1823. By 1824, Eugenia was definitely back at Riversdale, since both she and Julia were reported ill that fall, forcing cancellation of a planned visit to the Calvert plantation by the Marquis de Lafayette. Lafayette, on his grand tour of the United States, had been invited to stay at Riversdale, but the girls' illness forced him to lodge instead at a public inn (Rossburg) owned by Calvert, much to Calvert's embarrassment. Calvert wrote a lengthy letter to the *Federal Republican and Baltimore Telegraph* explaining his alleged lack of hospitality toward the popular French general (Undated newspaper clipping in possession of the Cristofane family of Bladensburg, Maryland).

3. CJS and JMvH to GC, Antwerp, 10 July 1821, from Johnson, *Ancestry,* vol. 2, p. 47.

4. Stier held a life interest in his wife's estate. At his death, her estate was divided into four parts; one went to each of her children or their heirs and the fourth part went into Stier's estate, there to be redivided into thirds.

5. Land Records of the General Court of the Western Shore, 1798–1800, Liber J. G. 5, fol. 492.

6. See Charles J. Stier's explanation of the distinction between the maternal and paternal successions to George Henry Calvert in a letter-draft, Antwerp, 21 December 1827, Cal S-V.

7. GC to CJS, [n.p.], October 3, 1821, Cal S-V.

8. CJS to GC, Antwerp, 11 January 1822, from Johnson, *Ancestry,* vol. 2, p. 49. Stier's American properties were two additions to Mount Albion purchased in 1812 and 1815 (from William White and Benjamin Plummer), Oatland, Spurrier's, and the Dorsey purchase near Spurrier's.

9. Division of the Estate of H. J. Stier and M. L. Peeters, 27 December 1822, Deeds of Notary J. J. Pinson, Notariaat no. 1024, State Archives, Antwerp (hereafter Stier-Peeters Estate, State Archives, Antwerp). Stier's largest holding was in the Bank of the United States, an investment of $50,000, valued at $60,000 at the time of his death; his second largest holding was $37,820 in the Bank of Washington, D.C., which his son-in-law Calvert served as director. His holdings in Treasury bonds show a regular pattern of investment through 1815, but none thereafter.

10. Measured by the Consumer Price Index and the Wholesale Price Index, one dollar in 1820 was worth about $10.22 in 1988. Such calculations are rough, however, depending on commodity. One dollar in Maryland farm land would be worth at least $75.00 in 1988. See U.S. Bureau of the Census, *Historical Statistics of the United States* (Washington, D.C., 1975), vol. 2, pp. 183–201.

11. GC to CJS, Riversdale, June 20, 1822, Cal S-V.

12. CJS to GC, Antwerp, 9 August 1822, in Johnson, *Ancestry,* vol. 2, p. 50. In the sale catalogue, no. 16, *Romulus et Rémus avec la louve,* is attributed to P. P. Rubens and Huysmans de Malines, and no. 55, *Chasse au Sanglier,* to P. de Vos and Wildens. See *Catalogue de la Collection de Tableaux,* sale, 29 July 1822 (Anvers, C. J. Binken, 1822). The third painting requested by Calvert is not known.

13. List of the proceeds of the sale of the H. J. Stier collection, Antwerp, 29 July 1822, prepared by Charles J. Stier for George Calvert, now in the possession of Mrs. Rosalie Calvert Ray, Fayetteville, North Carolina.

14. Stier-Peeters Estate, State Archives, Antwerp, fols. 11–12, 127–29, 132.

15. The valuations assigned to the properties in the estate division were generally at or close to their purchase price. Some cash from dividends and from the sale of the art collection was distributed, but it was a minor part of the whole.

16. Prince George's County Land Records, Liber A. B. 2, fols. 211–13. The tavern, built by Richard Ross in 1807, is now the Rossborough Inn, the Faculty Club of the University of Maryland at College Park.

17. GC to CJS and JMvH, Riversdale, July 10, 1822, Cal S-V.

18. See Prince George's County Land Records, Liber A. B. 3, fol. 422 for a 1824 transaction between George and Edward Henry Calvert involving ten thousand acres of the latter's land mortgaged for $84,800. Edward Henry also mortgaged slaves to his brother. Prince George's County Land Records, Liber A. B. 4, fols. 205–6.

19. The *1828 Tax List, Prince George's County, Maryland* (Prince George's County Genealogical Society, 1985) shows the four largest landholders in the county and the relative value of their holdings: (1) George Calvert, $53,762; (2) Benjamin Oden, $31,513; (3) William Dudley Digges, $30,450; and (4) Edward Henry Calvert, $29,321. The 1831 Prince George's County Tax Assessment shows George Calvert owning a seven thousand-acre tract of His Lordship's Kindness which had belonged to Edward Henry Calvert.

20. GC to CJS, [n.p.], November 2, 1822, and January 25, 1823, from Johnson, *Ancestry,* vol. 2, p. 54.

21. Information contained in a letter-draft from CJS to GHC advising the latter on his inheritance, Antwerp, 21 December 1827, Cal S-V.

22. Ida Gertrude Everson, *George Henry Calvert: American Literary Pioneer* (New York, 1975), pp. 60–64. Calvert received his degree thirty-two years later on special application, as did some of his classmates.

23. George Henry Calvert, *First Years in Europe* (Boston, 1866), p. 294.

24. The Calvert-Steuart relationship dated back to Benedict Calvert's arrival in Maryland when he was taken in by Dr. George Steuart of Annapolis. George Calvert's sister Elizabeth married Dr. Charles Steuart in 1780, son of Dr. George Steuart and older brother of Dr. James Steuart, whose daughter George Henry wished to marry.

25. GHC to CJS, Baltimore, November 12, 1827, Cal S-V.

26. CJS to GHC, Draft, Antwerp, 21 December 1827 and [n.d.] December 1827, Cal S-V.

27. GHC to CJS, Baltimore, January 22, 1828, Cal S-V.

28. Reported in a letter from Eugénie Stier to Louise van Havre della Faille, Paris, 3 June 1830, Cal S-V.

29. Charles Henry Carter's father was Bernard Carter of Shirley Plantation in Charles City County, Virginia, and his mother was Lucy Grimes (Lee). The young man had a double relationship with the Lees, since his aunt, Ann Hill Carter, became Light-Horse Harry's second wife and the mother of Robert E. Lee.

30. See Douglas Southall Freeman, *R. E. Lee: A Biography* (New York, 1934), vol. 1, pp. 97–99. The scandal became public in March 1830, when Henry Lee II (1787–1837), who had been nominated as consul to Morocco by President Andrew Jackson, was rejected by the Senate; not one senator cast a vote for him.

31. Bernard Carter was one of thirteen children of Charles Carter of Shirley by his second wife; Charles Carter's first marriage had already produced eight children.

32. Prince George's County Land Records, Liber A. B. 7, fols. 181–85. The contract made Eugenia's brother George Henry and her husband's father, Bernard, trustees of all property she had or would receive. By a will made at the same time, Eugenia Carter left all her property to her husband. Prince George's County Record of Wills, 1833–1854, Liber P. C. 1, fol. 293.

33. Prince George's County Land Records, Liber A. B. 11, fols. 32–40.

34. Prince George's County Land Records, Liber A. B. 10, fols. 306–8. The record reads as if Dr. Stuart paid for the transfer, but the figure mentioned is a valuation of the property.

35. C. Vann Woodward, editor, *Mary Chesnut's Civil War* (Binghamton, N.Y., 1981), p. 29.

36. Prince George's County Land Records, Liber J. R. M. 9, fol. 46.

37. Prince George's County Land Records, Liber A. B. 2, fol. 371.

38. Prince George's County Land Records, Liber A. B. 3, fols. 349–50. The children were to become free when they came of age: twenty-one for the males, eighteen for the females.

39. Prince George's County Land Records, Liber A. B. 4, fols. 24–25. Anne is identified here as "Anne or Anna"; hereafter I shall use Anne.

40. From Nellie Arnold Plummer, *Out of the Depths; or, The Triumph of the Cross* (Hyattsville, Md., 1927), p. 11. Miss Plummer's father, Adam Plummer, was a slave on the Riversdale plantation during Charles Benedict Calvert's time; her grandfather, Barney Plummer, a slave on the Goodwood plantation, married Sarah E. Norris, one of Eleanor Beckett's daughters by William Norris (see also Bianca P. Floyd, *Records and Recollections: Early Black History in Prince George's County, Maryland* [Maryland–National Capital Park and Planning Commission Publication, 1989], pp. 80–81).

41. Prince George's County Land Records, Liber A. B. 2, fols. 371–72, state that Charlotte and Sophia were daughters of Maria Norris, which I believe to be in error. Sophia's certificate of freedom, issued in 1827, says that she was sometimes called Maria, and perhaps this was the source of the error. Certificates were more detailed and more likely to be correct. Prince George's County Certificates of Freedom, 1806–29, fol. 244.

42. Prince George's County Certificates of Freedom, 1806–29, fol. 269.

43. Prince George's County Certificates of Freedom, 1806–29, fol. 250. Montgomery County Tax Assessments for 1826, 1831, and 1837 show a free black named William Beckett living in the Fourth District and owning one acre.

44. Calvert freed twenty Becketts, three Norrises, five Scotts (Ennis, Isabella and son Henry, Harriet, and Charlotte), and a Rachel Herbert. Four slaves freed in 1801—Nick, and Becky and her two children—had no identifying surnames. For Scotts, see Prince George's County Land Records, Liber A. B. 2, fols. 371–72, Liber A. B. 3, fol. 549, and Prince George's County Certificates of Freedom, 1806–29, fol. 248. For Rachel Herbert, Prince George's County Certificates of Freedom, 1806–29, fol. 269.

Calvert did not free all of his Beckett slaves, however. The inventory of Calvert's estate after his death in 1838 shows two Beckett slaves remaining at Riversdale: Will Beckett, valued at $150, and Jack Becket, valued at $1. And in what may or may not be coincidence, a William Beckett of Prince George's County was one of the persons making this inventory and was also one of three witnesses to George Calvert's last will and testament. See Prince George's County Inventories, Liber P. C. 3, fols. 410–21; Prince George's County Record of Wills, 1833–54, Liber P. C. 1, fols. 89–90.

45. Montgomery County Tax Assessments, Personal Property, 1813, fol. 37.

46. Population Schedules of the Fourth Census of the United States, 1820, Montgomery County, fol. 148.

47. Population Schedules of the Sixth Census of the United States, 1840, Montgomery County, fol. 303. The 1830 census schedule for Montgomery County no longer exists.

48. Both were located in Rock Creek Hundred in the vicinity of present-day Wheaton, Maryland.

49. See Chapter 5, above, letter dated 11 December 1806.

50. These were the same seven children manumitted by George Calvert in 1824: George, Caroline Elizabeth, John Henry, Henrietta Maria, Thomas Adolphus, Marietta, and Richard. Caroline and Thomas Cramphin had two more children, Hannah in 1825 and Robert in 1827. See *Prince George's County Maryland Indexes of Church Registers, 1686–1885,* comp. Helen W. Brown (Prince George's County Historical Society, 1979), vol. 2, p. 230. Caroline's last four children were christened in Prince George's (Rock Creek) Parish under the name Cramphin; one of Anne's children, Lucretia Ann, born in 1823, was also christened there, under the name Calvert. See ibid., p. 221.

51. See James M. Wright, *The Free Negro in Maryland, 1634–1860* (New York, 1971), p. 108.

52. Will of Thomas Cramphin, June 30, 1824, in the unrecorded papers of the Maryland Chancery Court, MS 7627.

53. Ibid.

54. See entry in *Biographical Dictionary of the Maryland Legislature, 1635–1789,* vol. 1.

55. Codicils to Thomas Cramphin's Will, November 1, 1824, and October 14, 1825, Maryland Chancery Court, MS 7627.

56. Montgomery County Land Records, Liber B. S. 33, fols. 89, 124–25, and petition of Caroline Calvert et al., 1838, Maryland Chancery Court, MS 7627.

57. One child, Richard, was now dead, and another, Caroline Elizabeth, had married. The two children, Hannah and Robert, born in 1825 and 1827, are not mentioned in the suit, possibly because they were not named in the 1824 will.

58. Maryland Chancery Court, unrecorded papers, MS 7627; Minutes of the Montgomery County Orphans Court, 1838, fol. 105.

59. The 1843 Liberian census is contained in Senate Document 150, 28th Cong., 2d sess., *Message from the President of the United States Communicating Information Relative to the Operations of the United States Squadron on the West Coast of Africa, the Conditions of the American Colonies There . . .* (Washington, D.C., 1845). Liberian passenger lists are found in a Register of Emigrants, 1835–1857, Microfilm Reel 314 of the Records of the American Colonization Society at the Library of Congress, Washington, D.C.

60. Prince George's County Record of Wills, 1833–1854, Liber P. C. 1, fols. 89–90.

61. Anne Arundel County Land Records, Liber W. S. G. 22, fols. 425–29; Prince

George's County Land Records, Liber A. B. 11, fols. 32–40, Liber A. B. 10, fols. 306–8. The Spurrier purchase had originally been 400 acres, but 116 acres had been added. The Goodwood transfer to Eugenia still left Calvert with 2,000 acres at Mount Albion, but he sold most of it before he died.

62. Thomas Willing Morris (hereafter TWM) to CJS, Philadelphia, February 5, 1839, Cal S-V. The property had cost twenty-one thousand dollars at purchase and generated twenty-five hundred dollars a year in its heyday, but Morris put its worth at less than ten thousand dollars in 1839 and said he could not find a buyer.

63. Ibid. Morris speaks of "a balance of $12,000 due" Caroline from her father that had not been paid at his death. Morris and Calvert probably could never agree on what was due.

64. Prince George's County Land Records, Liber A. B. 11, fols. 377–83.

65. Prince George's County Tax Assessments, 1838, show the following holdings for George Calvert's heirs: His Lordship's Kindness and Mount Airy, 6,721 acres; Mount Albion, 398 acres; Riversdale-Buck Lodge-Rossborough, 2,186 acres; and a mill site and several lots in Bladensburg. Calvert still owned 875 acres in Montgomery County and parcels of land on Pennsylvania Avenue, Sixth Street, and C Street, and a majority share in the National Hotel in the District of Columbia.

66. TWM to CJS, Glenthorne, November 6, 1842, Cal S-V. This twelve-page letter summarizes actions taken between 1838 and 1842.

67. Anne Arundel County Land Records, Liber W. S. G. 5, fols. 209–13.

68. State of Maryland Chancery Court, Liber 161, fols. 309–13.

69. State of Maryland Chancery Court, Unrecorded Papers, 1846, MS 9855.

70. For a complete account of Calvert's literary career, see Everson, *George Henry Calvert*.

71. See letters to the court from Charles Benedict and George Henry Calvert in State of Maryland Chancery Court, Unrecorded Papers, 1846, MS 9855.

72. TWM to CJS, Glenthorne, November 6, 1842, and November 3, 1843, Cal S-V.

73. In 1858 Charles Benedict Calvert and George Henry Calvert sold the 428-acre Rossborough Farm to the Maryland Agricultural College for its campus. This was the same land that George Calvert had bought in 1822 with Henri Stier's dividends.

74. A detailed account of Riversdale after the Calvert family is available in a Historic Structures report prepared by the History Division of the Maryland–National Capital Park and Planning Commission, Prince George's County, in 1979. This report, like the historical marker in the town of Riverdale, refers to H. J. Stier as a baron. Although two of his brothers were barons, Stier never possessed this title.

Appendix

THIS IS THE LIST OF PAINTINGS that Henri J. Stier prepared in June 1794 in preparation for bringing the collection of his late father-in-law to America. I have preserved Stier's arrangement and spellings as faithfully as legibility would allow. These paintings remained in America from 1794 to 1816.

A comparison of Stier's list of sixty-three paintings with the sale catalogue of the seventy-eight Peeters family paintings offered at public auction in Antwerp in 1817 reveals discrepancies in attribution for some of the paintings (see *Catalogue d'une Précieuse Collection de Tableaux,* Public sale, 27 August 1817 [Anvers, G. J. Binken, 1817]).

Liste des tablaux de la maison mortuaire de feu Monsieur Peeters

Premiere Caisse—grande

N° 1. la charite romaine	par Rubbens
2. le portrait de le roy	par Van dyk
3. un portrait de femme	par Van dyk
4. le portrait de L'amiral le roy	par Van dyk
5. le portrait de prekkius	par rubbens
6. un paysage de Vinkenboom	par Vinkenboom
7. un portrait de femme en chapeau	par rubbens
8. un portrait de femme avec un bonnet noir	par rubbens

9. un portrait d'homme faisant le pendant — p. Van dyk

10. un paysage nomme L'etable — par rubbens

11. romulus & remus — par rubbens

12. un portrait d'homme tenant un sac — par titien

13. une vierge que L'enfant regarde — par rubens

14. deux portraits se tenant la main — par Van dyk

Seconde Caisse

Nº 15. un portrait d'homme en mantau noir — par titien

Nᵒˢ 16, 17, 18, 19. quatre tablaux les 4 Saison — p. bruegel de velours

Nº 20. une vierge entourre de fleurs — par Seegers & Van bael

Nᵒˢ 21 & 22. deux paysages nomme les grottes — par momper & bruegel

23. L'arche de noé — par bruegel

24. diane sortant du bain — par poelenborg

25. une Eglise — par peeter neef

26. le jugement de paris — par rubbens

27. un paysage — par ruysdael

28. un tablau de conversation — par vanderlaenen

29. un ditto ou on fait de la musique — par le meme

Nº 30. une Esquisse — par Van dyk

31. moyse sauve — par breugel & le vieux van bael

32. une femme habille en satin jaune — pr. chev. vanderwerve

33. Jonas sortant de la baleine — pr. breugel de velours

34. une diane assise vue a dos — pr. poelemborg

35. une chasse — pr. ph: wouwersman

36. chutte d'au — pr. ruysdael

37. portrait de Van dyk — pr. Rubbens

38. portrait de femme vue de face — pr. chev. vanderwerve

39. bataille — pr. palamedes

40. un chasseur tenant son cheval — pr. ch: du jardin

41. un joueur de guitarre	pr. vanderheyden
42. un paysage	pr. teniers & van uden
43. Jaques le rieur	pr. otterlings
44. un homme & femme	pr. brouwer
45. une petitte vierge sur cuivre	pr. Van dyk
46. portrait d'homme en petit	- - - - -

3ieme Caisse

47. un portrait de femme en satin blanc	pr. brounkenhorst
48. un prêtre celebrant la messe	pr. le meme
49. Esquisse du tablau du grand autel de St. michel	p. rubbens
50. feulles & reptilles	p. Van huyssen
51. une figure pleurante	pr. tintoretti
52. un tablau de 2 figures	pr. rynbrandt
53. le plat de lentilles	p. rubbens
54. 13 enfants de goubau	- - - - -
55. - - - - - que depose son drapeau	Ecole holandaise
56. un mendiant	p. michelange
57. un paysage avec chutte d'au	
58. un paysage italien	ecole italien
59. la madelaine et son pendant	p. beschage
60. 2 tablaux ronds	p. brouwer
61. femme & homme avec un chien	Ecole hollandaise
62. diane se mirant	nicolas brehemberg
63. un petit paysage avec Etang	pr. poelemborg

Index

Designed by Martha Farlow

Composed by The Composing Room of Michigan, Inc., in Simoncini Garamond

Printed by Thomson-Shore, Inc., on 50-lb. Glatfelter Offset Eggshell

Library of Congress Cataloging-in-Publication Data

Calvert, Rosalie Stier, d. 1821.
  Mistress of Riversdale : the plantation letters of Rosalie Stier
Calvert, 1795–1821 / edited by Margaret Law Callcott.
      p.   cm.
  Letters translated from the French by M.L. Callcott.
  Includes bibliographical references.
  ISBN 0-8018-4093-7
  1. Calvert, Rosalie Stier, d. 1821—Correspondence.   2. Women plantation
owners—Chesapeake Bay Region (Md. and Va.)—Correspondence.
3. Plantation owners—Chesapeake Bay Region (Md. and Va.)—Correspondence.
4. Calvert family—Correspondence.   5. Plantation life—Chesapeake Bay Region
(Md. and Va.)—History.   6. Chesapeake Bay Region (Md. and Va.)—
History.   7. Chesapeake Bay Region (Md. and Va.)— Biography.   I. Title.
F187.C5C35   1991
975.5'1803'092—dc20
[B]

                                                    90-41099 CIP